FROMME

EasyGuide

to

COLORADO

by
Eric Peterson

Easy Guides are ✦ Quick To Read   ✦ Light To Carry
✦ For Expert Advice   ✦ In All Price Ranges

FrommerMedia LLC

Published by

FROMMER MEDIA LLC

ISBN 978-1-62887-098-5 (paper), 978-1-62887-099-2 (e-book)

Editorial Director: Pauline Frommer
Editor: Pauline Frommer
Production Editor: Heather Wilcox
Cartographer: Roberta Stockwell
Cover Design: Howard Grossman

For information on our other products or services, see www.frommers.com.

Frommer Media LLC also publishes its books in a variety of electronic formats. Some content that
appears in print may not be available in electronic formats.

Manufactured in the United States of America

5 4 3 2 1

CONTENTS

ABOUT THE AUTHOR

Eric Peterson has been writing about travel for more than 20 years. Beyond covering the Rockies in numerous Frommer's guidebooks, he's written about skiing, hiking, and other ways to get up and down mountains for such publications as "The New York Daily News," "Delta Sky," and his own "Ramble" series of travel books. When he's not on the road, he covers the arts, technology, and city-building for Confluence Denver, a hyper-local website. Eric lives in Denver with his wife, Jamie, and their trusted canines, Mini and Duncan.

ABOUT THE FROMMER'S TRAVEL GUIDES

For most of the past 50 years, Frommer's has been the leading series of travel guides in North America, accounting for as many as 24 percent of all guidebooks sold. I think I know why.

Although we hope our books are entertaining, we nevertheless deal with travel in a serious fashion. Our guidebooks have never looked on such journeys as a mere recreation, but as a far more important human function, a time of learning and introspection, an essential part of a civilized life. We stress the culture, lifestyle, history, and beliefs of the destinations we cover and urge our readers to seek out people and new ideas as the chief rewards of travel.

We have never shied from controversy. We have, from the beginning, encouraged our authors to be intensely judgmental, critical—both pro and con—in their comments, and wholly independent. Our only clients are our readers, and we have triggered the ire of countless prominent sorts, from a tourist newspaper we called "practically worthless" (it unsuccessfully sued us) to the many rip-offs we've condemned.

And because we believe that travel should be available to everyone regardless of their incomes, we have always been cost-conscious at every level of expenditure. Although we have broadened our recommendations beyond the budget category, we insist that every lodging we include be sensibly priced. We use every form of media to assist our readers and are particularly proud of our feisty daily website, the award-winning Frommers.com.

I have high hopes for the future of Frommer's. May these guidebooks, in all the years ahead, continue to reflect the joy of travel and the freedom that travel represents. May they always pursue a cost-conscious path, so that people of all incomes can enjoy the rewards of travel. And may they create, for both the traveler and the persons among whom we travel, a community of friends, where all human beings live in harmony and peace.

Arthur Frommer

THE BEST OF COLORADO

The old and the new, the rustic and the sophisticated, the wild and the refined—all these experiences exist practically side by side in Colorado, amid what is arguably the most breathtaking mountain scenery in America.

Colorado's booming cities—Boulder, Colorado Springs, and Denver—and its admittedly somewhat glitzy resorts—especially Vail and Aspen—offer much of the comfort and culture of New York or Los Angeles but at a more relaxed pace. Throughout the state, you'll also find testaments to another time, when life was simpler but rougher and only the strong survived: Victorian mansions, working steam trains, thousand-year-old adobe villages, and authentic Old West towns.

Enos Mills, an early-20th-century environmentalist and one of the driving forces behind the creation of Rocky Mountain National Park, said that knowledge of nature is the basis of wisdom. So climb on a horse or mountain bike, take a hike or a raft trip, or simply sit back and gaze at the mountains. Whatever you do, though, don't stay indoors.

COLORADO'S best AUTHENTIC EXPERIENCES

- **Skiing as Many Different Slopes as You Can:** Colorado gets twice as many skier days as any other state at its nearly 30 resorts. Ranging from mom-and-pop operations to some of the most fabled places in ski country, Colorado is just the place for a week, or even a month, on the slopes. See chapters 6, 7, 8, 9, and 10 for information on different resorts.

- **Exploring the Cities on the Front Range:** Plenty of mountain scenery lies between Fort Collins and Pueblo, and the majority of the top museums, hotels, and restaurants are found here. Spend a few days in Denver, Boulder, Colorado Springs, and elsewhere before ascending the Rockies. See chapters 4, 5, and 6.

- **Biking, Rafting, or Driving through Glenwood Canyon:** This masterwork of geology between Eagle and Glenwood Springs is home to an engineering marvel in I-70, but bike trails and the Colorado River provide alternate methods to see the stunning views. See chapter 8.

- **Gaping at the Views in Telluride:** Colorado has no shortage of incredible views, but for my money, the most beautiful town is Telluride. Waterfalls, forests, red rock, and jagged peaks comprise a picture-perfect landscape that begs for snapshot after snapshot. See chapter 9.

o **Experiencing Alpine Tundra in the Northern Rockies:** Once you pass timberline in such places as Rocky Mountain National Park, the ecosystem changes dramatically, and winter conditions persist for most of the year. No state in the Lower 48 has as much alpine tundra as Colorado, so a trip to the high country is a must. See chapter 7.

o **Driving the Million Dollar Highway to Durango:** This is the chunk of the famed San Juan Skyway that connects Ouray and Durango. Two great tourist towns, two stunning mountain passes, and tiny, historic Silverton in between make this a super-lative scenic drive. See chapter 9.

THE best HOTELS

o **Brown Palace Hotel** (Denver): Denver's finest hotel, the Brown Palace has been open continuously since 1892, serving high society and celebrities—from President Dwight Eisenhower to the Beatles—with elegance and charm. See p. 25.

o **The Broadmoor** (Colorado Springs): Colorado's top-rated resort hotel has it all—excellent dining, golf courses, pools, tennis courts, a state-of-the-art fitness center, full-service spa, and shopping, plus extraordinary service—in a magnificently restored historic building set in immaculate grounds. See p. 77.

o **Hotel Jerome** (Aspen): Historic hotels don't get any more luxurious than the Jerome, but don't expect Victorian frills: The 1889 hotel's red-brick facade belies the contemporary decor inside. See p. 171.

o **New Sheridan Hotel** (Telluride): With historic cachet to spare, the New Sheridan has been the place to hang your hat in Telluride for a dozen decades running. The place first opened in 1895—a year after the old Sheridan Hotel burned down—and has seen it all in the time since. See p. 215.

o **The Sebastian-Vail** (Vail): An architectural and artistic marvel that opened in early 2011, the Sebastian-Vail is among the best new luxury hotels in the West. It eschews Bavarian and New West motifs for a more contemporary look. See p. 157.

o **The Strater** (Durango): Opening in 1887, the red-brick-and-limestone Strater has long been the landmark piece of architecture in Durango. Most requested is room 222, favored by Western writer Louis L'Amour, who was inspired by the piano music and carousing at the Diamond Belle Saloon just below. See p. 198.

THE best RESTAURANTS

o **Beatrice & Woodsley** (Denver): This is one of the most quirky and creative restaurants you are going to find, and the food is uniformly excellent. See p. 34.

o **The Broadmoor** (Colorado Springs): The landmark resort offers no fewer than 19 restaurants, lounges, and cafes to pick from, and I highly recommend having at least one meal here to experience the splendid architecture and mountain scenery. See p. 77.

o **Campo de Fiori** (Aspen): Since 1994, this has been just the place to see and be seen in Aspen. The food is also first-rate, with the kitchen plating up such authentic Italian fare as fettuccine *bolognese,* shrimp and zucchini risotto, and fusilli pesto, plus steaks and seafood with similar preparations. See p. 172.

o **Frasca** (Boulder): Not only is slick, sociable Frasca one of the best-reviewed restaurants in Boulder, it's one of the best-reviewed in the country, landing on all sorts of national lists since its opening in 2004. The fare is inspired by Friuli–Venezia Giulia in northeast Italy. See p. 100.

o **Restaurant Kelly Liken** (Vail): Kelly Liken is one of the most celebrated chefs in Colorado—with appearances on such shows as "Iron Chef and "Top Chef"—and a meal at her eponymous Vail eatery makes it crystal-clear why her profile is so high. The seasonally shifting menu exudes creativity, and the wine pairings are pitch-perfect. See p. 159.

THE best SKI RESORTS

Large Resorts

o **Aspen:** Not only does Aspen have predictably superior ski terrain ranging from some of the most expert runs in Colorado to what "Ski" magazine has called the best mountain in America for beginners (Buttermilk), but it's also one of the most fun, genuinely historic ski towns in Colorado. Although it might come off at first as somewhat glitzy and certainly expensive, Aspen is a real town, with longtime, year-round residents and a history that goes beyond the slopes. See chapter 7.

o **Crested Butte:** My favorite ski town in Colorado also features some of the most challenging skiing and a complete dearth of lift lines. Although the untracked powder is legendary, the grooming is also some of the best in the state. See chapter 10.

o **Steamboat:** The snow at Steamboat is the stuff of legend: champagne powder that is perfect for skiing and snowboarding. The mountain has plenty of room to roam, and Steamboat Springs is an authentic cowboy town with more personality than most resort areas in Colorado. See chapter 7.

o **Telluride:** The funky historic town of Telluride at the bottom of the slopes and the posh Mountain Village at the mountain base offer the best of both worlds, as does the resort's diverse terrain, with plenty of snow for skiers of all levels. See chapter 9.

o **Vail:** This is it, the big one, America's flagship ski resort, as well as one of its largest, with 5,289 acres of skiable terrain, 193 trails, and 34 lifts. Every serious skier needs to ski Vail at least once. Its free bus system makes it easy to get around, but be prepared for steep prices, and don't look for historical charm—most everything is pretty new around here. See chapter 7.

Small Resorts

o **Arapahoe Basin:** One of the highest, snowiest, and longest-lasting resorts (it often stays open until midsummer), A-Basin, one of the few Summit County resorts not owned by Vail Resorts, is beloved by locals. See chapter 7.

o **Loveland:** Topping out just above 13,000 feet on "the Ridge," Loveland is one of the favorite resorts for Denver's day skiers, and it features low prices and plenty of terrain for every skill level. See chapter 7.

o **Wolf Creek:** The state's snowiest resort, Wolf Creek Ski Area is known for Alberta Peak's perfectly timbered terrain and the groomed slopes off the other chairs. See chapter 9.

o **Monarch Mountain:** Near the river-rat mecca of Salida, Monarch has some of the state's best snow, friendliest staff, and terrific bowl skiing. See chapter 10.

THE best ACTIVE ADVENTURES

o **Hiking in Rocky Mountain National Park:** There's something for everyone here, from short hikes around a lovely mountain lake to the difficult trek to the top of 14,259-foot Longs Peak. Trailheads can be accessed with the park's shuttle bus, from campgrounds, and from stops along Trail Ridge Road. See chapter 7.

o **Rafting the Arkansas River:** Running the rapids on the Arkansas River is one of the best and surely most exciting ways to see some of the most beautiful landscapes in the West. See chapter 10.

o **Skiing the San Juan Hut System:** Ambitious cross-country skiers who want to put a few miles behind them as well as take in the 14,000-foot alpine peaks love the San Juan Hut System's trail and series of shelters between Telluride and Moab, Utah. See chapter 9.

o **Backpacking in the Maroon Bells Wilderness Area:** Among the largest roadless areas in the Lower 48, the Maroon Bells and Snowmass wilderness areas occupy a sizable chunk of picture-perfect real estate between Aspen and Crested Butte. The Four Pass Loop is one of the best backpacking loops in the state, typically requiring 3 nights in the backcountry. See chapters 7 and 10.

o **Hiking the Colorado Trail:** For some 500 miles, this trail winds from Denver to Durango, through some of the state's most spectacular and rugged terrain, crossing the Continental Divide, eight mountain ranges, and six wilderness areas. See chapters 4, 7, and 9.

THE best FAMILY EXPERIENCES

o **Exploring the Denver Museum of Nature and Science:** The largest museum of its kind in the Rocky Mountain region, the Denver Museum of Nature & Science features scores of world-renowned dioramas, an extensive gems and minerals display, a pair of Egyptian mummies, and a terrific fossil collection. See chapter 4.

o **Feeding Giraffes at Cheyenne Mountain Zoo:** On the lower slopes of Cheyenne Mountain, at 6,800 feet above sea level—making it the nation's highest—Cheyenne Mountain Zoo in Colorado Springs is home to the largest and most prolific captive giraffe herd in the world, with about 200 live births since the 1950s. Visitors can actually feed the long-necked beasts. See chapter 5.

o **Riding an 1880s Narrow Gauge Steam Train:** There are two: The Durango & Silverton follows the Animas River from Durango up through the San Juan Mountains to historic Silverton; the Cumbres & Toltec chugs out of Antonito, Colorado, through the Toltec Gorge of the Los Piños River, and over Cumbres Pass into Chama, New Mexico. Scenery is stupendous over both lines, and each fulfills every train buff's greatest dream of smoke in your eyes and cinders in your hair. See chapters 9 and 10.

o **Playing in the Giant Sandbox That Is Great Sand Dunes National Park & Preserve:** About 40 miles northeast of Alamosa, this huge pile of sand is a great place to explore, camp, hike, or just play in the 750-foot-tall dunes. See chapter 10.

COLORADO IN CONTEXT

The Rocky Mountains are the backbone of North America, and with more than 50 peaks that soar above 14,000 feet—more mountains of such a magnitude than are present in the rest of the lower 48 states combined—Colorado is their heart. This dazzling constellation of high points, with its evergreen and aspen forests, racing streams and rivers, and wealth of wildlife, is perfect for recreation year-round—from summer hiking, mountain biking, and rafting to superlative winter skiing and snowboarding through deep and dry powder snow.

But Colorado isn't just mountains. It's also the wheat and cornfields of the vast eastern prairies, the high plateau country of the western slope, the numerous historic towns and American Indian communities, and the increasingly sophisticated cities of the Front Range.

THE HISTORY OF COLORADO

Early Inhabitants

The earliest people in Colorado are believed to have been nomadic hunters, who arrived some 12,000 to 20,000 years ago following the tracks of the now-extinct woolly mammoth and bison. Then, about 2,000 years ago, the ancestors of today's Pueblo people arrived, living in shallow caves in the Four Corners area, where the borders of Colorado, Utah, Arizona, and New Mexico meet.

Originally hunters, they gradually learned farming, basket making, pottery making, and the construction of pit houses. Eventually they built complex villages, such as those that can be seen at Mesa Verde National Park. For some unknown reason, possibly drought, they deserted the area by the end of the 13th century, probably moving southward into present-day New Mexico and Arizona.

Exploration & Settlement

Spanish colonists, having established settlements at Santa Fe and Taos in the 16th and 17th centuries, didn't immediately find southern Colorado attractive for colonization. Not only was there a lack of financial and military support from the Spanish crown, but also the freedom-loving, sometimes fierce Comanche and Ute also made it clear that they would rather be left alone.

Nevertheless, Spain still held title to southern and western Colorado in 1803, when U.S. President Thomas Jefferson paid $15 million for the vast Louisiana Territory, which included the lion's share of modern Colorado. Two years later, the Lewis and Clark expedition passed by. The first official exploration by the U.S. government occurred when Jefferson sent Captain Zebulon Pike to the territory. Pikes Peak, Colorado's landmark mountain and a top tourist attraction near Colorado Springs, was named for the explorer.

The Territory

Abraham Lincoln was elected president of the United States in November 1860, and Congress created the Colorado Territory 3 months later. Lincoln's Homestead Act brought much of the public domain into private ownership and led to the platting of Front Range townships, including Denver.

Controlling the American Indian peoples was a priority of the territorial government. A treaty negotiated in 1851 had guaranteed the entire Pikes Peak region to the nomadic plains tribes, but that was made moot by the arrival of settlers in the late 1850s. The Fort Wise Treaty of 1861 exchanged the Pikes Peak territory for 5 million fertile acres of Arkansas Valley land, north of modern La Junta. But when the Arapaho and Cheyenne continued to roam their old hunting grounds, conflict became inevitable. Frequent rumors and rare instances of hostility against settlers led the Colorado cavalry to attack a peaceful settlement of Indians—who were flying Old Glory and a white flag—on November 29, 1864. More than 150 Cheyenne and Arapaho, two-thirds of them women and children, were killed in what has become known as the Sand Creek Massacre.

Vowing revenge, the Cheyenne and Arapaho launched a campaign to drive whites from their ancient hunting grounds. Their biggest triumph was the destruction of the northeast Colorado town of Julesburg in 1865, but the cavalry, bolstered by returning Civil War veterans, managed to force the two tribes onto reservations in Indian Territory, in what is now Oklahoma—a barren area that whites thought they would never want.

Statehood

Colorado politicians began pressing for statehood during the Civil War, but it wasn't until August 1, 1876, that Colorado became the 38th state. Occurring less than a month after the 100th birthday of the United States, it was natural that Colorado would become known as "the Centennial State."

The state's new constitution gave the vote to blacks, but not to women, despite the strong efforts of the Colorado Women's Suffrage Association. Women finally succeeded in winning the vote in 1893, 3 years after Wyoming became the first state to offer universal suffrage.

At the time of statehood, most of Colorado's vast western region was still occupied by some 3,500 members of a half-dozen Ute tribes. Unlike the plains tribes, their early relations with white explorers and settlers had been peaceful. Chief Ouray, leader of the Uncompahgre Utes, had negotiated treaties in 1863 and 1868 that guaranteed them 16 million acres—most of western Colorado. In 1873, Ouray agreed to sell the United States a quarter of that acreage in the mineral-rich San Juan Mountains in exchange for hunting rights and $25,000 in annuities.

But a mining boom that began in 1878 led to a flurry of intrusions into Ute territory and stirred up a "Utes Must Go!" sentiment. Two years later, the Utes were forced onto small reserves in southwestern Colorado and Utah, and their lands opened to white settlement in 1882.

The Mining Boom

Colorado's real mining boom began on April 28, 1878, when August Rische and George Hook hit a vein of silver carbonate 27 feet deep on Fryer Hill in Leadville. Although the silver market collapsed in 1893, gold was there to take its place. In the fall of 1890, a cowboy named Bob Womack found gold in Cripple Creek, on the southwestern slope of Pikes Peak, west of Colorado Springs. He sold his claim to Winfield Scott Stratton, a carpenter and amateur geologist, and Stratton's mine earned a tidy profit of $6 million by 1899, when he sold it to an English company for another $11 million. Cripple Creek turned out to be the richest gold field ever discovered, ultimately producing $500 million in gold. By the early 1900s, like silver, the overproduction of gold began to drive the price of the metal down.

Environmentalism & Tourism

Another turning point for Colorado occurred just after the beginning of the 20th century. Theodore Roosevelt visited the state in September 1900 as the Republican vice-presidential nominee. Soon after he acceded the presidency in September 1901 (following the assassination of President McKinley), he began to declare large chunks of the Rockies as forest reserves. By 1907, when an act of Congress forbade the president from creating any new reserves by proclamation, nearly a quarter of Colorado was national forestland—16 million acres in 18 forests. Another project that reached fruition during the Roosevelt administration was the establishment in 1906 of Mesa Verde National Park, the first national park to preserve the works of humans.

Tourism grew hand in hand with the setting aside of public lands. Easterners had been visiting Colorado since the 1870s, when General William J. Palmer founded a Colorado Springs resort and made the mountains accessible via his Denver & Rio Grande Railroad.

Estes Park, northwest of Boulder, was among the first of the resort towns to emerge in the 20th century, spurred by a visit in 1903 by Freelan Stanley. With his brother Francis, Freelan had invented the Stanley Steamer, a steam-powered automobile, in Boston in 1899. Freelan Stanley shipped one of his steamers to Denver and drove the 40 miles to Estes Park in less than 2 hours, a remarkable speed for the day. Finding the climate conducive to his recovery from tuberculosis, he returned in 1907 with a dozen Steamers and established a shuttle service from Denver to Estes Park. Two years later he built the luxurious Stanley Hotel, still a hilltop landmark today, and in 1915 Rocky Mountain National Park was established down the road.

The Great Depression of the 1930s was a difficult time for many Coloradans, but it had some positive consequences. The federal government raised the price of gold from $20 to $35 an ounce, reviving Cripple Creek and other stagnant mining towns.

World War II and the subsequent Cold War were responsible for many of the defense installations that are now an integral part of the Colorado economy, particularly in the Colorado Springs area. The war also indirectly caused the other single greatest boon to Colorado's late-20th-century economy: the ski industry. Soldiers in the 10th Mountain Division, on leave from Camp Hale before heading off to fight in Europe, often crossed Independence Pass to relax in the lower altitude and milder climate of the 19th-century silver-mining village of Aspen. They tested their skiing skills, which they would need in the Italian Alps, against the slopes of Ajax Mountain.

In 1945, Walter and Elizabeth Paepcke—he the founder of the Container Corporation of America, she an ardent conservationist—moved to Aspen and established the Aspen Company as a property investment firm. Skiing was already popular in New

COLORADO'S GREEN RUSH: RECREATIONAL marijuana

On January 1, 2014, Denver was the site of the world's first legal sale of recreational marijuana. Other cities had decriminalized before Denver or otherwise looked the other way, but never before had the drug been fully legalized for recreational use.

Marijuana legalization kicked off a wave of cannabis-oriented tourism start-ups and initiatives—tour operators, marijuana-friendly bed-and-breakfasts, private smoking decks at a handful of ski lodges.

But not all in the tourist industry have been as welcoming of pot use. Most hotels consider marijuana the same as tobacco and fine guests who smoke it in their rooms. Some hotels, however, have opened new smoking rooms for marijuana use.

Denver is home to hundreds of marijuana dispensaries; many more are found in other cities and towns across the state, but some places (including Colorado Springs) have municipal bans in places. Many of the dispensaries are medical—only those with a doctor-approved red card can purchase from them—and others are recreational. The signage at front will be clear as to what type of dispensary you're visiting. All require that buyers show ID to, er, weed out those who are underage.

The dispensaries sell all manner of marijuana and marijuana products, including edibles of all descriptions—ice cream, candy bars, soda. These edibles can be extremely potent. Be sure not to exceed recommended dosage and ask for advice from employees at the dispensary on how fast they kick in.

A word to the wise: Driving under the influence is illegal, as is public consumption, supplying marijuana to minors, and transporting it out of the state.

England and the Midwest, but had few devotees in the Rockies. Paepcke bought a chairlift, the longest and fastest in the world at the time, and had it ready for operation by January 1947. Soon Easterners and Europeans were flocking to Aspen—and the rest is skiing history.

The Modern Era

Colorado continued its steady growth in the 1950s, aided by tourism and the federal government. The $200-million U.S. Air Force Academy, which opened to cadets in 1958, is Colorado Springs's top tourist attraction today. There was a brief oil boom in the 1970s, followed by increasing high-tech development and even more tourism.

In the 21st century, thoughts have turned to controlling population growth. With a growth rate of three times the national average—the state grew by about 2 million people during the 1990s and 2010s—residents and government leaders are questioning how this unabated influx of outsiders can continue without causing serious harm to the state's air, water, and general quality of life.

Since fiscal turmoil struck in 2008, the Colorado building boom has slowed but not stalled entirely. The region has weathered the recession better than most, with lower-than-average unemployment and a relatively vibrant economy.

One industry that has captured a fair amount of national media attention has been marijuana. Voters officially legalized recreational marijuana use in November 2012, and as of January 2014, anyone over 21 years of age can purchase it at one of the numerous recreational dispensaries throughout the state. (See "Colorado's Green Rush," above.)

Beyond this thriving sector, the state has seen tourism growth in recent years, with skier numbers rebounding along with hotel occupancy after the recession that began in 2008. While regional tourism took hits in 2011 (the mild winter kept skiers away) and 2012 and 2013 (the resulting drought lead to dreadful wildfire seasons, followed by major flooding), many attractions across Colorado enjoyed banner years in 2013 and 2014.

WHEN TO GO

Colorado has two main tourist seasons: warm and cold. Those who want to see the state's parks and other scenic wonders by hiking, mountain biking, or rafting usually visit from May through October; those who prefer skiing, snowboarding, and snow-mobiling will have to wait for winter, usually from late November through March or April, depending on snow levels. Although you can visit most museums year-round, some close in winter.

The best way to avoid crowds at the more popular destinations, such as Rocky Mountain National Park, Garden of the Gods, and Pikes Peak, is to try to visit during

FROM COWBOYS TO "MORK": COLORADO IN
popular culture

Those planning Colorado vacations can turn to a number of sources for background on the state and its major cities. Those who enjoy lengthy novels will want to get their hands on a copy of James Michener's 1,000-page "Centennial," inspired by the northeastern plains of Colorado. For a more bohemian point of view, look no further than Jack Kerouac's classic, "On the Road." Also engrossing is Wallace Stegner's Pulitzer Prize–winning 1971 novel, "Angle of Repose." Horror fans will surely appreciate a pair of Stephen King classics with Colorado ties: "The Stand" is set in Boulder and "The Shining" was inspired by the writer's stay at the Stanley Hotel in Estes Park. Much of Eric Schlosser's best-selling nonfiction book "Fast Food Nation" covers Colorado people and places.

Travelers interested in seeing wildlife will likely be successful with help from the "Colorado Wildlife Viewing Guide," by Mary Taylor Gray. You'll likely see a lot of historical sights here, so it's good to first get some background from the short, easy-to-read "Colorado: A History," by Marshall Sprague.

Movies set in Colorado range from numerous westerns—mostly filmed in the state's southwestern corner—such as the John Wayne classic "The Searchers," as well as "Butch Cassidy and the Sundance Kid" and "City Slickers." There's also "Things to Do in Denver When You're Dead," "Every Which Way But Loose," "About Schmidt," and "War Games." Television shows set in the state include "Dynasty" (Denver), "Mork & Mindy" (Boulder), and "South Park" (50 miles southwest of Denver).

Colorado also has a rich musical heritage and a diverse current scene. John Denver; Judy Collins; Earth, Wind & Fire; Big Head Todd and the Monsters; the Fray; 3OH!3; and the String Cheese Incident are among the bands that broke it big with strong ties to Denver or Boulder. In parts of the world, the "Denver Sound," a roots-based genre that melds gothic and country, has received critical acclaim, with bands like 16 Horsepower, Munly and the Lee Lewis Harlots, DeVotchKa, and Slim Cessna's Auto Club gaining an international following.

the shoulder seasons of March through May and October through mid-December. Generally, those traveling without children will want to avoid visiting during school vacations.

To hear Coloradans tell it, the state has perfect weather all the time. Although they may be exaggerating just a bit, the weather here is usually quite pleasant, with an abundance of sun and relatively mild temperatures in most places—just avoid those winter snowstorms.

Along the Front Range, where Denver and Colorado Springs are located, summer days are hot and dry, and evenings mild. Humidity is low, and temperatures seldom rise above 100°F (30°C). Evenings start to get cooler by mid-September, but even as late as November the days are often warm. Surprisingly, winters here are warmer and less snowy than winters in the Great Lakes or New England.

Most of Colorado is considered semi-arid, and overall the state has an average of 296 sunny days a year—more sunshine than San Diego or Miami Beach. The prairies average about 16 inches of precipitation annually; the Front Range, 14 inches; the western slope, only about 8 inches. Rain, when it falls, is commonly a short afternoon thunderstorm. However, if you want to see snow, simply head to the mountains, where snowfall is measured in feet rather than inches, and mountain peaks may still be white in July. Mountain temperatures can be bitterly cold, especially if it's windy, but even at the higher elevations of some of the nation's top ski resorts, you'll find plenty of sunshine.

eating & drinking IN COLORADO

Local delicacies include Rocky Mountain oysters (yes, they are deep-fried bull testicles), Mexican fare, beef, and game. Boulder and Paonia are on the forefront of numerous culinary trends, namely vegetarian, locavore, and organic, as are Denver and Colorado Springs and the ski towns, although to a lesser degree. There are also quite a few microbreweries throughout the state; Denver and the surrounding area has been dubbed "the Napa Valley of beer." On the western slope in and around Palisade and Paonia, there are numerous vineyards and wineries, but Colorado's fresh fruit and vegetables (namely, Paonia cherries, Palisade peaches, and Olathe sweet corn) are also among some of the nation's best.

SUGGESTED COLORADO ITINERARIES

At the risk of oversimplifying, let me suggest that there are essentially three activities for visitors to Colorado—viewing the scenery, visiting historic and cultural sites, and participating in outdoor sports. While there are some visitors whose only goal is to explore prehistoric American Indian sites or historic mining towns, and perhaps hardcore skiers or hikers who are interested solely in pursuing their preferred form of recreation, the vast majority of Colorado visitors want a smorgasbord of experiences. This might include a scenic drive over a mountain pass, a visit to a small-town museum in a Victorian mansion, and a hike to a picturesque lake.

My suggested itineraries assume that you're looking for a mix of experiences. I'll look at the most efficient routes and the must-see destinations.

These are almost all driving tours and, in fact, a motor vehicle is almost mandatory for anyone who wants to explore Colorado. Visitors to Denver don't necessarily need a car, and if you're heading to a major resort to ski for a week you can be car-less, but many of the best destinations here require that you drive.

Colorado has a well-maintained network of roadways that will take you to most places you want to visit, although not always directly. Unfortunately, Colorado is a big state, with everything spread out, so you may end up doing a lot of driving. One consolation is that traffic congestion, even in the cities, is not nearly as bad as in many other states. Services along rural highways are often limited, though, so be careful about checking fuel levels. Also, because of seasonal road closures, the tours that leave the Front Range are for summer use only, although parts of them can be adapted for winter use.

2 WEEKS OF COLORADO'S BEST

Yes, Colorado is a big state with a lot to offer, and you could stretch this itinerary beyond 2 weeks, but this driving tour hits many of the highlights—what you might call the best of the best. It will show you why Colorado is one of America's top vacation destinations.

Colorado

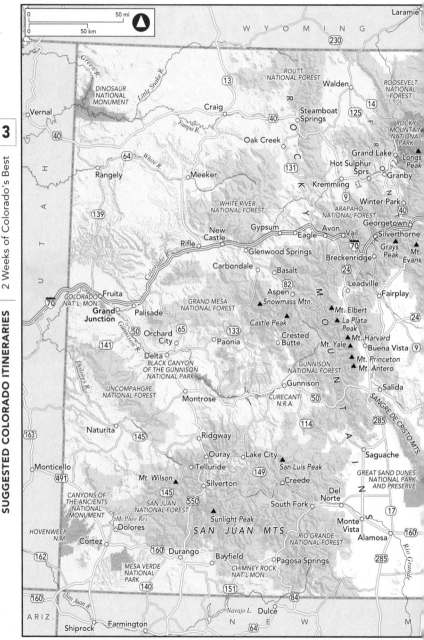

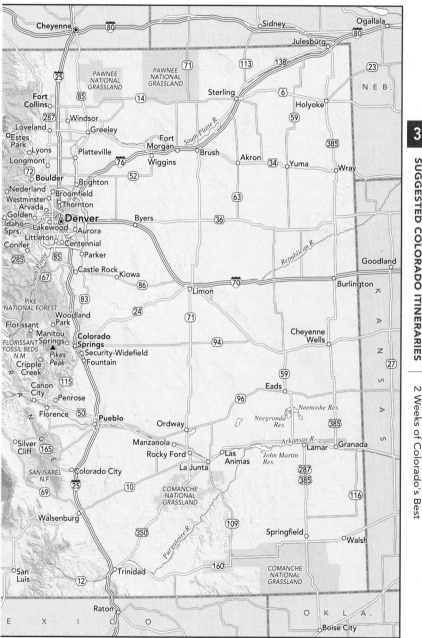

Days 1 & 2: Denver & Boulder ★★

Arrive in Denver, preferably in the late morning or early afternoon. Browse **Larimer Square** ★★ and the **16th Street Mall** (p. 53). The next morning, visit the **Denver Art Museum** ★★★ (p. 41) and the **state capitol** (p. 40). Take the short drive to Boulder and have lunch at **Boulder Dushanbe Teahouse** ★★ (p. 101); browse the **Pearl Street Mall** (p. 103), where you might see a juggler or mime (or just a sleeping University of Colorado student); and settle in for the night.

Day 3: Estes Park ★

Take Canyon Boulevard (Colo. 119) west to Nederland, then follow the foothills north on Colo. 72 and Colo. 7 to Estes Park, a gateway to Rocky Mountain National Park, where you can visit the **MacGregor Ranch Museum** ★ (p. 129) and **Estes Park Museum** ★★ (p. 129), and take in some breathtaking panoramic views on a ride on the **Estes Park Aerial Tramway** ★ (p. 128).

Day 4: Rocky Mountain National Park ★★★

In the morning, enjoy spectacular **Trail Ridge Road** through Rocky Mountain National Park (p. 120), across the Continental Divide to **Grand Lake** (p. 129). After lunch, proceed south on U.S. 40 to **Winter Park** ★★, **Berthoud Pass,** and **Georgetown** ★ (p. 66).

Day 5: Leadville ★

I-70 and Colo. 91 will take you up to Leadville, Colorado's 2-mile-high city. See the historic district and **National Mining Hall of Fame and Museum** (p. 166), then continue across Independence Pass to the famed resort town of **Aspen** (p. 168).

Day 6: Aspen ★★★

Give yourself a day in Aspen to shop, see the sights, hike, bike, or just enjoy the clean mountain air. Be sure to make it to the **Maroon Bells** (p. 175) and the **Woody Creek Tavern** ★★ for lunch or dinner (p. 173).

Day 7: Ouray ★★

From Aspen, the route follows the Roaring Fork River west to Carbondale, then south along scenic Colo. 133 over McClure Pass (elevation 8,755 ft.), and through the quaint historic village of Redstone. Try to complete the 140-mile drive by early afternoon, leaving time for a visit to the **Black Canyon of the Gunnison National Park** ★★ (p. 191). Spend the night in **Ouray** ★★, a charming Victorian town tucked into a beautiful box canyon (p. 220).

Day 8: The Million Dollar Highway to Durango ★★★

It's 98 miles via the **Million Dollar Highway** (p. 207), U.S. 550, to Durango. En route, between **Ouray** and **Silverton** ★ (p. 205), you'll cross spectacular **Red Mountain Pass** in the San Juan Mountains (p. 207). **Durango's historic district** (p. 200) is one of Colorado's largest and best preserved.

Day 9: Mesa Verde National Park ★★★

Visit the cliff dwellings of **Mesa Verde National Park** (p. 209), about 40 miles west of Durango. Camp or stay in the **Far View Lodge** ★ (p. 210).

Day 10: Great Sand Dunes National Park & Preserve ★★

Get an early start for the 150-mile drive across Wolf Creek Pass on U.S. 160 to Alamosa, and continue northeast to explore **Great Sand Dunes National Park & Preserve** ★★ (p. 236) before returning to **Alamosa** (p. 235), Crestone, or one of the valley's hot springs resorts for the night.

Day 11: Salida ★★

Head north to the rafting capital of Salida, perhaps stopping for a dip in the **hot springs pool** (p. 233) or getting in a half-day **whitewater excursion on the Arkansas River** (p. 233).

Days 12 & 13: Colorado Springs ★★

Spend 2 full days seeing the attractions in Colorado Springs and nearby Manitou Springs. Choose from the **Pikes Peak Cog Railway** ★★ (p. 82), the **U.S. Olympic Training Center** ★ (p. 82), the **Garden of the Gods** ★★★ (p. 82), and the **Cheyenne Mountain Zoo** ★★ (p. 80), among other sights. Stay at **The Broadmoor** ★★★ (p. 74) or **Cheyenne Mountain Resort** ★★ (p. 74).

Day 14: Back to Denver ★★

Stop and visit the **U.S. Air Force Academy** ★ (p. 84) on your way back to Denver, where your flight home awaits.

COLORADO'S BEST SKIING

Taking 2 weeks to ski the numerous slopes in Colorado will give you a great sampling of some of the best snow and terrain in the world.

Day 1: Denver ★★

Fly into Denver and take a shuttle to the slopes. You really can avoid a car for most of this trip, thanks to superlative mountain shuttle systems such as **Colorado Mountain Express** (p. 144). You can rent a car when you actually need it and save some money. The trip up will take about 2 hours, so if you want to ski that day, you will need to get an early flight.

Days 2, 3 & 4: Breckenridge & Summit County ★★

Ski **Breckenridge** ★★ (p. 150) for 2 days and then take local transportation to either **Copper Mountain** ★★ or **Keystone** ★ for your third day on the local slopes.

Days 5, 6 & 7: Vail & Beaver Creek ★★

Call the shuttle again for a ride to **Vail** ★★★ and ski both of these world-class resorts for 3 solid days. You will be able to ski all 3 days if you catch an early enough shuttle, or take a break if you need it. See p. 160.

Days 8, 9, 10 & 11: Aspen ★★★

Once again, you can take a ski shuttle and rely on free local transportation. **Aspen** is really four mountains (★ to ★★★), so devote a day to each, or take a break on your travel day in order to recover from 6 straight days on the slopes. Tamales and margaritas at the **Woody Creek Tavern** ★★ (p. 173) will help. See p. 174.

Days 12, 13 & 14: Steamboat Springs ★★ & Winter Park ★★

Now get yourself that rental car in Glenwood Springs and take a day to head to Steamboat Springs. Ski **Steamboat** ★★★ (p. 135) on day 13 of your trip, then get a final afternoon in at **Winter Park** ★★ (p. 143) the next day. From Winter Park it's about an hour and a half back to Denver International Airport.

COLORADO FOR FAMILIES

Denver, Boulder, and Colorado Springs are all great family-vacation destinations, with plenty of museums, kid-friendly restaurants and accommodations, and parks to romp around in—not to mention easy access to the Rocky Mountains.

Day 1: Arrive in Denver ★★

As with the 1-week itinerary above, start in Denver and base your time there out of downtown. However, kid-friendly destinations are more far-flung, so rent a car from the get-go.

Days 2 & 3: Explore Denver ★★

Start with a stop at **Confluence Park** before boarding the **Platte Valley Trolley** (p. 23); then hit the **Children's Museum** ★★ (p. 40) or the **Downtown Aquarium** ★ (p. 41). For dinner, **Casa Bonita** (p. 52) is a beloved birthday destination. On the third day, hit the **Colorado State Capitol** ★★★ (p. 40) and the **U.S. Mint** ★★ (p. 43) in the morning, and then head to the southern suburbs to **Wildlife Experience** ★★ (p. 51) or to **City Park,** home of the **Denver Zoo** ★★ (p. 45) and the **Denver Museum of Nature & Science** ★★★ (p. 44).

Days 4 & 5: Explore Colorado Springs ★★

Take your time leaving Denver on the fourth day, but make time to make it to Manitou Springs for lunch and a few vintage games at **Arcade Amusements** ★ (p. 80). In the afternoon, visit **Garden of the Gods** ★★★ (p. 82). Center your next day around Manitou Springs and a trip up **Pikes Peak** ★★ (p. 83) by car or rail.

Days 6 & 7: Explore Boulder ★★ & Rocky Mountain National Park ★★★

Return north on the sixth day of your trip. En route to Boulder, stop off U.S. 36 at the **Butterfly Pavilion** ★★ (p. 106) in Westminster. Visit **Pearl Street Mall** ★★★ (p. 103) and **Celestial Seasonings** ★★ (p. 105) in the afternoon. On the last day of your trip, make a trip up to Estes Park for a quick taste of the Rockies.

A WEEK IN SOUTHWESTERN COLORADO

This is Anasazi and red-rock country, often strikingly different than the high country and plains in central and eastern Colorado. With Durango as an anchor, you can easily spend a week exploring this spellbinding region.

Days 1, 2 & 3: Durango ★★★

Fly into Durango and then plan your second day around a trip on the **Durango & Silverton Narrow Gauge Railroad** ★★★ (p. 201) spending the afternoon in Silverton before returning to Durango for dinner at **Cyprus Cafe** ★★. Then spend day 3 in the **Vallecito Lake** area, hiking, horseback riding, or boating.

Day 4: Ouray ★★

Drive the **San Juan Skyway** ★★ (p. 206) over Molas Pass and past Silverton (unless you did not get your fill on day 2) to charming Ouray. Go gape at **Box Canyon Falls** before sundown, then soak and stay at **Wiesbaden Hot Springs** ★★ (p. 221) before you leave the next day.

Days 5 & 6: Telluride ★★★

Head to **Telluride** via Ridgway, and get in a hike or a jeep tour to **Bridal Veil Falls** that afternoon. Stay in the historic town at the **New Sheridan Hotel** (p. 215), but take a **gondola ride** to Mountain Village for a round of golf or more hiking the next day. See p. 213.

Day 7: Mesa Verde National Park ★★★

Here you can see the way of life of the Ancient Puebloan people, or Anasazi, who called the canyons of Southwestern Colorado home a millennia ago. Camp or stay in the park or return to Durango, less than an hour drive away. See p. 209.

DENVER

t's no accident that Denver is called "the Mile High City": When you climb up to the state capitol, you're precisely 5,280 feet above sea level when you reach the 13th step. Denver's location at this altitude was purely coincidental; Denver is one of the few cities not built on an ocean, a lake, a navigable river, or even (at the time) an existing road or railroad.

In the summer of 1858, eager prospectors discovered a few flecks of gold where Cherry Creek empties into the shallow South Platte River, and a tent camp quickly sprang up on the site. (The first permanent structure was a saloon.) When militia General William H. Larimer arrived in 1859, he claim-jumped the land on the east side of the Platte, laid out a city, and, hoping to curry political favors, named it after James Denver, governor of the Kansas Territory, which included this area. The plan didn't exactly work: Larimer was not aware that Denver had recently resigned.

Larimer's was one of several settlements on the South Platte. Three others also sought recognition, but Larimer had a solution. For the price of a barrel of whiskey, he bought out the other would-be town fathers, and the name "Denver" caught on.

Although the gold found in Denver was but a teaser for much larger strikes in the nearby mountains, the community grew as a shipping and trade center, in part because it had a milder climate than the mining towns it served. A devastating fire in 1863, a deadly flash flood in 1864, and American Indian hostilities in the late 1860s created hardships, but the establishment of rail links to the east and the influx of silver from the rich mines to the west kept Denver going. Silver from Leadville and gold from Cripple Creek made Denver a showcase city in the late 19th and early 20th centuries. The U.S. Mint, built in 1906, established Denver as a banking and financial center.

In the years following World War II, Denver mushroomed to become the largest city between the Great Plains and the Pacific Coast, with almost 650,000 residents within the city limits and over three million in the metropolitan area. It remains a growing city, with a booming downtown and suburbs. Denver is noted for its tree-lined boulevards, 200 city parks that cover more than 20,000 acres, and architecture ranging from Victorian to postmodern.

ESSENTIALS

Arriving

BY PLANE

Denver International Airport (DIA) is 23 miles northeast of downtown, usually a 35- to 45-minute drive. Covering 53 square miles (twice the size of Manhattan), DIA has one of the tallest flight-control towers in the world, at 327 feet. The airport, which has 95 gates and six full-service runways, can handle around 50 million passengers annually. Most major airlines serve Denver. For other information, call the Denver International Airport **information line** (📞 **800/247-2336** or 303/342-2000; www.flydenver.com).

GETTING TO & FROM THE AIRPORT Bus, taxi, and limousine services shuttle travelers between the airport and downtown, and most major car-rental companies have outlets at the airport. Because many major hotels are some distance from the airport, travelers should check on the availability and cost of hotel shuttle services when making reservations.

The **city bus** fare from the airport to downtown Denver is $11; from the airport to Boulder and suburban Park-n-Ride lots, it is about $13. The **SuperShuttle** (📞 **800/258-3826;** www.supershuttle.com) provides transportation to and from a number of hotels downtown and in the Denver Tech Center. The SuperShuttle has frequent scheduled service between the airport and downtown hotels for $22 per person each way. **Taxi** companies are another option (p. 24), with fares generally in the $50 to $60 range, and you can often share a cab and split the fare by calling the cab company ahead of time. For instance, **Yellow Cab** (📞 **303/777-7777;** www.yellowtrans.com) will take up to five people from DIA to most downtown hotels for a flat rate of $51.

BY CAR

The principal highway routes into Denver are **I-25** from the north (Fort Collins and Wyoming) and south (Colorado Springs and New Mexico), **I-70** from the east (Burlington and Kansas) and west (Grand Junction and Utah), and **I-76** from the northeast (Nebraska). If you're driving into Denver from Boulder, take **U.S. 36,** from Salida and the southwest, **U.S. 285.**

BY TRAIN

Amtrak serves the beautifully restored **Union Station,** at 17th and Wynkoop streets (📞 **800/872-7245** or 303/825-2583; www.amtrak.com), in the heart of LoDo. Denver is a stop for the **California Zephyr** (Chicago to Emeryville, California); there is one train daily in each direction.

BY BUS

Greyhound, 1055 19th St. (at Arapahoe St.; 📞 **800/231-2222;** www.greyhound.com), connects Colorado with cities coast to coast.

Visitor Information

Visit Denver operates a visitor center on the 16th Street Mall at 1600 California St. (📞 **303/892-1505**). It's open daily in summer and weekdays in winter. Information is also available at Denver International Airport. Ask for the Official Visitors Guide, a 150-plus-page full-color booklet with a comprehensive listing of accommodations, restaurants, and other visitor services in Denver and surrounding areas.

For maps and information, contact the Denver Metro Convention and Visitors Bureau, a.k.a. Visit Denver (📞 **800/233-6837** or 303/892-1112; www.denver.org).

City Layout

It's tough to get lost in Denver—just remember that the mountains, nearly always visible, are to the west. Nonetheless, getting around can sometimes be a challenge. One element of confusion is that Denver has both an older grid system downtown, which is oriented northeast-southwest to parallel the South Platte River, and a newer north-south grid system that surrounds the older one.

MAIN ARTERIES & STREETS

It's probably easiest to get your bearings from Civic Center Park. From here, Colfax Avenue (U.S. 40) extends east and west as far as the eye can see. The same is true for Broadway, which reaches north and south.

DOWNTOWN DENVER   North of Colfax and west of Broadway is the center of downtown, where the streets follow the old grid pattern. A mile-long pedestrian mall, **16th Street,** cuts northwest off Broadway just north of this intersection, with numbered streets running parallel in both directions. Intersecting the numbered streets at right angles are **Lawrence Street** (which runs one-way northeast) and **Larimer Street** (which runs one-way southwest). **I-25** skirts downtown Denver to the west, with access from Colfax or **Speer Boulevard,** which winds diagonally along Cherry Creek past Larimer Square.

OUTSIDE DOWNTOWN   Outside the downtown sector, the pattern is a little less confusing. But keep in mind that the numbered avenues that parallel Colfax to the north and south (Colfax is equivalent to 15th Ave.) have nothing in common with the numbered streets of the downtown grid. In fact, any byway labeled an "avenue" runs east-west, never north-south.

FINDING AN ADDRESS

NORTH-SOUTH ARTERIES   The thoroughfare that divides avenues into east and west is **Broadway,** which runs one-way south between 19th Street and I-25. Each block east or west adds 100 to the avenue address; thus, if you wanted to find 2115 E. 17th Ave., it would be a little more than 21 blocks east of Broadway, just beyond Vine Street.

Main thoroughfares that parallel Broadway to the east include **Downing Street** (1200 block), **York Street** (2300 block; it becomes **University Blvd.** south of 6th), **Colorado Boulevard** (4000 block), **Monaco Street Parkway** (6500 block), and **Quebec Street** (7300 block). Colorado Boulevard (Colo. 2) is the busiest street in the whole state, intersecting I-25 on the south and I-70 on the north. North-south streets that parallel Broadway to the west include **Santa Fe Drive** (U.S. 85; 1000 block); west of I-25 are **Federal Boulevard** (U.S. 287 N.; 3000 block) and **Sheridan Boulevard** (Colo. 95; 5200 block), the boundary between Denver and Lakewood.

EAST-WEST ARTERIES   Denver streets are divided into north and south at **Ellsworth Avenue,** about 2 miles south of Colfax. Ellsworth is a relatively minor street, but it's a convenient dividing point because it's just a block south of **1st Avenue.** With building numbers increasing by 100 each block, that puts an address like 1710 Downing St. at the corner of East 17th Avenue. **First, 6th, Colfax** (1500 block), and **26th avenues,** and **Martin Luther King Jr. Boulevard** (3200 block) are the principal east-west thoroughfares. There are no numbered avenues south of Ellsworth. Major east-west byways south of Ellsworth are **Alameda** (Colo. 26; 300 block), **Mississippi** (1100 block), **Louisiana** (1300 block), **Evans** (2100 block), **Yale** (2700 block), and **Hampden avenues** (U.S. 285; 3500 block).

The Neighborhoods in Brief

DOWNTOWN

For the purposes of this book, Downtown Denver is comprised of three areas. **LoDo,** a 25-block area surrounding Union Station, and encompassing **Wynkoop Street** southeast to **Market Street** and **20th Street** southwest to **Speer Boulevard,** is a delightful and busy historic district that was until recently a somewhat seedy neighborhood of deteriorating Victorian houses and

Denver Neighborhoods

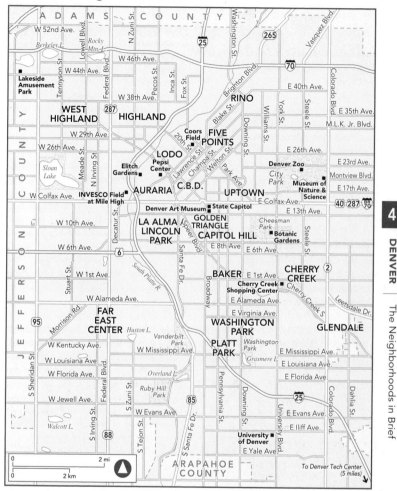

redbrick warehouses. A major restoration effort has brought it back to life. Today it is home to chic shops, art galleries, nightclubs, and restaurants. Listed as both a city and a county historic district, it boasts numerous National Historic Landmarks; skyscrapers are prohibited by law. Coors Field, the 50,000-seat home of the Rockies baseball team, opened here in 1995. East of LoDo is the **Central Business District.** This extends along **16th, 17th, and 18th streets between Lawrence Street and Broadway.**

The ban on skyscrapers certainly does not apply here. In this area you'll find the Brown Palace Hotel, the Westin Hotel at Tabor Center, and other upscale lodgings; numerous restaurants and bars; plus the popular 16th Street Mall. South of Colfax Avenue, west of Broadway, and west of Speer Boulevard is the **Golden Triangle,** home to the Denver Art Museum and numerous other attractions. There are also a number of art galleries here.

BAKER

Two miles south of downtown and centered on Broadway and 1st Avenue, Baker is the funky heart of south Denver. It is home to some great nightlife and shopping, a few excellent restaurants, and plenty of tattoo parlors and used bookstores.

FIVE POINTS

The "five points" actually meet at 23rd Street and Broadway, but the cultural and commercial hub of Denver's black community, from **23rd** to **38th streets,** northeast of downtown, covers a much larger area and incorporates four historic districts. Restaurants serve soul food, barbecued ribs, and Caribbean cuisine, while jazz and blues musicians and contemporary dance troupes perform in theaters and nightclubs. The Black American West Museum and Heritage Center is also in this area.

HIGHLANDS

Perched northwest of downtown from **32nd** to **38th avenues** between **Federal** and **Zuni streets,** the historic, increasingly chic Highlands neighborhood is the most densely populated neighborhood in the city outside of Capitol Hill. Mexican and Italian eateries brush elbows with stylish boutiques and galleries. In the neighboring West Highlands neighborhood, the eclectic retail district centered on 32nd Avenue and Lowell Boulevard is one of the most vibrant in the city.

LA ALMA/LINCOLN PARK/AURARIA

Latino culture, art, food, and entertainment predominate along this strip of **Santa Fe Drive,** between **West Colfax** and **West 6th avenues.** It's notable for its Southwestern character and architecture. This neighborhood is well worth a visit for its numerous restaurants, art galleries, and crafts shops. Denver's annual Cinco de Mayo celebration takes place here.

RINO

Short for "River North," this warehouse district **northeast of downtown and south of I-70** is one of the hottest addresses in Denver, thanks to the artists, tech startups, markets, and other businesses that have taken up residence in said warehouses. The brick warehouses are interspersed with contemporary new commercial and residential developments.

UPTOWN

Denver's oldest residential neighborhood, from **Broadway** east to **York Street** (City Park) and **23rd Avenue** south to **Colfax Avenue,** is best known today for two things: It's bisected by 17th Avenue, home to many of the city's finest restaurants, and several of its classic Victorian and Queen Anne–style homes have been converted to captivating bed-and-breakfasts.

WASHINGTON PARK

A grand Victorian neighborhood centered on the lush park of its namesake, "Wash Park" is one of Denver's trendiest and most popular neighborhoods. Bounded by **Broadway** east to **University Boulevard,** and **Alameda Avenue** south to **Evans Avenue,** it features a good deal of dining and recreational opportunities, but little in the way of lodging. The neighboring neighborhood of **Platt Park** also has good dining.

CAPITOL HILL

One of Denver's most diverse and oldest neighborhoods lies just southeast of downtown. Capitol Hill centers on the gold-domed Capitol Building, encompassing **Broadway** east to **York,** and **Colfax Avenue** south to **6th Avenue.** The north edge is improving after years of neglect and criminal activity, and now features such attractions as the Fillmore Auditorium and a lively restaurant and bar scene. There are several commercial and retail districts in the area, nestled amid Victorian houses and modern lofts and apartments. Also here are the Molly Brown House Museum (p. 44) and several lodging options, ranging from B&Bs to luxury hotels.

CHERRY CREEK

Home of the Cherry Creek Shopping Center and Denver Country Club, this area extends north from **East 1st Avenue** to **East 8th Avenue,** and from **Downing Street** east to **Steele Street.** You'll find huge, ostentatious stone mansions here, especially around Circle Drive (southwest of 6th and University), where many of Denver's wealthiest families have lived for generations.

DENVER TECH CENTER

At the southern end of the metropolitan area is the Denver Tech Center, along **I-25** between **Belleview Avenue** and **Arapahoe Road.** In this district, about a 25-minute drive from downtown, you will find the headquarters of several international and national companies, high-tech businesses, and a handful of upscale hotels heavily oriented toward business travelers.

GETTING AROUND

By Public Transportation

The **Regional Transportation District,** or **RTD** (✆ **303/299-6000;** www.rtd-denver.com), calls itself "The Ride." It operates bus routes and a light-rail system, with free transfer tickets available. It provides good service within Denver and its suburbs and outlying communities (including Boulder, Longmont, and Evergreen), as well as free parking at more than 60 Park-n-Ride locations throughout the Denver-Boulder metropolitan area. The light-rail service is designed to get buses and cars out of congested downtown Denver; many of the bus routes from outlying areas deliver passengers to light-rail stations rather than to downtown.

The local one-way fare is $2.25, seniors and passengers with disabilities pay $1, and children age 5 and under travel free. Regional bus fares vary—for example, Denver to Boulder costs $5. Day passes are $6.75. Exact change is required for buses, and train tickets can be purchased at vending machines beneath light-rail station awnings.

Depending on the route, the departure time of the last bus or train varies from 9pm to 2am. Maps for all routes are available at any time at the RTD **Civic Center Station,** 16th Street and Broadway, and the **Market Street Station,** Market and 16th streets. RTD also provides special service to Colorado Rockies (baseball) and Denver Broncos (football) games. All RTD buses and trains are completely wheelchair accessible.

Free buses run up and down the 16th Street Mall between the Civic Center and Market Street, daily from 6am to 1am.

The Light Rail is also useful for exploring downtown and the greater metro area. The **C Line** diverts from the main north-south **D Line** at Colfax Avenue, and it veers west and stops at Sports Authority Field at Mile High, the Pepsi Center, and Six Flags Elitch Gardens before chugging into Union Station at 17th and Wynkoop streets in lower downtown. The D Line continues along northeast through the east side of downtown before its terminus at 30th Avenue and Downing Street. The **E Line** runs along I-25 from Broadway to Lincoln Avenue in the south suburbs. The **F Line** connects 18th and California streets downtown with Lincoln Avenue. The **G Line** runs from Nine Mile in Aurora at I-225 and Parker Road to Lincoln; the **H Line** connects Nine Mile and 18th and California. New in 2013, the **W Line** connects downtown Denver and Golden. Projects are underway for lines to DIA and Boulder, but they will not open until 2016.

In 2010, the city installed numerous **B-Cycle kiosks** (http://denver.bcycle.com), which rent bicycles for a $5 daily fee plus fees for how long you use the bike before returning it to another kiosk. Check on the website for the kiosk locations—they are often right in front of prominent attractions, making this a viable means of getting from one place to another in the city.

The open-air **Platte Valley Trolley** (✆ **303/458-6255;** www.denvertrolley.org) operates year-round. From May to October between noon and 3:30pm Friday through Sunday, there's a 25-minute "Riverfront Ride" ($5 adults, $2 children under 13), which operates from 15th Street at Confluence Park, south to the Denver Children's Museum along the west bank of the Platte River.

By Taxi

The main companies are **Yellow Cab** (☏ **303/777-7777**; www.yellowtrans.com), **Union Taxi** (☏ **303/922-2222**; www.uniontaxidenver.net), and **Metro Taxi** (☏ **303/333-3333**; www.metrotaxidenver.com). Taxis can be hailed on the street, though it's preferable to call for a taxi or to wait for one at a taxi stand outside a major hotel.

By Car

Because cars are not necessary downtown, visitors can save money by staying downtown while in Denver, and then renting a car to leave the area. Most major car-rental agencies have outlets in or near downtown Denver, as well as at Denver International Airport. These include **Avis, Dollar, Enterprise, Hertz, National/Alamo,** and **Thrifty.** Per-day rentals for midsize cars typically range from $40 to $100, although discounts are often available, and weekend and multiday rates can also save money. Four-wheel-drive vehicles, trucks, and campers cost more.

PARKING Downtown parking-lot rates vary from around $1 per half-hour to $20 or more per full day. Many meters now accept credit cards, but not all.

[FastFACTS] DENVER

ATMs/Banks ATMs and banks are very common throughout the Denver area.

Dentists, Doctors & Hospitals Dentist and doctor referrals are available by calling ☏ **800/DOC-TORS** (362-8677). **Ask-A-Nurse Centura** (☏ **303/777-6877**) provides free physician referrals and answers health questions. Among Denver-area hospitals are **St. Joseph Hospital,** 1835 Franklin St. (☏ **303/837-7111**), just east of downtown, and **Children's Hospital,** 13123 E. 16th Ave., Aurora (☏ **720/777-1234**).

Emergencies Call ☏ **911.** For the **Colorado Poison Center,** call ☏ **303/739-1123.** For the

Rape Crisis and Domestic Violence Hotline, call ☏ **303/318-9989.**

Internet Access Most hotels and coffee shops have free Wi-Fi. Libraries have puclic computers.

Mail & Postage The main downtown post office is at 951 20th St. For other post office locations and hours, check with the U.S. Postal Service (☏ **800/275-8777**; www.usps.com).

Newspapers & Magazines **"The Denver Post"** (www.denverpost.com) is Denver's only daily newspaper. **"Westword"** (www.westword.com) is known as much for its coverage of local politicians and celebrities as its entertainment and dining listings. National

newspapers, such as **"USA Today"** and **"The Wall Street Journal,"** can be purchased at newsstands and at major hotels.

Pharmacies Throughout the metropolitan area, you will find Walgreens and other chain pharmacies, as well as Safeway and King Soopers grocery stores (which also have drugstores). The pharmacy at the **Walgreens** at 2000 E. Colfax Ave. (☏ **303/331-0917**) is open from 8am to 10pm daily.

Safety Although Denver is a relatively safe city, it is not crime-free. If you are unsure of the safety of a particular area you wish to visit, ask your hotel concierge or desk clerk.

WHERE TO STAY

Denver has its fair share of full-service hotels, most of them downtown and at the Denver Tech Center, as well as a few B&Bs in the central neighborhoods. Many more are in the works: The Union Station redevelopment includes a hotel and there are several projects underway slated for completion in late 2014 and beyond. Alas, most of these will be expensive chain properties—there are very few good budget lodgings in the city. That's why we suggest that budget travelers look at such websites as AirBnB.com and Wimdu.com that allow travelers to rent inexpensive rooms in local's homes (and sometimes an entire apartment for the cost of a hotel room). The app HotelTonight.com provides deeply discounted (up to 70 percent) rooms for travelers—but only those willing to book on the morning of their stay, a hair-raising idea for some.

Downtown

Hotels in downtown Denver, "the central business district of the Rocky Mountain West," generally cater to businesspeople, with high-tech amenities and locations convenient to the Convention Center or the financial district. These properties are more than adequate for leisure travelers, and especially enticing on weekends when they lower their rates.

EXPENSIVE

Brown Palace Hotel & Spa ★★★   This is the historic high point of hotels in Denver. The Brown Palace's doors opened in 1892 and in the 120-plus years of continuous operation, much has, happily, stayed the same. The lobby remains one for the ages, with iron grillwork panels surrounding the 8-story atrium on the way up to the ornate stained-glass dome. The original artesian well—drilled 720 feet into the ground below—still feeds every faucet and drinking fountain in the hotel. A few things have changed over the years, of course. Clad in sandstone and granite, the building is no longer the tallest in town. The guest rooms and suites, while still sporting a classic look, now have iPod docks, flatscreens, and other modern perks. The dining options—including the landmark Palace Arms and the less formal Ship Tavern—have gotten more adventurous. And there is now a beehive on the roof. The harvested honey is used to sweeten the traditional afternoon tea and in various spa treatments.

321 17th St. ⓒ **800/321-2599** or 303/297-3111. www.brownpalace.com. 241 units. $219–$410 double; $269–$1,400 suite. Lower weekend rates. Valet parking $26. Pets up to 20 lb. accepted. **Amenities:** 3 restaurants; 2 lounges; concierge; exercise room; room service; spa; Wi-Fi (free in lobby only).

Crawford Hotel ★★   Named for Dana Crawford, the legendary preservationist who spearheaded the restoration of Larimer Square, this 2014 entry into the Denver hotel landscape is a winner. Its location, right in historic Union Station and surrounded by boutiques and restaurants, couldn't be better (and don't worry, the entry points for the tracks are glassed in, so there's no train noise in the hotel). Rooms, lofts, and suites are contemporary but hark back to days past with handpicked Western art (including plenty of railroad relics and jackalope heads) and lots of wood and fine leathers. Even the smaller ones feel roomy, thanks to 14-foot ceilings. Contemporary touches include rainfall showers and smart TVs. The hotel even has a Tesla that will ferry you around downtown.

1701 Wynkoop St. ⓒ **800/228-5838.** www.thecrawfordhotel.com. 112 units, including 5 suites. $279–$669 double; $529–$1,800 suite. Valet parking $34. Dogs accepted ($50/night). **Amenities:** Concierge; fitness center; room service; free Wi-Fi.

On the Hoof

If you're in town for the National Western Stock Show, make sure to visit the Brown Palace Hotel for a study in contrasts—the champion steer is traditionally corralled in the lobby during one of the event's final mornings.

Denver Hotels & Restaurants

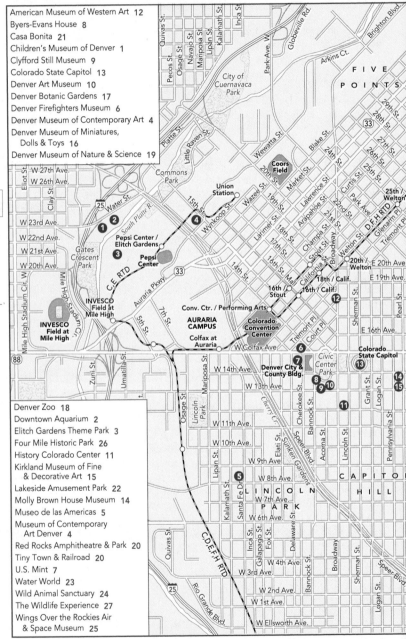

American Museum of Western Art 12
Byers-Evans House 8
Casa Bonita 21
Children's Museum of Denver 1
Clyfford Still Museum 9
Colorado State Capitol 13
Denver Art Museum 10
Denver Botanic Gardens 17
Denver Firefighters Museum 6
Denver Museum of Contemporary Art 4
Denver Museum of Miniatures,
    Dolls & Toys 16
Denver Museum of Nature & Science 19

Denver Zoo 18
Downtown Aquarium 2
Elitch Gardens Theme Park 3
Four Mile Historic Park 26
History Colorado Center 11
Kirkland Museum of Fine
    & Decorative Art 15
Lakeside Amusement Park 22
Molly Brown House Museum 14
Museo de las Americas 5
Museum of Contemporary
    Art Denver 4
Red Rocks Amphitheatre & Park 20
Tiny Town & Railroad 20
U.S. Mint 7
Water World 23
Wild Animal Sanctuary 24
The Wildlife Experience 27
Wings Over the Rockies Air
    & Space Museum 25

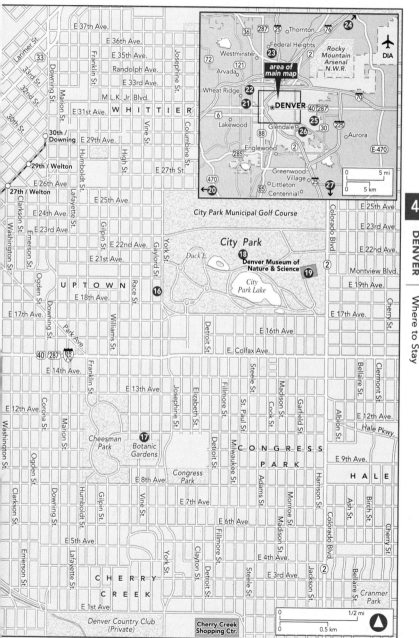

The Curtis, A DoubleTree by Hilton ★★ Few hotels take themselves less seriously than The Curtis, and that's a good thing. For starters, you might find the front desk staff hula-hooping or playing Guitar Hero in the lobby—it's part of the job description. Heading upstairs, every floor has a theme, from the Sci-Fi Floor to Dun Dun Dunnn!, the aptly named 13th floor with a creepy portrait of Jack Nicholson from "The Shining" greeting guests as they get off the elevator. There are classic board games you can borrow from the lobby, and wake-up calls from Yoda and Elvis. But it's not all fun and games: The freshly renovated guest rooms are sleek and contemporary, featuring custom artwork, and "hyper-themed" suites include nods to Jimmy Buffett and the "Talladega Nights" movie. The Theatre District location is convenient to the convention center and the performing arts complex.

1405 Curtis St. ℂ **800/525-6651** or 303/571-0300. www.thecurtis.com. 336 units. $159–$459 double; $600–$1,000 suite. Lower weekend rates. Valet parking $28. **Amenities:** Restaurant (New American); lounge; concierge; exercise room; room service; free Wi-Fi.

Hotel Monaco ★★ Melding alternately bright and bold colors, classical motifs, and a hint of Western chic, the Hotel Monaco is the cool kid on the Denver hotel block. Rooms manage to blend labyrinthine patterns, faux cowskin blankets, and oversized headboards into an aesthetically satisfying whole. The corner suites have similar eclectic style and plenty of space to spread out—675 square feet, to be precise. Among the facilities, the resident restaurant, **Panzano** (p. 31) is a standout. And if you are in need of company, the staff will deliver you a goldfish—they make great listeners.

1717 Champa St. (at 17th St.). ℂ **800/990-1303** or 303/296-1717. www.monaco-denver.com. 189 units. $170–$310 double; from $260 suite. Call for weekend rates. Valet parking $28 (hybrids $14). Pets accepted (no fee). **Amenities:** Restaurant; lounge; concierge; exercise room; room service; spa; Wi-Fi (free to Kimpton loyalty card members).

Hotel Teatro ★★★ Named for its proximity to the Denver Center for the Performing Arts, the boutique Hotel Teatro is Denver's most romantic hotel, still beaming from a slick renovation in 2012. A hotel since 1999, the former office building sports a stately exterior of red brick and gleaming white terra cotta as it did when it was built in 1911. Besides its moniker, the hotel pays homage to its theatrical neighbor with an assortment of props, photos, and costumes displayed throughout the public areas. With cherrywood details, Indonesian sandstone flooring, and mellow earth tones, the rooms are singularly striking. A new Colorado-centric restaurant, **The Nickel,** opened in 2014.

1100 14th St. (at Arapahoe St.). ℂ **303/228-1100.** www.hotelteatro.com. 109 units. $279–$409 double; $479–$1,500 suite. Valet parking $29 overnight. Pets accepted. **Amenities:** 2 restaurants; lounge; concierge; fitness center; room service; free Wi-Fi.

Oxford Hotel ★★ If you are looking to stay in the heart of LoDo, the venerable Oxford Hotel is the best pace to hang your hat. The 1891 hotel has been restored to its turn-of-the-20th-century heyday, down to the recently restored entry with "Oxford" in lights. Nodding to the 1920s and 1930s with reproductions and art, rooms have king or queen beds and a stylish air, but are a bit on the smallish side. No worries—the location begs for guests to get out and explore, the resident **McCormick & Schmick's** is known for its seafood, and the two bars—including the one and only **Cruise Room** (p. 58)—are among the best watering holes in the city.

1600 17th St. (at Wazee St.). ℂ **800/228-5838** or 303/628-5400. www.theoxfordhotel.com. 80 units. $190–$250 double; $290–$410 suite; presidential suite from $1,000. Valet parking $34. **Amenities:** Restaurant; 2 lounges; health club; room service; spa; free Wi-Fi.

Renaissance Denver Downtown City Center ★★ In the Colorado National Bank building (1915), the lobby is real showstopper, featuring marble columns and restored murals by legendary artist Allen True. The one-time bank reopened as a hotel in 2014 and deftly blends historic features—vaults are now meeting rooms, the teller counter has been transformed into a bar, and historic photos and documents abound—with contemporary art and decor, and even a bit of colorful whimsy. Sleek rooms include very comfortable, feather-topped king beds or two queens, workable desks, and minifridges; deluxe rooms have a bit more space. For those who like to sweat when they travel, the fitness room here is state-of-the-art. Even if you are not a guest, drop by for a drink or meal at the resident "New American West" **Range** restaurant, and then pull out your smartphone for a tour enabled by QR codes throughout the property.

918 17th St. ☎ **303/867-8100**. www.rendendowntown.com. 230 units, including 7 suites. $229–$499 double; $429–$1,000 suite. Valet parking $35. **Amenities:** Restaurant; 2 lounges; fitness center; room service; spa; free Wi-Fi.

MODERATE

Queen Anne Bed & Breakfast Inn ★★ Reinvented for the 21st century with contemporary design and a green bent, the Queen Anne has a sustainably minded philosophy, using local ingredients in the breakfasts and striving towards zero-waste. Rooms are in the 1879 Pierce-Tabor House and the 1886 Roberts house next door. Each of the four suites in the latter is designed by a local artist, adding some contemporary zing that meshes well with the Victorian vibe. My favorite is the Aspen Room, with a queen aspen-wood bed and a striking mural of turning aspen trees from the floor to the crux of the Victorian turret above.

2147–51 Tremont Place. ☎ **303/296-6666**. www.queenannebnb.com. 14 units. $135–$185 double; $215 suite. Rates include hot breakfast and evening wine. Free off-street parking. **Amenities:** Free Wi-Fi.

INEXPENSIVE

11th Avenue Hotel and Hostel ★ This budget hotel, a mile south of downtown, was built in 1903 and underwent a renovation adding hostel rooms a century later. Nicely maintained, the hotel includes such perks as access to a community kitchen and TV room (with Wi-Fi, a computer, and a small library) and coin laundry machines, as well as a patio out back. There are men's and women's dorm rooms with 22 bunks and about 100 modest but functional private rooms, some with baths and others that share them. Parking can be a bit difficult in the surrounding neighborhood, and the lack of air-conditioning can make for warm summer afternoons here.

1112 Broadway. ☎ **303/894-0529**. www.11thavenuehotelandhostel.com. 22 beds, 105 private units. $20–$22 per person; $53 double with shared bath; $60 double with private bath. **Amenities:** Free Wi-Fi.

Capitol Hill

MODERATE

Capitol Hill Mansion Bed & Breakfast ★★ This stunning Richardsonian Romanesque mansion on "Millionaire's Row" is an architectural gem with a great location for exploring the Civic Center area on foot. Just a block down the street from the Molly Brown House Museum, this is likewise a legacy to Denver's gilded Victorian era, featuring turrets, spires, and other touches that make it a great study of the so-called "Denver Style." Inside, the rooms are posh and romantic, each with unique decor. The unexpected Snowlover Balcony Room is a favorite, with a mural of a snowy forest and a balcony with city and mountain views (thus the name). Another fave is the

Pasque Flower Room, with floral stenciling, hardwoods, and a whirlpool for two built into the third-floor turret.

1207 Pennsylvania St. (© **800/839-9329** or 303/839-5221. www.capitolhillmansion.com. 8 units. $139–$219 double. Rates include full breakfast and evening wine and refreshments. Free off-street parking. **Amenities:** Free Wi-Fi.

Castle Marne Bed & Breakfast ★★   This inn wasn't named Castle Marne by accident. Architect William Lang crafted this true castle a mile east of downtown out of lava stone in 1889 and it remains one of the most distinctive addresses in the entire city. The more you look, the more details jump out at you, from the pagan Green Man carved into the mantel to the stained-glass Peacock Window strutting its stuff on the second floor. A real-estate bust in the 1980s led to the castle's abandonment, until the Peiker family lovingly breathed life into it as a B&B in 1988. A quarter-century later, Castle Marne is one of the best inns in the city, with a nice variety of antique-furnished rooms. It's a remarkable study in preservation and restoration.

1572 Race St. (© **303/331-0621.** www.castlemarne.com. 9 units, including 1 suite. $125–$285 double; $320 suite. Rates include full breakfast. Free off-street parking. **Amenities:** Free Wi-Fi.

West of Downtown

EXPENSIVE

Highland Haven Creekside Inn ★★   Evolving from a roadside motel in 1979 to a marvel of a lodging today, this B&B in Evergreen, about 30 miles southwest of downtown Denver in the Rocky Mountain foothills, is just the spot for those who are looking for a getaway from the city. Centered on a historic (1884) cabin, this completely unfussy (even a bit rugged) inn has no doilies but plenty of first-rate woodwork. You can pick from a wide variety of room options, including standard rooms, luxurious suites, cottages, and the magical TreeHouse, a one-of-a-kind unit that is nestled between two huge spruce trees with a two-person steam shower and a Jacuzzi in the cupola.

4359 Independence Trail, Evergreen. (© **800/459-2406** or 303/674-3577. www.highlandhaven. com. 18 units, including 3 suites and 6 cottages. $160–$250 double; $265–$565 suite or cottage. Rates include full breakfast. **Amenities:** Free Wi-Fi.

WHERE TO EAT

Denver abounds with Mexican holes in the wall, chain eateries, steak joints, and even a few bison joints, and the restaurants in LoDo and Cherry Creek become more like those in Los Angeles and Manhattan every year. Below, I've listed primarily independent restaurants, unique to this area and a cut above others in their price ranges. If you'd like to get a taste of several restaurants, **Culinary Connectors** (© **303/495-5487;** www.culinaryconnectors.com) leads walking tours of Denver on Friday and Saturday afternoons, as well as other tours. Pricing is typically $99 per person.

Downtown

Downtown encompasses three downtown-area neighborhoods as far as the following reviews are concerned: **Lower Downtown (LoDo),** the **Central Business District,** and the **Golden Triangle,** as well as a few nearby neighborhoods. This area is the densest concentration of restaurants in Denver, and there is plenty to choose from: Steakhouses, microbreweries, and cutting-edge eateries abound. Beyond the restaurants that follow, **The Kitchen Denver,** 1530 16th St. (© **303/623-3127;** www.

thekitchencommunity.com), is the highly recommended younger sister restaurant of the original **Kitchen** in Boulder (p. 101).

EXPENSIVE

Buckhorn Exchange ★★ STEAKS/GAME   No eatery in Denver has the historic cachet of the Buckhorn Exchange. Open since 1893, the place earned its name for cashing the checks of miners and others fresh off the adjacent railroad. Buffalo Bill drank here, and it has the first electric beer sign on the planet in the bar upstairs. The dining room, its walls populated with trophy heads of every description, is just the spot for carnivores. The Buckhorn has made its name on succulent steaks and savory game dishes. Of the former, some are meant for the table—weighing up to 4 pounds and costing up to $215—and the latter includes elk, venison, and buffalo as well as exotic specials like yak and rattlesnake.

1000 Osage St. (at W. 10th Ave.). ℂ **303/534-9505.** www.buckhorn.com. Main courses $10–$20 lunch, $25–$56 dinner. Mon–Fri 11am–2pm; Mon–Thurs 5:30–9pm; Fri–Sat 5–10pm; Sun 5–9pm. Bar open all day. Light Rail: 10th and Osage.

Panzano ★★★ ITALIAN   The best Italian eatery in the city, Panzano is a terrific pick for a downtown dinner that balances a casual, contemporary atmosphere with inventive fare inspired by the cuisine of Northern Italy. Chef Elise Wiggins has helmed the kitchen here since 2004, with reliably electrifying results. Seqared sea scallops, fried brussels sprouts, and Caesar salad set the stage for dishes like gnocchi with rabbit confit, slate-grilled salmon, and vegetarian lasagna.

In Hotel Monaco, 909 17th St. ℂ **303/296-3525.** www.panzano-denver.com. Main courses $10–$16 breakfast and brunch, $14–$25 lunch, $20–$30 dinner. Mon–Fri 6:30–10am and 11am–2:30pm; Mon–Thurs 5–10pm; Fri–Sat 5–11pm; Sat–Sun 8am–2:30pm; Sun 4:30–9:30pm Bus: 28. Light Rail: D/F, 18th St. stations.

Rioja ★★★ MEDITERRANEAN   Rioja chef-owner Jennifer Jasinski took top honors for best chef in the Southwest at the 2013 James Beard awards in New York. It's easy to see why when you visit the sleek Larimer Square spot, with a menu brimming with creativity and unexpected flavors. The Mediterranean serves as a culinary launching point, but the food often veers through other culinary traditions en route to the finish line. You might get tempura-fried green tomatoes, or cucumber carpaccio with feta mousse, or Peking duck with caramelized eggplant and a delectable orange-olive puree. Jasinski changes the menu on a regular basis, but you can count on tantalizing tastes and impeccable service.

1431 Larimer Sq. ℂ **303/820-2282.** www.riojadenver.com. Main courses $11–$24 brunch and lunch, $19–$29 dinner. Wed–Fri 11:30am–2:30pm; Sat–Sun 10am–2:30pm; Sun–Thurs 5–10pm; Fri–Sat 5–11pm. Bus: 6. Light Rail: D/F, Theatre District.

The Squeaky Bean ★★★ NEW AMERICAN   After a stint in the Highlands, the Squeaky Bean relocated to LoDo in 2012, where it remains one of the most creative eateries in Denver. In a space bedecked with an electric Bingo board (it is in use during the standout Sunday brunch), the restaurant has a fun atmosphere, and the kitchen loves to break rules. You'll see what I mean when you peruse the menu, which includes such starters as twice-fried chicken wings and red and yellow beet salad, plus such innovative entrees as pork-lemongrass sausage and local lamb shank with peas, lentils, and mint yogurt. Leave room for an artful dessert—I recommend the delectable chocolate pot au crème.

1500 Wynkoop St. ℂ **303/623-2665.** www.thesqueakybean.com. Main courses $24–$38. Tues–Thurs 4–10pm; Fri–Sat 4–11pm; Sun 10am–3pm. Bus: 28, 30X, 41X. Light Rail: C/E, Union Station.

TAG ★★★ NEW AMERICAN   Chef-owner Troy Guard is one of Denver's most prolific restaurateurs. He's also one of the best. His flagship—open since 2009 and named for his initials—TAG is a brick-laden, contemporary space that meshes Guard's experience under the legendary Roy Yamaguchi in Hawaii and his love for local Colorado ingredients. The results are stunning, from "TAG Fry"—octopus confit with shishito peppers and sweet potatoes—to inventive sushi rolls to larger plates like Colorado ranch steak with local fingerling potatoes.

1441 Larimer St. ⓒ **303/996-9985.** www.tag-restaurant.com. Main courses $14–$32 lunch, $19–$32 dinner. Mon–Thurs 11:30am–10pm; Fri–Sat 5–11pm; Sun 5–9pm. Bus: 6. Light Rail: D/F, Theatre District.

MODERATE

Euclid Hall ★★ GASTROPUB   Plating up the best in comfort foods from the owners of Rioja, Euclid Hall is a bustling two-story restaurant off Larimer Square that balances a casual—and often loud—atmosphere with delectable fare. Housemade pickles, sausages, and poutines are complemented by chicken and waffles, *pad Thai* pig ears, and gourmet sandwiches. The beer menu is impressive, with a dozen on tap and many more in cans and bottles, and there is an emphasis on beer parings.

1317 14th St. ⓒ **303/595-4255.** www.euclidhall.com. Main courses $10–$18. Mon–Thurs 11:30am–midnight; Fri 11am–1am; Sat 2pm–1am; Sun 2pm–midnight. Bus: 6. Light Rail: D/F, Theater District.

Red Square Euro Bistro ★★ RUSSIAN/NEW AMERICAN   Tucked in the back of Writer Square, Red Square elevates Russian standards with an dollop of contemporary world cuisine. That means the menu has Russian classics like golubtsi (a cabbage roll stuffed with ground beef) and stroganoff alongside pan-seared swordfish and a mean veal osso bucco. The vodka list is a regional standout, sporting infusions made in house like beet, pineapple, and horseradish, as well as labels from Russia, Poland, Sweden, England, Iceland, and even El Salvador lining the back bar.

1512 Larimer St. (at Writer Sq.). ⓒ **303/595-8600.** www.redsquarebistro.com. Main courses $18–$32. Daily 5–10pm. Bar open later. Bus: 6. Light Rail: D/F, Theater District.

Wynkoop Brewing Company ★★ AMERICAN/BREWPUB   This is ground zero for the amazing revitalization of LoDo. In 1988, the 1888 warehouse was converted into one of the best brewpubs anywhere, and the place has now been pouring first-rate suds and plating up an eclectic menu of inventive pub grub for a quarter-century. Get mac and asiago and cheddar cheese, fish and chips, or buffalo meatloaf, and wash it down with the flagship Railyard Ale or—my favorite—Patty's Chile Beer, sporting a spicy kick. They also make a wide array of small-batch beers, including a zany Rocky Mountain Oyster Stout that debuted in 2012. Then you have the political connections: In 2010, founder John Hickenlooper became the nation's first brewer-governor since Sam Adams left office in Massachusetts in 1797.

1634 18th St. (at Wynkoop St.). ⓒ **303/297-2700.** www.wynkoop.com. Main courses $10–$19. Mon–Thurs 11am–11pm; Fri–Sat 11am–midnight; Sun 11am–10pm. Bar open later Bus: 28, 30X, 41X. Light Rail: C/E, Union Station.

INEXPENSIVE

In addition to the options that follow, there are a number of great breakfast and lunch spots in the downtown area. **Snooze,** 2262 Larimer St. (ⓒ **303/297-0700;** www.snoozeeatery.com), and other locations (including Union Station), serves delicacies like pineapple upside-down pancakes and bison meatball subs. Established in 1942, **Pete's Kitchen,** 1962 E. Colfax Ave. (ⓒ **303/321-3139;** www.petesrestaurants.com), is a prototypical urban diner, with checkerboard floors, a breakfast bar, booths, plenty of local color, and killer breakfast burritos. Pete's is open 24 hours on weekends, making it a favorite of the barhopping crowd. And there is perhaps no more remarkable value-oriented restaurant than the nonprofit **SAME Cafe,** 2023 E. Colfax Ave. (✆ **720/530-6853;** www.soallmayeat.org), where there is no cash register: Customers pay donations of their own choosing for a healthy lunch. The socially conscious proprietors are committed to alleviating hunger and promoting healthy eating for all.

Biker Jim's Gourmet Dogs ★ AMERICAN/HOT DOGS/GAME   Jim Pittenger, a.k.a. Biker Jim, got his start selling hot dogs from a cart on the 16th Street Mall. Not just any hot dogs: wild boar hot dogs, reindeer hot dogs, pheasant hot dogs, buffalo, rattlesnake, you name it. Pittenger still has the cart (and a food truck), but he also opened permanent digs on Larimer, serving his trademark dogs, overflowing with all manner of toppings (wasabi aioli, pinto beans, cactus, and cream cheese among them), as well as guilty-pleasure side dishes like fried mac and cheese, charred cauliflower, and Biker Jim's transcendent baked beans. The formula is working: Pittenger's earned a fiercely loyal following, as well as praise from Anthony Bourdain and countless critics. There is a full bar.

2148 Larimer St. ✆ 720/746-9355. www.bikerjimsdogs.com. Hot dogs $6–$9; side dishes $2–$4. Mon–Thurs and Sun 11am–10pm; Fri–Sat 11am–3am. Light Rail: D/F 20th and Welton.

Baker

A few years ago, Baker was home to a couple of greasy spoons and that was about it. What a difference a decade makes: Now you can get everything from a gourmet dinner to sushi to a slice of pizza on this funky Broadway strip.

A GOOD CITY FOR green chile FIENDS

Green chile (green chil-ay): n. a fiery-sweet stew made of chile peppers and other ingredients, often but not always including chunks of pork, tomato, and onion. Denver's eateries serve bowl after bowl of good green chile, stuff that ranges from merely spicy to flat-out nuclear. If you have a serious weakness for a bowl of green (as I do), here are five hot spots in the Mile High City, in no particular order:

1. **Brewery Bar II,** 150 Kalamath St. (✆ **303/893-0971**): Inconspicuously nestled in a warehouse district, the Brewery Bar serves some of the hottest green chile in Denver. It also happens to be some of the tastiest. There are also two Brewery Bars in the south suburbs.

2. **El Tejado,** 2651 S. Broadway (✆ **303/722-3987**): This locals' favorite in the southern reaches of the city serves a unique thick green chile plate as well as some of the best authentic Mexican dishes in the Rockies.

3. **Jack-N-Grill,** 2524 N. Federal Blvd. (✆ **303/964-9544**): Sweet and typically served in a bowl with beans, Jack Martinez's green chile is excellent, as is his red. There are three Denver-area locations. See p. 35.

4. **Las Delicias,** 439 E. 19th Ave. (✆ **303/839-5675**): A Denver tradition, Las Delicias serves some of the city's best green chile from its downtown location among its five metro-area eateries.

5. **Little Anita's,** 1550 S. Colorado Blvd. (✆ **303/691-3337**): This long-time New Mexico-based eatery offers wicked green and red chile from a strip mall in southeast Denver and three other metro-area locations.

EXPENSIVE

Beatrice & Woodsley ★★★ NEW AMERICAN   This is one of the most quirky and creative restaurants you are going to find, and the food is uniformly excellent. Aspen trees sprout from the floor in the front of the room as part of a wilderness-meets-city motif, the bathrooms are perplexingly camouflaged and marvels of design, and the aesthetic is hyper-contemporary meets fun. The fare incorporates plenty of local and organic ingredients into inventive dishes like wild boar burgers, catfish with grits and fried pickles, and cider-brined pork porterhouse. The small plates, cocktails, and desserts are similarly superlative, worthy a stop for happy hour or late at night. The wine list is short but excellent.

38 S. Broadway. (℃ **303/777-3505.** www.beatriceandwoodsley.com. Main courses $18–$32. Daily 5–9 or 10pm; Sat–Sun 10am–2pm. Bus: 0. Light Rail: Alameda.

Cherry Creek
EXPENSIVE

Elway's ★★ STEAKS/SEAFOOD   No. 7 worked wonders with a pigskin, but John Elway has demonstrated he knows how to make a restaurant score as well with his eponymous Cherry Creek steakhouse. This is just the place to see and be seen, with a focus squarely on top-quality beef and fresh seafood as well as comfort foods like creamed corn, Brussels spout hash, and broccoli and cheese. Beyond the flagship location in Cherry Creek, you'll also find an **Elway's Downtown** in the Ritz-Carlton Denver, 1881 Curtis St. (℃ **303/312-3107**), as well as a new-in-2013 Denver International Airport location in Concourse B (℃ **303/342-7777**).

2500 E. 1st Ave. (immediately west of the Cherry Creek Shopping Center). (℃ **303/399-5353.** www.elways.com. Main courses $9–$34 lunch and brunch, $14–$60 dinner. Mon–Thurs 11am–10pm; Fri–Sat 11am–11pm; Sun 11am–9pm. Bus: 3.

Highlands

The hippest and hottest restaurant scene outside downtown, Highlands is likewise the hippest and hottest neighborhood in Denver. New American is the cuisine of choice here, but there is everything from neighborhood bar-and-grills to fun Mexican joints.

MODERATE

Linger ★★ NEW AMERICAN   In the historic Olinger Mortuary, Linger is known for several superlatives: the city views, especially from the rooftop patio; the creative menu of "globally inspired street food," ranging from fish tacos to wagyu sliders to shrimp and grits; and the slick decor, equal parts industrial chic and speakeasy. Dinner reservations are hard to come by—make them at least 2 weeks in advance—but lunch is easy for walk-ins. Skip dessert and head to **Little Man Ice Cream** (www.littleman icecream.com), shaped like a 28-foot-tall cream can, in the adjacent plaza.

2030 W. 30th Ave. (℃ **303/993-3120.** www.lingerdenver.com. Main courses $9–$17 brunch and lunch, $11–$22 dinner. Tues–Fri 11:30am–2:30pm; Tues–Sun 5:30–10pm; Sat–Sun 10am–2:30pm. Bar open later. Bus: 32.

Lola ★★ SEAFOOD/MEXICAN   Lola planted its flag in the Lower Highlands neighborhood in 2007 and, in the time since, it has emerged as one of the best places for a meal or just a margarita with a city view. Start off with guacamole, prepared fresh table-side, and then take your pick of one of the delectable specialties—lobster enchiladas, seared sea bass, and caldo de mariscos, a stew with shrimp, crab, mussels, and more. Landlubbing tastes will appreciate pork, beef, and vegetarian options. But it's the cocktails that make the place shine, with seven margaritas and unique drinks like the Fuego Verde—yes, green fire—with tequila, muddled jalapenos, and fresh lime.

1575 Boulder St. © **720/570-8686.** www.loladenver.com. Main courses $8–$16 brunch, $17–$30 dinner. Mon–Thurs 5–10pm; Fri 5–11pm; Sat 10am–11pm; Sun 9am–9pm. Bar open later. Bus: 32.

Root Down ★★ NEW AMERICAN What was until recently an abandoned garage is now one of the best eateries in Denver. Perched on an off-the-beaten High-lands location, Root Down is colorful inside and out, but perhaps best defined by a single hue: green. This is one of the most sustainable restaurants I've ever encountered, from the reverse-osmosis water system to the local foods, to the recycled materials throughout. Featuring a number of vegetarian selections, the fare is healthy and utterly distinctive, from sliders made of veggies and Colorado lamb to country-fried tofu to roast chicken with a green chile grit cake. There is also a new Root Down at Denver International Airport in Concourse C (© **303/342-6959**).

1600 W. 33rd Ave. © **303/993-4200.** www.rootdowndenver.com. Main courses $5–$14 brunch; $13–$28 dinner. Mon–Thurs 5–10pm; Fri–Sat 5–11pm; Sun 5–9pm; Sat–Sun 10am–2:30pm. Bar open later. Bus: 32.

INEXPENSIVE

Jack-N-Grill ★ NEW MEXICAN There is a credo that Jack Martinez, proprietor of Jack-N-Grill, lives by: "Comida sin chile, no es comida," meaning "A meal without chile is not a meal." This means few options are lacking this key ingredient, roasted on the premises every September during harvest season and stocked in a freezer to last the year. Served in a dining room decorated with jacks of all kinds—from Nicholson to the jack of hearts—hearty Mexican options like burritos and rellenos are complemented by less expected items such as stuffed sopapillas and posole stew. The burgers are also some of the biggest and best in Denver, and competitive eaters may want to try the 7-pound breakfast burrito ($22).

2524 N. Federal Blvd. © **303/964-9544.** www.jackngrill.com. Main courses $8–$14. Sun–Thurs 7am–9pm; Fri–Sat 7am–10pm. Bus: 31.

River North (North of Downtown)

River North (RiNo) is dominated by warehouses, but is a fast up-and-coming area with a number of startups and new developments, and a few good restaurants.

MODERATE

Fuel ★★ NEW AMERICAN This new restaurant at the TAXI redevelopment in River North (a new mixed-use rebirth of a former run-down taxi HQ) is an interesting place a bit out of the way, but right off the Platte River Trail if you are on bike or foot. The colorful, contemporary, industrial interior is a nice match for the menu, with a diverse and proprietor-described "intensely seasonal" dinner menu with an emphasis on creative recipes and local ingredients. The results are excellent, including lamb steak, gnocchi with mint and fava beans, and local striped bass with cauliflower risotto. Brunch includes smoked trout and a bagel, sausage stuffed brioche French toast, and the PBR breakfast, with two eggs, home fries, choice of meat, toast, and a Pabst Blue Ribbon for $9, or $10 without the beer (yes, I know).

3455 Ringsby Ct., Ste. 105. © **303/296-4642.** www.fuelcafedenver.com. Main courses $9–$15 brunch and lunch, $14–$25 dinner. Mon–Fri 11am–3pm; Wed–Sat 5–9pm; Sat–Sun 10am–2pm. Bus: 44.

Uptown

Just east of downtown and west of City Park, Uptown is a great destination for dining and nightlife. Most establishments are on 17th Avenue.

East 17th Avenue has long been a great stretch for restaurants east of downtown. The one-way street has several options, on both sides of the street. All points of the culinary spectrum (vegetarian to burgers) are here, and there are a number of gems tucked in neighborhoods away from the prime strip.

MODERATE

Jonesy's Eat Bar ★ GASTROPUB   Cuisine doesn't get much more comforting than this: Cashew curry and Thai ginger fries, lamb, beef, and shrimp sliders, and roasted beet salads are complemented by bigger plates like low country grits with crawfish and meatloaf (or meatless loaf). Beer is another strong point: The bar stocks more than 30 craft labels. The setting is casual, and the location is just a few blocks east of downtown.

400 E. 20th Ave. ⓒ **303/863-7473.** www.jeatbar.com. Main courses $8–$12 lunch and brunch, $10–$19 dinner. Daily 11am–3pm; Sun–Tues 5–10pm; Wed–Sat 5–11pm. Bus 20.

INEXPENSIVE

WaterCourse Foods ★★ VEGETARIAN   Serving a 100 percent vegetarian menu with plenty of vegan options, WaterCourse is a Denver institution. The bright and cheery space, bedecked with original art depicting rabbits and bison on an idyllic prairie, is perfect for the superlative food. Breakfast burritos are available with eggs or tofu, vegetarian grinders come with seitan and po' boys with polenta, and there are also a few Mexican specialties like black bean tacos. Besides the healthy and tasty vittles, local draft microbrew, bar and table seating, and a friendly tattooed staff make Water-Course a local favorite, whether the local in question is vegetarian or not.

837 E. 17th Ave. ⓒ **303/832-7313.** www.watercoursefoods.com. Main courses $6–$11. Mon–Thurs 11am–10pm; Fri–Sun 8am–10pm. Bus: 20.

Washington Park/Platt Park

Located about 3 miles southeast of the Colorado State Capitol downtown, Washington Park and Platte Park have several neighborhood strips with good restaurants.

South Pearl Street and South Gaylord Street each have a commercial strip nestled in a residential neighborhood with several restaurants on each. Also in the vicinity for burrito aficionados and budget travelers: The world's first **Chipotle** is located near the University of Denver, at 1644 E. Evans Ave. (ⓒ **303/722-4121**).

EXPENSIVE

Sushi Den ★★ SUSHI/JAPANESE   Brothers Toshi and Yasu Kizaki are the masterminds behind the best sushi joint in the Mile High City, if not the West. The key is fresh fish, flown in daily from Fukuoka, Japan, complemented by fresh greens from the Den Farm north of the city. With these ingredients in hand, the chefs show off their skills in the form of seaweed salad, sushi, sashimi, tempura, and other Japanese dishes. Fish-averse types need not stay away, however, as the menu also includes short ribs and beef carpaccio for carnivores and vegetarian sushi for vegetarians. In 2013, the always-evolving spot saw one of its biggest changes since opening in 1985: The Kizaki brothers bought and knocked down the longstanding Pearl Street Grill to make way for the **Izakaya Den,** 1487-A S. Pearl St. (ⓒ **303/777-0691;** www.izakayaden.net), a contemporary spot that focuses on Asian-inspired small plates.

1487 S. Pearl St. ℂ **303/777-0826.** www.sushiden.net. Main courses $9–$19 lunch, $10–$35 dinner; sushi rolls $5–$19. Mon–Fri 11:30am–2:30pm; Mon–Thurs 4:45–10:30pm; Fri 4:45–11pm; Sat 4:30–11pm; Sun 5–10:30pm. Light Rail: E/F, Louisiana and Pearl.

South of Downtown

A mile southeast of downtown, you will find a number of good restaurants in the Cheesman Park, Congress Park, and Speer neighborhoods on and around 6th Avenue.

EXPENSIVE

Fruition ★★★ NEW AMERICAN   Alex Seidel has been on the front end of the farm-to-table charge since opening Fruition in 2010. He raises everything from bees to lamb at Fruition Farms in Larkspur, about 50 miles south of Denver, and sources a wide range of local produce. He lets the ingredients shine in dishes like local chicken with house-made rigatoni, pork tenderloin with a Carolina BBQ lentil vinaigrette, and walleye pike with mushroom chips and Brusselks sprouts slaw. Seidel also makes superlative cheeses and other dairy products at his farm, and you will find plenty of them on the menu. Soon Fruition will have a sister eatery: In 2014, Seidel opened a new place in Union Station, **Mercantile Dining & Provision.**

1313 E. 6th Ave. ℂ **303/831-1962.** www.fruitionrestaurant.com. Main courses $24–$35. Tues–Sat 5–10pm; Sun 5–8pm. Bus 6.

Mizuna ★★ ITALIAN/NEW AMERICAN   Dinky Mizuna is the apex of Frank Bonanno's ever-growing Denver restaurant empire, spanning no less than 9 establishments. The small space turns out to be the perfect stage for some of the headiest fare in the West. He calls it "a food laboratory," and the menu—which changes monthly—is a reflection of that ethos. A recent edition included asparagus bisque, seared scallops with saffron-braised onions, an ostrich strip steak. A nice match for the fare, the ambiance is romantic but simple, with a "wine library" and an open kitchen.

225 E. 7th Ave. ℂ **303/832-4778.** www.mizunadenver.com. Main courses $28–$40; prix-fixe dinners $80–$160. Tues–Thurs 5–10pm; Fri–Sat 5–11pm. Bus: 6.

West of Downtown

EXPENSIVE

The Fort ★★★ STEAKS/GAME   The grand dame of Colorado's wild game restaurants, this replica of Bent's Fort near **Red Rocks Amphitheatre** in Morrison (p. 57) opened its doors in 1963 and has been on Denver's short list ever since. Known for elk, quail, and buffalo (the kitchen plates up 80,000 dishes of the latter annually), The Fort is a Colorado original, thanks in large part to the legacy of late founder Sam Arnold, whose vision still helps guide the menu today. Appetizers venture into uncharted territory of bison tongue and jalapenos with peanut butter, and the game is matched by a number of beef, pork, and poultry dishes. Once dessert rolls around—if you still have room—the triple-layer chocolate chile bourbon cake is a spectacularly decadent closer.

19192 Colo. 8 (just north W. Hampden Ave./U.S. 285), Morrison. ℂ **303/697-4771.** www.thefort. com. Main courses $20–$60. Mon–Fri 5:30–9:30pm; Sat 5–9:30pm; Sun 5–9pm.

EXPLORING DENVER

Most of the city's big attractions are located in and around Downtown Denver, and the adjacent neighborhoods of Capitol Hill (to the east) and the Golden Triangle (to the south). Start in the city center, then maybe pick a few of the outlying attractions to sample after you have visited the main attractions.

Denver Attractions

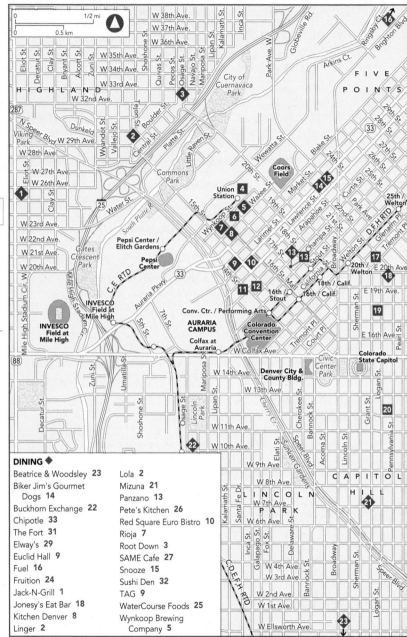

DINING ◆

Beatrice & Woodsley **23**
Biker Jim's Gourmet
    Dogs **14**
Buckhorn Exchange **22**
Chipotle **33**
The Fort **31**
Elway's **29**
Euclid Hall **9**
Fuel **16**
Fruition **24**
Jack-N-Grill **1**
Jonesy's Eat Bar **18**
Kitchen Denver **8**
Linger **2**

Lola **2**
Mizuna **21**
Panzano **13**
Pete's Kitchen **26**
Red Square Euro Bistro **10**
Rioja **7**
Root Down **3**
SAME Cafe **27**
Snooze **15**
Sushi Den **32**
TAG **9**
WaterCourse Foods **25**
Wynkoop Brewing
    Company **5**

ACCOMMODATIONS ■

Brown Palace Hotel **19**

Capitol Hill Mansion B&B **20**

Castle Marne **28**

Crawford Hotel **4**

The Curtis **12**

Highland Haven Creekside Inn **30**

Hotel Monaco **13**

Hotel Teatro **11**

Oxford Hotel **6**

Queen Anne B&B Inn **17**

Renaissance Denver Downtown
City Center **13**

Downtown

American Museum of Western Art ★★   Debuting to the public in May 2012, this museum displays the works from the renowned Anschutz Collection, one of the best collections of Western art on the planet, in the historic Navarre Building, a one-time bordello across from the Brown Palace. Pre-purchase your tickets on the website. Allow 2 hours.

1727 Tremont Place. ℰ **303/293-2000.** www.anschutzcollection.org. Admission $10 adults, $7 students and seniors. Guided tours Mon and Wed at 10am and 1:30pm; self-guided tours Mon and Wed at 11:45am and 3pm. Bus: 0.

Byers-Evans House ★   This elaborate Victorian home, built by "Rocky Mountain News" founding editor William Byers in 1883, has been restored to its appearance of 1912–24, when it was owned by William Gray Evans, son of Colorado's second territorial governor, John Evans. (The Evans family continued to reside here until 1981.) Guided tours describe the architecture and explain the fascinating lives of these prominent Denver families; you can still explore a public gallery if you cannot go on a tour. There is a gift shop. Allow 45 minutes.

1310 Bannock St. (in front of the Denver Art Museum). ℰ **303/620-4933.** www.historycolorado.org. Admission $6 adults, $5 seniors, $4 children 6–16, free for children 5 and under. Mon–Sat 10am–4pm; guided tours every hour 10:30am–2:30pm. Closed state holidays. Bus: 7, 9, or 12.

Children's Museum of Denver ★★   Targeting kids up to 8, this spot is good for parents looking for an interactive and educational experience for the family. Visitors get a taste of everything from art to bubbles to recycling with a wide range or ingenious exhibits. Summers bring outdoor playscapes. Allow at least 2 hours.

2121 Children's Museum Dr. ℰ **303/433-7444.** www.mychildsmuseum.org. Admission $9 ages 2–59, $7 for 1-year-olds and seniors 60 and over, free for children under 1. Mon–Fri 9am–4pm (until 7:30pm Wed); Sat–Sun 10am–5pm. Bus: 28.

Clyfford Still Museum ★★   Established in 2011, the Clyfford Still Museum displays pieces from its collection of 2,400 works from the eponymous abstract expressionist. Still rarely sold his creations; thus, the museum possesses over 90 percent of his body of work, the highest percentage for any museum dedicated to a single major artist. The sequential displays showcase Still's evolution from landscapes to distorted figures to large-scale abstractions that are held on critical par with those of his contemporaries, Jackson Pollock and Willem de Kooning. While Still withdrew from the art world in 1951, he was a prolific artist until he died in 1980, so the museum has a vast reservoir of his works to display on rotation. Allow 1 hour.

1250 Bannock St. ℰ **720/354-4880.** www.clyffordstillmuseum.org. Admission $10 adults, $8 seniors 65 and over, $6 students, $3 children 6–17, free for children 5 and under. Tues–Sun 10am–5pm (until 8pm Fri). Bus: 0, 2, 6, 16, or 52.

Colorado State Capitol ★★★   Built to last 1,000 years, the capitol was constructed in 1886 of granite from a Colorado quarry. The dome, which rises 272 feet above the ground, was first sheathed in copper and then replaced with gold leaf after a public outcry: Copper was not a Colorado product. Inside, murals depicting the history of water in the state adorn the walls of the first-floor rotunda, which offers a splendid view upward to the underside of the dome. Out front, the 13th step has a marker commemorating the elevation: exactly 1 mile above sea level. On the first floor, the west lobby hosts revolving temporary exhibits. To the right of the main lobby is the governor's reception room. The second floor has main entrances to the House, Senate, and old Supreme Court chambers. On the third floor are entrances to the public and visitor galleries for the House and Senate. 45-minute guided tours are available.

Lincoln St. and Colfax Ave. ℰ **303/866-2604.** www.colorado.gov/capitoltour. Free admission. Building hours Mon–Fri 7:30am–5pm. Tours offered year-round (more frequently in summer) Mon–Fri 10am–3pm. Bus: 0, 2, 3, 5, 15, or 16.

Denver Art Museum ★★★ If you are only going to experience just one museum in Denver, this should be it. The largest art museum between Chicago and California, the Denver Art Museum has landed a number of world-class shows in recent years, putting it on the international map in a big way. In 2011, an Yves St. Laurent retrospective was featured, after a run in Paris. And that was it: Denver and Paris. From 2012 to 2013, "Becoming Van Gogh" was a sold-out Denver exclusive, featuring works from more than 60 collections, and 2014 brought "Modern Masters," with works from Warhol, Picasso, Dali, Pollock, O'Keeffe, and other contemporary notables. But no matter the current exhibits, the museum is highly recommended. The building is a work of art, with its 1971 tiled tower by Gio Ponti and jagged, platinum-clad 2006 expansion by Daniel Libeskind. Inside, the Western art collection is world-class and outside are numerous works of distinctive public art. On the last Friday of the month, "Untitled" takes over the museum after hours, featuring interactive art projects and performances from actors with **Buntport Theater** (p. 56). Allow 2 to 3 hours.

100 W. 14th Ave. Pkwy. (at Civic Center Park). ℰ **720/865-5000.** www.denverartmuseum.org. Non-resident admission $13 adults, $10 college students and seniors 65 and over, $5 children 6–18, free for children 5 and under. Tues–Thurs and Sat–Sun 10am–5pm; Fri 10am–8pm. Bus: 0, 2, 6, 16, or 52.

Denver Firefighters Museum ★ Denver Firehouse Number 1, established in 1909, is a great family destination, with all of the tools of the real firefighting trade as well mini-uniforms for kids to don and slide down the pint-sized pole. Exhibits cover the history of firefighting in Denver and beyond, including a replica of a firefighter's living quarters from the early 1900s on the second floor. There are rotating temporary exhibits. Allow 45 minutes.

1326 Tremont Place. ℰ **303/892-1436.** www.denverfirefightersmuseum.org. Admission $6 adults, $5 students and seniors, $4 children 2–12, and free for kids 1 and under. Mon–Sat 10am–4pm. Located 2 blocks west of Civic Center Park just north of Colfax. Bus: 7.

Downtown Aquarium ★ Denver's state-of-the-art aquarium—the largest between Chicago and Monterey, California—opened in 1999 as a nonprofit, went belly-up, and in 2003 was sold to the for-profit Landry's seafood restaurant chain. The sale brought the aquarium stability, not to mention new exhibits and a theme restaurant and lounge on-site. Residents include greenback cutthroat trout (the Colorado state fish), river otters, nurse sharks, sea turtles, and moray eels swimming in 1 million of gallons of water here. At "Stingray Reef," visitors can pet and feed the slippery denizens. On Saturdays, divers and novices can swim in the big tanks for a fee ($185 for divers, $85 for snorkelers). Allow 2 hours.

700 Water St. (just east of I-25 via 23rd Ave., exit 211). ℰ **303/561-4450.** www.aquarium restaurants.com. Admission before 6pm $18 adults, $17 seniors, $12 children 3–11, free for children 2 and under. Discounts available after 6pm or with receipt from restaurant. Sun–Thurs 10am–9pm; Fri–Sat 10am–9:30pm. Closed Dec 25. Bus: 28. Light Rail: Pepsi Center/Elitch Gardens.

Elitch Gardens Theme Park ★ The venerable Elitch Gardens was founded in northwest Denver in 1890, then moved and opened at its current Central Platte Valley location in 1995, before downtown Denver enjoyed a residential boom. Now it's the only downtown amusement park in the country. A bit of the historic luster has been chipped away over the years, but the offerings have expanded with a water park, more thrill rides, and other facilities. Six Flags divested the park, so the licensed characters are gone, but there are still plenty of worthwhile thrills to be had here, including the Twister II, a super-sized replica of Mister Twister from the park's previous incarnation across town. New for 2014: the Brain Drain coaster, a 7-story continuous loop. Allow 3 hours.

Speer Blvd. (at I-25, exit 212A). © **303/595-4386.** www.elitchgardens.com. Gate admission with unlimited rides $46 for those taller than 4 ft., $32 for those 4 ft. and under or 61 and older, free for children under 4 ft. and under and seniors 70 and older. Parking $15. Memorial Day to Labor Day Mon–Thurs 10am–7pm, Fri–Sun 10am10pm; early to late May and early Sept to Oct weekends (call for hours). Light Rail: C Line, Pepsi Center/Elitch Gardens.

History Colorado Center ★
Opening in spring 2012 after the demolition of the maligned Colorado History Museum, the History Colorado Center is a stunning new facility, from the striking (and green) architecture to the "Great Map of Colorado" inlaid in the lobby (you can interact with it via movable multimedia "time machines") to the exhibits (including the state's original constitution). The permanent "Colorado Stories" gallery covers skiing with a ski jump simulator, Lincoln Hills, a segregation-era resort for African-Americans, Bent's Fort on the southeastern plains, and the Sand Creek Massacre. Many of the galleries are empty, awaiting sponsors for expansion. New in 2013 is the "Living West" exhibit covering the environmental history of Colorado from the Anasazi era forward. Allow 1 to 2 hours.

1200 Broadway. © **303/447-8679.** www.historycoloradocenter.org. Admission $12 adults, $10 students and seniors 65 and over, $8 children 6–12, free for children 5 and under. Mon–Sat 10am–5pm; Sun noon–5pm. Bus: 0, 2, 6, 16, or 52.

Larimer Square ★★
This is where Denver began. Larimer Street between 14th and 15th streets was the entire community of Denver City in 1858, with false-fronted stores, hotels, and saloons to serve gold-seekers and other pioneers. In the mid-1870s it was the main street of the city and the site of Denver's first post office, bank, theater, and streetcar line. By the 1930s, however, this part of Larimer Street had deteriorated so much that it had become a skid row of pawnshops, gin mills, and flophouses. Plans had been made to tear these structures down, when a group of investors purchased the entire block in 1965. The Larimer Square project subsequently became Denver's first major historic preservation effort. All 16 of the block's commercial buildings, constructed in the 1870s and 1880s, were renovated, providing space for street-level retail shops, restaurants, and nightclubs, as well as upper-story offices. A series of courtyards and open spaces was created, and in 1973 it was added to the National Register of Historic Places. There are special events all year. Allow at least a half-hour—but this is a great spot for a meal if you have more time.

1400 block of Larimer St. © **303/534-2367.** www.larimersquare.com. Bus: 2, 10, 12, 15, 20, 28, 32, 38, or 44. Light Rail: D/F, Theatre District.

Museum of Contemporary Art Denver ★★
Quirky, independent, and intellectual, Denver's resident contemporary art museum has risen in recent years, catalyzed by a move from the Central Business District to a slick new building in the Central Platte Valley on the west side of downtown in 2007, then the hiring of Adam Lerner as director in 2009. Today MCA Denver is one of the city's hippest cultural institutions, with a great slate of rotating exhibits and event series like "Mixed Taste," a Thursday night speaker series featuring two divergent experts—recent events have teamed soul food with Salvador Dali and minimalism with giant wombats. Expect to spend about an hour or two here.

A New Union Station

A $500-million restoration and redevelopment project has remade **Denver Union Station,** the historic railroad depot in the heart of Lower Downtown, in grand fashion.

Originally built in the early 1900s after a pair of predecessors burned to the ground, Union Station was nearly forgotten until a redevelopment plan emerged. Five years after groundbreaking, it reopened in July 2014 as a multimodal transit hub with Light Rail and bus service and great walkability to Denver's urban core.

Along with daily Amtrak service, the station has light-rail connectivity to the south suburbs of Denver. In 2016, trains will start running to DIA and Westminster and eventually connect to Boulder and Longmont.

The project included the slickly designed **Crawford Hotel** (p. 25) and numerous local retailers and several local restaurants, including Stoic & Genuine from the proprietors of **Rioja** (p. 31) and Mercantile Dining & Provision from Alex Seidel of **Fruition** (p. 37). It also houses several bars.

1485 Delgany St. ✆ **303/298-7554.** www.mcadenver.org. Admission $8 adults, $5 seniors and college students, free for children 18 and under. Tues–Thurs noon–7pm; Fri noon–9pm; Sat–Sun 10am–5pm.

U.S. Mint ★★   There are four mints in the United States, but the Denver Mint is one of only two (the other is the Philadelphia Mint) where one can actually see the process of turning lumps of metal into shiny coins. It's a fascinating sight.

Opened in 1863, the Mint originally melted gold dust and nuggets into bars. In 1904 the office moved to this site, and 2 years later began making gold and silver coins. Copper pennies were added a few years later. The last silver dollars (containing 90 percent silver) were coined in 1935. In 1970, all silver was eliminated from dollars and half dollars (today they're made of a copper-nickel alloy). The Denver Mint stamps billions of coins each year, and each has a small D on it.

Although visitors today don't get as close as they once did, a self-guided tour along the visitors' gallery provides a good look at the process, with a bird's-eye view from the mezzanine of the actual coin-minting process. A variety of displays help explain the minting process, and an adjacent **gift shop** on Cherokee Street offers a variety of souvenirs. Allow 1 hour.

320 W. Colfax Ave. (btw. Cherokee and Delaware sts.). ✆ **303/405-4761** or 303/572-9500 for gift shop. www.usmint.gov. Free admission. Tours Mon–Thurs 8am–3:30pm. Gift shop 8am–3pm. Reservations required; online reservations available. Closed holidays. Bus: 2, 7, or 16L.

Capitol Hill

Kirkland Museum of Fine & Decorative Art ★★★   Vance Kirkland is undoubtedly the dean of Colorado artists. The late University of Denver professor and artist underwent a stylistic transformation over the course of his long career. Beginning with watercolors of Western landscapes in the 1920s to psychedelic interpretations of nebulae and other interstellar areas that only existed in Kirkland's mind in the 1940s and 1950s. Then from the 1960s until his death in 1981 came his best known works: "dot" paintings with perfectly round globules of oil paints in geometric patterns. The museum also houses one of the most extensive collections of decorative art in the U.S. and has a large gallery dedicated to Colorado artists other than Kirkland. Expect to spend about 90 minutes here. *Note:* The museum will be moving to 1225 Bannock St. in 2017.

1311 Pearl St. ✆ **303/832-8576.** www.kirklandmuseum.org. Admission $8 adults, $6 students, teachers, and seniors. Children 13–17 must be accompanied by an adult. Children under 13 are not permitted due to the fragile nature of the collection. Tues–Sun 11am–5pm. Guided tour Wed–Thurs and Sat at 1:30pm. Closed major holidays. Bus: 10.

Molly Brown House Museum ★★ "The Unsinkable Molly Brown"—who actually was only known as Margaret during her lifetime (the Molly moniker was an invention of Broadway)—ascended from modest beginnings as the wife of miner J.J. Brown in Leadville, who struck it big in the 1890s and moved to Mansion Row in Denver, the site of this museum now dedicated to life and times of Molly, er, Margaret Brown. She was known for her commitment to social causes before earning her immortal nickname after surviving the Titanic disaster in 1912. Today the house celebrates Brown's amazing life and times while providing a glimpse into life in Denver in the early 20th century with rooms decorated just as they were in their famous owner's heyday. Allow 1 hour.

1340 Pennsylvania St. ✆ **303/832-4092.** www.mollybrown.org. Guided tour $8 adults, $6 seniors 65 and older, $4 children 6–12, free for children 5 and under. Tues–Sat 10am–4pm, Sun noon–4pm. Guided tours every 30 min.; last tour of the day begins at 3:30pm. Bus: 10.

La Alma/Lincoln Park/Auraria

Museo de las Americas ★★ This is the place to experience Latin American Art, with works stemming from cultures ancient and contemporary in media of every description. Rotating exhibitions take over most of the floor space, but works from the permanent collection are also always on display. The nights of **First Fridays** are a great time to visit, when the surrounding Art District on Santa Fe is abuzz with activity. Allow 1 to 2 hours.

861 Santa Fe Dr. ✆ **303/571-4401.** www.museo.org. Admission $5 adults, $3 seniors and students, free for children under 13. Tues–Fri 10am–5pm; Sat–Sun noon–5pm. Open with free admission 5–9pm on the 1st Fri of the month. Bus: 1.

East of Downtown

Denver Museum of Miniatures, Dolls & Toys ★ Kids of all ages will enjoy a trip to this museum in a converted Victorian in the Uptown neighborhood east of downtown. The permanent collection is a rich retrospective on toys through the ages, with a wide range of historic dollhouses, vintage board games, and dolls from all over the world. Allow 45 to 60 minutes.

1880 Gaylord St. (just west of City Park). ✆ **303/322-1053.** www.dmmdt.org. Admission $6 adults, $5 seniors, $4 children 5–16, free for children 4 and under. Wed–Sat 10am–4pm; Sun 1–4pm.

Denver Museum of Nature & Science ★★★ Dinosaur and fossil aficionados will love this top-notch natural history museum in City Park, and even the most casual fan of science will find something of interest here. The permanent exhibits showcase Egyptian mummies, gems and minerals, and custom plastinated people climbing a rock wall from the creator of "Body Worlds." The favorite of the aforementioned Jurassic nuts, "Prehistoric Journey" covers 3.5 billion years of history with interactive and cutting-edge exhibits detailing not only the big feathered reptilians, but also climate history, the rise of mammals, and the techniques of paleontologists in the field. A 2014 expansion added 126,000 square feet of exhibit space, featuring the interactive "Discovery Sone" for young kids on the second floor, and you'll also find a planetarium and an IMAX theater here Allow 2 to 6 hours.

City Park, 2001 Colorado Blvd. ℂ **303/370-6000.** www.dmns.org. Admission to museum $13 adults, $10 seniors 65 and older, $8 children 3–18 or student with ID, and free for children 2 and under; IMAX $10 adults, $8 children, students and seniors; planetarium $18 for adults, $14 for seniors, $12 for children and students. Combination tickets available. Daily 9am–5pm. Closed Dec 25. Bus: 32 or 40.

Denver Zoo ★★   More than 650 species of animals (nearly 3,500 individuals) live in this spacious zoological park, home to the rare deerlike okapi as well as to North American otters, Komodo dragons, and western lowland gorillas. The newest (and most ambitious) habitat here is the Toyota Elephant Passage, a 10-acre complex featuring Asian elephants, rhinos, and gibbons in a re-creation of their natural habitat, as well as a simulation of a rural village coexisting with the pachyderms. The zoo has long been an innovator in re-creating realistic habitats: Bear Mountain, built in 1918, was the first naturalistic animal habitat in the United States and is now a National Historic Landmark. The zoo is also home to the nation's first natural gas–powered train ($2). An especially kid-friendly attraction is the Conversation Carousel ($2), featuring wood-carved renditions of such endangered species as okapi, polar bears, Komodo dragons, and hippos. A cafeteria serves full meals, and picnicking is popular, too. Feeding times are posted near the zoo entrance so you can time your visit to see the animals when they are most active. Allow from 2 to 4 hours.

City Park, 2300 Steele St. (main entrance btw. Colorado Blvd. and York St. on 23rd Ave.). ℂ **720/337-1400.** www.denverzoo.org. Admission $15 adults; $12 seniors 62 and over, $10 children 3–11 accompanied by an adult, free for children 2 and under. Lower prices in winter. Apr–Sept daily 9am–5pm; Oct–Mar daily 10am–4pm. Bus: 24, 32, or 40.

Wings Over the Rockies Air & Space Museum ★   Set in a historic hangar on what was once Lowry Air Force Base (and is now the upscale Lowry development) "Wings" keeps getting better and better. At one time a fairly standard air and space museum, it now boasts an impressive collection of rare aircraft (from a B-1A Lancer to a RF-84K Thunderflash Parasite), a cutting-edge flight simulator, and even an X-wing that was a prop in "Star Wars"—thanks to a local fan club of the movie that is in possession of this piece of sci-fi lore. The best days to visit are the cockpit demo days on the second Saturday of each month. Allow 1 hour.

7711 E. Academy Blvd., Hangar No. 1. ℂ **303/360-5360.** www.wingsmuseum.org. Admission $11 adults, $9 seniors, $6 children 4–12, free for children 3 and under. Mon–Sat 10am–5pm; Sun noon–5pm. Bus: 65.

North of Downtown

Lakeside Amusement Park ★   Among the most historic amusement parks in the U.S., Lakeside has about 40 rides, including the Cyclone roller coaster, a midway with carnival and arcade games, and a rare steam-powered miniature train from the early 20th century that circles the lake. It is rougher around the edges than Elitch Gardens, but the retro style and historic cachet of the rides makes it worth a visit. There are also food stands and picnic facilities, plus a separate Kiddie's Playland with 15 rides. Allow 3 hours.

4601 Sheridan Blvd. (just south of I-70, exit 271). ℂ **303/477-1621.** www.lakesideamusementpark. com. Admission $3. Ride coupons 50¢ (rides require 1–6 coupons each); unlimited rides $11–$15 Mon–Fri, $18–$23 Sat–Sun and holidays. May Fri 6–10-pm, Sat–Sun and holidays noon–10pm; June to Labor Day Mon–Fri 6–10-pm, Sat–Sun and holidays noon–10pm. Closed early Sept to Apr.

Rocky Mountain Arsenal National Wildlife Refuge ★★ Once a site where the U.S. Army manufactured chemical weapons such as mustard gas and GB nerve agent, and later leased to a private enterprise to produce pesticides, the Rocky Mountain Arsenal has become an environmental success story. The 15,000-acre site, an area of open grasslands and wetlands just west of Denver International Airport, is home to more than 330 species, including deer, coyotes, prairie dogs, birds of prey, and bison. This is one of the country's largest bald eagle-roosting locales during the winter. The Rocky Mountain Arsenal Wildlife Society Bookstore is at the visitor center, and there is a scenic 9-mile drive and about 10 miles of hiking trails as well as catch-and-release fishing. Allow at least an hour.

64th Ave. (at Quebec St.). ✆ **303/289-0930.** www.fws.gov/refuge/rocky_mountain_arsenal. Free admission. Daily sunrise–sunset. Visitor center Tues–Sun 9am–4pm. Bus: 88.

South of Downtown

Denver Botanic Gardens ★★ Twenty-three acres of outstanding outdoor and indoor gardens display plants native to the desert, plains, mountain foothills, and alpine zones. There's also a traditional Japanese garden, an herb garden, a water garden, a fragrance garden, and a garden that melds art and agriculture. Even in the cold of winter, the greenhouses house thousands of species of tropical and subtropical plants. Huge, colorful orchids and bromeliads share space with a collection of plants used for food, fibers, dyes, building materials, and medicines. There is a 3-acre kid's garden where kids can race pinecones down a stream or hunt for bugs in a small-scale grassland. The Botanic Gardens also have a gift shop, a library, and an auditorium. Special events, scheduled throughout the year, include garden concerts in summer, a spring plant sale, and a fall cornfield maze southwest of Denver. Allow 1 to 2 hours.

1007 York St. ✆ **720/865-3501.** www.botanicgardens.org. Admission $13 adults, $9.50 seniors, $9 children 4–15 and students, free for children 3 and under. May–Sept Mon–Fri 9am–9pm, Sat–Sun 8am–9pm; Oct–Apr daily 9am–5pm. Bus: 2, 10, or 24.

Four Mile Historic Park ★ Four miles southeast of downtown Denver—thus the name—the city's oldest extant log home (1859) serves as the centerpiece for this 12-acre open-air museum. Everything is authentic to the period from 1859 to 1883, including the house (a former stagecoach stop), its furnishings, outbuildings, and farm equipment. There are draft horses and chickens in the barn, and crops in the garden. Seasonal "Heritage Events" feature pioneer-era musicians and actors as well as many food and craft demonstrations. Big events include July 4th and an outdoor theater series. Allow 1 hour.

715 S. Forest St. ✆ **720/865-0800.** www.fourmilepark.org. Admission and guided tour $5 adults, $4 seniors, $3 children 7–17, free for children 6 and under. Apr–Sept Wed–Fri noon–4pm, Sat–Sun 10am–4pm; Oct–Mar Wed–Sun noon–4pm.

ORGANIZED TOURS

Visitors who want to be personally guided to the attractions of Denver and the surrounding areas by those in the know have a variety of choices.

Half- and full-day bus tours of Denver and the nearby Rockies are offered by the ubiquitous **Gray Line** (✆ **800/348-6877;** www.grayline.com). A 4-hour tour, leaving at 8:30am, takes in Denver's mountain parks: Red Rocks Park, Bergen Park, and Buffalo Bill's grave atop Lookout Mountain. It costs $45 for adults. The 3-hour Denver city tour, which departs daily at 8:30am and 2pm, gives you a taste of both old

Denver—through Larimer Square and other historic buildings—and the modern-day city. It's $35 for adults. The city tour combined with the mountain-parks tour costs $75. Kids pay half, and those 1 and under are free.

The **Colorado Sightseer** (℗ **303/423-8200;** www.coloradosightseer.com) leads guided tours of Denver and environs. The main Denver tour includes a visit to LoDo and some of the city's earliest buildings, the State Capitol, the Molly Brown House, and other attractions. It lasts about 4 hours and costs $40 per person. A Rocky Mountain National Park tour, lasting about 8 hours, costs $85 per person, including a box lunch. The 5-hour Foothills Tour includes stops at Coors Brewery, the Buffalo Bill memorial, and scenic Red Rocks Park. The cost is $45 per person.

Banjo Billy's Bus Tours (℗ **720/938-8885;** www.banjobilly.com) offers 90-minute tours in a funky bus (complete with couches and a disco ball) covering all sorts of nooks and crannies of Denver history, especially the most bizarre ones. Tickets are $22 adults, $20 seniors, $14 children 6 to 12, and free for children under 6. Summer tours depart the Colorado Convention Center at 14th and California sts. Tuesday to Sunday at 1pm and 3pm, and less frequently at other times of year. There is also an adults-only brewery tour ($40).

The **LoDo District** (℗ **303/628-5428;** www.lodo.org) leads guided walking tours of the storied area June to October. Tours depart from Union Station (17th and Wynkoop sts.) on every other Saturday at 1pm; the cost is $10 adults, $5 students, and free for those 12 and under. They also offer adults-only tours focusing on the seamy side of the city's history on Saturday afternoons for $20, $15 for seniors.

Walk2Connect (℗ **303/908-0076;** www.walk2connect.com) is the place to go for informative and invigorating walking tours around the city for $25 to $55 per person. Some tours include lunch.

Bikalope Tours (℗ **800/979-3370;** www.bikalope.com) will take visitors on 9-mile bike tours of downtown and vicinity for $50 per person, bike included.

OUTDOOR ACTIVITIES

Denver's proximity to the Rocky Mountains makes it possible to spend a day skiing, snowmobiling, horseback riding, hiking, river running, sailing, fishing, hunting, mountain climbing, or rockhounding and return to the city by nightfall. Within the city limits and nearby, visitors will find more than 200 miles of jogging and bicycle paths, more than 100 free tennis courts, and several dozen public golf courses. Beyond city limitd, Denver also has an excellent system of **Mountain Parks** (℗ **720/865-0900**), covering more than 14,000 acres (p. 50).

Campsites are easy to reach from Denver, as are suitable sites for hang gliding and hot-air ballooning. Sailing is popular within the city at Sloan's Lake (a Denver park), and the Platte River is clear for many miles of river running in rafts, kayaks, and canoes.

Visit Denver (p. 19) can supply detailed information about activities in the city. Information on nearby outdoor activities is available from **Colorado Parks and Wildlife** (℗ **720/297-1192;** http://cpw.state.co.us); the **U.S. Forest Service,** Rocky Mountain Region (℗ **303/275-5350;** www.fs.usda.gov); the **U.S. Bureau of Land Management** (℗ **303/239-3600;** www.blm.gov/co); and the **National Park Service** (℗ **303/969-2500;** www.nps.gov).

Visitors who don't bring the necessary equipment should hit the **REI Flagship** store, 1416 Platte St. (℗ **303/756-3100**); its rental department is stocked with tents, backpacks, stoves, mountaineering equipment, kayaks, and other gear.

BALLOONING It is hard to top a hot-air balloon ride for viewing the magnificent Rocky Mountain scenery. **Rocky Mountain Hot Air** (① **303/936-0292;** www.rocky mountainhotair.com) offers sunrise flights daily, launching from Chatfield State Park south of town. The cost is usually $195 to $225 per person.

BICYCLING & SKATEBOARDING The paved bicycle paths that crisscross Denver include a 12-mile scenic stretch along the bank of the South Platte River and along Cherry Creek beside Speer Boulevard. All told, the city has more than 100 miles of off-road trails for bikers and runners. Bike paths link the city's 205 parks, and many streets have bike lanes. For mountain bikers, one option is **Waterton Canyon,** where single track connects metro Denver and Deckers. For more information, contact **BikeDenver** (www.bikedenver.org) or **Bicycle Colorado** (① **303/417-1544;** www. bicyclecolo.org). Bike tours are available from several companies and clubs (see "Organized Tours," p. 46). **Bicycle Doctor,** 860 Broadway (① **303/831-7228;** www. bicycledr.com), offers rentals ($20–$70 a day), service, and assorted gear. There are also numerous **B-Cycle kiosks** (http://denver.bcycle.com), renting bicycles for a $8 a day (or $20 a week) plus fees for how long you use the bike before returning it to another kiosk (rides under 30 min. are included). Kiosks are often right in front of prominent attractions, making this a viable means of getting around in the city.

Denver also has the one of the largest free skateboarding parks (3 acres) in the country, the **Denver Skatepark,** 19th and Little Raven sts. (① **720/913-1311;** www. denverskatepark.com). It is quite popular and open from 5am to 11pm.

BOATING Kayaking is a popular pursuit on the Platte River. Near Confluence Park you can rent a kayak ($25 a day) and take kayaking classes ($59 per session and up) at **Confluence Kayaks,** 2373 15th St., Unit B (① **303/433-3676;** www.confluence kayaks.com).

For a different watersports experience, try riverboarding with **RipBoard** (① **866/311-2627;** www.ripboard.com), which entails going down Clear Creek in Golden face-first with flippers on your feet and a helmet on your head. It's exciting and exhausting, but can be a lot of fun in the right water. Lessons (including equipment) are $65 for 2½ hours.

For information on other boating opportunities, contact Colorado State Parks, the National Park Service, or the U.S. Forest Service (p. 47).

FISHING A couple of good bets in the metropolitan area are Chatfield State Park, with trout, bass, and panfish, and Cherry Creek State Park, which boasts trout, walleye pike, bass, and crappie. In all, there are more than 7,100 miles of streams and 2,000 reservoirs and lakes in Colorado. For information on other angling opportunities, contact Colorado State Parks, the National Park Service, or the U.S. Forest Service (p. 47). Within Denver city limits, the **Denver Department of Parks and Recreation** (① **720/913-1311**) stocks a number of lakes with fish.

A number of sporting-goods stores can provide more detailed information. The skilled and experienced staff at **Trout's** 1303 E. 6th. Ave. (① **877/464-0034;** www. troutsflyfishing.com), can help with equipment choices and recommendations for where to go.

GOLF Throughout the Front Range, it's often said that you can play golf at least 320 days a year, because the sun always seems to be shining, and even when it snows, the little snow that sticks melts quickly. There are more than 50 courses in the Denver area, including seven municipal golf courses, with nonresident greens fees from $22 to $35 for 18 holes and $8 to $18 for 9. City courses are **City Park Golf Course,** East 25th

Avenue and York Street (© 720/865-3410); **Evergreen Golf Course,** 29614 Upper Bear Creek Rd., Evergreen (© 720/865-3430); the par-3 **Harvard Gulch Golf Course,** East Iliff Avenue and South Clarkson Street (© 303/698-4078); **Kennedy Golf Course,** 10500 E. Hampden Ave. (© 720/865-0720); **Overland Park Golf Course,** South Santa Fe Drive and West Jewell Avenue (© 720/865-0430); **Wellshire Golf Course,** 3333 S. Colorado Blvd. (© 303/757-1352); and **Willis Case Golf Course,** 4999 Vrain St., near West 50th Avenue (© 720/865-0700). Wellshire is the best overall course, notorious for tricky trees, but I also like Willis Case for its panoramic mountain views. You can make reservations by visiting **www.denvergov.org/golf** up to 14 days in advance, or 7 days in advance by calling the course of your choice.

HIKING & BACKPACKING   For hikes in the Denver area, contact the city **Department of Parks and Recreation** (© **720/913-1311**) for information on Denver's mountain park system (p. 50). Or contact any of the following agencies: Colorado Parks and Wildlife, National Park Service, U.S. Bureau of Land Management, or U.S. Forest Service (see the introduction to this section). Another good source for advice and the many published area maps and hiking guides is **REI,** 1416 Platte St., Denver (© **303/756-3100**).

Part of Jefferson County Open Space, 4,000-acre **Mount Falcon Park** (© **303/271-5925**) offers excellent trails that are rated easy to moderate in difficulty, making this a good place for families with children. There are also picnic areas, shelters, and ruins of an old castlelike home of late local entrepreneur John Brisben Walker, the visionary behind Red Rocks Amphitheatre. From Denver, go west on U.S. 285 (Hampden Ave.), north on Parmalee Gulch Road, and follow the signs; the park is open daily from dawn to dusk, and admission is free. Mountain bikes and horseback riding are permitted, as are leashed dogs.

Other good trails near Denver are in **Roxborough State Park** (© **303/973-3959**), 10 miles south of Littleton—the 1-mile **Willow Creek Trail** and the 2.3-mile **Fountain Valley Trail.** There are several more strenuous trails connected through Roxborough, most notably the 13-mile trail up Waterton Canyon, which is worth the effort if you enjoy beautiful red rocks and the chance to see wildlife. To get to Roxborough Park, exit Colo. 470 south onto U.S. 85, turn west onto Titan Road, and then go south again at Roxborough Park Road to the main entrance. Admission is $7 per passenger vehicle. The park is open daily from 7am to 8pm in summer, with shorter hours the rest of the year. Dogs, bikes, and horseback riding are not permitted.

The **Colorado Trail** is a hiking, horse, and mountain-biking route stretching 500 miles from Denver to Durango. The trail is also open to cross-country skiing, snowshoeing, and llama-pack hiking. Opened in 1988, the trail is still being fine-tuned. It took 15 years to establish, using volunteer labor, and crosses eight mountain ranges and five river systems, winding from rugged terrain to pristine meadows. It begins in Waterton Canyon. For information, contact the **Colorado Trail Foundation** (© **303/384-3729;** www.coloradotrail.org).

RECREATION CENTERS & SWIMMING   The **Denver Department of Parks and Recreation** (© **720/913-1311**) operates about 30 recreation centers around the city, several of which have swimming pools. Browse **www.denvergov.org/recreation** for additional information.

SKIING   Several ski resorts close to the Front Range target predominately locals. Personally, I primarily ski **Loveland Basin and Valley,** 56 miles west of Denver on I-70, exit 216 (© **800/736-3754** or 303/569-3203; www.skiloveland.com), covering

1,800 acres and with 93 trails, rated 13 percent beginner, 41 percent intermediate, and 46 percent advanced. Full-day lift tickets are $61 for adults, and the $99 "Day Tripper" package includes a ticket, gear rentals, and even a jacket and snowpants.

TENNIS   The Denver Department of Parks and Recreation (✆ **720/913-1311**) manages or owns close to 150 tennis courts, more than one-third of them lit for night play. For more information, contact the **Colorado Tennis Association** (✆ **303/695-4116;** www.coloradotennis.com).

Outlying Attractions

Denver Mountain Parks ★★★   Formally established in August 1913, the city's Mountain Parks system immediately began acquiring land in the mountains near Denver to be set aside for recreational use. Today it includes more than 14,000 acres, with 24 developed mountain parks and 22 unnamed wilderness areas that are wonderful places for hiking, picnicking, bird-watching, golfing, or lazing in the sun.

The first and largest, **Genesee Park,** is 20 miles west of Denver off I-70, exit 254; its 2,413 acres contain the Chief Hosa Lodge and Campground (the only overnight camping available in the system), picnic areas, a scenic overlook, and an elk-and-buffalo enclosure. Among the system's other parks are **Echo Lake,** about 45 minutes from downtown Denver on Colo. 103. At 10,600 feet elevation on Mount Evans, the park has good fishing, hiking, and picnicking, plus a restaurant and curio shop; 1,000-acre **Daniels Park** (23 miles south of Denver; take I-25 to Castle Pines Pkwy., and then go west to the park), which offers picnic areas, a bison enclosure, and a scenic overlook; and **Dedisse Park** (2 miles west of Evergreen on Colo. 74), which provides picnic facilities, a golf course, a restaurant, a clubhouse, and opportunities for ice-skating, fishing, and volleyball.

Dept. of Parks and Recreation. ✆ **720/868-0900.** www.denvergov.org. Free admission.

Red Rocks Amphitheatre & Park ★★★   Not just a spectacular concert venue, Red Rocks is part of the Denver Mountain Parks system (see above) and a bona fide tourist attraction. Everyone from The Beatles to Willie Nelson has taken to the stage here, framed by 400-foot-high red sandstone rocks; the amphitheater was constructed by the Civilian Conservation Corps in the 1930s. There is a terrific **visitor center** at the top, with amazing views and displays covering the varied performances that have taken place here since it opened in 1941. There's also a restaurant, a network of hiking trails, and the **trading post,** carrying a good selection of curios and souvenirs.

18300 W. Alameda Pkwy., Morrison. ✆ **720/865-2494.** www.redrocksonline.com. Free admission (except during concerts). May–Sept 8am–7pm; Oct–Apr 9am–4pm.

Tiny Town and Railroad ★   Originally built by George Turner for his daughter in 1915, Tiny Town is exactly what its name implies—a one-sixth-scale Western village of about 100 colorful buildings. There is also a steam-powered locomotive that visitors can ride for an additional $2. Allow 1 hour.

6249 S. Turkey Creek Rd., Tiny Town. ✆ **303/697-6829.** www.tinytownrailroad.com. Admission $5 adults, $3 children 2–12, free for children 1 and under. Memorial Day to Labor Day daily 10am–5pm; May and Sept Sat–Sun 10am–5pm. Closed Oct–Apr. Located 20 miles southwest of downtown via U.S. 285 (Hampden Ave.).

Water World ★   This 64-acre complex, billed as America's largest family water park, has two oceanlike wave pools, river rapids for inner tubing, twisting water slides, several kids' play areas, a gondola to the country's first water-based fun house, plus other attractions—more than 40 in all—as well as food service and other amenities. Allow at least 4 hours.

88th Ave. and Pecos St., Federal Heights. © **303/427-7873.** www.waterworldcolorado.com. Admission $41 for those 48 in. and taller, $36 for those 40–47 in., $10 seniors, free for children under 40 in. tall. Memorial Day to Labor Day daily 10am–6pm. Closed rest of year and some school days in Aug. Take the Thornton exit (exit 219, 84th Ave.) off I-25 north.

The Wild Animal Sanctuary ★ This lauded sanctuary is home to about 350 animals, including lions, tigers, bears, and wolves, rescued from illegal and abusive situations. The animals have 700 acres on which to romp, and visitors can see them via a mile-long elevated walkway that opened in 2012. The best times to come is morning or near dusk, when the animals are most active. Allow at least an hour.

1946 County Rd. 53, Keenesburg (30 miles northeast of Denver). © **303/536-0118.** www.wild animalsanctuary.org. Admission $15 adults, $7.50 children 3–12. Year-round daily 9am–sunset. Take I-76 northeast to Colo. 52 east, turn right (south) on County Road 53 for 3 miles.

The Wildlife Experience ★★ More than worth the 20-mile trip from downtown for young animal fanatics, this suburban museum gives its visitors an in-depth look into the ways of wild animals with interactive exhibits and an "Extreme Screen" theater. Among the permanent displays are Cub's Corner, aimed squarely at kids 5 and under, and the outdoor Wildlife Walk, as well as Globeology, a state-of-the-art exhibit spanning 10,000 square feet of murals, animatronics, and replica ecosystems from alpine tundra to the rainforest. Allow 1 or 2 hours.

10035 S. Peoria St. © **720/488-3300.** www.thewildlifeexperience.org. Admission $10 adults, $9 seniors, $6 children; theater tickets combination museum/theater tickets $14 adults, $13 seniors, $9 children. Daily 9am–5pm. Closed major holidays. Located 1 mile east of I-25 via Lincoln Ave. (exit 193).

Great Nearby State Parks

Colorado has a number of excellent state parks offering a wide range of activities and scenery. Eldorado Canyon State Park, near Boulder, is also an excellent hiking and climbing area (p. 106). Information on state parks is available at **http://cpw.state.co.us.**

Castlewood Canyon State Park ★★ Steep canyons, a meandering stream, a waterfall, lush vegetation, and considerable wildlife distinguish this 2,000-acre park. You can see the remains of Castlewood Canyon Dam, which was built for irrigation in 1890; it collapsed in 1933, killing two people and flooding the streets of Denver. The park, 30 miles south of Denver on Colo. 83, east of Castle Rock in Franktown, provides picnic facilities and hiking trails. The entrance is at 2989 S. State Hwy. 83; admission is $7 per vehicle. Call © **303/688-5242** for more information.

Chatfield State Park ★ Sixteen miles south of downtown Denver on U.S. 85 in Littleton, this park occupies 5,600 acres of prairie against a backdrop of the Rocky Mountains. Chatfield Reservoir, with a 26-mile shoreline, invites swimming, boating, fishing, and other watersports. The area also has 12 miles of paved bicycle trails, plus hiking and horseback-riding paths. In winter, there's ice fishing and cross-country skiing. The park also has a hot-air-balloon launchpad, a radio-controlled model aircraft field, an off-leash dog area, and a 21-acre man-made wetlands area. Campsites are also available. Admission is $8 per vehicle; the camping fee is $20 to $26 nightly. The entrance is 1 mile south of C-470 on Wadsworth Boulevard (© **303/791-7275**). Call © **800/678-2267** or 303/470-4144 for camping reservations ($10 fee).

Cherry Creek State Park ★   The 880-acre Cherry Creek Reservoir is the central attraction of this popular park, which draws 1.5 million visitors each year. Located at the southeast Denver city limits (off Parker Rd. and I-225) about 12 miles from downtown, the park encompasses 4,200 acres in all. Watersports include swimming, waterskiing, boating, and fishing. There's a nature trail, an off-leash dog area, model-airplane field with paved runways, jet-ski rental facility, and shooting areas. Twelve miles of paved bicycle paths and 12 miles of bridle trails circle the reservoir (horse rentals are available). Rangers offer guided walks by appointment, as well as evening campfire programs. In winter, there's skating, ice fishing, and ice boating. Campsites are available and many lakeshore day-use sites have picnic tables and grills. Admission is $9 per vehicle; campsites are $16 to $24 nightly. The entrance is at 4201 S. Parker Rd. in Aurora. Call ℂ **303/690-1166** for general information, or ℂ **800/678-2267** or 303/470-4144 for camping reservations ($10 fee).

Golden Gate Canyon State Park ★★   About 30 miles west of Denver, this 12,000-acre park ranges in elevation from 7,400 to 10,400 feet and offers 35 miles of trails through dense forest and aspen-lined meadows. There are around 160 developed campsites, with a limited number of electrical hookups. Reverend's Ridge, the park's largest campground, has coin-operated showers and laundry facilities. A daily vehicle pass costs $7, and camping fees range from $16 to $22 in developed campgrounds, $10 to $12 for backcountry camping, and $70 for a cabin or a yurt. There is also a 4-bedroom guest house for $260 nightly. To get to Golden Gate Canyon, take Colo. 93 north from Golden 1 mile to Golden Gate Canyon Road. Turn left and continue 13 miles to the park. For more information, call ℂ **303/582-3707.** Call ℂ **800/678-2267** or 303/470-4144 for camping reservations ($10 fee).

Roxborough State Park ★★★   This 4,000-acre park is a wonderland of spectacular red-rock fins jutting from the forested grassland at a noticeable angle. Roxborough is a great destination for hikers, with a challenging 6.4-mile hike up Carpenter Peak in park boundaries, as well as a plethora of trails that lead out of the park, including the popular 13-mile round-trip hike up Waterton Canyon. A daily vehicle pass costs $7; there is no camping, and dogs, bikes, and horses are not permitted. (Bikes are permitted in Waterton Canyon.) To get to Roxborough, take Wadsworth to Waterton Road (past Chatfield), and drive east to Rampart Range Road, then head south 2 miles to Roxborough Park Rd. and turn right into the park. For more information, call ℂ **303/973-3959.**

ESPECIALLY FOR KIDS

Denver is full of child-oriented activities and attractions. They include the Children's Museum of Denver, History Colorado Center, Downtown Aquarium, Denver Art Museum, Denver Museum of Miniatures Dolls & Toys, Denver Museum of Nature and Science, Denver Zoo, Elitch Gardens, Four Mile Historic Park, Lakeside Amusement Park, Tiny Town and Railroad, the U.S. Mint, and Water World. Some of the Denver Mountain Parks and local state parks have trails fit for short legs, as well as Mount Falcon Park, part of Jefferson County Open Space.

Kids will go bananas for **Casa Bonita,** and not because of the food. Equal parts amusement park and family restaurant—and famously featured on "South Park" in 2003—this is the largest restaurant in the Western Hemisphere, complete with fake cliffs in the middle of the action where actors regularly take swan dives into the pool below. That is just the beginning of the entertainment, ranging from mariachi bands to a video arcade to Black Bart's Cave, where spelunking comes with a few thrills and chills. Served cafeteria style, the all-you-can-eat menu ($13–$24, children's meals $5) spans Mexican and American standards like enchiladas, burritos, fajitas, fried chicken, and country-fried steak; you raise a little red flag at your table when you want seconds. Open Sunday through Thursday 11am to 9pm and Friday and Saturday 11am to 10pm, Casa Bonita is located in the JCRS Shopping Center, 6715 W. Colfax Ave. in Lakewood (📞 303/232-5115; www.casabonitadenver.com).

SHOPPING

If you're in Denver on foot, you'll find that most visitors do their shopping along the **16th Street Mall** (the mile-long pedestrian walkway between Market St. and Tremont Place) and adjacent areas, including **Larimer Square, Writer Square,** and the newest retail development downtown, **Denver Pavilions.** Outside the downtown area there are more options, primarily the huge **Cherry Creek Shopping Center.** There are also numerous funky urban retail areas within the city limits, as well as suburban shopping malls.

Malls & Markets

Cherry Creek Shopping Center ★   This is the only traditional shopping mall in the city limits, with big department stores like Macy's, Nordstrom, and Neiman Marcus, as well as an Apple Store and other usual suspects. Hours are Monday through Saturday from 10am to 9pm, and Sunday from 11am to 6pm. 3000 E. 1st Ave. (btw. University Blvd. and Steele St.). 📞 303/388-3900. www.shopcherrycreek.com.

Denver Pavilions ★   The southern anchor of downtown shopping, this complex covers 2 city blocks on three levels, with a wide range of local and national retailers, including Gap, H&M, and the terrific I Heart Denver Store (p. 54), as well as a jazz club and movie theaters. Hours are Monday to Saturday from 10am to 9pm and Sunday from 11am to 6pm; restaurants and theaters are open later. 500 16th St. (btw. Welton and Tremont sts.). 📞 303/260-6000. www.denverpavilions.com.

Park Meadows Mall ★   Dominating the southern suburban fringes, this is the biggest mall in the Rockies, surrounded by big boxes and smaller shopping strips. There are big department stores like Nordstrom as well as such specialty shops as Brookstone and Pottery Barn. Hours are Monday through Saturday from 10am to 9pm, Sunday from 11am to 6pm. 8401 Park Meadows Center Dr. (south of C-470 on Yosemite St.), Littleton. 📞 303/792-2999. www.parkmeadows.com.

Shopping A to Z
ANTIQUES

Denver's main antiques area is **Antique Row** (www.antique-row.com) along **South Broadway,** between Mississippi and Colorado avenues, with dozens of dealers selling all sorts of fine antiques, collectibles, and junk. Wandering through the wide variety of stores, where each dealer has his or her own unique bent, is great fun. Just remember that prices are often negotiable; unless you're quite knowledgeable about antiques, it wouldn't hurt to do some comparison shopping before making a major purchase.

ART & FINE CRAFTS

The top arts destination in Denver is the **Art District on Santa Fe** (www.artdistricton santafe.com). In recent years, Santa Fe Drive has attracted about 60 galleries and studios between 5th and 11th avenues. Most of the galleries are contemporary or Latin American and there is a popular First Friday Art Walk here on the first Friday night of every month.

A mile to the southeast, the Golden Triangle neighborhood, bordered by Lincoln Street, Speer Boulevard, and Colfax Avenue, has more than 25 galleries and museums, including the Denver Art Museum. The **Golden Triangle Museum District** (✆ **303/534-0771;** www.gtmd.org) puts together an open gallery event the first Friday night of every month, complete with a free shuttle.

The most recent neighborhood to blossom with studios is **River North Art District** (www.rivernorthart.com), a.k.a. "RiNo," in the formerly industrial nether-regions north of downtown; the neighborhood has an open gallery event on the first Friday of the month.

BOOKS

There is a sizable, well-stocked and expertly run downtown **Barnes & Noble ★★** anchoring the Denver Pavilions at 500 16th St. (✆ **303/825-9166**), with a coffee shop and free Wi-Fi.

Tattered Cover ★★★   The Tattered Cover is always near the top of the list when it comes to the country's best bookstores. The flagship is on the east side of town in a converted performing arts center, but the LoDo location is also excellent. 2526 E. Colfax Ave. ✆ **303/322-7727.** www.tatteredcover.com. There are also locations at Denver's LoDo at 16th and Wynkoop sts. (✆ **303/436-1070**) and in Union Station, as well as in the Town Center development in Highlands Ranch (✆ **303/470-7050**).

FASHION

Rockmount Ranch Wear ★★   Jack A. Weil invented the Western snap shirt in 1946 and headed the company until he died at age 107 in 2008. In the intervening 61 years, everyone from Elvis Presley to Woody Harrelson has worn a Rockmount shirt. Today Weil's grandson Steve Weil runs the business, which sells its signature snap shirts at its historic LoDo warehouse. The 1908 brick building doubles as a museum of Western shirts, and the embroidery is nothing short of artful. The inventory also includes cowboy hats, belt buckles, and scarves. 1626 Wazee St. ✆ **303/629-7777.** www.rockmount.com.

FOOD & DRINK

The Market at Larimer Square ★   Hit here to grab coffee, baked goods, or a sandwich for your rambles in downtown Denver. There are also shelves stocked with a variety of gourmet specialty foods. 1445 Larimer Sq. ✆ **303/534-5140.** www.themarketat larimer.com.

The Source ★★   Located north of downtown in RiNo, this 26,000-square-foot warehouse is the latest, greatest market in Denver, with local providers like the Crooked Stave brewery, a bakery, a butcher, and several shops and restaurants. The focus is squarely on local and artisan products. 3350 Brighton Blvd. ✆ **720/443-1135.** www. thesourcedenver.com.

GIFTS & SOUVENIRS

I Heart Denver Store ★   Samuel Schimek has created the most original souvenir and gift shop in the city by working exclusively with local crafters and artists. Most of the T-shirts, posters, cards, and other products have a Denver or Colorado theme. On Level 2 of the Denver Pavilions, 500 16th St., #264. ✆ **720/317-2328.** www.iheartdenver.info.

SPORTING GOODS

Sports fans looking for that Rockies cap or Broncos shirt will have no trouble finding it at **Bill's Sports Collectibles,** 2335 S. Broadway (✆ **303/733-4878**).

REI ★★★ The flagship REI store in the Central Platte Valley is one of the best outdoors stores in the country. At the entry, shoppers are greeted with a massive climbing wall before going on to peruse the camping gear, bicycles, skis, snowboards, and clothing populating the shelves and racks. Rentals are available, and there is a full calendar of classes and lectures. 1416 Platte St. ℂ **303/756-3100.**

Sports Authority Sportscastle ★ Five stories of sporting goods fill this long-standing retail location just south of downtown, located in a former Chrysler dealership. Besides sales of skis, bikes, clothing, and camping equipment, the store offers a wide range of services, from tank refills to hunting licenses. 1000 Broadway. ℂ **303/863-2260.**

TOYS & HOBBIES

Caboose Hobbies ★★★ Here in the Baker neighborhood is the world's largest train store, with nearly 20,000 square feet of floor space and 100,000 train related products in every scale. Even if you're not a certified train-iac, the store is worth a peek for the numerous showcase displays of model-train dioramas that are out of this world. 500 S. Broadway. ℂ **303/777-6766.** www.caboosehobbies.com.

Wizard's Chest ★ There are three areas of focus at this castle-themed shop in Cherry Creek North: costumes, magic, and toys and games. Upstairs, the costumes run the gamut from princesses to monsters, and the lower level has all sorts of miniature animals and dragons, a wide range of board and role-playing games, and a dedicated magic counter where old pros reveal their secrets to prospective buyers. 230 Fillmore St. ℂ **303/321-4304.** www.wizardschest.com.

NIGHTLIFE

Denver has an especially vibrant entertainment scene for a city its size, and the same could be said for the nightlife. With great venues downtown and in outlying areas (yes, I am talking about Red Rocks) and a wide variety of watering holes, it is not hard to find after-dark diversions in the Mile High City.

The Performing Arts

The anchor of Denver's performing arts scene, an important part of this increasingly sophisticated city, is the 4-square-block **Denver Performing Arts Complex,** located downtown just a few blocks from major hotels. In all, Denver has more than 30 theaters, and dozens of concert halls, nightclubs, and bars. Clubs offer country-and-western music, jazz, rock, and comedy.

Current entertainment listings appear in special Friday-morning sections of the "Denver Post." "Westword," the alternative weekly newspaper distributed free throughout the city every Wednesday evening, has perhaps the best listings: It focuses on the arts, entertainment, and local politics.

CLASSICAL MUSIC & OPERA

Colorado Symphony Orchestra ★ Denver's orchestra performs about 100 concerts a year at venues all over the metro area, including the Denver Performing Arts Complex. ℂ **303/623-7876.** www.coloradosymphony.org.

Opera Colorado ★ From February to May, Opera Colorado produces three different operas, typically performing at the Ellie Caulkins Opera House at the Denver Performing Arts Complex. ℂ **303/468-2030** for tickets, or 303/778-1500. www.operacolorado.org.

THEATER & COMEDY

Buntport Theater ★★ This is the best—and zaniest—original theater company in Denver. At their warehouse-turned-theater in the Art District on Santa Fe, Buntport stages four plays a year as well as events like "The Great Debate," with actors debating bacon the food versus Kevin Bacon, for example, on the third Tuesday of the month. Recent productions have included an off-kilter adaptation of Shakespeare's "The Tempest" and a play starring a life-sized Tommy Lee Jones puppet. 717 Lipan St. © **720/946-1388.** www.buntport.com.

Comedy Works ★ Comedy Works is one of the anchors of Larimer Square. Top touring comedians and rising stars of Denver's local laugh scene take the stage here. 1226 15th St. © **303/595-3637.** www.comedyworks.com.

Denver Center for the Performing Arts ★★★ The wide-ranging theater organization includes the **Denver Center Theatre Company,** the largest in Colorado, as well as **Denver Center Attractions,** featuring touring productions, including the off-Broadway premiere of "The Book of Mormon" in 2012, and the edgier **Off-Center @ The Jones** (www.denveroffcenter.org). 14th and Curtis sts. © **800/641-1222** or 303/893-4100. www.denvercenter.org.

Denver Puppet Theater ★★ This beloved theater in the Highlands area showcases puppets of all kinds in regular performances of fairy tales and other kid-oriented fare, as well as more mature entertainment in the evenings. Tickets cost $7. There is an ice cream parlor onsite. 3156 W. 38th Ave. © **303/458-6446.** www.denverpuppettheater.com.

Su Teatro Cultural and Performing Arts Center ★ One of the pillars of the local Hispanic arts community, El Centro produces bilingual performances that include poetry festivals, film screenings, dramas, and musicals at the historic Denver Civic Theatre in the Art District on Santa Fe. 721 Santa Fe Dr. © **303/296-0219.** www.suteatro.org.

Lannie's Clocktower Cabaret ★★ Named for Lannie Garrett, a.k.a. "Patsy DeCline," this eclectic venue in the basement of the landmark D&F Tower on the 16th Street Mall serves up burlesque, comedy, and musical theater. In the D&F Tower, 1601 Arapahoe St. © **303/293-0075.** www.lannies.com.

DANCE

Cleo Parker Robinson Dance ★★ The eponymous founder of this contemporary dance company has been one of the shining stars in Denver since launching it in the 1970s, and her international reputation is well deserved. Annual spring and summer productions are the hallmark of the local calendar, but the company tours the country as well. 119 Park Ave. W. © **303/295-1759.** www.cleoparkerdance.org.

Colorado Ballet ★★ The state's top professional resident ballet company, the Colorado Ballet produces both classical and contemporary works as well as "The Nutcracker" in December. 1278 Lincoln St. © **303/837-8888.** www.coloradoballet.org.

MAJOR CONCERT HALLS & AUDITORIUMS

Denver Performing Arts Complex ★★★ This is not only the biggest and best performing arts facility in the Rocky Mountain region, it is on the short list of the tops in the country. The complex houses nine theaters, a concert hall, and what may be the nation's first symphony hall in the round. It is home to the Colorado Symphony, Colorado Ballet, Opera Colorado, and Denver Center for the Performing Arts (an umbrella organization for resident and touring theater companies). Theaters range from intimate to cavernous, and local and touring productions fill out the calendar. The rising reputation is demonstrated by numerous world premieres in recent years, including "The Laramie Project" and "Tantalus," and "The Book of Mormon." 14th and Curtis sts. ✆ **800/641-1222** or 303/893-4100. www.denvercenter.org.

Fillmore Auditorium ★   Formerly a roller-skating rink, this theater got a slick redo in 1999 and has emerged as one of the top music venues in the downtown area. Jam bands like to stop here for multiday stands, but musical talents ranging from Slayer to Robin Thicke have played here in recent years. 1510 Clarkson St. ✆ **303/837-1482.** www.fillmoreauditorium.com.

Paramount Theatre ★   This has been a focal point of local culture since it opened in 1929. Now an anchor of the 16th Street Mall, the venue has recently been graced by the likes of Tom Waits and Queens of the Stone Age. 1621 Glenarm Place. ✆ **303/623-0106.** www.paramountdenver.com.

Red Rocks Amphitheatre ★★★   With a scenic view of the city and incredible scenery in every direction, there is no finer outdoor music venue in the United States. Flanked by fins of red rock that provide near-perfect acoustics, the 9,000-seat amphitheater is the place to see a concert in Colorado in the summer. The Beatles played here in 1964—it was the only non-sellout on their initial U.S. tour—and in the time since has been the site of concerts by everyone from Jimmy Cliff to The Flaming Lips to Widespread Panic. For the record, however, Willie Nelson has played here more than anyone else, a title he took from The Grateful Dead in 2003. Whether there is a concert or not, Red Rocks is a great attraction, featuring trails, a museum, a restaurant and more (p. 50). 18300 W. Alameda Pkwy., Morrison. ✆ **720/865-2494.** www.redrocksonline.com.

The Bar Scene

The first permanent structure on the site of modern Denver was supposedly a saloon, and the city has built on that tradition ever since. Today, there are sports bars, dance bars, lots of brewpubs, outdoor cafe bars, English pubs, Old West saloons, bars with views of the city, Art Deco bars, gay bars, and a few bars we probably shouldn't even discuss here.

Appropriately, the newest Denver "in" spot for barhopping is also the oldest part of the city—LoDo—which has been renovated and upgraded, and now attracts all the young partiers and upwardly mobile professionals. Its trendy nightspots are often noisy and crowded, but if you're looking for action, this is where you'll find it.

Other popular "strips" are along Broadway at 10th and Ellsworth avenues, and along East Colfax Avenue between Ogden and Monroe streets. For those who prefer caffeine to alcohol, a number of good coffee bars abound throughout downtown Denver, as well as in the Capitol Hill and Uptown neighborhoods.

Black Crown Lounge ★★   This gay-friendly lounge south of downtown doubles as a high-end antique and decor store (Crown Accents) during the day. Come nightfall, it's undoubtedly the best-decorated piano bar in the Rockies, with a labyrinthine layout, board games on the second level, and outdoor areas as thoughtfully designed as the interior. 1446 S. Broadway. ✆ **720/353-4701.** www.blackcrownlounge.com.

Charlie Brown's ★   A friendly piano bar with one of the best patios around, Charlie Brown's has been serving Denver's tipplers since Prohibition ended—or even a few years before, if you believe the legends. The grill serves Mexican, Greek, and American standards, and does a good job of it. 980 Grant St. (at 10th Ave.). ✆ **303/860-1655.** www. charliebrownsbarandgrill.com.

DENVER: THE NAPA VALLEY OF beer

Denver has an ever-growing collection of microbreweries, brewpubs, and nano-breweries, not to mention the largest beer festival in the country in the **Great American Beer Festival** (✆ **303/447-0816**; www.greatamericanbeerfestival. com), held annually at the Colorado Convention Center in early fall. The 4-day festival attracts tens of thousands of beer nuts to sample the wares of more than 500 breweries from all over the country.

If the festival is not in session, however, your first stop should be Denver's first modern microbrewery, the **Wynkoop Brewing Co.,** in LoDo at 1634 18th St., at Wynkoop Street (✆ **303/297-2700**; www.wynkoop.com), offering tours every Saturday between 1 and 5pm (see "Where to Eat," p. 30). At least 10 beers are always on tap, including a few unusual recipes—the spicy chile beer is my favorite. Also downtown, **Great Divide Brewing Co.,** 2201 Arapahoe St. (✆ **303/296-9460**; www.greatdivide. com), has a terrific taproom and some of the best beer in the state. Tours are offered Monday through Friday at 3, 4, and 5pm and on the hour on Saturdays and Sundays from 2 to 6pm.

On the west side of downtown, **Denver Beer Co.,** 1695 Platte St. (✆ **303/433-2739**; www.denverbeerco.com), has a social vibe and a great patio, not to mention the top-notch suds. Northeast of downtown in the up-and-coming RiNo neighborhood, **Crooked Stave Artisan Beer Project**, 3350 Brighton Blvd., at The Source (✆ **720/508-3292**; www. crookedstave.com), is one of the best-reviewed breweries in the country, specializing in small batches with unusual ingredients. South of downtown in Baker, **TRVE Brewing,** 227 Broadway (✆ **303/351-1021**; www.trvebrewing. com), is a neighborhood nanobrewery playing loud music and pouring excellent beers in a spare, funky room. Further south, **Former Future Brewing Company,** 1290 S. Broadway (✆ **720/441-4253**; www.formerfuture-brewingcompany.com), is a new entry winning fans with its innovative approach to time-tested recipes.

If you would like to sample several Denver microbreweries without the hassle of getting yourself there, hop on **Banjo Billy's brewery tours** (✆ **720/938-8885**; www.banjobilly.com), which leave the Wynkoop every Thursday at 6pm and cost $40 per person. The fee includes a ride on the one-and-only Banjo Billy bus and three pints of beer. Reservations are recommended.

For more information on the brewers in Denver and Colorado, contact the **Colorado Brewers Guild** (✆ **303/507-7664**; www.coloradobeer.org).

Churchill Bar ★★   With a rarified atmosphere, the resident cigar bar at the Brown Palace is one of the few places you can smoke and drink indoors in the city. There are wide selections of cigars, single-malt scotches, and small-batch bourbons on the menu. In the Brown Palace Hotel, 321 17th St. ✆ **303/297-3111.**

Cruise Room Bar ★★   The Cruise Room opened in 1933 on the very day Prohibition was repealed and today it remains the best place to quaff a martini in Denver. Its walls are clad in Art Deco panels depicting how to say "cheers" all over the world and the red light gives the place that perfectly sinful vibe that newer bars strive, and most often fail, to duplicate. In the Oxford Hotel, 1600 17th St. (at Wazee St.). ✆ **303/825-1107.**

Falling Rock Tap House ★★★   Famously featuring more than 75 beers on tap, Falling Rock is the best beer hall in all of beer-crazed Denver. The bar food is a cut above, and the location near Coors Field makes it a popular and busy hangout on game day. 1919 Blake St. ℐ **303/293-8338.** www.fallingrocktaphouse.com.

My Brother's Bar ★   Jack Kerouac loved this bar when he rambled in Denver in the 1940s, and it will be hard not to do the same yourself when you belly up to one of the least pretentious bars in the West. Purportedly the oldest watering hole in the city— it's been serving booze since the 1880s—the establishment grills some mean burgers and has a stash of Girl Scout cookies all year long. 2376 15th St. ℐ **303/455-9991.**

Williams & Graham ★★   This retro-looking Highlands hotspot is a blast from the past, taking its cues for design and cocktails from the 1920s and 1930s. The speakeasy-style bar is accessed from a moving bookshelf in an actual bookstore focusing on cocktail tomes and bar gear. 3160 Tejon St. ℐ **303/997-8886.** www.williamsandgraham. com.

Wynkoop Brewing Company ★★   This cavernous converted warehouse across from Union Station, famously founded in 1988 by Colorado Governor John Hickenlooper, is the soul of LoDo. With 15 of its house-brewed beers on tap and another 5 or so from local breweries for good measure, most tastes can be satisfied here. They've even brewed a stout with Rocky Mountain oysters—bull testicles for the uninformed. Beyond the beer, the place has three levels, with an improv theater downstairs, the restaurant on the main floor, and a 21-and-over pool hall on the second floor. 1634 18th St. (at Wynkoop St.). ℐ **303/297-2700.** www.wynkoop.com.

The Club & Music Scene
ROCK, JAZZ & BLUES

Bluebird Theater ★   This small historic theater has emerged as the centerpiece of revitalization of East Colfax. The performers who take to the stage are primarily rockers, but you will also catch a country or hip-hop show on some nights. 3317 E. Colfax Ave. (at Adams St.). ℐ **303/377-1666.** www.bluebirdtheater.net.

The Church ★   So named because it was a church before a conversion to a nightclub, the historic 1865 building wears its new purpose well. The cavernous facility includes multiple dance floors and bars, and the religious ambiance lends it an interesting vibe, to say the least. 1160 Lincoln St. ℐ **303/832-8628.** www.coclubs.com.

El Chapultepec ★★   No cover and great jazz make this one of the best nightspots downtown. It's a picture-perfect bar, complete with checkerboard flooring and black-and-white photos of jazz greats who have played here over the years. 1962 Market St. ℐ **303/295-9126.** www.thepeclodo.com.

hi-dive ★★   Hipster central in Denver, the hi-dive is also the best space to catch rising stars of the local and national indie scene. Next door (and under the same ownership) is **Sputnik,** featuring DJs, bingo nights, and a good menu of relatively healthy bar snacks. Tickets run $6 to $10. 7 S. Broadway. ℐ **303/733-0230.** www.hi-dive.com.

Larimer Lounge ★   The Larimer Lounge planted its flag in RiNo before it was cool, and the neighborhood has finally caught up to it a decade later. The hard-rocking acts that play here are usually underground and off the radar, but the space—with a great barbecue area out back—hits all of the right notes for a dive-meets-venue-meets-hangout. 2721 Larimer St. ℐ **303/291-1007.** www.larimerlounge.com.

Mercury Café ★   Proprietor Marilyn Megenity has booked eclectic acts in Denver for more than 30 years. Located in Five Points, "The Merc" still serves fresh and healthy fare while booking one of the most adventurous calendars in the city, delivering blues, poetry, world music, flamenco classes, and film screenings. Credit cards are not accepted. 2199 California St. (at 22nd St.). ℂ **303/294-9258.** www.mercurycafe.com.

3 Kings Tavern ★★ This funky joint in Baker isn't just the rough-and-tumble music venue—it's a veritable museum of oddball art and pop-culture collectibles with comic book covers and musician head shots wallpapering various walls, and there is pinball games, pool tables, and a calendar that veers from burlesque and jazz to rowdy rockabilly, punk, and metal shows. 60 S. Broadway. ℂ **303/777-7352.** www.3kingstavern.com.

COUNTRY MUSIC

Grizzly Rose ★★ The Grizzly Rose dates back to the halcyon days of sprawling, Texas-sized country-and-western compounds—the 1980s—but it is still going strong 25 years after it opened. It packs them in for touring country acts on weekends, and the free dance lessons on Wednesday night at 7pm attract hoofers of all skill levels. 5450 N. Valley Hwy. (at I-25, exit 215). ℂ **303/295-1330.** www.grizzlyrose.com.

Stampede ★★★ Those in need of a line-dancing fix should head over to Stampede Wednesday through Saturday for the metro area's top country bar. Live performers and DJs offer a jangly soundtrack that goes especially well with a couple of drinks from any one of the six bars on the spacious premises. 2430 S. Havana St. (at Parker Rd.), Aurora. ℂ **303/696-7686.** www.stampedeclub.net.

The Gay & Lesbian Scene

Denver has a thriving gay culture, and most of the bars and other establishments covered in this book are gay-friendly. Of the above bars, the Black Crown Lounge, Charlie Brown's, and the Cruise Room are most popular with gays and lesbians.

Spectator Sports

Sports-crazed Denver is the smallest of the 12 cities in the U.S. with teams in each of the four major professional team sports: football, baseball, basketball, and hockey. Tickets to many sporting events in Denver can be obtained from **Ticketmaster** (ℂ **800/745-3000;** www.ticketmaster.com), which has several outlets in the Denver area. **Craigslist** (http://denver.craigslist.org) and **StubHub** (www.stubhub.com) are also good place to find tickets.

BASEBALL The **Colorado Rockies** (ℂ **800/388-7625** or 303/762-5437; www.coloradorockies.com) play in Major League Baseball's National League West. The team plays at Coors Field, located at 20th and Blake streets in LoDo. The 50,000-seat stadium, with its old-school looks and on-site microbrewery, is one of the best baseball stadiums in the country. Tickets are readily available for most games, from either the box office or the scalpers on the street.

BASKETBALL The **Denver Nuggets** (ℂ **303/287-3865;** www.nuggets.com) of the National Basketball Association have become a perennial playoff team in recent years. The Nuggets play their home games at the Pepsi Center (downtown at Speer Blvd. and Auraria Pkwy.) from fall to spring.

FOOTBALL The **Denver Broncos** (ℂ **720/258-3333;** www.denverbroncos.com) of the National Football League play home games at Sports Authority Field at Mile High just northwest of I-25 and Colfax Avenue. This is without a doubt Denver's favorite home team: Home games are sold out months in advance, so call early; there are also a few tickets sold on game day. You can often find an enterprising individual selling tickets outside the stadium entrance on game day. Scalping is illegal in Denver, but police rarely enforce the ban.

HOCKEY Denver's National Hockey League team, the **Colorado Avalanche** (📞 **303/428-7645;** www.coloradoavalanche.com), plays at the Pepsi Center (Speer Blvd. and Auraria Pkwy.) from fall to spring. For a cheaper ticket (and a fun atmosphere), the **University of Denver** men's hockey team (📞 **303/871-2336;** www.denverpioneers.com) is consistently good and plays a competitive schedule between October and mid-March at the Ritchie Center. The new **Denver Cutthroats** of the Central Hockey League (📞 **303/295-3474;** www.denvercutthroats.com) skate at the Denver Coliseum (I-70 and Brighton Blvd.).

RODEO Held in Denver since 1906, the **National Western Stock Show** (📞 **303/295-6124;** www.nationalwestern.com) takes over the city the second and third weeks of January. While a possible move is on the drawing board, the rodeo takes place at the Denver Coliseum, with other activities happening at the National Western Complex and the Event Center. Both facilities are located about 2 miles north of downtown at Brighton Boulevard and I-70. The purse is rich—more than $500,000—and the event is popular, attracting some 600,000 people (along with 15,000 head of livestock) each year.

SOCCER The Colorado Rapids (📞 **303/727-3500;** www.coloradorapids.com), of Major League Soccer, play at Dick's Sporting Goods Park, a soccer-only stadium about 10 miles northeast of downtown at Quebec Street and 60th Avenue.

DAY TRIPS FROM DENVER

Golden, Idaho Springs, and **Georgetown** make up most of the fabled Gold Circle—those towns that boomed with the first strikes of the gold rush in 1859. **Central City,** once the richest of the four towns but now the least attractive, completes the circle. Central City is trying to relive its glory days with a return to gambling, largely supported by locals from Denver, and although the exteriors of its historic buildings remain appealing, the rows of electronic slot machines and other gambling devices inside are a turnoff.

Golden ★★

Golden, 15 miles west of downtown Denver by way of U.S. 6 or Colo. 58 off I-70, is better known for the Coors Brewery (founded in 1873) and the Colorado School of Mines (established in 1874) than for its years as territorial capital. Today, it sports a spiffy downtown, numerous compelling attractions, and a vibrant recreational scene, newly connected to Denver with the arrival of the Light Rail in 2013.

ESSENTIALS

For tourist information, contact the **Greater Golden Area Chamber of Commerce** (📞 **303/279-3113;** www.goldencochamber.org).

EXPLORING GOLDEN

Historic downtown Golden centers on the **Territorial Capitol** in the **Loveland Building,** 12th Street and Washington Avenue. Built in 1861, it housed the first state legislature from 1862 to 1867, when the capital was moved to Denver. Today it contains offices and a restaurant. The **Armory,** 13th and Arapahoe streets, is probably the largest cobblestone structure in the United States; 3,300 wagonloads of stone and quartz went into its construction. The **Rock Flour Mill Warehouse,** 8th and Cheyenne streets, dates from 1863, built with red granite from nearby Golden Gate Canyon and still has its original cedar beams and wooden floors.

In addition to the attractions that follow, see the section on **Golden Gate State Park** (p. 52) and **RipBoard** (p. 48).

Astor House Museum ★ This 1867 boardinghouse now serves as a lens into Colorado's territorial days and ways. The basic stone facade belies the fascinating exhibits within, centered on rooms decorated just as they might have been in the 1860s. Allow about 30 minutes.

822 12th St. ℂ **303/278-3557.** www.goldenhistory.org. Admission $3, free for children under 7. There is also a combo ticket that includes admission to the Golden History Center for $5. Tues–Sat 10am–4:30pm; Sun noon–4:30pm.

Boettcher Mansion ★ This historic Jefferson County estate was built by Charles Boettcher in 1917 as a summer home and hunting lodge. It contains displays of furnishings and other items from the American Arts and Crafts period of the late 1800s and early 1900s. Other exhibits explore the history of Golden and the Boettcher family. Allow 1 hour.

900 Colorow Rd. (on Lookout Mountain). ℂ **720/497-7630.** http://mansion.jeffco.us. Free admission, donations accepted. Mon–Fri 8am–4pm or by appointment.

Bradford Washburn American Mountaineering Museum ★★ Golden is a fitting location for this museum detailing the history of mountaineering and some of the greatest achievements of the sport. On display: Peter Schoening's legendary ice axe that saved five mountaineers from certain death on K2 in 1953; a wealth of artifacts from the Tenth Mountain Division when they trained near Leadville, Colorado, during World War II; and a miniature model of Mount Everest that showcases the mountain's extreme topography. Allow 1 hour.

710 10th St. ℂ **303/996-2755.** www.bwamm.org. Admission $5 adults, $1 children under 12. Mon–Thurs 9am–6pm (until 7pm Tues); Fri 9am–4pm; Sat noon–5pm.

Buffalo Bill Museum & Grave ★★ Likely the most famous person on the planet when he died in 1917, William "Buffalo Bill" Cody defined modern American celebrity. That's probably why his sister sold his body to the "Denver Post" and the city of Denver to make a tourist attraction of his grave on Lookout Mountain. While many say he wanted to be buried in Wyoming near the city that bears his name, Cody was laid to rest in Golden, where his grave was later buried under 20 tons of concrete to thwart would-be grave-robbers. Exhibits in the museum cover the life and times of this consummate showman and his one-of-a-kind "Wild West Show." Allow up to 2 hours.

987½ Lookout Mountain Rd. ℂ **303/526-0744.** www.buffalobill.org. Admission $5 adults, $4 seniors, $1 children 6–15, free for children 5 and under. May–Oct daily 9am–5pm; Nov–Apr Tues–Sun 9am–4pm. Closed Dec 25. I-70, exit 256.

Clear Creek History Park ★ This 3-acre creek-side park illustrates the history of the area's ranching, with two log cabins, several animal barns, a blacksmith's shop, and a one-room schoolhouse from the 1870s. The buildings, which were moved to this site to save them from development in their original site in nearby Golden Gate Canyon, are open during special events. Allow about an hour.

11th and Arapahoe sts. (in downtown Golden). ℂ **303/278-3557.** www.goldenhistory.org. Free admission; $3 suggested donation. Daily sunrise–sunset.

Colorado Railroad Museum ★★ Housed in a replica of an 1880s railroad depot, this museum covers the fascinating world of Colorado railroads. The state's rugged mountains made for a challenge, and the resulting work-arounds are things of

Day Trips from Denver

DENVER

serious engineering beauty. Outside is a nice collection of railcars and locomotives, including an 1880 steam locomotive that pulled Denver Leadville & Gunnison trains over the Continental Divide. Visitors can also take a ride on one of the original "Galloping Goose" engines that delivered freights to remote corners of southwestern Colorado. Allow 1 to 2 hours.

17155 W. 44th Ave. ✆ **800/365-6263** or 303/279-4591. www.coloradorailroadmuseum.org. Admission $10 adults, $8 seniors, $5 children 3–16, free for children under 2, $20 families. Daily 9am–5pm. Closed major holidays. Follow signs from I-70, exit 265, westbound; exit 266, eastbound.

Colorado School of Mines Geology Museum ★

On the campus of the Colorado School of Mines, this first-rate geology museum has rocks from all over the planet, not to mention the Moon. On two floors of exhibits, visitors can delve into carbon dating, meteorites, and a striking array of ultraviolet rocks. The outdoor geology trail is marked by fossils, petrified logs, dinosaur tracks, and other geological attractions. Allow 1 hour.

1310 Maple St. ✆ **303/273-3815** or 303/273-3823. www.mines.edu/Geology_Museum. Free admission. Mon–Sat 9am–4pm; Sun 1–4pm. Closed Colorado School of Mines holidays.

Coors Brewing Company ★

One of the world's largest breweries, this facility produces 1.5 million gallons of beer each day. Coors conducts free public tours, followed by free samples of the various beers produced. The 30-minute prerecorded walking tour covers the history of the Coors family and company, the barley malting process, and the entire production process all the way to packaging. Children are welcome, and arrangements can be made for visitors with disabilities. There's also a gift shop and an interactive timeline in the reception area. Allow about 2 hours—unless you take the "short tour" which actually skips the tour altogether and heads straight to the hospitality lounge for your freebies.

13th and Ford sts. ✆ **866/812-2337** or 303/277-2337. www.millercoors.com/golden-brewery-tour.aspx. Free admission. Tours Memorial Day to Labor Day Mon–Sat 10am–4pm, Sun noon–4pm; rest of the year Thurs–Sat and Mon 10am–4pm, Sun noon–4pm. Closed holidays. Visitors under 18 must be accompanied by an adult.

Foothills Art Center ★★

This small art museum has risen in reputation in recent years, culminating with a standout Edgar Degas exhibit in spring 2013. The community gallery showcases Colorado artists, and fall brings a worthwhile holiday market. Allow 30 minutes.

809 15th St. ✆ **303/279-3922.** www.foothillsartcenter.org. Admission $5 adults, $3 seniors, free for students and children. Special exhibitions have different pricing. Tues–Sat 10am–5pm; Sun 1–5pm.

Golden History Center ★

Covering the history of the Golden area from the Jurassic epoch onward, this is a cut above your average small history museum. Displays include relics from Coors Brewing Company, terrifying antique dentists' tools, and a small-scale diorama of Golden when it served as the territorial capital. Allow 1 hour.

923 10th St. ✆ **303/278-3557.** www.goldenhistory.org. Admission $3 adults, free for children under 7. A combo ticket includes admission to the Astor House Museum for $5. Tues–Sat 10am–4:30pm; June–Aug also open Sun noon–4:30pm.

Heritage Square ★

A family-oriented shopping, dining, and entertainment village with a Wild West theme, Heritage Square features some Victorian specialty shops, a Ferris wheel, pony rides, laser maze, rope course, go-carts, and bumper boats. The big attraction is a 2,350-foot alpine slide with bobsled-style carts, and there's also a nostalgic ice-cream parlor. Allow 1 to 2 hours.

18301 Colfax Ave. (U.S. 40). ☏ **303/727-8437.** www.heritagesquare.info. Free admission; separate charges for individual activities. Memorial Day to Labor Day Mon–Sat 10am–8pm; Sun 11am–8pm. Shorter hours rest of year. I-70, exit 259.

Lookout Mountain Nature Center ★
A 1.5-mile self-guided nature trail winds through this 110-acre preserve among ponderosa pines and pretty mountain meadows. A free trail guide is available at the Nature Center when it's open, and a map is on display at a kiosk for those walking the trail at other times. The nonprofit Nature Center has displays on the pine beetle, pollination, and Colorado wildlife, plus an interactive exhibit on the ponderosa pine forest. The building is also worth a look—it's constructed of used and recycled materials such as ground-up plastic soda containers and the pulp of aspen trees. Allow at least 1 hour.

910 Colorow Rd. (on Lookout Mountain). ☏ **720/497-7600.** http://lmnc.jeffco.us. Free admission. Trail daily 8am–dusk; Nature Center Tues–Sun 10am–4pm (summer Sat–Sun 9am–5pm).

Mother Cabrini Shrine ★
A 22-foot statue of Jesus stands at the top of a 373-step stairway adorned by carvings representing the Stations of the Cross and mysteries of the rosary. The shrine is dedicated to the country's first citizen saint, St. Frances Xavier Cabrini, who founded the Order of the Missionary Sisters of the Sacred Heart. The order has a convent here with a gift shop that's open from 9am to 5pm daily and mass is open to the public. Allow 45 to 90 minutes.

20189 Cabrini Blvd. (I-70, exit 259), Lookout Mountain. ☏ **303/526-0758.** www.mother cabrinishrine.org. Free admission, donations welcome. Daily 7am–6pm.

National Earthquake Information Center ★
The U.S. Geological Survey operates this facility to collect rapid earthquake information, transmit warnings over the Earthquake Early Alerting Service, and publish and disseminate earthquake data. Tours of 30 to 45 minutes can be scheduled by appointment when a guide is available.

1711 Illinois St. ☏ **303/273-8420.** http://neic.usgs.gov. Free tours Mon and Thurs, by appointment only.

National Renewable Energy Laboratory Education Center ★★
Those interested in green energy will find the wide range of interactive exhibits fascinating. Energy options ranging from solar to hydrogen fuel cells are covered, and this public face of the federal clean-energy lab practices what it preaches, with an energy-efficient design that maximizes daylighting and makes use of wind power and evaporative cooling. Allow 1 hour.

15013 Denver W. Pkwy. ☏ **303/384-6565.** www.nrel.gov/education_center. Free admission. Mon–Fri 9am–4pm.

Rocky Mountain Quilt Museum ★
Quilting fanatics and crafts lovers will appreciate the permanent collection of more than 500 quilts at this small museum. Temporary exhibits cover the work of standout quilters from Colorado and elsewhere. Allow 30 minutes.

1213 Washington Ave. ☏ **303/277-0377.** www.rmqm.org. Admission $6 adults, $5 seniors, $4 children 6–12, free for children 5 and under. Mon–Sat 10am–4pm; mid-May to Aug also Sun 11am–4pm.

WHERE TO EAT

For a good meal in a historic setting, try the **Old Capitol Grill** in downtown Golden, 1122 Washington Ave., at 12th Street (☏ **303/279-6390**), which offers steak and burgers plus a good selection of sandwiches. Located in the Territorial Capitol Building constructed in 1862, the restaurant is open daily for lunch and dinner, with dinner prices in the $8 to $20 range. A more upscale dinner choice is the **Bridgewater Grill,** in the Golden Hotel, 800 11th St. (*C* **303/279-2010**). It serves creative regional fare in the $10 to $30 range.

Idaho Springs

This community 35 miles west of Denver was the site of a major gold strike in 1859. Idaho Springs today beckons visitors to try their luck at panning for any gold that may remain. The quaint Victorian downtown is worth a look; don't miss the Bridal Veil Falls tumbling through the largest water wheel in Colorado across from City Hall.

ESSENTIALS

For visitor information, contact the **Idaho Springs Chamber of Commerce** (*C* **303/567-4447;** www.idahospringschamberofcommerce.com).

EXPLORING IDAHO SPRINGS

The scenic **"Oh My God" dirt road,** a steep, winding thoroughfare, runs from Central City through Virginia Canyon to Idaho Springs, although most visitors prefer to take I-70 directly.

The **Argo Gold Mine, Mill, and Museum** is listed on the National Register of Historic Places and offers tours daily from mid-April to October from 9am to 6pm. Visitors can see the Double Eagle Gold Mine, relatively unchanged since the early miners first worked it more than 100 years ago, and the mill, where ore was processed into gold. Everyone is welcome to take part in gold- and gemstone-panning. Admission is $16 for adults, $8 for children 6 to 12, and free for kids 5 and under. Allow at least 45 minutes. The museum is at 350 Riverside Dr. (*C* **303/567-2421;** www.historic argotours.com).

At the **Phoenix Gold Mine** you can don a hard hat and follow a working miner through narrow tunnels to experience mining in the 1800s. You can also pan for gold on the property and relax in the picnic area. Weather permitting, the mine is open daily from 10am to 5pm in the summer (until 4pm in the winter); the tours are informal and entertaining. Cost for the tour and panning is $15 for adults, $5 for children 8 to 11, and free for children 7 and under. Panning without the tour is $8. The mine is on Trail Creek Road (*C* **303/567-0422;** www.phoenixgoldmine.com). Allow about 1 hour.

Just outside Idaho Springs is **Indian Springs Healing Waters Spa,** a fine spot for a relaxing soak in the hot springs after a long day of skiing or hiking. The resort has a covered swimming pool, indoor and outdoor private baths, and a vapor cave with soaking pools. Rates are $19 to $25 per person for an hour in the private baths or all-day use of the vapor cave, $15 to $17 for all-day use of the pool, and $11 to $13 for a mud bath in "Club Mud." Lodging is in rooms and cabins ($65–$120 for two) or a campground ($25 nightly); meals and weekend entertainment are also offered. The resort, located at 302 Soda Creek Rd. (*C* **303/989-6666;** www.indianspringsresort.com), is open daily from 7:30am to 10:30pm year-round.

Idaho Springs is the starting point for a 28-mile drive to the summit of 14,260-foot **Mount Evans.** From I-70, exit 240, follow Colo. 103—also called Mt. Evans Highway—as it winds along Chicago Creek through Arapahoe National Forest to **Echo Lake Park,** a unit of Denver Mountain Parks (p. 50) with picnic areas, hiking trails, and fishing. From here, Colo. 5—the highest paved auto road in North America—climbs to the Mount Evans summit. Views along this highway are of spectacular snowcapped peaks (even in June), and you're likely to see mountain goats, bighorn sheep, marmots, eagles, and other wildlife. The road is generally open from Memorial Day to Labor Day, and there is a $10 fee per vehicle. Allow at least 4 hours.

Another way to see this area's great scenery is by horseback. **A&A Historical Trails Stables,** 5 miles up Virginia Canyon from Idaho Springs (☎ 303/567-4808; www.aastables.com), offers a variety of trail rides, including breakfast and moonlight rides. A 1-hour ride costs $40 per person, plus $30 for each additional hour.

WHERE TO EAT

An après-ski institution and the first of a regional chain, **Beau Jo's Colorado Style Pizza,** 1517 Miner St. (☎ 303/567-4376; www.beaujos.com), offers a wide variety of so-called mountain pizzas, including standard pepperoni; "Skier Mike's," with Canadian bacon, green peppers, and chicken breast; and a roasted-garlic and veggie combo. Sandwiches are also available, plus a salad bar set up in a pair of old claw-foot bathtubs. The bill usually comes out to $10 to $20 per person. Another good place for a meal and/or a beer is the **Buffalo Restaurant & Bar,** 1617 Miner St. (☎ 303/567-2729; www.buffalorestaurant.com), an upscale bar and grill housed in a slickly restored 1881 building and featuring plenty of buffalo on the menu. Lunch and dinner main courses run $10 to $25.

Georgetown ★

A pretty village of Victorian-era houses and stores, Georgetown, 45 miles west of Denver on I-70 at an elevation of 8,500 feet, is named for an 1860 gold camp. Among the best preserved of the foothill mining towns, Georgetown is one of the few that didn't suffer a major fire during its formative years. Perhaps to acknowledge their blessings, townspeople built eye-catching steeples on top of their firehouses, not their churches.

ESSENTIALS

Georgetown is accessed via I-70, exit 228. For information on attractions and travel services, drop by or contact the **Georgetown Gateway Visitors Center** at 1491 Argentine St. (☎ 303/569-2405; www.town.goeorgetown.co.us); or **Historic Georgetown, Inc.** (☎ 303/569-2840; www.historicgeorgetown.org). The latter offers free lectures and occasional tours.

EXPLORING GEORGETOWN

The Georgetown–Silver Plume Mining Area was declared a National Historic Landmark District in 1966, and more than 200 of its buildings have been restored.

A convenient place to begin a **walking tour** is the Old County Courthouse, at 6th and Argentine streets. Now the community center and tourist information office, it was built in 1867. Across Argentine Street is the Old Stone Jail (1868); 3 blocks south, at 3rd and Argentine, is the Hamill House.

Sixth Street is Georgetown's main commercial strip. Walk east from the Old Courthouse. On your left are the Masonic Hall (1891), the Fish Block (1886), the Monti and Guanella Building (1868), and the Cushman Block (1874); on your right, the Hamill Block (1881) and the Kneisel & Anderson Building (1893). The Hotel de Paris is at the corner of 6th and Taos. Nearly opposite, at 6th and Griffith, is the Star Hook and Ladder Building (1886), along with the town hall and marshal's office.

Georgetown Energy Museum ★   Not merely a museum, this is a fully operational hydroelectric power plant that covers the history of water power around the world. The water wheels that have powered Georgetown since 1900 are the main attraction, but there are also antique electrical appliances of the same vintage. Allow 30 minutes.

600 Griffith St. ✆ **303/569-3557.** www.georgetownenergymuseum.org. Free admission, donations accepted. Memorial Day to early Oct Mon–Sat 11am–4pm, Sun noon–4pm; rest of the year weekdays by appointment only.

Georgetown Loop Railroad ★★   This historic railroad makes as many as nine round-trips daily between Georgetown and Silver Plume during peak summer season. The route gains about 600 feet in elevation over the course of the 2-mile ride (the views are terrific); riders spend some time in the tiny mining town of Silver Plume before returning by rail to Georgetown. Dinner rides and other special events occur throughout the year.

606 Loop Dr. ✆ **888/456-6777.** www.georgetownlooprr.com. Tickets $26–$38 adults, $19–$31 children 3–12, free for children under 3. Memorial Day to early Oct daily 10am–3pm, shorter hours rest of the year. Closed early Jan to early May.

Hamill House ★   Built in Country Gothic Revival style, this house dates from 1867, when silver speculator William Hamill owned it. When Historic Georgetown, Inc., acquired it in 1971, the house had its original woodwork, fireplaces, and wallpaper. A delicately carved outhouse had two sections: one with walnut seats for the family, the other with pine seats for servants. Allow 30 to 60 minutes.

305 Argentine St. ✆ **303/569-2840.** www.historicgeorgetown.org. Admission $4 adults, $3 seniors 65 and older and students, free for children 11 and under. Memorial Day to June Sat–Sun noon–4pm; July to early Sept Mon–Fri noon–5pm and Sat–Sun 11am–5pm; early Sept to mid-Dec Sat–Sun 11am–5pm. Closed mid-Dec to late May except for prearranged tours.

Hotel de Paris ★★   The builder of the hotel, Louis Dupuy, once explained his desire to build a French inn so far away from his homeland: "I love these mountains and I love America, but you will pardon me if I bring into this community a remembrance of my youth and my country." The hotel opened in 1875 and soon became famous for its French Provincial luxury. Today it's a historical museum run by the National Society of Colonial Dames of America, embellished with many of its original furnishings, including Haviland china, a big pendulum clock, paintings and etchings, photographs by William Henry Jackson, and carved walnut furniture. The kitchen contains an antique stove and other cooking equipment, and the wine cellar houses early wine barrels, with their labels still in place. Allow 45 to 60 minutes.

409 6th St. (at Taos St.). ✆ **303/569-2311.** www.hoteldeparismuseum.org. Admission $5 adults, $3 seniors 60 and older and children 6–17, free for children 5 and under. June–Sept Mon–Sat 10am–5pm, Sun noon–5pm; Oct –Dec and May Sat 10am–5pm and Sun noon–5pm, weather permitting. Closed Jan–Apr and major holidays.

WHERE TO EAT

The **Happy Cooker,** 412 6th St. (✆ **303/569-3166;** www.happycookerrestaurant. com), serves soups, sandwiches on homemade breads, crepes, quiches, and more substantial fare such as frittatas and eggs Benedict, for breakfast and lunch in a converted home in Georgetown's historic business district. Prices are in the $5 to $10 range. **Lucha Cantina @ the Red Ram,** 606 6th St. (✆ **303/569-2300;** www.luchacantina. com), is a good casual option, offering historic barroom atmosphere and good Mexican grub, steaks, and burgers, as well as a slate of unique grilled cheese sandwiches. Main courses are $9 to $17.

COLORADO SPRINGS

Magnificent scenic beauty, a favorable climate, and dreams of gold have lured visitors to Colorado Springs and neighboring Pikes Peak Country for well over 100 years. And, while the gold mining has nearly disappeared, the beauty and weather remain prime lures to this day.

In 1806, Army Lt. Zebulon Pike led a company of soldiers on a trek around the base of an enormous mountain. He called it "Grand Peak," declared it unconquerable, and moved on. Today, the 14,110-foot mountain we know as Pikes Peak has been conquered so often that an auto highway and a cog railway take visitors to the top.

Unlike many Colorado towns, neither mineral wealth nor ranching was the cornerstone of Colorado Springs' economy during the 19th century—tourism was. In fact, Colorado Springs, founded in 1871, was the first genuine resort community west of Chicago. Gen. William J. Palmer, builder of the Denver & Rio Grande Railroad, established the resort on his rail line, at an elevation of 6,035 feet. The state's growing reputation as a health center, with its high mountains and mineral springs, convinced him to build at the foot of Pikes Peak. To lure affluent easterners, he named the resort Colorado Springs, because most fashionable eastern resorts were called "springs."

In the 1890s, gold strikes at Cripple Creek, on the southwestern slope of Pikes Peak, added a new dimension to life in Colorado Springs. Among those who cashed in on the boom was Spencer Penrose. To show the effectiveness of cars in the mountains, he built the Pikes Peak Highway (1913–15), using more than $250,000 of his own money. Then, during World War I and at a cost of more than $2 million, he built the luxurious Broadmoor hotel at the base of Cheyenne Mountain. World War II brought the military and defense industry to the area, and in 1958 the U.S. Air Force Academy opened.

Modern Colorado Springs is a growing city of about 420,000, with over 650,000 in the metropolitan area. To many visitors, the city retains the feel and mood of a small Western town. Most tourists come to see the Air Force Academy, marvel at the scenery at Garden of the Gods and Pikes Peak, and explore the history of the West. I'm also pleased to report that Colorado Springs also has some of the best lodging and dining in the state.

ESSENTIALS

Arriving
BY PLANE
Major airlines offer nearly 100 flights a day to **Colorado Springs Airport,** located 11 miles southeast of downtown via Fountain Boulevard

(C 719/550-1900; www.flycos.com). Airlines serving Colorado Springs are **Alaska, Allegiant, American, Delta,** and **United.**

GETTING TO & FROM THE AIRPORT **Advantage, Avis, Budget, Enterprise, Hertz,** and **National/Alamo** offer rental cars. Taxis include **Yellow Cab** (C 719/777-7777) and **Spring Cab** (C 719/444-8989). **Colorado Springs Shuttle** (C 719/687-3456) offers transportation to downtown hotels for $15 one-way.

BY CAR

The principal artery to and from the north and south, I-25, bisects Colorado Springs. Denver is 70 miles north; Pueblo, 42 miles south. U.S. 24 is the principal east-west route through the city. Visitors arriving on I-70 from the east can take exit 359 at Limon and follow U.S. 24 into the Springs. Arriving on I-70 from the west, the most direct route is exit 201 at Frisco, then Colo. 9 through Breckenridge 53 miles to U.S. 24 (at Hartsel), and finally east 66 miles to the Springs.

Visitor Information

The **Colorado Springs Convention and Visitors Bureau** (C 800/888-4748 or 719/635-7506; www.visitcos.com) operates a visitor center downtown at 515 S. Cascade Ave., open from 8:30am to 5pm and Saturday from 9am to 1pm.

Visitors to Manitou Springs—and every Colorado Springs visitor should also get to Manitou Springs—can get information from the **Manitou Springs Chamber of Commerce & Visitors Bureau,** 354 Manitou Ave., Manitou Springs (C 719/685-5089; www.manitousprings.org). You can also contact **Pikes Peak Country Attractions,** 337 Manitou Ave. (C 800/525-2250; www.pikes-peak.com).

City Layout

It's easy to get around central Colorado Springs, which is laid out on a classic grid pattern. If you focus on the intersection of I-25 and U.S. 24, downtown Colorado Springs lays in the northeast quadrant, bounded on the west by I-25 and on the south by U.S. 24 (Cimarron St.). Boulder Street to the north and Wahsatch Avenue to the east complete the downtown frame. Nevada Avenue parallels the freeway for 15 miles through the city, intersecting it twice; Tejon Street and Cascade Avenue also run north-south through downtown between Nevada Avenue and the freeway.

West of downtown, Colorado Avenue extends through the historic Old Colorado City district and the quaint foothill community of **Manitou Springs,** rejoining U.S. 24—a busy but less interesting artery—as it enters Pike National Forest.

South of downtown, Nevada Avenue intersects Lake Avenue, the principal boulevard to the Broadmoor, and proceeds south as Colo. 115 past Fort Carson to Cañon City.

North and east of downtown, Academy Boulevard is a good street name to remember. From the south gate of the Air Force Academy north of the Springs, it winds through residential hills, crosses Austin Bluffs Parkway, and then runs without a curve 8 miles due south, finally bending west to intersect I-25 and Colo. 115 at Fort Carson. Austin Bluffs Parkway extends west of I-25 as Garden of the Gods Road, leading to that natural wonder.

City street addresses are divided by Pikes Peak Avenue into north and south, by Nevada Avenue into east and west.

The Neighborhoods in Brief

Downtown has come a long way in recent years and is home to a number of attractions, as well as plenty of dining and nightlife and a few good hotels. This can be a

Colorado Springs

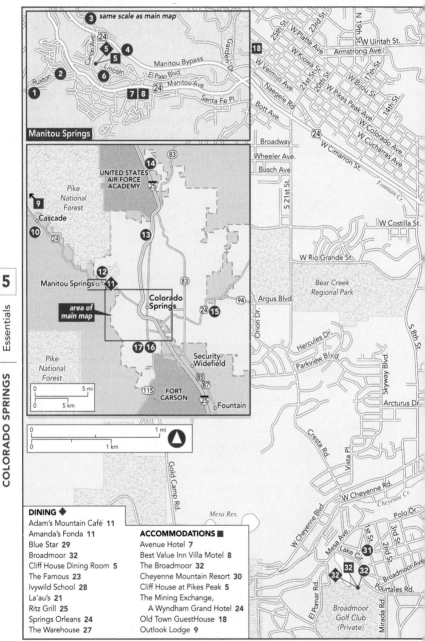

Manitou Springs

UNITED STATES AIR FORCE ACADEMY

Pike National Forest

Cascade

Manitou Springs

Colorado Springs

Security-Widefield

FORT CARSON

Fountain

Pike National Forest

Bear Creek Regional Park

Broadmoor Golf Club (Private)

Mesa Res.

DINING ◆
Adam's Mountain Café **11**
Amanda's Fonda **11**
Blue Star **29**
Broadmoor **32**
Cliff House Dining Room **5**
The Famous **23**
Ivywild School **28**
La'au's **21**
Ritz Grill **25**
Springs Orleans **24**
The Warehouse **27**

ACCOMMODATIONS ■
Avenue Hotel **7**
Best Value Inn Villa Motel **8**
The Broadmoor **32**
Cheyenne Mountain Resort **30**
Cliff House at Pikes Peak **5**
The Mining Exchange,
  A Wyndham Grand Hotel **24**
Old Town GuestHouse **18**
Outlook Lodge **9**

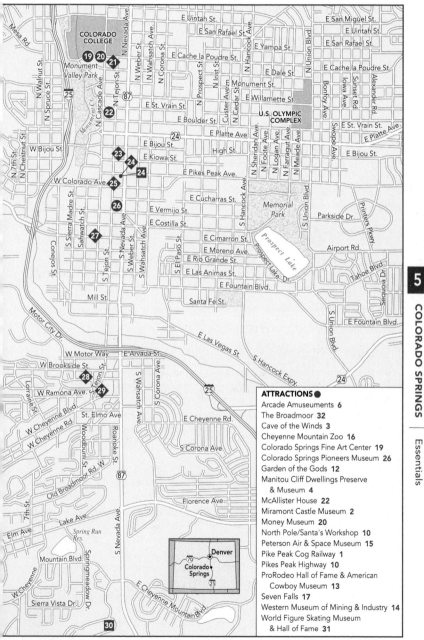

ATTRACTIONS ●

Arcade Amuseuments **6**
The Broadmoor **32**
Cave of the Winds **3**
Cheyenne Mountain Zoo **16**
Colorado Springs Fine Art Center **19**
Colorado Springs Pioneers Museum **26**
Garden of the Gods **12**
Manitou Cliff Dwellings Preserve
 & Museum **4**
McAllister House **22**
Miramont Castle Museum **2**
Money Museum **20**
North Pole/Santa's Workshop **10**
Peterson Air & Space Museum **15**
Pike Peak Cog Railway **1**
Pikes Peak Highway **10**
ProRodeo Hall of Fame & American
 Cowboy Museum **13**
Seven Falls **17**
Western Museum of Mining & Industry **14**
World Figure Skating Museum
 & Hall of Fame **31**

good place to start your tour of the city, followed by excursions to central attractions such as Garden of the Gods before perhaps heading to the attractions to the west in Old Colorado City, Manitou Springs, and beyond.

The **Broadmoor area,** named for the famed resort of the same name, is 3 miles southwest of downtown at the foot of Cheyenne Mountain (home of NORAD). The resort is at the center of a residential neighborhood, and area attractions include the Cheyenne Mountain Zoo and Seven Falls.

Old Colorado City, Colorado Avenue between 21st and 31st streets, was founded in 1859, 12 years before Colorado Springs. The town boomed as a red-light district in the 1880s after General Palmer's railroad came through. Today this historic district has an interesting assortment of shops, galleries, and restaurants.

At the foot of Pikes Peak, **Manitou Springs,** which centers on Manitou Avenue off U.S. 24 W., is a separate town with its own government. It is one of the country's largest National Historic Districts. Legend has it that Utes named the springs Manitou, their word for "Great Spirit," because they believed that the deity had breathed into the waters to create the natural effervescence of the springs. It boasts numerous Victorian buildings, many of which house delightful shops, galleries, restaurants, and lodgings.

GETTING AROUND

Although Colorado Springs has public transportation, most visitors prefer to drive. Parking and roads are good, and some of the best attractions, such as the Garden of the Gods (p. 82), are accessible only by car (or foot or bike for the truly ambitious).

By Taxi

Call **Yellow Cab** (© 719/777-7777). Hailing a cab on the street is difficult.

By Car

A car is a near-necessity in Colorado Springs, as the attractions are spaced far apart and public transportation is limited. Car-rental agencies in Colorado Springs, some of which have offices in or near downtown as well as at the airport, include **Avis, Budget, Enterprise,** and **Hertz.** Most downtown streets have parking meters; the usual rate is 25¢ for 15 minutes to a half-hour. Look for city-run parking lots, which offer hourly and day rates. Outside downtown, free parking is generally available on side streets.

By Bus

Mountain Metropolitan Transit (© 719/385-7433; www.springsgov.com) provides city bus service. Buses operate Monday through Friday from about 5am to 7:30pm, except major holidays. Fares on in-city routes are $1.75 for adults; 85¢ youth 6 to 18, seniors, and passengers with disabilities; and free for kids 5 and under.

By Bike

Bicycles are more a form of recreation than transportation in Colorado Springs. There are trails all over town, but they don't necessarily connect.

On Foot

Each of the main sections of town can easily be explored without a vehicle. It's fun, for instance, to wander the winding streets of Manitou Springs or explore the Old Colorado City "strip." Between neighborhoods, however, distances are considerable.

[FastFACTS] COLORADO SPRINGS

ATMs/Banks ATMs and banks are very common throughout the Colorado Springs area.

Dentists For referrals for dentists who accept emergency patients, contact the **Colorado Springs Dental Society** (✆ **719/598-5161**).

Doctors & Hospitals **Memorial Hospital,** 1400 E. Boulder St. (✆ **719/365-5000**), offers full medical services, including 24-hour emergency treatment, as does **Penrose–St. Francis Hospital,** 2222 N. Nevada Ave. (✆ **719/776-5000**).

Emergencies For police, fire, or medical emergencies, dial ✆ **911.**

Internet Access Most hotels and coffee shops have free Wi-Fi.

Mail & Postage The main post office is downtown at 201 E. Pikes Peak Ave. Contact the U.S. Postal Service (✆ **800/275-8777;** www.usps.com) for hours and locations of other post offices.

Newspapers & Magazines "The Gazette" (www.gazette.com), published daily in Colorado Springs, is the city's most widely read newspaper. "The Denver Post" is also available at newsstands throughout the city, as is the alt-weekly "Independent."

Pharmacies There is a 24-hour pharmacy at **Walgreens,** 3840 N. Academy Blvd. (✆ **719/380-9438**).

Safety Although Colorado Springs is generally a safe city, it is not crime-free. Try to be aware of your surroundings at all times, especially after dark.

Also see "Fast Facts" in Planning Your Trip (p. 242).

WHERE TO STAY

You'll find a wide range of lodging possibilities here, from Colorado's ritziest resort—the Broadmoor—to basic budget motels. Downtown Colorado Springs has a few good options for those looking for a full-service hotel.

The rates listed here are the officially quoted prices ("rack rates") and don't include any discounts. Generally, rates are highest from Memorial Day to Labor Day, and lowest in spring. During graduation and special events at the Air Force Academy, rates can jump markedly, and you may have trouble finding a room at any price.

Downtown

EXPENSIVE

The Mining Exchange, A Wyndham Grand Hotel ★★ In May 2012, this spiffy hotel opened in the old Mining Exchange building. It's now the hippest place to hang your hat in downtown Colorado Springs. Thanks to all of the gold in the nearby Rockies, the Mining Exchange was the highest volume stock exchange in North America after opening in 1900; the hotel retained such historic touches as vault doors, exposed brick, and ornate ceilings and added new ones in the form of original art by Louisiana artist Eddie Mormon and a slick lobby and courtyard. Classic but contemporary, the rooms are sizable, with the original windows and granite countered bathrooms with two-headed showers. Off the courtyard, the restaurant, **Springs Orleans** (p. 76), is also a standout.

8 S. Nevada Ave. ✆ **877/999-3223** or 719/323-2000. www.miningexchangehotel.com. 117 units, including 16 suites. $209–$239 double; $229–$369 suite. Valet parking $18. **Amenities:** Restaurant; lounge; free Wi-Fi.

Broadmoor Area

The Broadmoor resort is tucked into an upscale neighborhood of the same name, and there are a few other lodgings in the area, about 3 miles southwest of downtown.

EXPENSIVE

The Broadmoor ★★★   Philadelphia-bred tycoon Spencer Penrose opened this landmark hostelry in 1918 and it remains one of the country's top resorts under the ownership of magnate Philip Anschutz, who bought it in 2011. The Broadmoor spans 3,000 acres at the foot of Cheyenne Mountain, featuring 779 rooms and three renowned golf courses. Anschutz has looked back to Penrose for guidance as he poured more than $120 million into the resort, renovating its onsite pub the Golden Bee and Broadmoor West (one of the lodging towers), hanging paintings from his heralded art collection on the walls, and adding a bowling alley, while revisiting the founder's mountain properties in the new-for-2013 **Ranch at Emerald Valley,** an all-inclusive guest ranch 9 miles away. While it's certainly not inexpensive, The Broadmoor's mix of luxury, history, and service make it hard not to recommend. Even if the room rates eclipse your budget, don't pass on a meal here at one of the **19 restaurants, lounges, and cafes** (p. 77), or just a walk around the picture-perfect lake at the center of the resort.

1 Lake Circle (at Lake Ave.). ⓒ **855/634-7711** or 719/634-7711. www.broadmoor.com. 744 units. May–Oct $420–$650 double, $625–$1,200 1-bedroom suite, from $1,400 cottage suite; Nov–Apr $300–$450 double, $475–$900 1-bedroom suite, from $950 cottage suite; $435 per person per night at the all-inclusive Ranch at Emerald Valley; year-round up to $3,400 large suite. Pets accepted (75-lb. limit; $50/night). Self-parking $16; valet $18. **Amenities:** 10 restaurants; 6 lounges; 3 cafes; bikes; children's program; concierge; 3 18-hole golf courses; health club; 2 outdoor Jacuzzis; 3 swimming pools (indoor, outdoor w/water slide, outdoor lap pool); room service; spa; 6 all-weather tennis courts (2 clay courts); watersports equipment; free Wi-Fi.

Cheyenne Mountain Resort ★★   This family-friendly and conveniently located resort is a top pick for travelers looking for easy access to both Cheyenne Mountain and downtown Colorado Springs. Rooms are plush and modern, adorned in earth tones and granite counters in the oversized bathrooms, and there's a long list of facilities and amenities, highlighted by a Pete Dye-designed golf course and a private lake.

3225 Broadmoor Valley Rd. ⓒ **888/588-0250** or 719/538-4000. www.cheyennemountain.com. 321 units. Summer $189–$279 double; $485–$750 suite. Lower rates fall–spring. **Amenities:** 4 restaurants (American/buffet); 2 lounges; bikes; children's program; concierge; 18-hole golf course; health club; indoor Jacuzzi; 4 pools (3 outdoor, 1 indoor); room service; sauna; 18 tennis courts (6 indoor, 2 clay courts); free watersports equipment; free Wi-Fi.

Old Colorado City

MODERATE

Old Town GuestHouse ★   Don and Shirley Wick have been running the Old Town GuestHouse in Colorado City since it was built in 1997, and they've got inn-keeping down pat at this point. Despite its young age, the GuestHouse blends in nicely in the surrounding historic neighborhood. The inn offers a hybrid of boutique hotel privacy and B&B intimacy. Named for flowers and their undersea and desert cousins, the rooms showcase art and artifacts from all over the world. Coral Reef is the smallest, with a shower and a queen, and Paintbrush is the roomiest, with a second small bed in an alcove and superb views of Pikes Peak.

115 S. 26th St., Colorado Springs. ⓒ **888/375-4210** or 719/632-9194. www.oldtown-guesthouse. com. 8 units. $99–$199 double. Free off-street parking. Children 11 and under not accepted. **Amenities:** Free Wi-Fi.

Manitou Springs

Manitou Springs is a tourist-oriented community, and it has a plethora of overnight options. You will find historic hotels and B&Bs, budget motels, and everything in between here.

MODERATE

Avenue Hotel ★ My B&B pick for B&B-packed Manitou, the Avenue Hotel opened as a boardinghouse in 1886 and now is ideal for modern travelers looking for a little more elbow room than your average hotel. Located in the inn and a carriage house behind it, the colorful rooms have private baths (two are detached), with fir floors and handsome claw-foot tubs. The stately building is perched above a steep staircase with easy walking access to all of the restaurants, shops, and watering holes in town.

711 Manitou Ave. © **800/294-1277** or 719/685-1277. www.avenuehotelbandb.com. 9 units. $120–$155 double. **Amenities:** Free Wi-Fi.

The Cliff House at Pikes Peak ★★ The Cliff House opened in 1874 and was shut down by a catastrophic fire in 1982. After sitting vacant for 15 years, it reopened as a hotel in 1999 and continues to comeback from what once looked like a sure date with the wrecking ball. Now it's the place to stay in Manitou Springs, right in the thick of the touristy action but a world away. Standard rooms have classy, historic reproduction furnishings and such modern comforts as heated toilet seats. A number of the suites named for celebrities from the Cliff House's heyday. The Clark Gable Suite is my favorite, with animal-skin wallpaper and all sorts of perks the rugged star would definitely approve. **The Cliff House Dining Room** (p. 78) is one of the best eateries in the Pikes Peak region.

306 Cañon Ave. © **888/212-7000** or 719/685-3000. www.thecliffhouse.com. 54 units. $99–$149 double; $240–$400 suite. Children 12 and under stay free in parent's room. Rates include breakfast buffet. **Amenities:** 2 restaurants; lounge; concierge; exercise room; room service; free Wi-Fi.

INEXPENSIVE

Best Value Inn Villa Motel ★ There are scads of motels on Colorado Avenue heading into Manitou Springs, and more after it turns the corner and becomes Manitou Avenue, and quality varies considerably. This is my pick, thanks to well-kept, comfortable rooms, reasonable rates, and a great location: The Villa Motel is within walking distance of the center of town.

481 Manitou Ave. © **719/685-5492.** www.villamotel.com. 7 units. $69–$139 double. **Amenities:** Large outdoor heated pool (seasonal); free Wi-Fi.

West of Manitou Springs

There are a number of options on the north flank of Pikes Peak in towns like Cascade, Chipita Park, and Green Mountain Falls. This has the best of both worlds: You have good city access and great mountain scenery to boot.

MODERATE

Outlook Lodge ★★ Originally built in 1889, this former church rectory underwent a transformation into a boutique hotel in 2012. Sandwiched between the tiny town of Green Mountain Falls and the Pikes Peak foothills, the location is just about ideal, and the rooms are stunners as well. History meshes nicely with contemporary touches, with well-chosen antiques alongside modern art. The staff is hands-off: Guests pick up their keys from a lockbox, and may never encounter an employee face-to-face. The low-key approach works nicely, as this is a place designed for relaxation, from the wraparound porch, lined with rocking chairs, to the fire pit, surrounded by recycled chairs and aspen trees.

6975 Howard St., Green Mountain Falls. © **855/463-2557.** www.outlookgmf.com. 6 units, including 2 suites. $134–$144 double; $199–$279 suite. Lower rates in winter. 11 miles west of I-25, then 1 mile south in Green Mountain Falls. **Amenities:** Free Wi-Fi.

WHERE TO EAT

Colorado Springs has an excellent variety of above-average restaurants, with a good sampling of Continental cuisine, Mexican restaurants, and steak joints.

Downtown

Downtown Colorado Springs has exploded with good restaurants in recent years, and is the best place for a meal and some after-dark entertainment. Your choices run the gamut from hip urban eateries to Mexican food, and steakhouses to college haunts.

EXPENSIVE

The Famous ★★ STEAKS   This swank, chic spot feels like it belongs in a bigger city. It focuses on top-quality beef from the Midwest and lamb, pork, and chicken from Colorado, and the kitchen staff is talented in giving it all just the right amount of sear. Lighter fare includes fresh seafood, but strict vegetarians will want to look elsewhere.

31 N. Tejon St. © **719/227-7333.** www.thefamoussteakhouse.net. Main courses $12–$22 lunch, $29–$52 dinner. Mon–Fri 11am–3pm; Mon–Thurs 5–10pm; Fri 5–11pm; Sat 4–11pm; Sun 4–10pm.

Springs Orleans ★★ CAJUN   This contemporary Cajun eatery at the Mining Exchange hotel has an avid local following, thanks to a social atmosphere, low-key live piano music, and delectable interpretations of bayou classics. Beyond the gumbo, blackened catfish, and red beans and rice, the menu offers toothsome pasta dishes, lobster, and a cast-iron filet mignon. The breakfast and lunch menus also tip their hats to Louisiana, as do the craft cocktails: passion-fruit-puree hurricane, anyone?

At the Mining Exchange Hotel, 123 E. Pikes Peak Ave. © **719/520-0123.** www.springsorleans. com. Main courses $7–$10 breakfast; $9–$36 lunch and dinner. Sun–Thurs 6:30am–10pm; Fri–Sat 6:30am–11pm.

The Warehouse ★★ NEW AMERICAN   Dubbed a "restaurant and gallery," this converted—you guessed it—warehouse on the southern fringe of downtown has some of the best food in the city and artwork inside and out. The kitchen plates up a wide range of creative cuisine, with influences near and far: For starters, there's fajita steak and caprese salad, and entrees range from local beef and chicken dishes to such exotic offerings as peppered elk tenderloin and macadamia halibut. The gallery offerings include eye-catching murals on the exterior and contemporary art on the walls.

25 W. Cimarron St. © **719/475-8880.** www.thewarehouserestaurant.com. Main courses $9–$18 lunch; $11–$35 dinner. Mon–Fri 11:30am–9pm; Sat 5–10pm. Closed Sun.

MODERATE

Ritz Grill ★★ NEW AMERICAN   The Ritz has been a Tejon Street institution for more than 15 years. Countless business lunches, happy hours, and late-night snacks later, the Ritz has seen a long list of its downtown peers come and go, but it still packs people in with creative burgers and salads and entrees with pizzazz, including a brown-sugar salmon and a top-notch steak and frites.

15 S. Tejon St. © **719/635-8484.** www.ritzgrill.com. Main courses $9–$23. Mon–Fri 11:30am–11pm; Sat–Sun noon–11pm. Bar open later with a limited menu.

INEXPENSIVE

La'au's ★ HAWAIIAN TACOS Yes, it's fusion food at its wackiest, but this unlikely combination works well at this fun spot near the Colorado College campus. The menu is simple: Take your pick of tacos, a bowl, burrito, or salad, add a protein from mahi-mahi to pork (or go vegetarian) then top it with Pacific Rim-inspired ingredients like green papaya, Napa cabbage, and mango as well as Mexican-inspired salsa. The flavor combinations range from subtle to fiery, and beer and margaritas are available for a cool-down from the latter.

830 N. Tejon St., Ste. 110. © **719/578-5228.** www.laaustacoshop.com. Plates $6–$10. Daily 11am–9pm.

Broadmoor Area

With nearly 20 places to eat, The Broadmoor features dining for every budget, from the relatively affordable to the heights of the Penrose Room atop the South Tower.

MODERATE TO EXPENSIVE

The Broadmoor ★★★ NEW AMERICAN/CONTINENTAL The Broadmoor is the historic heart of Colorado Springs' time-tested tourism industry, and its dining is a highlight. There are no less than 19 restaurants, lounges, and cafes to pick from at the landmark resort, and I highly recommend having at least one meal here to experience the splendid architecture and mountain scenery.

The **Penrose Room** is a highlight, atop Broadmoor South. The jacket-required formality, a rarity in Colorado, is matched by splendid views and prix-fixe dinners that marry culinary tradition and innovation. **The Tavern,** where the focus is squarely on beef, is another standout, with an authentic garden room and original Toulouse-Latrecs. **Summit** is the bold, contemporary eatery here, with outside-of-the-box design and cuisine. In Broadmoor West, **Ristorante del Lago** opened in 2014, serving upscale Italian fare.

There are more affordable options at **Play,** a new-for-2013 bowling alley and gastropub, and **The Golden Bee,** an authentic British pub shipped to, and reassembled in, Colorado; it was expanded in 2013 and is known for fish and chips and nightly piano sing-alongs (p. 89). **Lake Terrace** features breakfast buffets, and there are several slick bars to have a drink and an appetizer. **Natural Epicurean** offers healthy fare with local ingredients.

The Broadmoor, 1 Lake Circle. © **719/577-5773.** www.broadmoor.com. Breakfast and lunch $8–$40; dinner main courses $15–$50; Penrose Room 4- to 5-course tasting menus $78–$88, plus $45–$55 for wine pairings. Daily 7am–10pm.

West of Downtown

Manitou Springs and Old Colorado City have dining options for every budget. You can find quick bites at touristy snack bars, grab a seat at a bar for a burger and a beer, or have a fine-dining experience as exquisite as any in the Pikes Peak region.

MODERATE TO EXPENSIVE

Adam's Mountain Cafe ★★ AMERICAN/VEGETARIAN Since 1984, Adam's has been the place to hit for vegetarian—but not exclusively vegetarian—food in Manitou Springs. A sign at each table explains why the food takes so long: The kitchen doesn't take any shortcuts, as everything is prepared fresh to order. The casual creekside atmosphere serves as an ideal platform for the artfully prepared food. Adam's serves three meals a day, with healthful and tasty options for each, from whole-grain pancakes to pear-pecan salads to crepes with squash, caramelized onions, and red chile. Many items are available with meat, largely local free-range chicken.

26 Manitou Ave. ✆ **719/685-1430.** www.adamsmountain.com. Main courses $7–$12 breakfast and lunch, $10–$19 dinner. Daily 8am–3pm; Tues–Sat 5–9pm. Closed Mon Oct–Apr.

Cliff House Dining Room ★★★ NEW AMERICAN   The historic Cliff House hits all of the right notes with its resident restaurant, with an emphasis on expertly crafted game dishes like bacon-wrapped elk rib-eye with brussels sprouts with a hint horseradish. Breakfast is traditional American, and lunch is more casual, with quiche, burgers, and a spicy pulled-pork burrito.

At the Cliff House, 306 Cañon Ave., Manitou Springs. ✆ **719/785-2415.** www.thecliffhouse.com. Breakfast and lunch main courses $7–$20; dinner main courses $18–$32. Daily 6:30–10:30am, 11:30am–2:30pm, and 5:30–9pm.

INEXPENSIVE

Amanda's Fonda ★ MEXICAN   Convenient and affordable, this West Side institution is a good bet for lunch or dinner, with a full menu of Mexican standards like enchiladas and fajitas as well as steaks and a few sandwiches. The salsa is spicy, the atmosphere lively and kid-friendly, and the bar mixes a pretty good margarita to boot.

3625 W. Colorado Ave. ✆ **719/227-1975.** www.amandasfonda.com. Main courses $8–$17. Sun–Thurs 11am–9pm, Fri–Sat 11am–10pm; winter Mon–Sat 11:30am–9pm, Sun noon–9pm.

South of Downtown

There is a terrific destination area on Tejon Street south of I-25, including a culinary pacesetter of the city, as well as a microbrewery and a few others.

EXPENSIVE

The Blue Star ★★★ NEW AMERICAN   Since 1995, The Blue Star has elevated the Colorado Springs dining scene to a higher level. The menu changes monthly, and there are nightly specials depending on what's fresh and in season. Clever pairings like butternut squash and shiitake mushroom bruschetta and wild boar pasta with pappardelle pasta enliven the menu, which always includes at least one meatless option. The dining room has a quiet atmosphere, while the happening bar has several less expensive options as well as selections from the dining room menu.

1645 S. Tejon St. ✆ **719/632-1086.** www.thebluestar.net. Main courses $12–$34. Dining room daily 5:30–9pm; bar daily 3–10pm.

MODERATE

Ivywild School ★★ MICROBREWERY   Ivywild School saw its last students in 2009 after a 93-year run, and underwent a $5 million makeover into a culinary destination and emerging community hub in 2013. Today it houses several eateries, including the pub and taproom for award-winning **Bristol Brewing Company,** as well as a butcher shop, bakery, cocktail bar, and other businesses from the same ownership as The Blue Star (see above). The food focuses on local ingredients, and most everything, from the mustard to the sausages, are made in-house.

1604 S. Cascade Ave. ✆ **719/368-6100.** www.ivywildschool.com. Main courses $8–$20. Mon–Thurs 11am–10pm; Fri–Sat 11am–11pm; Sun 11am–8pm.

EXPLORING COLORADO SPRINGS

Most of the attractions of the Pikes Peak region fit in two general categories: natural, such as Pikes Peak, Garden of the Gods, and Cave of the Winds; and historic/educational, including the Air Force Academy, Olympic Complex training center, museums, historic homes, and art galleries. There are also gambling houses in Cripple Creek.

Downtown

Colorado Springs Fine Arts Center ★★   In 2007, when the Colorado Springs Fine Arts Center significantly increased its footprint with an expansion, it was overshadowed by the expansion at the Denver Art Museum. But many architecture critics actually preferred the work by David Tryba to that of Daniel Libeskind in Denver—form does not compete with function here. The resulting space is ideal for showcasing an impressive collection featuring Georgia O'Keeffe, Dale Chihuly, and a number of Native American artists and artisans. There's a top-flight performing arts venue here as well. The focus of changing exhibits is squarely on local artists. Expect to spend about 1 to 3 hours here.

30 W. Dale St. (west of N. Cascade Ave.). ⓒ **719/634-5583.** www.csfineartscenter.org. Admission $10 adults; $8.50 seniors, students, and children 5–17; free for children 4 and under. Tues–Sun 10am–5pm.

Colorado Springs Pioneers Museum ★   Housed in the landmark 1903 El Paso County Courthouse, one of the defining structures downtown, the Pioneers Museum tells the intriguing history of the area, beginning as a gold-mining camp, then attracting tuberculosis patients seeking a cure, to its more recent military boom. The exhibits include the late-1800s home of Helen Hunt Jackson, the famed local author of "Ramona." Those particularly interested in history can spend a couple of hours here, but for most an hour will do.

215 S. Tejon St. ⓒ **719/385-5990.** www.cspm.org. Free admission, donations accepted. Year-round Tues–Sat 10am–5pm.

McAllister House ★   This Gothic cottage, listed on the National Register of Historic Places, is a good place for a quick look at the Colorado of the late 19th century. It was built in 1873, and the builder, an army major named Henry McAllister, decided to construct the house with brick when he learned that the local wind was so strong it had blown a train off the tracks nearby. The house has many original furnishings, including three marble fireplaces. It is now owned by the Colonial Dames of America, whose knowledgeable volunteers lead guided tours. Allow about an hour.

423 N. Cascade Ave. (at St. Vrain St.). ⓒ **719/635-7925.** www.mcallisterhouse.org. Admission $5 adults, $4 seniors 62 and older, $3 children 6–12, free for children 5 and under. Summer Tues–Sat 10am–4pm; winter Thurs–Sat 10am–4pm. Closed Jan.

Money Museum ★   Coin collectors will love this place, but this museum's exhibits will capture the attention of most anyone who has handled money. There are about one-quarter million coins here, with specimens as old as money itself (about 4,500 years old, to be precise) in "The History of Money" exhibit, as well as U.S. currency dating back to the late 1700s. New is the Mini-Mint that gives visitors a look at minting processes from centuries past, with demonstrations on the third Saturday of each month. Allow about an hour.

818 N. Cascade Ave. (on the campus of Colorado College). ⓒ **719/482-9834.** www.money.org. Admission $5 adults, $4 seniors and students, free for children 5 and under. Tues–Sat 10:30am–5pm.

Broadmoor Area

Longstanding tourist attraction **Seven Falls** (www.sevenfalls.com) was damaged by floods but is expected to reopen in spring of 2015.

The Broadmoor ★★   This famous Italian Renaissance–style resort hotel has been a Colorado Springs landmark since Spencer Penrose built it in 1918. (See "Where to Stay," p. 73.) A walking tour brochure is available from the front desk; one of the top stops is the free **El Pomar Heritage Museum,** featuring Penrose's carriage collection (including five with motors). After the guided tour, stroll around the lake, have a drink at one of the watering holes, and look at the "Walk of Fame" near the new **Play** bowling alley, a hallway of photographs of celebrities at the resort, everyone from Jonathan Winters to Barack Obama.

Lake Circle, at 1 Lake Ave. ✆ **719/623-5112.** www.broadmoor.com. Free admission. Daily.

Cheyenne Mountain Zoo ★★   On the lower slopes of Cheyenne Mountain, at 6,800 feet above sea level—making it the nation's highest—this medium-size zoological park is my top pick for families. The 700-plus animals, many in "natural" environments, include wolves, lions, leopards, red pandas, elephants, hippos, monkeys, snakes, mountain lions, grizzly bears, and moose. The zoo's giraffe herd is the largest and most prolific captive herd in the world; there have been more than 200 live births since the 1950s. Visitors can actually feed the long-necked beasts ($2 for lettuce or crackers), whose prehensile tongues are quite the sight to behold. There's also a colorful antique **carousel,** built in 1926, the year the zoo was founded (rides are $2), and a new chairlift dubbed the **Mountaineer Sky Ride** ($5 adults, $4 kids 3–11). A stroller- and wheelchair-accessible tram makes a full loop of the zoo in about 15 minutes; it operates from Memorial Day to Labor Day. Admission to the zoo includes road access to the nearby **Will Rogers Shrine of the Sun,** a granite tower built in 1937, with photos and information on the American humorist. The tower also affords great views of the city and surrounding countryside. Strollers, double strollers, wheelchairs, and wagons are available for rent. Allow 2 to 4 hours for the zoo and an extra 45 minutes for the shrine.

4250 Cheyenne Mountain Zoo Rd. ✆ **719/633-9925.** www.cmzoo.org. Peak-season admission $17 adults, $15 seniors 65 and over, $12 children 3–11, free for children 2 and under. Summer daily 9am–6pm; off season daily 9am–5pm.

World Figure Skating Museum & Hall of Fame ★   From inaugural inductees like Dick Button and Peggy Fleming to Denise Biellman, the champion Swiss skater elected in 2014, this attraction honors all of the ice-skating greats. The museum side has exhibits detailing the history, art, and science of the sport. Allow 30 minutes to an hour.

20 1st St. ✆ **719/635-5200.** www.worldskatingmuseum.org. Admission $5 adults, $3 seniors 60 and over and children 6–12, free for children 5 and under. Summer Tues–Fri 10am–4pm; closed Mon rest of year. Closed Sat–Sun and major holidays.

Manitou Springs

Arcade Amusements ★   Among the West's oldest and largest amusement arcades, this game complex just might be considered a hands-on arcade museum as well as a fun place for kids of all ages. Some 250 machines range from original working penny pinball machines to Pac-Man and Q*bert to modern video games, along with Skee-Ball, kiddie rides, and 12-player horse racing. There is a food concession with ice cream, candy, and basic fast food. Allow an hour or two here.

900 block of Manitou Ave., Manitou Springs. © **719/685-9815.** Free admission; arcade games from a penny to $2. Early May to Labor Day daily 10am–10pm. Call for winter hours.

Cave of the Winds ★ Discovered by two boys on a church outing in the 1880s, this impressive underground cavern has offered public tours for well over a century. The 45-minute Discovery Tour takes visitors along a well-lit ¾-mile passageway through 20 subterranean chambers, complete with handsome stalagmites, stalactites, crystal flowers, and limestone canopies. In the Adventure Room, modern lighting techniques return visitors to an era when spelunking was done by candle and lantern. The more strenuous 1½-hour Lantern Tour follows unpaved and unlighted passageways and corridors, with some stooping required in areas with low ceilings; it might muddy your shoes, but not your clothes. Outside and aboveground is the Wind Walker Challenge Course where harnessed participants navigate a maze 600 feet above the canyon below, and a Bat-a-Pult thrill ride ($20 for both); new for 2014 was the Terrordactyl thrill ride.

U.S. 24, Manitou Springs. © **719/685-5444.** www.caveofthewinds.com. Memorial Day to Labor Day daily 9am–9pm; early Sept to late May daily 10am–5pm. Discovery Tour $20 adults, $12 children 6–11, free for children 5 and under. Lantern Tour $30 adults, $15 children 6–11, children 5 and under not permitted. Visitors with heart conditions, visual impairment, or other physical limitations are advised not to take Lantern Tour.

Manitou Cliff Dwellings Preserve & Museums ★ The cliff-dwelling ruins here are real, although originally they were located elsewhere. This put me off at first—they would be more authentic if they were in their original location—but the move here may have saved them. In the early 1900s, archaeologists, who saw such dwellings being plundered by treasure hunters, dismantled some of the ancient buildings, gathered artifacts found there, and hauled them away. Some of these ruins, constructed from A.D. 1200 to 1300, can be seen here in a village reconstructed by archaeologists. There are also two museums with exhibits on prehistoric American Indian life, and several gift shops that sell American Indian–made jewelry, pottery, and other crafts, plus Colorado souvenirs. American Indian dancers perform during the summer. There are usually printable coupons for discounted tickets on the website. Allow 2 hours.

10 Cliff Rd. (5 miles west of Manitou Springs). © **800/354-9971** or 719/685-5242. www.cliffdwellingsmuseum.com. Admission $9.50 adults, $8.50 seniors 60 and over, $7.50 children 7–11, free for children 6 and under. May–Sept daily 9am–6pm; Oct–Nov and Mar–Apr daily 9am–5pm; Dec–Feb daily 10am–4pm. Closed Thanksgiving and Dec 25.

Miramont Castle Museum ★ Built in the 1890s with very few square corners, Miramont Castle is today a museum that showcases this one-of-a-kind structure. An unusual architectural specimen to say the least, it fuses Queen Anne, Romanesque, Tudor, and Gothic styles into an intriguingly satisfying whole. Tours give visitors an up-close look at the nooks and crannies of this 14,0000-square-foot castle, including a 16-sided room and hidden passageways. Allow at least 1 hour.

9 Capitol Hill Ave., Manitou Springs. © **888/685-1011** or 719/685-1011. www.miramontcastle.org. Admission $8 adults, $7 seniors 60 and over, $5 children 6–15, free for children 5 and under. Memorial Day to Labor Day daily 9am–5pm; rest of year Tues–Sat 10am–4pm; Sun noon–4pm. Guided tours at 11am and 1pm; reservations recommended.

Pikes Peak Cog Railway ★★   Spectacular scenery—and the thrill of mountain climbing without all the work—is this attraction's potent lure. The first passenger train climbed 14,110-foot Pikes Peak on June 30, 1891, and diesel slowly replaced steam power between 1939 and 1955. Four custom-built Swiss twin-unit rail cars, each seating 216 passengers, went into service in 1989.

Passengers tend to begin oohing and aahing when the track leaves the forest, creeping above timberline at about 11,500 feet. The view from the summit takes in Denver, 75 miles north; New Mexico's Sangre de Cristo range, 150 miles south; the Cripple Creek mining district, on the mountain's western flank; wave after wave of Rocky Mountain subranges to the west; and the seemingly endless sea of Great Plains to the east. Up top, watch for Rocky Mountain bighorn sheep and yellow-bellied marmots. The Summit House at the top of Pikes Peak has a restaurant and a gift shop.

Take a jacket or sweater—it can be cold and windy on top, even on warm summer days. The round trip requires 3 hours and 10 minutes (including a 40-min. stopover at the top) and is not recommended if you have cardiac or respiratory problems—even those in good health may feel lightheaded.

515 Ruxton Ave., Manitou Springs. ☏ **719/685-5401.** www.cograilway.com. $36 adults, $20 children 3–12, free for children 2 and under held on an adult's lap. Year-round, with 2–8 departures daily late May to Sept and less frequent trains the rest of the year; call or check schedules online. Reservations required (available online).

Peterson Air & Space Museum ★   We'd say this little museum, on the grounds of Peterson Air Force Base, is strictly for aerospace aficionados. There's little explanation given, and those without military I.D. must apply 24-hours in advance to get on base, a real hassle. The collection features more than 25 aircraft and missiles from the 1950s onward, including an exhibit on Intercontinental Ballistic Missiles (ICBMs) and a Lockheed F-94 C Starfire. You can see the entire exhibit in about an hour.

Peterson Air Force Base main gate, off U.S. 24 7 miles east of downtown. ☏ **719/556-4915.** www.petemuseum.org. Free admission. Tues–Sat 9am–4pm. Closed holidays and occasionally during military exercises; call ahead.

United States Olympic Complex ★   Thousands of athletes train in a variety of Olympic sports at this state-of-the-art center. On the free, daily 45-minute tour, you'll see the indoor shooting ranges (the largest of their kind in the Western Hemisphere), the aquatics center (containing a 50×25m pool with more than 900,000 gallons of water), a film on what it takes to become an Olympian, and more. A highlight (which doesn't always happen) is when visitors get to see the athletes in training. The visitor center includes the U.S. Olympic Hall of Fame, interactive kiosks on Olympic-related subjects, and a gift shop that sells Olympic-logo merchandise.

1 Olympic Plaza (corner of Boulder St. [entrance] and Union Blvd.). ☏ **719/866-4618.** www.teamusa.org. Free admission. Complex Mon–Sat 9am–6pm; Sun 11am–6pm (until 5pm Aug–May). Guided tours begin every half-hour Mon–Sat 9am–4:30pm (hourly with last tour at 4pm Aug–May).

North of Downtown

Garden of the Gods ★★★   One of the West's unique geological sites, the 1,300-acre Garden of the Gods is a giant rock garden composed of spectacular red sandstone formations sculpted by rain and wind over millions of years. Located where several life zones and ecosystems converge, the beautiful city-run park is a can't-miss attraction for Colorado Springs visitors.

Highly recommended are a number of hiking trails—mostly easy to moderate—that offer an opportunity to get away from the crowds. Leashed dogs, horses, and mountain bikes are permitted on some trails. There are trail maps at the **Garden of the Gods Visitor & Nature Center,** which also offers exhibits on the history, geology, plants, and wildlife of the area; a cafeteria; and other conveniences. A short **multimedia theater presentation** ($5 adults, $3 children 5–12, free for children 4 and under) is an excellent introduction to the geologic and cultural history of the area. In summer, park naturalists lead free 45-minute walks through the park and conduct free afternoon interpretive programs. You can also take a van or jeep tour of the park for $10 per person, or a Segway tour for $75 to $105 per person. You may spot technical rock climbers on some of the park spires; they are required to register at the visitor center.

Also in the park is the **Rock Ledge Ranch Historic Site** (*C* **719/578-6777;** www. rockledgeranch.com). Admission is $8 adults, $5 seniors, $4 children 6–17, and free for kids 5 and under. Allow 2 hours, longer if you want to hike or bike.

1805 N. 30th St. *C* **719/634-6666.** www.gardenofgods.com. Free admission. Park May–Oct daily 5am–11pm; Nov–Apr daily 5am–9pm. Visitor Center Memorial Day to Labor Day daily 8am–8pm; rest of the year daily 9am–5pm.

ProRodeo Hall of Fame & American Cowboy Museum ★   From animals like Descent, a bucking horse who was in the first class of inductees in 1979, to bareback rider Chuck Logue, a 2013 inductee, the ProRodeo Hall of Fame honors the legends of the rodeo. Also onsite, the **American Cowboy Museum** traces the history of rodeo from the late 1800s to today with a collection of exhibits and artwork. There is also an outdoor arena that hosts rodeo demonstrations and events from May to October. Expect to spend about 2 hours here.

101 ProRodeo Dr. (off Rockrimmon Blvd.). *C* **719/528-4764.** www.prorodeohalloffame.com. Admission $8 adults, $7 seniors 55 and older, $5 children 6–12, free for children 5 and under. Memorial Day to Aug daily 9am–5pm; Sept to day before Memorial Day Wed–Sun 9am–5pm. Closed major holidays.

Outlying Attractions

North Pole/Santa's Workshop ★   A Christmas-themed amusement park, Santa's Workshop is busy from mid-May until December 24. Not only can kids visit shops where elves have some early Christmas gifts for sale, they can see Santa and whisper their requests in his ear. This 26-acre village features numerous rides, including a miniature train, a 60-foot Ferris wheel (claimed to be the highest in the world), and a space-shuttle replica that swings to and fro, as well as magic shows and music, snack shops, and an ice-cream parlor Expect to spend 2 to 4 hours here.

At the foot of Pikes Peak Hwy. off U.S. 24 (5 miles west of Manitou Springs). *C* **719/684-9432.** www.santas-colo.com. Admission (includes all rides, shows, and attractions) $21 ages 2–59, free for seniors 60 and over and children 1 and under. Mid-May to late Aug and mid-Dec to Dec 23 daily 10am–5pm (until 6pm on peak weekends); late Aug to mid-Dec (weather permitting) Thurs–Mon 10am–5pm; Dec 24 10am–4pm. Closed Dec 25 to mid-May.

Pikes Peak Highway ★★   Perhaps no view in Colorado equals the 360-degree panorama from the 14,110-foot summit of Pikes Peak. Whether you go by cog railway, hiking trail, or private vehicle, the ascent is a spectacular, exciting experience— although not for those with heart or breathing problems or a fear of heights. The 19-mile, paved toll highway starts at 7,400 feet, some 4 miles west of Manitou Springs. There are numerous photo-op stops as you head up the mountain, and deer, mountain sheep, marmots, and other animals often appear on the slopes, especially above the timberline (around 11,500 ft.). Allow 3 hours minimum.

Off U.S. 24 at the town of Cascade (10 miles west of Colorado Springs). *C* **719/385-7325.** www. pikespeakcolorado.com. Admission $12 adults, $5 children 6–15, free for children 5 and under, $40 per car up to 5 passengers. Fri before Memorial Day to Labor Day daily 7:30am–6pm; rest of Sept daily 7:30am–5pm; Oct to late May daily 9am–3pm, weather permitting.

United States Air Force Academy ★   Located 12 miles north of downtown, Colorado Springs' pride and joy got its start in 1954 when Congress authorized the establishment of a U.S. Air Force Academy and chose this 18,000-acre site from among 400 prospective locations. The first class of cadets enrolled in 1959, and each year since, about 4,000 cadets have enrolled for the 4 years of rigorous training required to become Air Force officers.

Open daily, the visitor center offers a variety of exhibits and films on the academy's history and cadet life, extensive literature and self-guided tour maps, and the latest information and schedules on academy activities. There's also a large gift shop and coffee shop. A short trail from the visitor center leads to the unmistakable Cadet Chapel. Its 17 gleaming aluminum spires soar 150 feet, and within the building are separate chapels for the major Western faiths as well as an "all faiths" room. Military buffs should expect to spend at least 2 hours here; non-military buffs might spend about an hour exploring.

West of I-25, exit 156B. ☎ **719/333-2025.** www.usafa.af.mil. Free admission. Visitor center daily 9am–5pm; grounds daily 8am–6pm; chapel Mon–Sat 9am–5pm, Sun 1–5pm.

Western Museum of Mining & Industry ★   This is the best mining museum in Colorado outside of Leadville. There are thousands of artifacts on the 27-acre campus, ranging from antique hand tools to a monstrous 1928 steam shovel to Nugget and Chism, the donkeys who serve as mascots for the museum. Special exhibits have recently included a look at Cripple Creek mining baron W.S. Stratton. Allow 1 hour.

225 N. Gate Blvd., at I-25, exit 156A (off Gleneagle Dr., just east of the U.S. Air Force Academy). ☎ **719/488-0880.** www.wmmi.org. Admission $8 adults, $6 seniors 60 and older and students, $4 children 3–12, free for children 2 and under. Mon–Sat 9am–4pm. Guided tours at 10am and 1pm.

Organized Tours

Adventures Out West, 1680 S. 21st St. (☎ **800/755-0935;** www.advoutwest.com), offers a wide range of tours in the Colorado Springs area, including guided hikes, jeep and van tours of the city and surrounding mountains, and Segway tours of Garden of the Gods. Day tours are typically $75 to $150 per person, and more for some activities.

You can bike down Pikes Peak ($110 per adult) or go mountain biking on a tour with Challenge Unlimited (☎ **800/798-5954;** www.bikithikit.com) or **Pikes Peak Mountain Bike Tours** (☎ **719/337-5311;** www.bikepikespeak.com) for about $100 per rider, or else get a city tour with **Springs Bike Tours** (☎ **719/464-2514;** www.springsbike tours.com) for $30 to $50.

Outdoor Activities

For information on the city's parks and programs, contact **Colorado Springs Parks, Recreation & Cultural Services** (☎ **719/385-5940;** www.springsgov.com). There are offices in Colorado Springs for **Colorado Parks and Wildlife,** 4255 Sinton Rd. (☎ **719/227-5200;** http://parks.state.co.us); and the **U.S. Forest Service,** Pikes Peak Ranger District of the Pike National Forest, 601 S. Weber St. (☎ **719/636-1602**).

You can get hunting and fishing licenses at many sporting-goods stores, as well as at the Colorado Parks and Wildlife office listed above.

BALLOONING   The area's commercial ballooning companies include **High but Dry Balloons** (☎ **719/260-0011;** www.highbutdryballoons.com), for tours, champagne flights, and weddings. Sunrise flights are scheduled daily year-round, weather permitting. Cost depends on the number of passengers, locations, and type of flight, but start at about $200 per person. Generally, flights last 2 or 3 hours, with a minimum of 1 hour. On Labor Day weekends since 1977, the **Colorado Springs Balloon Classic** (✆ **719/471-4833;** www.balloonclassic.com) sees over 100 hot-air balloons launched from the city's Memorial Park. Admission is free.

BICYCLING   The 4.3-mile loop trail around Monument Valley Park at 170 W. Cache La Poudre St. is a good one, and there are numerous other urban trails for bikers. For rentals, contact **Colorado Kite & Ski,** 2820 W. Colorado Ave. (✆ **719/633-6227;** www.ckski.com).

FISHING   Most serious Colorado Springs anglers drive south 40 miles to the Arkansas River or west to the Rocky Mountain streams and lakes, such as those found in **Eleven Mile State Park** and **Spinney Mountain State Park** (✆ **719/748-3401** for both; http://parks.state.co.us) on the South Platte River west of Florissant. Bass, catfish, walleye pike, and panfish are found in the streams of eastern Colorado; trout is the preferred sport fish of the mountain regions. **Angler's Covey,** 295 S. 21st St. (✆ **719/471-2984;** www.anglerscovey.com), is a good source of general fishing information for southern Colorado. It offers guided trips ($350 for two people for a full day; half-days are also available), as well as licenses, rentals, flies, tackle, and clinics.

GOLF   Public courses include the **Patty Jewett Golf Course,** 900 E. Española St. (✆ **719/385-6950;** www.pattyjewettgolfshop.com); and **Valley Hi Golf Course,** 610 S. Chelton Rd. (✆ **719/385-6967;** www.valleyhigolfcourse.com). Nonresident greens fees range from $28 to $30 for 18 holes (not including a cart). **Pine Creek Golf Club,** 9850 Divot Trail (✆ **719/594-9999;** www.pinecreekgc.com), is another public course, with greens fees of $34 to $54 for 18 holes.

The finest golf courses in the Colorado Springs area are private. Guests of the Broadmoor hotel (p. 74) can play the 54-hole **Broadmoor Golf Club** (✆ **719/577-5790**), and guests at **Cheyenne Mountain Resort** can play its resident Pete Dye course (✆ **719/538-4095**).

HIKING   Opportunities abound in municipal parks, state parks, and Pike National Forest, which borders Colorado Springs to the west. The **U.S. Forest Service district office,** 601 S. Weber St. (✆ **719/636-1602**), can provide maps and general info.

Especially popular are the 4.75-mile **Seven Bridges Trail,** which starts in North Cheyenne Cañon Park at the parking lot at the end of North Cheyenne Cañon Rd.; the 6-mile **Mount Manitou Trail,** starting in Ruxton Canyon above the hydroelectric plant; and the 12-mile **Barr Trail** to the summit of Pikes Peak. (The latter's first stretch, the Manitou Incline, gains about 2,100 ft. over the first mile.) There are 13 miles of trails in the new **Red Rock Canyon Open Space,** just south of U.S. 24 and east of Manitou Springs. **Mueller State Park** (✆ **719/687-2366**), 3½ miles south of Divide en route to Cripple Creek, has 50 miles of trails, and **Cheyenne Mountain State Park,** south of the city via Colo. 115 (✆ **719/576-2016**), has about 20 miles of trails. See p. 86.

HORSEBACK RIDING   You'll find good opportunities at city parks, including Garden of the Gods, North Cheyenne Cañon Park, and Palmer Park, plus **Mueller State Park** (p. 86). The **Academy Riding Stables,** 4 El Paso Blvd., near the Garden of the Gods (✆ **888/700-0410;** www.academyridingstables.com), offers guided trail rides of nearby Garden of the Gods. One-hour rides are $49 for adults.

5

COLORADO SPRINGS

Exploring Colorado Springs

ICE SKATING   The **Sertich Ice Center** at Memorial Park (☎ **719/385-5983**) is open daily and offers prearranged instruction and rentals. (Admission is $5.25–$6.25; skate rentals are $3.25.) The U.S. Olympic Complex operates the **Colorado Springs World Arena Ice Hall,** 3185 Venetucci Blvd. (☎ **719/477-2150;** www.worldarena.com), with public sessions daily. Admission is $2 to $4; skate rentals are $2. If you have hockey equipment, you can join a pickup game ($7); call for times.

MOUNTAIN BIKING   There are abundant mountain-biking opportunities in the Colorado Springs area; contact the U.S. Forest Service, 601 S. Weber St. (☎ **719/636-1602**). For rentals, contact **Colorado Kite & Ski,** 2820 W. Colorado Ave. (☎ **719/633-6227;** www.ckski.com).

Parks

Cheyenne Mountain State Park ★   One of the newest state parks in Colorado, Cheyenne Mountain State Park is easily accessible, with 20 miles of trails meandering through 1,680 acres of plains and mountain woodland on the south side of Cheyenne Mountain. The ecosystem is a transition zone, meaning you have species from both plains and mountain environments, with wildlife ranging from prairie dogs to mountain lions. There are campsites ($16–$26) and coin-operated showers and laundry machines.

410 JL Ranch Heights Rd. ☎ **719/576-2016.** http://cpw.state.co.us. Admission $7 per vehicle. Daily 9am–5pm. Take Colo. 115 south from Colorado Springs to JL Ranch Heights Rd. and turn right (west).

Mueller State Park ★★   Somewhat like a junior version of Rocky Mountain National Park, Mueller contains over 5,000 acres of prime scenic beauty along the west slope of Pikes Peak. The 55 miles of uncrowded trails, designated for hikers, horseback riders, and mountain bikers, provide great mountain views and opportunities to observe the park's wildlife (including elk, bighorn sheep, and black bears). The best times to spot wildlife are spring and fall, just after sunrise and just before sunset. In the summer, rangers lead hikes and offer campfire programs in a 100-seat amphitheater. The park has 132 campsites (☎ **800/678-2267** for reservations), with fees ranging from $18 for walk-in sites to $22 for drive-in sites with electricity; coin-operated pay showers and coin laundry are available from mid-May to mid-October. Also available are two- to four-bedroom cabins for $140 to $260 a night.

21045 Colo. 67 South, Divide. ☎ **719/687-2366.** http://cpw.state.co.us. Admission $7 per vehicle. Daily 9am–5pm. Take U.S. 24 west 25 miles from Colorado Springs to Divide and then go 3½ miles south on Colo. 67.

North Cheyenne Cañon Park and Starsmore Discovery Center ★★   A delightful escape on a hot summer day, this 1,600-acre park includes North Cheyenne Creek, which drops 1,800 feet over the course of 5 miles in a series of cascades and waterfalls. The heavily wooded park contains picnic areas and about 15 miles of hiking/biking/horseback riding trails. The visitor center at the foot of scenic Helen Hunt Falls has exhibits on history, geology, flora, and fauna. The **Starsmore Discovery Center** at the entrance to the park holds maps, information, and interactive exhibits for both kids and adults, including audiovisual programs and a climbing wall where you can learn about rock climbing. The park also has excellent rock-climbing areas for experienced climbers.

2120 S. Cheyenne Cañon Rd. (west of 21st St.). ☎ **719/578-6086.** www.springsgov.com. Free admission. Park daily year-round. Starsmore Discovery Center summer daily 9am–5pm; rest of year Tues–Sat 9am–3pm. Helen Hunt Falls Visitor Center Memorial Day to Labor Day daily 9am–5pm; closed rest of year. Located just west of the Broadmoor via Cheyenne Blvd.

florissant fossil beds
NATIONAL MONUMENT

Approximately 35 miles west of Colorado Springs on U.S. 24 is the small village of Florissant, which means "flowering" in French. It couldn't be more aptly named—every spring its hillsides virtually blaze with wildflowers. Just 2 miles south is one of the most spectacular, yet relatively unknown, fossil deposits in the world, Florissant Fossil Beds National Monument.

The fossils in this 6,000-acre National Park Service property are preserved in the rocks of ancient Lake Florissant, which existed 34 million years ago. Volcanic eruptions spanning 500,000 years trapped plants and animals under layers of ash and dust; the creatures were fossilized as the sediment settled and became shale. The detailed impressions, first discovered in 1873, offer the most extensive record of its kind in the world.

Scientists have removed thousands of specimens, including 1,100 separate species of insects. There are dragonflies, beetles, and ants, more fossil butterflies than anywhere else in the world, plus spiders, fish, mammals, and birds, all perfectly preserved for millions of years.

Mudflows also buried forests during this long period, petrifying the trees where they stood. Nature trails pass petrified tree stumps; one sequoia stump is 10 feet in diameter and 11 feet high. The national monument also has over 14 miles of hiking trails. Admission to the monument is $3 per adult for a week and free for children 14 and under. It's open from 8am to 6pm daily in summer and 9am to 5pm daily the rest of the year (closed major holidays). Contact Florissant Fossil Beds National Monument (© **719/748-3253;** www.nps.gov/flfo).

Especially for Kids

Kids will enjoy the **Cheyenne Mountain Zoo** (p. 80), **Arcade Amusements** (p. 80), and the **North Pole/Santa's Workshop** (p. 83).

SHOPPING

Five principal areas attract shoppers in Colorado Springs. The Manitou Springs and Old Colorado City neighborhoods are fun places to browse for art, jewelry, arts and crafts, books, antiques, and other specialty items. The Chapel Hills and Citadel malls combine major department stores with a variety of national chain outlets. Downtown Colorado Springs also has numerous shops. Sales taxes total about 7.6 percent in the city of Colorado Springs.

Malls

Local malls include **Chapel Hills Mall,** 1710 Briargate Blvd. at North Academy Boulevard and I-25 (© **719/594-0110;** www.chapelhillsmall.com); and the **Citadel,** 750 Citadel Dr. E., at North Academy Boulevard and East Platte Avenue (© **719/591-5515;** www.shopthecitadel.com).

Arts & Crafts

Commonwheel Artists Co-op ★★ There are artists galore in Manitou Springs, and this co-op showcases works from a good many of them. Of the galleries dotting the streets, this is the best place to start. 102 Cañon Ave., Manitou Springs. ℂ **719/685-1008.** www.commonwheel.com.

Michael Garman's Museum and Gallery ★★   Michael Garman has made a name for himself with his sculptures of down-and-out types, cowboys, and blue-collar everyday joes. Stop here for a great selection of his work, but the can't-miss attraction is **Magic Town,** a room-sized city with so many details it's hard to take them in in less than a half-hour. Entry to Magic Town is $5 for adults, $4 for seniors, $3 for children 7 to 12, and free for younger kids. If you feel like really exploring, get a scavenger hunt card from the cashier. 2418 W. Colorado Ave., Old Colorado City. ℂ **800/731-3908** or 719/471-9391. www.michaelgarman.com.

Van Briggle Pottery & Tile ★★   The late Artus Van Briggle took Far Eastern techniques of matte glaze to locally sourced clay starting in 1899, and his Art Nouveau results are the thing of legend. The kilns are still active today, and you can see artists in action. 1024 S. Tejon St. ℂ **719/633-7729.** www.vanbriggle.com.

Books

Five miles east of downtown near the Citadel Mall, **Barnes & Noble** ★★, 795 Citadel Dr. E. (ℂ **719/637-8282**), offers a wide selection of books and magazines.

Poor Richard's Bookstore ★★★   The best used bookstore in Colorado Springs is the tip of the iceberg for the Poor Richard's complex, with everything from toys to coffee to tapas as well. 320 N. Tejon St. ℂ **719/578-5549.** www.poorrichardsdowntown.com.

Sporting Goods

Mountain Chalet ★   In business since 1968, the independent store has everything you need for a hike or overnight camping trip, as well as a nice array of mountain-centric Colorado souvenirs. 226 N. Tejon St. ℂ **719/633-0732.** www.mtnchalet.com.

Western Wear

Lorig's Western Wear ★   For cowboys real and faux, Lorig's has long been the place to get your duds for work, play, or a night on the town. 15 N. Union Blvd. ℂ **719/633-4695.** www.lorigscolorado.com.

NIGHTLIFE

Performing Arts Venues

The **Colorado Springs World Arena,** 3185 Venetucci Blvd., at I-25, exit 138 (ℂ **719/520-7469** for the ticket office, or 719/477-2100; www.worldarena.com), is the city's largest indoor venue, featuring ice skating as well as national touring bands and other well-known entertainers.

Downtown, the **Pikes Peak Center,** 190 S. Cascade Ave. (ℂ **719/520-7469** for the ticket office, or 719/477-2100; www.pikespeakcenter.org), is home to a symphony orchestra and dance theater. Touring productions also often perform here.

The **Colorado Springs Fine Arts Center,** 30 W. Dale St. (ℂ **719/634-5583;** www.csfineartscenter.org), is another great performing arts venue in the downtown area. Located at the excellent art museum of the same name (p. 79), productions include theater aimed at kids as well as adults, and it's also a top venue for culinary events.

SYMPHONY, THEATER & DANCE

Colorado Springs Dance Theatre ★★ This excellent company stages several productions from fall to spring at several venues in Colorado Springs. The style runs the gamut from classical to contemporary. ℭ **719/630-7434.** www.csdance.org.

Colorado Springs Philharmonic ★ The well-regarded civic orchestra plays at numerous venues and events all year long, including outdoor concerts in the summer and "The Nutcracker" come December. ℭ **719/575-9632** or 719/520-7469 for tickets. www.csphilharmonic.org.

DINNER THEATERS

The beloved **Flying W Ranch** was completely destroyed by a ferocious wildfire in 2012, but the owners have pledged to rebuild. Check the website (www.flyingw.com) for up-to-date information.

Iron Springs Chateau Melodrama ★ It's cowboys in white hats versus stereo-typical mustachioed villains at this longstanding Manitou Springs theater. Quirky titles like "Danger Ranger Granger" and "The Pigskin Perils of Old P.U." are preceded by a hearty dinner. 444 S. Ruxton Ave., Manitou Springs. ℭ **719/685-5104.** www.ironspringschateau. com. Reservations required. Dinner and show $30 adults, $28 seniors, $17 children 12 and under; show only $16 adults, $15 seniors, $9.50 children. Tues–Sun 6pm; show at 8pm. Closed winter.

The Bar Scene

Cowboys ★ Line dancers, country karaoke stars, and bowlers form the trifecta here, with a hopping dance floor on the main floor and a bowling alley upstairs. 25 N. Tejon St. ℭ **719/596-1212.**

Golden Bee ★★★ This is the real deal, built in the 1800s in Great Britain and taken apart, shipped to Colorado, and put together again in 1961 at The Broadmoor. The place saw a significant expansion in late 2012 that tripled the square footage and added a rooftop deck. There's a great ham and cheddar on a pretzel roll, burgers, and other British pub fare like chicken curry masala and bangers and mash. After dinner, the piano player leads the bar in old standards and more contemporary hits as the staff deftly flings bee-shaped stickers at the shirts of guests. The Broadmoor, 1 Lake Circle. ℭ **719/577-5773.**

The Keg Bar & Grill ★ For drinks or dinner, this fun neighborhood hangout on the main drag in Manitou is a reliable pick, serving burgers, steaks, and a good berry salad. 730 Manitou Ave., Manitou Springs. ℭ **719/685-9531.**

Meadow Muffins ★★ This is one of those spots where everything but the kitchen sink hangs from the rafters, and it somehow seems to fit. The burgers and beer are the specialties here, and it's typically the busiest bar in Old Colorado City. 2432 W. Colorado Ave., in Old Colorado City. ℭ **719/633-0583.**

Phantom Canyon Brewing Co. ★★ This landmark brewpub downtown is part of the empire of the Wynkoop Brewing Company in Denver, and it produces similarly scintillating variety of beers on-site, with a solid menu to match. 2 E. Pikes Peak Ave. ℭ **719/635-2800.**

Tony's ★ Green Bay Packers fans overrun this Badger State-loving bar on game days, but this downtown bar is more than memorabilia and fried cheese curds. It's got a friendly vibe and harks back to neighborhood bars of decades past. 311 N. Tejon St. ℭ **719/228-6566.**

The Underground   This is one of the longest lasting gay bars in the Springs area, with drag shows and other entertainment most Friday nights. 110 N. Nevada Ave. ✆ **719/578-7771.**

Spectator Sports

Air Force Academy Falcons football, basketball, and other sports (✆ **800/666-8723** or 719/472-1895; www.goairforcefalcons.com) are the focal point of sports in Colorado Springs.

AUTO RACING   First staged in 1916, the **Pikes Peak International Hill Climb** (✆ **719/685-4400;** www.ppihc.com) is held annually in summer and is one of the scariest races in motorsports, thanks to 2,000 foot plunges and nary a guardrail in sight. The brave drivers zig and zag their way around more than 150 turns on the last 12 miles of the Pikes Peak Highway, with the finish line appropriately at the 14,110-foot summit.

RODEO   The **Pikes Peak or Bust Rodeo** (✆ **719/884-1199;** www.pikespeakorbust. org) started in the 1940s and continues to attract top rodeo talent. Held in June or July at **Norris-Penrose Events Center,** 1045 Lower Gold Camp Rd., the highlight is the offsite kickoff parade with a horde of cowboys, cowgirls, and rodeo clowns.

DAY TRIPS FROM COLORADO SPRINGS

There are several great day trips from Colorado Springs beyond the usual outings of Pikes Peak and Garden of the Gods. An old mining mecca turned gambling town, Cripple Creek can be a fun day trip for casino fans and history buffs, and the precipitous Royal Gorge is one of the great natural wonders of the West.

Cripple Creek ★

Located 45 miles west of Colorado Springs via U.S. 24 west and Colo. 67 south, this old mining town on the southwestern flank of Pikes Peak was known as the world's greatest gold camp after the precious metal was first discovered here in 1890. During its heyday at the beginning of the 20th century, Cripple Creek (elevation 9,494 ft.) had a stock exchange, two opera houses, five daily newspapers, 16 churches, 19 schools, and 73 saloons, plus an elaborate streetcar system and a railroad depot that saw 18 arrivals and departures a day. By 1961, more than $800 million worth of ore had been taken from the surrounding hills.

Today Cripple Creek has several dozen limited-stakes gambling casinos, most lining Bennett Avenue. They cash in not only on the lure of gambling but also on the nostalgia for the gambling houses that were once prominent throughout the Old West. Although gamblers must be at least 21 years old, some casinos offer special children's areas, along with other family activities.

EXPLORING CRIPPLE CREEK

One of the town's unique attractions is a herd of wild donkeys, descendants of the miners' runaways, which roam freely through the hills and into the streets. The year's biggest celebration, **Donkey Derby Days** in late June, culminates with a donkey race.

Although gambling takes place year-round, many of the historic attractions are open in summer only or have limited winter hours. Among those you'll want to check out is the 1891 **Mollie Kathleen Gold Mine,** 1 mile north of Cripple Creek at 9388 Colo. 67 (✆ **719/689-2466;** www.goldminetours.com). It offers visitors a rare chance to join hard-rock miners on a 1,050-foot underground descent into a genuine gold mine and take home a gold-ore specimen as a souvenir. Tours last about 40 minutes; temperatures in the mine are 45°F to 50°F (7°C–10°C), and jackets are provided. Admission is $18 for adults, $10 for children 3 through 12, and free for children 2 and under. The mine is open from mid-May to mid-September daily from 9am to 5pm with shorter hours the rest of the year.

The **Cripple Creek District Museum,** at the east end of Bennett Ave (℃ **719/689-2634;** www.cripplecreekmuseum.com), is just the spot to explore the area's fascinating, rough-and-tumble history. The museum is open daily from 10am to 5pm Memorial Day through September, and Saturday and Sunday from 10am to 4pm the rest of the year. Admission is $5 adults, $3 seniors and children 11 and under. The surprisingly family-friendly **Old Homestead Museum,** 353 Myers Ave. (℃ **719/689-9090**), delves into the red-light history of brothels that attracted the miners in centuries past. Admission is $5 adults and $2 for kids 11 and under. The museum is open daily in summer from 11am to 4pm.

The **Cripple Creek & Victor Narrow Gauge Railroad Co.,** at the Midland Terminal Depot, 520 E. Carr St. (℃ **719/689-2640;** www.cripplecreekrailroad.com), takes visitors on a 4-mile narrated tour. The route runs past abandoned mines and over a reconstructed trestle to the ghost town of Anaconda, powered by a 15-ton "iron horse" steam locomotive. The train operates daily from mid-May to mid-October. The first train leaves the station at 10am and subsequent trains leave every 40 minutes until 5pm. Tickets are $12 for adults, $11 for seniors, $8.25 for children 3 to 12, and free for kids 2 and under.

WHERE TO EAT

Most of the casinos have restaurants, but my pick is **The Creek,** 317 E. Bennett Ave. (℃ **719/689-9595**) for burgers or pizza in a historic room. For additional information, contact the **Cripple Creek Chamber of Commerce** (℃ **877/858-4653;** www.cripplecreek.co.us).

NEARBY SCENIC DRIVES

When you leave Cripple Creek, two drives of particular beauty offer alternatives to Colo. 67. Neither is paved and both are narrow and winding, but both are usually acceptable for everyday vehicles under dry conditions. Each is roughly 30 miles long but requires about 90 minutes to negotiate. First, take Colo. 67 south out of Cripple Creek for 6 miles to the historic mining town of **Victor,** a picturesque destination.

The **Gold Camp Road** leads east from Victor to Colorado Springs via the North Cheyenne Cañon. Theodore Roosevelt said that this trip up the old Short Line Railroad bed had "scenery that bankrupts the English language." The **Phantom Canyon Road** leads south from Victor to Florence, following another old narrow-gauge railroad bed, the Gold Belt Line. A number of ghost towns and fossil areas mark this route.

The Royal Gorge ★★

Located 45 miles southwest of Colorado Springs, this narrow canyon, 1,053 feet deep, was cut through solid granite by 3 million years of water and wind erosion. When Zebulon Pike saw the gorge in 1806, he predicted that man would never conquer it. But by 1877 the Denver & Rio Grande Railroad had laid a route through the canyon, and it soon became a major tourist attraction.

ESSENTIALS

From Colorado Springs, the breathtaking **Royal Gorge** and **Royal Gorge Bridge and Park** and the historic town of **Cañon City** make an easy day trip. The Royal Gorge, one of the most impressive natural attractions in the state, lies 8 miles west of Cañon City off U.S. 50, at the head of the Arkansas River valley. From the Springs, head southwest on Colo. 115 for about 33 miles, turn west for about 12 miles on U.S. 50 to Cañon City, and then go south to the Royal Gorge.

The gorge is spanned by what is said to be the world's highest suspension bridge and an aerial tramway, built for no other reason than to thrill tourists. The ¼-mile-long bridge was constructed in 1929, suspended from two 300-ton cables, and reinforced in 1983. An incline railway, believed to be the world's steepest, was completed in 1931; it plunges from the rim of the gorge 1,550 feet to the floor at a 45-degree angle, giving passengers the view from the bottom as well as from the top. The 35-passenger tram, added in 1968, provides views of the gorge and the bridge from a height of 1,178 feet above the Arkansas River. *Note:* A forest fire in 2013 ravaged the rim of the Royal Gorge and destroyed numerous attractions. Restoration was underway at press time.

For more information, contact the **Cañon City Chamber of Commerce,** 403 Royal Gorge Blvd. (© **800/876-7922** or 719/275-2331; www.canoncity.com).

EXPLORING THE ROYAL GORGE AREA

Owned by Cañon City, **Royal Gorge Bridge and Park** has been a mainstay of Colorado tourism, but was essentially destroyed in a forest fire in June 2013; the park was slated for a full reconstruction in 2014. For current information, contact **Royal Gorge Bridge & Park** (© **888/333-5597** or 719/275-7507; www.royalgorgebridge.com).

An interesting way to view the canyon is from the **Royal Gorge Route Railroad,** 401 Water St. (south of U.S. 50 on 3rd St.), in Cañon City (© **888/724-5748;** www.royalgorgeroute.com). The train takes passengers on a 2-hour, 24-mile trip through the canyon. From early May to early October, the train departs daily at 9:30am and 12:30pm; there are also 3:30pm departures in summer and 7pm dinner rides on select evenings. Coach tickets cost $39 for adults, $28 for children 3 to 12, and are free for children 2 and under. Reservations are recommended. Observation-dome tickets are $25 more and dinner rides are $89 a person ($115 in the observation dome). You can ride in the locomotive with the engineer for $150, or $250 for two.

To see this beautiful gorge from the river while also enjoying some thrills, consider a raft trip. Adult rates run about $125 for a full-day trip, including lunch; half-day trips are about $75. Most Royal Gorge raft trips include rough white-water stretches of the river. Major outfitters include **Arkansas River Tours** (© **800/321-4352;** www.arkansasrivertours.com), **Echo Canyon River Expeditions** (© **800/755-3246;** www.raftecho.com), and **Wilderness Aware Rafting** (© **800/462-7238;** www.inaraft.com).

An interesting Cañon City stop, the **Museum of Colorado Prisons,** 201 N. 1st St. (© **719/269-3015;** www.prisonmuseum.org), is in a former women's prison. If you are into the history of capital and/or cruel and unusual punishment, the exhibits are sure to captivate, but others might do well to steer clear. A shop sells goods made by inmates at an adjacent prison. The museum has hours from mid-May through Labor Day daily from 10am to 6pm; Labor Day through October 10am to 5pm daily; and the rest of the year Wednesday to Sunday 10am to 5pm. Admission is $7 for adults, $6 for seniors 65 and older, $5 for children 6 to 12, and free for children 5 and under. Allow about an hour.

WHERE TO EAT

Royal Gorge Brewing Co. & Restaurant, 413 Main St. (© **719/345-4141;** www.royalgorgebrewing.com), is a solid brewpub in downtown Cañon City serving hose beers as well as burgers, fish and chips, and sandwiches. Most dishes are $8 to $12.

BOULDER

Although Boulder is known primarily as a college town (the University of Colorado is here), it would be inaccurate to begin and end the description there. Sophisticated and artsy, Boulder is home to numerous high-tech companies and research concerns; it also attracts countless outdoor sports enthusiasts with its delightful climate, vast open spaces, and proximity to Rocky Mountain National Park.

Set at the foot of the Flatirons of the Rocky Mountains, just 30 miles northwest of downtown Denver and only 74 feet higher than the Mile High City, Boulder was settled by hopeful miners in 1858 and named for the large rocks in the area. Welcomed by Chief Niwot and the resident southern Arapaho, the miners struck gold in the nearby hills the following year. By the 1870s, Boulder had become a regional rail and trade center for mining and farming. The university, founded in 1877, became the economic mainstay of the community after mining collapsed around the beginning of the 20th century.

In the 1950s, Boulder emerged as a national hub for scientific and environmental research. The National Center for Atmospheric Research and the National Institute of Standards and Technology are located here, as are dozens of high-tech and aerospace companies. Alongside the ongoing high-tech boom, the university and attendant vibrant culture have attracted a diverse mix of intellectuals, individualists, and eccentrics. Writers William S. Burroughs, Jr., Stephen King, and Allen Ginsberg, cofounder of the city's Naropa Institute, all called Boulder home at one time or another, as have numerous triathletes, reincarnated lamas, and jam bands.

Today's residents are a mix of students attending the University of Colorado (called CU by locals); employees of the many computer, biotech, and research firms; and others attracted by the casual, bohemian, environmentally aware, and otherwise hip lifestyles that prevail here. Whatever differences exist among the residents, they are united by a common love of the outdoors. Within its city limits, Boulder has over 40,000 acres of open space, 56 parks, and 200 miles of trails. On any given day, seemingly three-quarters of the population is outside making great use of this land, generally from the vantage point of a bicycle seat, the preferred mode of transport—there are about 100,000 bicycles in Boulder, about one for each of the city's 97,000 residents.

ESSENTIALS

Arriving
BY PLANE
Boulder doesn't have a commercial airport. Air travelers must fly into Denver International Airport and make ground connections to Boulder, a trip of about an hour.

GETTING TO & FROM THE AIRPORT SuperShuttle Boulder (© 303/227-0000; www.supershuttle.com) offers rides between Boulder and Denver International Airport. One-way fare is about $30 per person; round-trips run around $50.

Boulder Yellow Cab (© 303/777-7777; www.boulderyellowcab.com) charges $84 one-way to the airport for up to five passengers.

Buses operated by the **Regional Transportation District,** known locally as **RTD** (© 303/299-6000; www.rtd-denver.com), charge $13 for a one-way trip to the airport (exact change required); those 15 and under ride free if accompanied by a paying adult.

BY CAR

The Boulder Turnpike (U.S. 36) branches off I-25 north of Denver and passes through the suburbs of Westminster, Broomfield, and Louisville before reaching Boulder. The trip takes about 30 minutes. If you are coming from Denver International Airport, take E-470 west, which becomes the Northwest Parkway (both are no-stop toll roads; car owners are automatically billed by mail, but renters should review their contract) to U.S. 36. If you're arriving from the north, take the Longmont exit from I-25 and follow Colo. 119 all the way. Longmont is 7 miles due west of the freeway; Boulder is another 15 miles southwest on the Longmont Diagonal Highway.

Visitor Information

The **Boulder Convention and Visitors Bureau,** 2440 Pearl St. (at Folsom St.), Boulder, CO 80302 (© **800/444-0447** or 303/442-2911; www.bouldercoloradousa.com), provides maps, brochures, and information.

City Layout

The north-south streets increase in number going from west to east, beginning with Third Street. Where U.S. 36 enters Boulder and turns north, it becomes 28th Street, a major commercial artery. The Longmont Diagonal Highway (Colo. 119) enters Boulder from the northeast and intersects 28th Street at the north end of the city.

To reach downtown Boulder from U.S. 36, turn west on Canyon Boulevard (Colo. 119 west) and north on Broadway, which would be 12th Street if it had a number. It's 2 blocks to the Pearl Street Mall, a 4-block, east-west pedestrian-only strip from 11th to 15th streets that constitutes the historic downtown district. Boulder's few one-way streets circle the mall: 13th and 15th streets are one-way north, 11th and 14th one-way south, Walnut Street (a block south of the mall) one-way east, and Spruce Street (a block north) one-way west.

Broadway continues across the mall, eventually joining U.S. 36 north of the city. South of Arapahoe Avenue, Broadway turns southeast, skirting the University of Colorado campus and becoming Colo. 93 (the Foothills Hwy. to Golden) after crossing Baseline Road. Baseline follows a straight line from east Boulder, across U.S. 36 and Broadway, past Chautauqua Park and up the mountain slopes. To the south, Table Mesa Drive takes a similar course.

The Foothills Parkway (not to be confused with the Foothills Hwy.) is the principal north-south route on the east side of Boulder, extending from U.S. 36 to the Longmont Diagonal.

Boulder Neighborhoods

Downtown Boulder is between 1st (west) and 28th (east) streets and centered on Pearl Street. **University Hill,** or "The Hill," is south of downtown adjacent to the campus of the University of Colorado and north of **Chautauqua. Eastern Boulder** is more industrial. **Mapleton** is largely residential and north of downtown

GETTING AROUND

By Taxi

Boulder Yellow Cab (✆ **303/777-7777**) operates 24 hours, but you need to call for service—there are no taxi stands, and taxis won't stop for you on the street. Other companies that serve Boulder are **Freedom Cab** (✆ **303/444-4444**) and **Metro Taxi** (✆ **303/333-3333**).

By Car

Most people who fly to Colorado land at **Denver International Airport** (p. 240) and rent a car there. Most downtown streets have parking meters, with rates of about 25¢ per 20 minutes. Downtown lots cost $1 to $3 for 3 hours. Parking can be hard to find around the Pearl Street Mall, but new lots have eased the pain. Outside downtown, free parking is generally available on side streets.

By Bus

The **Regional Transportation District** (**RTD;** ✆ **800/366-7433** or 303/299-6000; www.rtd-denver.com) provides bus service throughout Boulder as well as the Denver greater metropolitan area. The hub is the Boulder Transit Center at 14th and Walnut streets. Fares within the city are $2.25 ($1.10 for seniors and passengers with disabilities, free for children 5 and under). Buses are wheelchair accessible.

The city of Boulder runs a shuttle bus service called the **HOP** (✆ **303/447-8282**), connecting downtown, University Hill, the University of Colorado, and 30th and Pearl. The HOP operates weekdays from 7am to 10pm, Saturdays from 9am to 10pm, and Sundays from 10am to 6pm. While CU is in session, a late-night bus runs Thursday through Saturday nights until 3am. Buses run about every 10 to 15 minutes during the day, every 15 to 20 minutes at night; fares are as above.

The RTD runs a free local shuttle, the **SKIP,** Monday through Friday from 5:30am to 12:30am, Saturday from 7am to 12:30am, and Sunday from 7am to 11:30pm. Buses run north and south along Broadway every 10 minutes during peak weekday times and less frequently in the evenings and on weekends.

By Bike

Boulder is a wonderful place for bicycling; there are bike paths throughout the city and an extensive trail system leading for miles beyond Boulder's borders (see "Bicycling" under "Outdoor Activities," p. 106).

You can rent and repair mountain bikes and buy trail and city maps at **University Bicycles,** 839 Pearl St., about 2 blocks west of the Pearl Street Mall (✆ **303/444-4196;** www.ubikes.com). Bike rentals cost $30 to $85 daily.

On Foot

You can walk to most of the attractions in downtown Boulder, especially around the Pearl Street Mall and University of Colorado campus. Books and brochures covering historic walking tours are available at the Boulder CVB, 2440 Pearl St.

WHERE TO STAY

You'll find a good selection of comfortable lodgings in Boulder, with a wide range of rates to suit almost every budget. Be aware, though, that the town fills up during the

Boulder

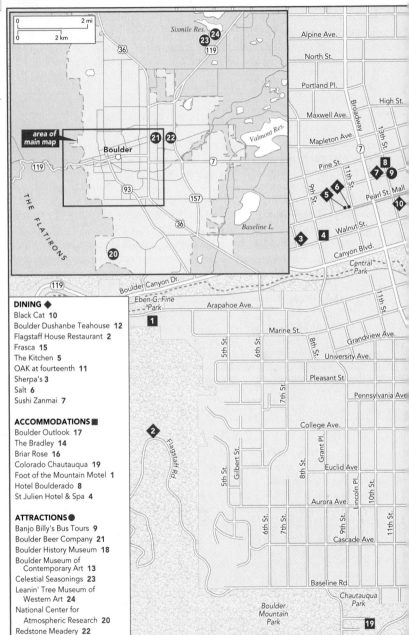

DINING ◆
Black Cat **10**
Boulder Dushanbe Teahouse **12**
Flagstaff House Restaurant **2**
Frasca **15**
The Kitchen **5**
OAK at fourteenth **11**
Sherpa's **3**
Salt **6**
Sushi Zanmai **7**

ACCOMMODATIONS ■
Boulder Outlook **17**
The Bradley **14**
Briar Rose **16**
Colorado Chautauqua **19**
Foot of the Mountain Motel **1**
Hotel Boulderado **8**
St Julien Hotel & Spa **4**

ATTRACTIONS ●
Banjo Billy's Bus Tours **9**
Boulder Beer Company **21**
Boulder History Museum **18**
Boulder Museum of
    Contemporary Art **13**
Celestial Seasonings **23**
Leanin' Tree Museum of
    Western Art **24**
National Center for
    Atmospheric Research **20**
Redstone Meadery **22**

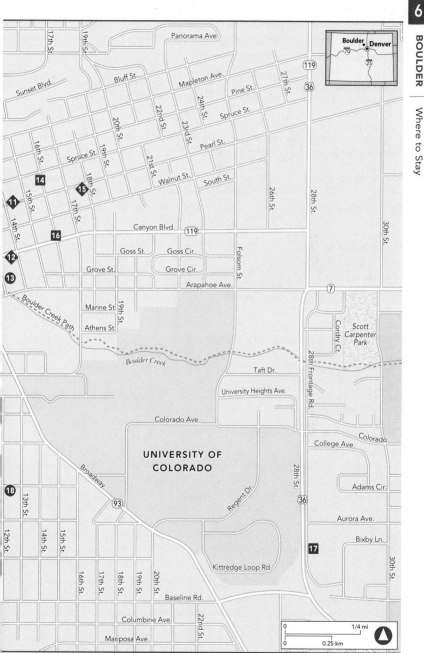

Panorama Ave.

17th St.

19th St.

Bluff St.

Mapleton Ave.

Pine St.

27th St.

119

36

Sunset Blvd.

22nd St.

24th St.

Spruce St.

20th St.

23rd St.

16th St.

Spruce St.

19th St.

21st St.

Pearl St.

18th St.

14

17th St.

15

Walnut St.

South St.

26th St.

28th St.

30th St.

11

15th St.

16

14th St.

Canyon Blvd.

119

12

Goss St.

Goss Cir.

Folsom St.

13

Grove St.

Grove Cir.

Arapahoe Ave.

7

Boulder Creek Path

Marine St.

19th St.

Cordry Ct.

Scott
Carpenter
Park

Athens St.

Boulder Creek

Taft Dr.

University Heights Ave.

28th Frontage Rd.

Colorado Ave.

Colorado

College Ave.

UNIVERSITY OF
COLORADO

18

13th St.

Broadway

Regent Dr.

28th St.

36

Adams Cir.

93

Aurora Ave.

12th St.

14th St.

15th St.

Bixby Ln.

16th St.

17th St.

18th St.

19th St.

20th St.

17

30th St.

Kittredge Loop Rd.

Baseline Rd.

Columbine Ave.

22nd St.

Mariposa Ave.

Boulder

Denver

70

25

0   1/4 mi

0   0.25 km

[FastFACTS] BOULDER

ATMs/Banks ATMs and banks are very common throughout the Boulder area.

Doctors & Hospitals Full medical services, including 24-hour emergency treatment, are available at **Boulder Community Hospital,** 1100 Balsam Ave., at North Broadway (✆ 303/440-2273; www.bch.org).

Emergencies For police, fire, or medical emergencies, dial ✆ **911.** To reach **Poison Control,** call ✆ **800/332-3073.**

Internet Access Most hotels and coffee shops have free Wi-Fi.

Mail & Postage The main downtown post office is at 1905 15th St. Contact the U.S. Postal Service (✆ **800/275-8777;** www.usps.com) for hours and other locations.

Newspapers & Magazines Newspapers include the Daily Camera and the Boulder Weekly. Many Boulderites also read the campus paper, the Colorado Daily, available all over town. The Denver Post is also available at newsstands throughout the city. You can also find the New York Times and Wall Street Journal.

Pharmacies There are no 24-hour pharmacies in Boulder. The pharmacy at **King Soopers Supermarket,** 1650 30th St., in Sunrise Plaza (✆ 303/444-0164), is open from 8am to 9pm weekdays, 9am to 6pm Saturdays, and 10am to 6pm Sundays.

Safety Although Boulder is generally a safe city, it is not crime-free. Be aware of your surroundings, especially if walking alone at night.

Also see "Fast Facts" in Planning Your Trip (p. 242).

popular summer season, so making advance reservations essential. It's also almost impossible to find a place to sleep during any major event at the University of Colorado, particularly graduation. Those who do find themselves in Boulder without lodging can check with the Boulder Convention and Visitors Bureau (see "Visitor Information," p. 94), which keeps track of availability. You can usually find a room in Denver, a half-hour or so away.

Downtown & Vicinity
EXPENSIVE

The Bradley Boulder Inn ★★★   Although it's nearly a century newer than many of its Victorian neighbors, The Bradley has the same grace as its neighbors. That goes for the rooms, all of which come with handsome, solid-wood furnishings and, in some, such romance-enhancing amenities as working fireplaces, deep soaking tubs, and pretty balconies. Every evening at 5pm, the congenial staff holds a wine and cheese reception. A block north of Pearl Street, the location is likewise superb, balancing the intimacy of a residential neighborhood with easy walking access to all the downtown attractions.

2040 16th St. ✆ 303/545-5200. www.thebradleyboulder.com. 12 units. $195–$235 double. Rates include full breakfast. **Amenities:** Concierge; access to nearby health club; free Wi-Fi.

Briar Rose ★★   This Zen-like B&B is as green as they come, from the organic breakfasts served every morning to refillable bath amenities; there's also a meditation room. It makes sense: Innkeeper Gary Hardin is a practicing Buddhist and, if the level of his hospitality is any indication, a very old soul. Rooms are comfortably appointed with antiques, and a doily-free atmosphere that's hipper than most inns; the Huron Room has a hot tub for two. Of special note are the xeriscaped gardens (they need no additional water), designed as a contemplative getaway right in the middle of town.

2151 Arapahoe Ave. ✆ **888/786-8440** or 303/442-3007. www.briarrosebb.com. 10 units. $164–$219 double. Rates include full breakfast. **Amenities:** Free Wi-Fi.

Hotel Boulderado ★★★   The Boulderado has been the place to hang your hat in downtown Boulder for more than a century. Rooms cost $1 to $2.50 when it opened in 1909 and an annex was added in 1989, but otherwise the hotel has changed very little over the years. It still sports a distinctive red sandstone exterior and Spanish Revival architecture, stained-glass canopy above the lobby, and the original Otis elevator. The rooms and suites have taken advantage of the perks of modern technology (iPod docking stations and Wi-Fi, to name two) but retain a turn-of-the-20th-century charm with Victorian-style wallpapers, antique reproduction furnishings, and handsome heavy drapes. The resident eating and drinking establishments are first-rate, with **a fine-dining restaurant,** a casual atmosphere at the **Corner Bar,** and a great basement haunt dubbed **License No. 1** (p. 112).

2115 13th St. (at Spruce St.). ✆ **800/433-4344** or 303/442-4344. www.boulderado.com. 160 units. $215–$329 double; $323–$419 suite. **Amenities:** 2 restaurants; 3 lounges; fitness center; free Wi-Fi.

St Julien Hotel & Spa ★★★   This sleek hotel has been the cornerstone of southwest downtown Boulder since it opened in 2005. The contemporary furnishings (think: neutral colors, fine linens, workable desks, good seating areas), local art, and architecture complement the mountain views, which are the best of any hotel in the city. The rooms feature oversized bathrooms and pillowtop mattresses that were custom-made for the property. The facilities hit all the right notes, from Jill's Restaurant to the T-Zero Lounge to the resident spa and fitness facilities, and the location is ideal, on the fringe of the hustle and bustle but a world away.

900 Walnut St. ✆ **877/303-0900** or 720/406-9696. www.stjulien.com. 201 units, including 6 suites. $239–$369 double; $339–$559 suite. Valet parking $20 per night. **Amenities:** Restaurant; lounge; bikes (free); concierge; exercise room; indoor Jacuzzi; indoor heated pool; spa; free Wi-Fi.

West of Downtown
INEXPENSIVE
Foot of the Mountain Motel ★   Some roadside motels age remarkably well. This is one of them. One of Boulder's first motels (established in 1936), the log-cabin inspired exterior, bedecked with bright red trim, has the prettiest location of any budget lodging, at the scenic mouth of Boulder Canyon across from Eben G., Fine Park (which features a network of short hiking trails). It's as far west you can get in Boulder without ascending into the Rockies, and it's tucked away on a little-trafficked street. Rooms are neat as a pin and comfy.

200 Arapahoe Ave. ✆ **866/773-5489** or 303/442-5688. www.footofthemountainmotel.com. 20 units. $90 double; $115–$185 suite. Rates include complimentary continental breakfast. Pets accepted ($5 nightly fee, $50 refundable deposit). **Amenities:** Free Wi-Fi.

East of Downtown
INEXPENSIVE
Boulder Outlook ★★   It's hard to get any more Boulder than this: How many hotels have dog runs and bouldering rocks on their list of facilities? This colorful place came to be in 2002 when local hotel-management company HVS took its collective know-how and plowed it—along with a cool $1.5 million—into a 40-year-old chain property in their hometown. Rooms are comfortable and well maintained, if fairly typical motel accommodations. There's a great bar with local microbrews and live blues, and the Outlook strives to be a zero-waste facility.

800 28th St. ℂ **800/542-0304** or 303/443-3322. www.boulderoutlook.com. 162 units. $99–$169 double. Lower rates in winter. Rates include continental breakfast. Pets accepted. **Amenities:** Restaurant (American); lounge; bikes (complimentary); exercise room; indoor Jacuzzi; indoor heated pool; room service, saunas; free Wi-Fi.

South of Downtown
MODERATE

Colorado Chautauqua ★★ This is a great pick for history buffs and hikers. One of the last remnants of the Chautauqua movement of a century ago—gatherings to educate and inform—the Colorado Chautauqua (est. 1898) is frozen in that heyday on the southern fringes of Boulder. Nestled in aptly named Chautauqua Park below the Flatirons, the location is stunning, with plenty of elbow room. Laid out like a small town separated from the city by open space, accommodations are in a wide range of historic cottages that sleep up to 8 comfortably; there are also lodge rooms. Trails radiate from the cabins into the mountains to the west, and there are concerts in the acoustically renowned auditorium year-round.

900 Baseline Rd. (at 9th St.). ℂ **303/952-1611.** www.chautauqua.com. 82 units. $81–$130 lodge room; $123–$176 efficiency cottage; $151–$281 1- to 3-bedroom cottage. Pets accepted in most cottages ($10 per night). Pets not accepted in lodges. **Amenities:** Restaurant (New American); children's programs during summer; 2 outdoor tennis courts; Wi-Fi (free for 2 hr./day).

WHERE TO EAT

"Bon Appétit" named Boulder the foodiest town in the U.S. in 2010, and we'd say that title still applies: From the farmer's market to the great restaurants to the strong natural foods industry, good food is hard-wired into the local culture. At Boulder's chef-owned-and-operated establishments, innovative and often-changing cuisine is the rule. The farm-to-table and craft cocktail movements have also exploded in Boulder in recent years.

Downtown & Vicinity
EXPENSIVE

Frasca ★★★ ITALIAN Not only is sociable Frasca one of the best reviewed restaurants in Boulder, it's one of the best-reviewed in the country, landing on all sorts of national lists since its opening in 2004.The fare is inspired by Friuli-Venezia Giulia in northeast Italy, and the name comes from *frascas*—informal gathering places—there. Naturally, wine is a big thing here—the restaurant won the 2013 James Beard Award for Outstanding Wine Program. Adjacent and under the same ownership, **Pizzeria Locale,** 1730 Pearl St. (ℂ **303/442-3003**), is more casual, but is equally authentic in its pursuit of the perfect pizza.

1738 Pearl St. ℂ **303/442-6966.** www.frascafoodandwine.com. Main courses $38, $78 for 4-course dinner ($50 on Mon). Mon–Sat 5:30–10:30pm. Closed Sun. Bus: HOP.

Black Cat ★★ NEW AMERICAN Owner Eric Skokan started with a dinky little farm just outside town in 2007. Now he has 130 acres, with heirloom crops of all kinds, as well as chickens, pigs, turkeys, ducks, and sheep, and he even runs a community-supported agriculture program. It goes without saying that the Black Cat serves some of the freshest fare in Boulder, but Skokan's eye for invention is what makes this restaurant soar. The menu changes on a weekly basis, with farm-to-table specials with some serious flair. Expect delectable house-made sausage, a vegetarian entree, and such unusual dishes as braised leg of rabbit with beluga lentils and braised leeks or chilled turnip soup with leek panna cotta.

1964 13th St. © **303/444-5500.** www.blackcatboulder.com. Main courses $19–$31. Daily 5:30–10pm. Bus: HOP, SKIP.

The Kitchen ★★ NEW AMERICAN Kimbal Musk started PayPal with his brother Elon and then decided to go to culinary school and open a restaurant in Boulder. The results speak for themselves: Musk might be better working in a kitchen than he is at a tech startup. Since opening The Kitchen in 2004, he's opened an upstairs cocktail lounge and a pub next door (aptly named [Upstairs] and [Next Door]); sister restaurants in Denver, Chicago, Glendale, and Fort Collins; and a nonprofit that is planning to build 180 learning gardens at schools around the country. As for the food, it would best be described as veggie-heavy American gourmet. Elon has a talent for making those good-for-you products (kale, Swiss chard, beets) taste as rich as foie gras. Vegetarians are well-served here, but so are carnivores who like creatively cooked proteins served with a lot of greens (and yellows and purples).

1039 Pearl St. © **303/544-5973.** www.thekitchencommunity.com. Main courses $11–$21 lunch or brunch, $18–$33 dinner. Mon 11am–9pm; Tues–Fri 11am–10pm; Sat–Sun 9am–2pm; Sun 5:30–9pm. Bar open later. Bus: HOP, SKIP.

OAK at fourteenth ★★ NEW AMERICAN Opening in December 2011 after a fire shut it down in its first incarnation (it was open for a short spell the year before), OAK is one of the most social eating spots in Boulder. Grab a table on one of the best people-watching patios on the Pearl Street Mall, or eat inside at the long bar along the open kitchen, where the chefs prepare fare from the menu of the week. After a salad or a small plate, pick from Italian and comfort-food standbys like braised meatballs on grits, alongside creative dishes that are largely based on what's fresh, what's local, and what's in season. Colorado lamb and local chicken are often on the menu. The bartenders take their cocktails seriously here; the wait staff is professional but casual, in white shirts and jeans.

1400 Pearl St. (at 14th St.). © **303/444-3622.** www.oakatfourteenth.com. Main courses $12–$15 lunch; $20–$28 dinner. Mon–Sat 11am–10pm; Sun 5:30–10pm. Bus: HOP, SKIP.

MODERATE

Boulder Dushanbe Teahouse ★★★ INTERNATIONAL The only authentic Persian teahouse in the country, the Boulder Dushanbe Teahouse is a stunning work of architecture, with soaring pillars, hand-painted paneling, and ornate craftsmanship around every turn. It makes sense: It was a gift from Boulder's sister city of Dushanbe, Tajikistan, in 1990, with every piece shipped in crates, and assembled by Tajik workers who came over for the task. The food is also artful, inspired by culinary traditions from all over the planet, from Bengali Shrimp to Mexican braised pork shoulder. And the tea list is staggering—there are more than 100 loose-leaf teas to be steeped here.

1770 13th St. © **303/442-4993.** www.boulderteahouse.com. Main courses $5–$10 breakfast, $10–$15 lunch, $13–$21 dinner. Daily 8am–9pm. Bus: HOP.

Salt ★★ NEW AMERICAN Salt opened its doors in 2009 and has dazzled Boulder ever since. The emphasis is on fresh, local ingredients, with the kitchen plating up roasted beet salads, sweet pea ravioli, and saffron risotto with calamari and mussels, as well as flatiron steaks that have been braised for 7 hours—a lot of attention goes into preparation here. The same can be said for the cocktails, crafted by the city's top mixologists. Make mine a Mountain Manhattan.

1047 Pearl St. (just west of the mall). © **303/444-7258.** www.saltthebistro.com. Main courses $12–$15 lunch and brunch, $14–$34 dinner. Mon–Fri 11am–10pm; Sat–Sun 10am–11pm. Bus: HOP, SKIP.

Sushi Zanmai ★ SUSHI/JAPANESE   The staff greets you in unison, sings along to karaoke, and otherwise entertains patrons at this longstanding sushi joint near the Hotel Boulderado. But the zany antics of the employees are no distraction—the sushi rolls (many of which draw inspiration from the Rockies or Boulder's tie-dye-tinged culture), tempura, and noodle dishes are uniformly first-rate. You'll find a traditional Japanese izakaya at the sister restaurant, **Amu** (☎ **303/440-0807;** www.izakayamu. com), located just one door to the west.

1221 Spruce St. (at Broadway). ☎ **303/440-0733.** www.sushizanmai.com. Main courses $8–$15 lunch, $14–$28 dinner; sushi rolls $2–$16. Mon–Fri 11:30am–2pm; Sun–Fri 5–10pm; Sat 5pm–midnight. Bus: HOP, SKIP.

INEXPENSIVE

Sherpa's ★ TIBETAN/NEPALESE   Owner Pemba Sherpa guided dozens of expeditions to the Himalayas, and completed countless feats of endurance. (Yes, he's an authentic sherpa who was born in Nepal.) With this in mind, it's hard to argue with his culinary vision. The fare takes Tibetan, Nepalese, and Indian traditions and delivers spicy, satisfying, and healthful selections like dall baht (traditional Nepalese lentil soup and basmati rice), curry dishes, and tandoori. The front patio is host to one of the best happy hours in Boulder and there's a library catering to world adventurers inside.

825 Walnut St. ☎ **303/440-7151.** www.sherpasrestaurant.com. Main courses $7–$14. Daily 11am–3pm; Sun–Wed 5–9:30pm; Thurs–Sat 5–10pm. Bus: HOP, SKIP.

South of Downtown

EXPENSIVE

Flagstaff House Restaurant ★★★ NEW AMERICAN   There are many superlatives when it comes to describing the Flagstaff House. The mountainside location on the peak of the same name makes for the best views of any Boulder restaurant. Same goes for the wine cellar at 12,000 bottles—it wouldn't be a stretch to say it's the best in the state. But it's the food that sets the stage for all else: The regularly changing menu starts with Continental standards and adds a dollop of contemporary verve, with items like Colorado lamb, pan-seared duck, and buffalo filet mignon, all prepared with a distinctive culinary spin. The Monette family has run the restaurant since 1971, transforming what was once a 1920s cabin into one of the most revered eateries in the Rockies.

1138 Flagstaff Rd. (west up Baseline Rd.). ☎ **303/442-4640.** www.flagstaffhouse.com. Main courses $34–$74. Sun–Fri 6–10pm; Sat 5–10pm.

EXPLORING BOULDER

Most of Boulder's attractions are downtown along the **Pearl Street Mall** or on the **University of Colorado campus;** the **Boulder Creek Path** connects these two areas. There are also several attractions, like **Celestial Seasonings** and the **Redstone Meadery,** in the more industrial areas on the east side of the city.

Downtown Boulder & Vicinity

Banjo Billy's Bus Tours ★   A rollicking journey through Boulder and its storied history, Banjo Billy's Bus Tours uses one of the funkiest vehicles you've ever seen. Featuring armchairs for guests inside, the exterior looks like the offspring of a log cabin and a school bus—and features 13 disco balls, five saddles, and a rubber chicken! The 90-minute tours delve into ghost stories and lurid tales of crime, but the tone is tongue-in-cheek and entertaining. Banjo Billy also offers Denver tours.

Tours depart from the Hotel Boulderado, 13th and Spruce sts. (p. 99). © **720/938-8885.** www. banjobilly.com. Tickets $22 adults, $20 seniors, $14 children 6–12, and free for children 5 and under. Summer tours depart Tues–Sun at 2pm and 4pm; less frequently at other times of year.

Boulder Creek Path ★★★ Following Boulder Creek, this nature corridor provides about a 6-mile-long oasis and recreation area through the city and west into the mountains. With no street crossings (there are bridges and underpasses instead), the path is popular with Boulder residents, especially on weekends, when you'll see numerous walkers, runners, bicyclists, and in-line skaters. (Walkers should stay to the right; the left lane is for faster traffic.) The path links the CU campus, several city parks, and office buildings. Near the east end, watch for deer, prairie-dog colonies, and wetlands, where some 150 species of birds have been spotted. You might see Canada geese, mallard ducks, spotted sandpipers, owls, and woodpeckers.

At 30th Street, south of Arapahoe Road, the path cuts through **Scott Carpenter Park** (named for the astronaut and Colorado native), where you can enjoy swimming in summer and sledding in winter. Just west of Scott Carpenter Park, you'll find **Boulder Creek Stream Observatory.** In addition to observing trout and other aquatic wildlife, you're invited to feed the fish with trout food purchased from a coin-operated vending machine. **Central Park,** at Broadway and Canyon Boulevard, preserves some of Boulder's history with a restored steam locomotive.

Traveling west, watch for the **Charles A. Heartling Sculpture Garden** (with the stone image of local Indian Chief Niwot) and the **Kids' Fishing Ponds;** the Boulder Fish and Game Club stocks the ponds, which are open only to children 11 and under, who can fish for free and keep what they catch.

The **Eben G. Fine Park** is named for the Boulder pharmacist who discovered Arapaho Glacier on nearby Arapaho Peak. To the west, **Red Rocks Settlers' Park** marks the beginning of the **Boulder Canyon Pioneer Trail,** which leads to a continuation of Boulder Creek Path. The park is named for Missouri gold-seekers who camped at this spot in 1858 and later found gold about 12 miles farther west. The path ends at **Four Mile Canyon,** the old town site of Orodell. *Note:* The trail sustained serious damage during flooding in September 2013, but it has reopened in its entirety.

55th St. and Pearl Pkwy. (to the mouth of Boulder Canyon). © **303/413-7200.** Free admission. Daily 24 hr. Bus: HOP.

Pearl Street Mall ★★★ This 4-block-long tree-lined pedestrian mall marks Boulder's downtown core and its center for dining, shopping, strolling, and people-watching. Musicians, mimes, jugglers, and other street entertainers hold court on the landscaped mall day and night, year-round. Buy your lunch from one of the many vendors and sprawl on the grass in front of the courthouse to relax and eat. Locally owned businesses and galleries share the mall with trendy boutiques, sidewalk cafes, and national chain stores. There's a wonderful play area for youngsters, with climbable boulders set in gravel. Don't miss the bronze bust of Chief Niwot (of the southern Arapaho) in front of the Boulder County Courthouse between 13th and 14th streets. Niwot, who welcomed the first Boulder settlers, was killed in southeastern Colorado during the Sand Creek Massacre of 1864.

Pearl St. (from 11th to 15th sts.). Bus: HOP.

South of Downtown

Boulder History Museum ★★ From Chief Niwot to the Colorado Chautauqua, Boulder's fascinating history is unraveled here in the permanent "Storymakers" exhibit on the second floor of the 1899 Harbeck-Bergheim House in southwest Boulder. The museum also features one or two temporary exhibits every year; the 2014 slate included a retrospective on the evolution of outdoor apparel. Expect to spend 30 minutes here, or more for serious history buffs.

1206 Euclid Ave. (℃ **303/449-3464.** www.boulderhistorymuseum.org. Admission $6 adults, $4 seniors, $3 children and students, free for children 4 and under. Tues–Fri 10am–5pm; Sat–Sun noon–4pm. Guided tours by appointment. Closed Mon and major holidays. Bus: HOP.

Boulder Museum of Contemporary Art ★★

Well worth a visit, "B-MoCA" spotlights some of the quirkier nooks and crannies of the arts world with a special exhibition or two at a time. A recent one, entitled "Game Changer," featured 11 contemporary artists and their often critical take on sports. Outside on summer Saturday nights, **Boulder Outdoor Cinema** (℃ **855/262-9324;** www.boulderoutdoorcinema. com) screens cult classics like "Monty Python and the Holy Grail" and "The Big Lebowski." There's a $5 suggested donation. Expect to spend an hour here.

1750 13th St. (℃ **303/443-2122.** www.bmoca.org. Admission $5 adults, $4 students and seniors, free for children 11 and under. Tues–Sun 11am–5pm (until 8pm Wed in summer). Hours change seasonally; call for current information. Closed Sun–Mon and major holidays. Bus: HOP, SKIP.

National Center for Atmospheric Research ★★

Inspired by the cliff dwellings at Mesa Verde National Park, I. M. Pei designed this striking pink-sandstone building, which overlooks Boulder from high atop Table Mesa in the southwestern foothills. (You might recognize the center from Woody Allen's "Sleeper," as some scenes were shot here.) World-class scientists study such important phenomena as the greenhouse effect, wind shear, and ozone depletion to gain a better understanding of the earth's atmosphere. Among the technological tools on display are satellites, weather balloons, interactive computer monitors, robots, and supercomputers that can simulate the world's climate. There are also hands-on, weather-oriented exhibits and a theater. Outside, the **Walter Orr Roberts Weather Trail** takes visitors on a .4-mile, wheelchair-accessible loop along a path with interpretive signs describing various aspects of weather and climate plus the plants and animals of the area. The center also houses a changing art exhibit and a cafeteria. Allow 1 to 2 hours.

1850 Table Mesa Dr. (℃ **303/497-1000** or 303/497-1174. www.spark.ucar.edu/visit. Free admission. Mon–Fri 8am–5pm; Sat–Sun and holidays 9am–4pm. 1-hr. guided tours Mon, Wed, and Fri at noon; there is also a self-guided audio tour.

University of Colorado ★★

The largest university in the state, with more than 30,000 students, "CU" dominates the city. Its student population, cultural and sports events, and intellectual atmosphere have helped shape Boulder into the city it is today. The school boasts 20 alumni astronauts who have flown in space and five Nobel laureates on the faculty.

Old Main, on the Norlin Quadrangle, was the first building erected after the university was established in 1876; at that time, it housed the entire school. Later, pink-sandstone Italian Renaissance–style buildings came to dominate the campus. On the third floor, the **CU Heritage Center** (℃ **303/492-6329;** www.cuheritage.org) covers the university's history. Admission is free.

The **CU Museum of Natural History ★,** in the Henderson Building just east of Broadway and 15th Street (℃ **303/492-6892;** http://cumuseum.colorado.edu), is another campus highlight, with an extensive collection of 4 million objects that includes everything from fossilized turtle shells to Navajo rugs. Admission is $3 for adults, $1 for seniors and children 6–18, and free for kids 5 and under.

The **CU Art Museum** (© 303/492-8300; http://cuartmuseum.colorado.edu) displays the work of CU students and faculty as well as pieces from the Colorado Collection, more than 8,000 works in all. There are also rotating exhibits. The museum is located in the new Visual Arts Complex; admission is free.

The **Sommers-Bausch Observatory** (© 303/492-6732 during the day, or 303/492-2020 at night; http://lyra.colorado.edu/sbo) offers tours and Friday-evening open houses, and the **Fiske Planetarium** (© 303/492-5002; http://fiske.colorado.edu) reopened in fall 2013 after a year-long renovation.

East side of Broadway (btw. Arapahoe Ave. and Baseline Rd.). © **303/492-1411.** www.colorado. edu. Bus: HOP, SKIP, STAMPEDE, and Denver buses.

East of Downtown

Boulder Beer Company ★   From the grinding of the grain to the bottling of the beer, the 25-minute tour of Colorado's original microbrewery ends as all brewery tours should: in the pub. Tours pass by glistening copper vats that turn out hundreds of kegs of Boulder Beer a day. The pub overlooks the bottling area, so even if you visit without taking a tour, you still get a good view of the brewing process. The menu includes burgers, burritos, salads, and appetizers; most entrees run $7 to $10.

2880 Wilderness Place. © **303/444-8448.** www.boulderbeer.com. Free admission. Tours Mon–Fri 2pm, Sat 2pm and 4pm; pub Mon–Fri 11am–9pm, Sat noon–8pm. Take U.S. 36 north to Valmont Rd.; then head east to Wilderness Place.

Celestial Seasonings ★★   The nation's leading producer of herbal teas, housed in a modern building in northeastern Boulder, offers tours that are an experience for the senses. The company began in a Boulder garage in 1969 and now steeps in more than 1.6 billion cups of tea a year, sourcing more than 100 different herbs and spices from 35 countries. You'll understand why the company invites you to "see, taste, and smell the world of Celestial Seasonings" as you move from a consumer taste test in the lobby to their famed tea-box art, and finally into the production plant where millions of tea bags are made daily. The exhilaratingly aromatic "Mint Room" is a highlight. The tour lasts 45 minutes, and there is a cafe and gift shop on-site.

4600 Sleepytime Dr. © **303/581-1266.** www.celestialseasonings.com. Free admission. Mon–Sat 10am–4pm; Sun 11am–3pm; tours on the hour. Gift shop Mon–Fri 9am–6pm; Sat 9am–5pm; Sun 10am–5pm. Reservations required for groups of 8 or more. Exit Colo. 119, Longmont Diagonal, at Jay Rd.; go east to Spine and then north to Sleepytime. Bus: 205.

Leanin' Tree Museum of Western Art ★   This is the personal art collection of Ed Trumble, the founder of Leanin' Tree, a greeting card company; it features about 400 paintings and bronze sculptures. Subject matter ranges from cowboys to wild animals, and the outdoor sculpture garden offers a chance to experience some art and fresh air at the same time. You'll probably spend about 30 minutes here.

6055 Longbow Dr. (exit Jay Rd. and Longmont Diagonal). © **303/530-1442.** www.leanintreemuseum.com. Free admission; donations suggested. Mon–Fri 8am–5pm; Sat–Sun 10am–5pm. Bus: 205.

Redstone Meadery ★   Drunk by Beowulf and Shakespeare, mead is one of the oldest fermented beverages. There are now over 100 active meaderies in the United States, including this standout in Boulder. Founded by David Myers in 2000, the meadery crafts several beverages that quickly demonstrate why this amateur mead-maker turned pro. The meadery offers free 30-minute tours and tastings, and sells its wares and other regional foods and gifts.

4700 Old Pearl St., #2A. ✆ **720/406-1215.** www.redstonemeadery.com. Free admission. Tours Mon–Fri 1 and 3pm, Sat 12:30pm; tasting room Mon–Fri noon–6:30pm, Sat noon–5pm. Located 1 block northeast of Pearl St. exit off Foothills Pkwy.

Outlying Attractions

Butterfly Pavilion ★★   A world of grace, beauty, and constant mists awaits visitors here. Those mists create a hazy habitat to support the lush green plants that are both food and home to the 1,600 butterfly inhabitants representing 100 species at any given time. If you stand still for a few minutes, a butterfly might land on you, but don't try to pick up the butterflies—the oils on your hands contaminate their senses, interfering with their ability to find food. One display describes the differences among butterflies, moths, and skippers, and color charts help with identification. In the "Crawl-A-See-Um," meet bugs that are native to Colorado, and see (and touch) exotic species from around the world. The pavilion also includes a snack bar. Outside, a half-mile nature trail meanders amid cactuses and other desert-friendly plants. Allow 2 hours.

6252 W. 104th Ave., Westminster. ✆ **303/469-5441.** www.butterflies.org. Admission $9.50 adults, $7.50 seniors, $6.50 children 2–12, free for children under 2. Daily 9am–5pm. Take U.S. 36 to 104th Ave.

ORGANIZED TOURS

Hop on one of **Banjo Billy's Bus Tours** (p. 102) for a decidedly Boulder kind of tour. Pedestrians should contact the pros at **Boulder Walking Tours** (✆ **720/243-1376;** www.boulderwalkingtours.com) if you would like a guide who's knowledgeable of the city's history and geography.

OUTDOOR ACTIVITIES

In 2014, Outdoor magazine named Boulder one of its top 10 communities for outdoor enthusiasts in North America. The city manages more than 40,000 acres of parklands, including more than 200 miles of hiking trails and bicycle paths. Several canyons lead down from the Rockies directly into Boulder, attracting mountaineers and rock climbers. Families enjoy picnicking and camping in the beautiful surroundings. It seems that everywhere you look, people of all ages are running, walking, biking, skiing, or engaged in other active sports.

The **Boulder Parks and Recreation Department** (✆ **303/413-7200;** www. bouldercolorado.gov) manages numerous parks, pools, and recreation centers and schedules a variety of year-round activities for children as well as adults.

One of the best (and most scenic) outdoor destinations on the Front Range, **Eldorado Canyon State Park,** just 5 miles southwest of Boulder in Eldorado Springs, is a favorite of technical rock climbers, but the 850-foot-high canyon's beauty makes it just as popular with hikers, picnickers, and others who want to get away from it all. The 1,448-acre park features about 10 miles of hiking and horseback-riding trails, with about 6 miles of trails suitable for mountain bikes; I recommend hiking Eldorado Canyon Trail (3.5 miles one-way) for a workout and canyon views. Fishing is permitted, but camping is not. An exhibit at the visitor center describes the history of the park; there's also a bookstore and rotating displays covering topics from wildflowers to climbing. *Note:* A few trails and the picnic area were closed by floods in 2013 and had yet to reopen at press time. Admission is $8 per vehicle and $3 per pedestrian; the park is open daily from dawn to dusk. For further information, contact Eldorado Canyon State Park (✆ **303/543-8882;** http://parks.state.co.us).

BALLOONING   Float above the majestic Rocky Mountains in a hot-air balloon, watching as the early-morning light gradually brightens to full day. Flights often include champagne and an elaborate continental breakfast or brunch. **Fair Winds Hot Air Balloon Flights** (© 303/939-9323; www.hotairballoonridescolorado.com) flies 7 days a week year-round, weather permitting. Prices are typically $195 to $275 per person, and include a certificate, T-shirt, and photograph.

BICYCLING   On some days, you see more bikes than cars in Boulder. Paths run along many of the city's major arteries, and local racing and touring events are scheduled year-round. Bicyclists riding at night are required to have lights; perhaps because of the large number of bicyclists in Boulder, the local police actively enforce traffic regulations that apply to them. Generally, bicyclists must obey the same laws that apply to operators of motor vehicles.

For current information on biking events, maps of the city's trails, tips on the best places to ride, and equipment sales and repairs, check with **University Bicycles,** 839 Pearl St., about 2 blocks west of the Pearl Street Mall (© 303/444-4196; www.ubikes. com), and **Full Cycle,** 1211 13th St. (© 303/440-7771; www.fullcyclebikes.com). Daily bike rentals cost $30 to $90.

CLIMBING & BOULDERING   If you want to tackle the nearby mountains and cliffs with ropes and pitons, contact **Neptune Mountaineering,** 633 S. Broadway (© 303/499-8866; www.neptunemountaineering.com), which sells clothing and technical equipment, and can also provide maps and advice on climbing and trail running. Another good information source is **Total Climbing,** 2829 Mapleton Ave. (© 800/836-4008; www.totalclimbing.com), home to the Boulder Rock Club, featuring 10,000 square feet of indoor climbing surfaces, and offers guiding services. Boulderers (those who climb without ropes) flock to the **Spot,** billed as the country's largest bouldering gym, at 3240 Prairie Ave. (© 303/379-8806; www.thespotgym.com). Lessons and guide service are available, and there are a cafe and a yoga studio on-site.

The **Flatiron Range** (easily visible from downtown Boulder) and nearby Eldorado Canyon are two favorite destinations for expert rock scalers. The Third Flatiron is 1,400 feet high, taller than the Empire State Building, and has been climbed by people without using their hands, on roller skates, and naked. For bouldering, Carter Lake (30 miles north on U.S. 36) and Boulder Canyon (west of the city on Canyon Blvd.) are two of the top spots.

FISHING   Favored fishing areas near Boulder include **Boulder Reservoir,** North 51st Street, northeast of the city off the Longmont Diagonal, where you can try your luck at walleye, catfish, largemouth bass, bluegill, crappie, and carp. The Boulder Parks and Recreation Department (© 303/441-3461; www.bouldercolorado.gov) manages the reservoir. Other favorite fishing holes include **Lagerman Reservoir,** west of North 73rd Street off Pike Road, about 15 miles northeast of the city, where only nonmotorized boats can be used; **Barker Reservoir,** just east of Nederland on the Boulder Canyon Drive (Colo. 119), for bank fishing; and **Walden Ponds Wildlife Habitat,** about 6 miles east of downtown on North 75th Street. Fly-fishing is also popular in the area; guide service is available through **Front Range Anglers** (© 303/494-1375; www.frontrangeanglers.com) for $370 for two for a full day.

GLIDER FLYING & SOARING   The atmospheric conditions generated by the peaks of the Front Range are ideal for year-round soaring and gliding. **Mile High Gliding,** 5534 Independence Rd. (© 303/527-1122; www.milehighgliding.com), offers rides and lessons on the north side of Boulder Municipal Airport, 2 miles northeast of downtown. Rides for one person range from $99 to $299 and last from 15 minutes to an hour or more; a 40-minute ride for two costs $259.

GOLF   Local courses include the 18-hole **Flatirons Golf Course** (run by Boulder Parks and Recreation), 5706 E. Arapahoe Ave. (© **303/442-7851**; www.flatironsgolf. com), and the 9-hole **Haystack Mountain Golf Course,** 5877 Niwot Rd. in Niwot, 5 miles north of Boulder (© **303/530-1400**; www.golfhaystack.com). Nonresident greens fees range from $23 to $38 at Flatirons for 18 holes, and $14 to $16 for 9 at Haystack.

HIKING & BACKPACKING   There are plenty of opportunities in the Boulder area—the **Boulder Mountain Parks** system includes 4,625 acres bordering the city limits, including the Flatirons and Flagstaff Mountain. If you're not afraid of a little exercise, **Mount Sanitas** is a popular trail rated moderate to strenuous, accessible via Mapleton Avenue a half-mile west of 4th Street (about a 3-mile loop). **Enchanted Mesa,** accessible via Chautauqua Park (Baseline Rd. and 9th Ave.), is a gentler option, winding a mile until connecting with the longer Mesa Trail (6.9 miles one-way). You can obtain a map with trail descriptions from the **Boulder Convention and Visitors Bureau,** 2440 Pearl St. (© **303/442-2911**).

Numerous Roosevelt National Forest trailheads leave the Peak-to-Peak Scenic Byway (Colo. 72) west of Boulder. Check with the **U.S. Forest Service,** Boulder Ranger District, 2140 Yarmouth Ave. (© **303/541-2500**; www.fs.usda.gov/arp), for hiking and backpacking information. During dry weather, check on possible fire and smoking restrictions before heading into the forest. The trailheads leading to Long, Mitchell, and Brainard lakes are among the most popular, as is the 2-mile hike to Isabel Glacier.

RUNNING   Boulder is one of the country's true running meccas. The **Boulder Creek Path** (p. 103) is one of the most popular routes for runners in Boulder. A good resource for the traveling runner is **Boulder Road Runners** (www.boulderroadrunners.org). They organize group runs in the area and can provide information. The **Bolder Boulder** (© **303/444-7223**; www.bolderboulder.com), held every Memorial Day, attracts 50,000 runners who circle its 10km (6.3-mile) course. The **Boulder Running Company,** 2775 Pearl St. (© **303/786-9255**; www.boulderrunningcompany. com), sells a wide variety of running shoes and gear, going as far as analyzing customers' strides on a treadmill to find the perfect shoe.

SKIING   Friendly **Eldora Mountain Resort** (© **303/440-8700**; www.eldora.com) is 21 miles west of downtown Boulder, a 40-minute drive on Colo. 119 through Nederland. RTD buses leave Boulder for Eldora four times daily during ski season. For downhill skiers and snowboarders, Eldora has 53 trails, rated 30 percent novice, 50 percent intermediate, and 20 percent expert terrain on 680 acres, as well as a terrain park. The area has two quad lifts, two triple and four double chairlifts, two surface lifts, and a vertical rise of 1,500 feet. Lift tickets (2013–14 rates) were $79 for adults, $46 for seniors 65 to 74 and children 6 to 15, and $12 for those 5 and under and 75 and over. The season runs from mid-November to mid-April, snow permitting.

For cross-country skiers, Eldora has 25 miles of groomed and backcountry trails, and an overnight hut available by reservation. About 15 percent of the trails are rated easy, 50 percent intermediate, and 35 percent difficult. The trail fee is $24, $13 for children 6 to 15 and seniors 65 to 74, and $5 for those 5 and under and 75 and over. Snowshoers pay a reduced rate.

You can rent all your ski, snowboard, and snowshoeing equipment at the ski-rental center, and Nordic equipment at the Eldora Nordic Center. A free base-area shuttle runs throughout the day from the lodge to the Little Hawk area and the Nordic Center.

WATERSPORTS For both motorboating and human-powered boating, sailboard instruction, or swimming at a sandy beach, head for the square-mile **Boulder Reservoir** (② 303/441-3461), on North 51st Street off the Longmont Diagonal northeast of the city. Human-powered boats and canoes (no personal watercraft) can be rented at the **boathouse** (② 303/441-3468). Rates are $10 to $35 per hour. There's also a boat ramp and other facilities.

Tubing is huge on Boulder Creek on hot summer days. You'll see Bermuda shorts–and bikini-clad students heading down to cool off. Join them with the help of the **Whitewater Tubing Company,** 3600 Arapahoe Ave. (② 720/239-2179; www.white watertubing.com), offering tube rentals ($16–$21 daily).

ESPECIALLY FOR KIDS

On the **Boulder Creek Path** (p. 103), the underwater fish observatory behind the Millennium Harvest House fascinates youngsters. They can feed the huge trout swimming behind a glass barrier on the creek (machines cough up handfuls of fish food for quarters).

Likewise, the **Pearl Street Mall** (p. 103) is a terrific spot for kids, featuring giant beaver and snail sculptures to frolic with, massive faux boulders to climb, and a pop-jet fountain to cool off in on hot summer days, not to mention such kid-friendly shops as Into the Wind and the Rocky Mountain Chocolate Factory.

On the north end of town, at **Gateway Park Fun Center,** 4800 N. 28th St. (② 303/442-4386; www.gatewayfunpark.com), you'll find go-karts, a human maze, batting cages, miniature golf, and more.

SHOPPING

Malls

For some of the best shopping in Boulder, head to the **Pearl Street Mall** (p. 103), where you'll find not only shops and galleries galore but also street entertainers.

The other major shopping destination in Boulder, **Twenty Ninth Street** is centered on the former site of the Crossroads Mall at the intersection of Canyon Boulevard and 29th Street (② 303/444-0722; www.twentyninthstreet.com). Tenants include Apple, Macy's, Coldwater Creek, Sur La Table, Eddie Bauer, Trader Joe's, Smashburger, Chipotle, and Century Theatres. Hours are 10am to 9pm Monday through Saturday and 11am to 6pm on Sunday.

The indoor-outdoor, 1.5-million-square-foot **FlatIron Crossing** (② 720/887-7467; www.flatironcrossing.com), an upscale mall featuring Nordstrom, Dillard's, and Brookstone among its 200 shops, is a more comprehensive option for the devout shopper. It's 9 miles southeast of Boulder off U.S. 36 in Broomfield. Hours are 10am to 9pm Monday through Saturday and 11am to 6pm on Sunday.

Arts & Crafts

Boulder Arts & Crafts Cooperative ★ For 4 decades, this longstanding Pearl Street Mall store has offered a wide selection of artwork, most made by locals. 1421 Pearl St. ② **303/443-3683.** www.boulderartsandcrafts.com.

Books

Barnes & Noble ★★★, 2999 Pearl St. (✆ **303/444-0349**), is one of Boulder's treasured one-stop shops, carrying books and magazines as well as toys, games, and coffee.

Boulder Book Store ★★★ A Boulder institution and community hub, the Boulder Book Store has more than 100,000 new and used tomes on its shelves, as well as a full calendar of lectures and readings, and a definitive Boulder vibe. 1107 Pearl St. ✆ **303/447-2074.** www.boulderbookstore.net.

Hardware

McGuckin Hardware ★★ Open since 1955, this is the anti-Home Depot. Fiercely independent and ultra-supportive of local products, McGuckin is a cavernous hardware store that harkens back to a pre-Big Box era. You'll find tools and lumber alongside outdoor gear, housewares, art supplies, and toys in the 60,000-square-foot space. 2525 Arapahoe Ave. ✆ **303/443-1822.** www.mcguckin.com.

Kitchenware

Peppercorn ★★★ Bar none, this is the best kitchen store in the Rocky Mountain region. You will find every imaginable pot, pan, and cooking gadget, plus plenty for other rooms in your home in this sizable space. 1235 Pearl St. ✆ **303/449-5847.** www.peppercorn.com.

Kites & Toys

Into the Wind ★★★ Into the Wind is known for its kites, and with good reason—it likely has the best selection in the state—but that's just the beginning of the whimsical catalog available here. Wind-up gorillas? Check. Black-light posters? Check. Hacky-sacks, inflatable taxidermy, and propeller beanies? Check, check, and check. 1408 Pearl St. ✆ **303/449-5906.** www.intothewind.com.

Sporting Goods

Boulder Army Store ★ Sure, this store started as a military surplus outlet, but today it is one of the premiere spots to get outdoor gear in one of the premiere outdoor cities in the country. The selection spans tents, boots, sunglasses, and most any other item you'll need before wandering into the nearby wild. 1545 Pearl St. ✆ **303/442-7616.** www.boulderarmystore.com.

NIGHTLIFE

As a cultured and well-educated community (almost 60 percent of adult residents have at least one college degree), Boulder is especially noted for its summer music, dance, and Shakespeare festivals. Major entertainment events take place year-round, both downtown and on the University of Colorado campus. There's also a wide choice of nightclubs and bars, but it hasn't always been so: Boulder was dry for 60 years, from 1907 (13 years before national Prohibition) to 1967. The first new bar in the city opened in 1969, in the Hotel Boulderado. The notoriously healthy city banned smoking in public places in 1995, 11 years before the state did the same thing.

Entertainment schedules can be found in the "Daily Camera," the "Denver Post," "Westword," and the "Boulder Weekly."

Performing Arts Venues

Top venues in Boulder include **Macky Auditorium** at the University of Colorado (✆ **303/492-8008;** www.colorado.edu/music) and other campus venues as well as **Chautauqua Auditorium,** 900 Baseline Rd. (✆ **303/440-7666;** www.chautauqua.com), and the **Dairy Center for the Arts,** 2590 Walnut St. (✆ **303/440-7826;** www.thedairy.org).

CLASSICAL MUSIC & OPERA

Boulder Bach Festival ★★   The oeuvre of Johann Sebastian Bach is the focal point at this longstanding event. The main slate of festival events takes place in February and March, but there are recitals and concerts all year long. ✆ **303/776-9666.** www.boulderbachfestival.org.

Boulder Philharmonic Orchestra ★★★   Founded in 1958, this community orchestra is one of the best in the West. Their annual concert series spotlights contemporary and time-tested classical works, typically performing at Macky Auditorium at CU. ✆ **303/449-1343.** www.boulderphil.org.

Colorado MahlerFest ★   Aficionados of Gustav Mahler mass in Boulder in May of each year for a far-flung slate of performances, lectures, and other events dedicated to the legendary director of the Vienna Opera. ✆ **303/492-8970.** www.mahlerfest.org.

Colorado Music Festival ★★★   This showcase event for the umbrella organization, the Colorado Center for Musical Arts, is one of the best music festivals in the state. The calendar stretches from late June to early August, covering all sorts of musical grounds in 6 weeks. ✆ **303/665-0599** for general information, or 303/440-7666, or visit website for tickets. www.comusic.org.

CU Presents ★   The CU College of Music stages a wide range of concerts at Macky Auditorium and other campus venues year-round. Performers include students as well as a wide range of pro musicians from near and far. University of Colorado. ✆ **303/492-8008.** www.cupresents.org.

THEATER

Colorado Shakespeare Festival ★   The Bard gets his due at this annual summer festival at CU that sees several productions at the Mary Rippon Outdoor Theatre and the indoor University Theatre Main Stage. The 2014 lineup included "The Tempest," "The Merry Wives of Windsor," "Henry IV," and the comedic "I Hate Hamlet." University of Colorado ✆ **303/492-8008.** www.coloradoshakes.org.

The Bar Scene

Conor O'Neill's ★★   Live music, trivia nights, and a social atmosphere complement the traditional Irish pub fare and taps of Irish beer. Just when you thought it couldn't

---

Sellout Picnic

As the revered Chautauqua Auditorium opens up to let the breeze in during summer performances, the sound carries out into the surrounding public parkland. In the event of a sellout (or if you just are pinching pennies), pack a picnic dinner and head to the park to get a free listen as you watch the sunset over the Flatirons.

get more Irish, you find out that the actual place is Irish, designed and crafted in Ireland and installed by Irish laborers. 1922 13th St. ✆ **303/449-1922.** www.conoroneills.com.

License No. 1 ★   In the bowels of the Hotel Boulderado, the former Catacombs serves a long list of local beers and spirits. Formerly a jazz and blues venue, entertainment now tends towards DJs, trivia, and movie nights. At the Hotel Boulderado, 13th and Spruce sts. ✆ **303/443-0486.**

Mountain Sun Pub & Brewery ★★   Boulder's best microbrewery offers some interesting suds to say the least. Beyond the flagship Colorado Kind Ale, there are beers brewed with chocolate, coffee, and raspberries flowing from the tap, and seasonal experiments are the norm. The menu includes burritos, burgers, and a make-your-own grilled cheese option. The empire extends south to the **Southern Sun** in south Boulder at 627 S. Broadway (✆ **303/543-0886**). 1535 Pearl St. (east of the mall). ✆ **303/546-0886.** www.mountainsunpub.com.

The Sink ★★   Since opening in 1923, this venerable college hangout has seen it all: CU dropout Robert Redford was once the janitor, and President Barack Obama made a surprise appearance in 2012. But celebrity trivia aside, this is the best place to get a whiff of Boulder's culture while knocking back a beer or two, and the psychedelic murals on the walls are a bonus. 165 13th St. ✆ **303/444-7465.** www.thesink.com.

West End Tavern ★   A picture perfect neighborhood bar with a legendary rooftop deck, the West End Tavern is named for its location on the far fringe on the Pearl Street Mall. The Southern-tinged menu is also notable. Chicken and biscuits, anyone? 926 Pearl St. ✆ **303/444-3535.** www.thewestendtavern.com.

The Club & Music Scene

Boulder Theater ★   Eclectic is the best adjective for the calendar here, where performers in 2014 ranged from Lauryn Hill to George Thorogood & The Destroyers. 2032 14th St. ✆ **303/786-7030.** www.bouldertheater.com.

Fox Theatre and Café ★★★   The best music venue on "The Hill" and one of the most acoustically endowed old theaters anywhere, the Fox is a beloved institution. Jam bands tend to dominate the calendar. 1135 13th St. ✆ **303/443-3399** or 303/447-0095. www.foxtheatre.com.

Spectator Sports

The **University of Colorado** fields teams in most college sports. For tickets, contact the ticket office (✆ **303/492-8337;** www.cubuffs.com).

A DAY TRIP TO FORT COLLINS

A fun college town 55 miles north of Boulder, Fort Collins was founded in 1864 as a military post on the Cache la Poudre (pronounced Poo-der) River, named for a powder cache left by French fur traders. The fort was abandoned in 1867, but the settlement prospered, first as a center for quarrying and farming, then for sugar-beet processing after 1910. Colorado State University (CSU) was established in 1870; today it is nationally known for its veterinary medicine and forestry schools, as well as its research advances in space engineering and bone cancer. The population of the city grew from 43,000 in 1970 to roughly 150,000 today, not including the many students.

The city, just below 5,000 feet in elevation, makes a good base for fishing, boating, rafting, or exploring **Rocky Mountain National Park** (p. 118). It also has several historic sites and offers a treat for beer lovers, with tours of breweries ranging from micro to "macro" micro to the huge facility operated by Anheuser-Busch.

Essentials

GETTING THERE   By Car   Coming from Boulder, take Colo. 119 northeast to I-25 north to exit 269 (Mulberry St. for downtown Fort Collins), exit 268 (Prospect Rd. for CSU), or exit 265 (Harmony Rd. for south Fort Collins). The drive takes about 1 hour.

GETTING AROUND   Fort Collins is located on the Cache la Poudre River, 4 miles west of I-25. College Avenue (U.S. 287) is the main north-south artery and the city's primary commercial strip; Mulberry Street (Colo. 14) is the main east-west thoroughfare. Downtown extends north of Mulberry Street on College Avenue to Jefferson Street; Old Town is a triangle bounded on the west by College Avenue, 4 blocks north of Mulberry. The main CSU campus covers a square mile west of College Avenue 2 blocks south of Mulberry.

VISITOR INFORMATION   The **Fort Collins Convention and Visitors Bureau** operates a visitor center at 19 Old Town Sq., Ste. 137 (✆ **800/274-3678** or 970/232-3840; www.visitftcollins.com). The state operates a **Colorado Welcome Center** (✆ **970/491-3583**), just east of I-25 at 3745 E. Prospect Rd. (exit 268); the angular, two-story building's unique architecture makes it hard to miss. Both are open daily.

Exploring Fort Collins

Anheuser-Busch Brewery ★   This brewery produces some 6 million barrels of Budweiser and other brands each year, distributed to 10 Western states. Tours end at the tasting room with a free sample. You can also visit the barn and see the giant Clydesdale horses used to promote Anheuser-Busch beers since 1933, but their busy promotional schedule means they are often out of pocket in the summer.

2351 Busch Dr. (I-25 exit 271). ✆ **970/490-4691.** www.budweisertours.com. Free admission. June–Sept daily 10am–4pm; Oct–May Thurs–Mon 10am–4pm. Closed some major holidays.

THE great stupa OF DHARMAKAYA & THE SHAMBHALA MOUNTAIN CENTER

Founded by Chögyam Trungpa Rinpoche, a Tibetan Buddhist teacher who was a major figure in bringing his religion to the U.S., the **Shambhala Mountain Center** is about an hour's drive northwest of Fort Collins and a world apart. Located in a rocky, forested mountain valley, the center offers a curriculum ranging from meditation and yoga to gardening and storytelling.

The center is also home to a unique structure: The **Great Stupa of Dharmakaya,** dedicated to Shambhala founder Rinpoche, is the largest and most ornate *stupa* (a spire built in honor of a deceased Buddhist teacher) in the Western Hemisphere. Engineers who had a hand in building nuclear plants were called in to design a structure out of reinforced concrete that would stand for 1,000 years, and artisans hand-painted every last detail. The stupa is open from 10am to 6pm daily; donations are requested. Guided tours are offered by appointment ($10).

For lodging, dining, and program information, contact the Shambhala Mountain Center (✆ **970/881-2184;** www.shambhalamountain.org).

Colorado State University ★ Fort Collins revolves around this university, with its roughly 30,000 students from every state and close to 100 foreign countries. Founded in 1870 as Colorado Agricultural College, it was renamed Colorado A&M in 1935 and became Colorado State University in 1957. The A constructed on the hillside behind Hughes Stadium by students and faculty in 1923 stands for "Aggies" and remains a cherished tradition, even though the school's athletic teams have been called the Rams for decades.

Those wanting to see the campus should stop first at the **University Welcome Center,** at College Avenue and Pitkin Street (☎ **970/491-4636**), for information, maps, and parking passes. Among suggested stops are the **Administration Building,** on the Oval where the school began, and the **Lory Student Center,** at University and Center avenues, which houses a food court, bookstore, art gallery, and other facilities. Allow an hour for a stroll around campus. Guided tours are offered daily.

Appointments can be made to visit the renowned **Veterinary Teaching Hospital** and the **Equine Teaching Center.** The **Art Department** has several galleries with revolving exhibits, and the **University Theatre** in Johnson Hall, on East Drive (☎ **970/491-2787;** www.csuartstickets.com), presents student productions year-round. The university's **Environmental Learning Center** (☎ **970/491-1661;** www.csuelc. com) covers 200 acres and has 2.5 miles of trails, with opportunities to see wildlife such as golden eagles, muskrats, and white-tail deer, and a variety of plants.

University and College aves. ☎ **970/491-6444.** www.colostate.edu.

Fort Collins Municipal Railway ★ One of the few remaining original trolley systems in the nation, this restored 1919 Birney streetcar runs on its original route, along Mountain Avenue for 1½ miles from City Park to Howes Street. Today it's more for fun than practical urban transport. Allow 30 minutes.

Oak and Roosevelt, at City Park. www.fortnet.org/trolley. Admission $2 adults, $1 seniors and children 2–12, free for children under 2. May–Sept Sat–Sun and holidays only noon–5pm.

The Fort Collins Museum of Discovery ★ This joint history and science museum boasts a large collection of Folsom points of any Western museum. There are historical artifacts from Fort Collins as well as pioneer and Victorian objects, a number of cool hands-on science exhibits in the Schatz Family Exploration Zone, and a special exhibit on a landmark local archaeological discovery, Folsom man. Also on-site: a movie theater, a Theremin to play with at the music lab, and a packed calendar of special events.

408 Mason Ct. ☎ **970/221-6738.** www.fcmod.org. Admission $9.50 adults, $7 seniors, $6 children 3–12, free for children 2 and under. Tues–Sun 10am–5pm.

Old Town ★★ A redbrick pedestrian mall flanked by streetlamps and centered on a bubbling fountain is the focus of this restored historic district. The main plaza, which covers several square blocks, extends diagonally to the northeast from the intersection of College and Mountain avenues; on either side are shops and galleries, restaurants, and nightspots. Outdoor concerts and a string of special events keep the plaza lively all summer long. Allow about an hour, more if you want to do some serious shopping.

Btw. College and Mountain aves. and Jefferson St. www.downtownfortcollins.com.

Outdoor Activities

With its prime location, nestled in the foothills of the Rockies, Fort Collins is ideally situated for those who want to get out under Colorado's clear blue sky and experience

brewery TOURS

There's no denying that Fort Collins is a beer town. Not only is it home to the giant **Anheuser-Busch Brewery,** with its famous Clydesdale horses (p. 113), but the city also boasts several excellent microbreweries.

The heart and soul of Old Town, **CooperSmith's Pub & Brewing Co.** (p. 116) provides patrons a view of the brewing process from inside the restaurant and offers tours by appointment. Using English malted barley and hops from the Pacific Northwest, CooperSmith's brews from 6 to 10 ales. For those averse to beer, the brewery also makes its own root beer, ginger ale, and cream soda.

Just northeast of Old Town, across the railroad tracks, **New Belgium Brewing Company,** 500 Linden St. (℃ **970/221-0524;** www.newbelgium.com), is the local "macro" microbrewery—it ranks in the country's top 10 brewers by volume—producing top-quality Belgian-style ales including the very popular Fat Tire. The always-lively brewery's "Liquid Center" is open Tuesday through Sunday from 10am to 6pm, offering four 3-ounce samples to visitors. Hour-long tours are offered every half-hour 11am to 4:30pm (they fill up quickly, so make reservations online), with self-guided tours anytime. Beer can be purchased, along with glasses, caps, T-shirts, and other souvenirs.

Next up: **Odell Brewing Company,** Fort Collins's oldest craft brewery, at 800 E. Lincoln Ave. (℃ **970/498-9070;** www.odellbrewing.com). Specializing in English-style ales, Odell produces locally beloved lineup of beers, including 90 Shilling Ale and 5 Barrel Pale Ale. Tours are given daily at 1, 2, 3, and 4pm, and the tasting room is open from 11am to 6pm (7pm Wed–Sat). The beer isn't free, but you can sample before making your choice, plus beer glasses, shirts, and other souvenirs are all available.

Another good stop is the **Fort Collins Brewery,** 1900 E. Lincoln Ave., #B (℃ **970/472-1499;** www.fortcollinsbrewery.com), which has a comfortable tasting room that's open from noon to 7pm Friday and Saturday. Free 20-minute tours ending with free samples are offered from noon to 6pm on the hour.

Other breweries with public taprooms in Fort Collins include saison specialists **Funkwerks,** 1900 E. Lincoln Ave., Unit B (℃ **970/482-3865;** www.funkwerks.com); **Pateros Creek Brewing Company,** 242 N. College Ave. (℃ **970/484-7222;** www.pateroscreekbrewing.com); **Black Bottle Brewery,** 1611 S. College Ave. (℃ **970/493-2337;** www.blackbottlebrewery.com); and **Equinox Brewing,** 133 Remington St. (℃ **970/484-1368;** www.equinoxbrewing.com).

the delights of nature. There are several convenient multiuse trails. The **Poudre River Trail** is a 10-mile paved trail that follows the Poudre River from North Taft Hill Road to East Drake Road and the CSU Environmental Learning Center, passing Lee Martinez Park along the way. The paved **Spring Creek Trail** runs 6.9 miles along Spring Creek, passing through several city parks, from West Drake Road to East Prospect Road at the Poudre River, where you can pick up the Poudre River Trail.

There is a vast amount of public land under the jurisdiction of the U.S. Forest Service within easy access of Fort Collins, offering opportunities for hiking, mountain biking, horseback riding, fishing, camping, snowshoeing, and cross-country skiing. For details, check with the information center (℃ **970/295-6600**).

Among the most popular areas for outdoor recreation are **Poudre Canyon,** west of town and the site of a devastating wildfire in 2012, and **Horsetooth Reservoir** (℃ **970/679-4570;** www.larimer.org/parks/horsetooth.cfm), also west of town, just over the first ridge of the Rocky Mountain foothills. Along the northwest edge of the reservoir, **Lory State Park** (✆ **970/493-1623;** http://cpw.state.co.us) is known for its scenic beauty and 26-mile trail system.

BICYCLING & MOUNTAIN BIKING   There are more than 75 miles of designated bikeways in Fort Collins, including the Spring Creek and Poudre River trails, both paved (p. 115). A good choice for mountain bikers is the **Foothills Trail,** which runs along the east side of Horsetooth Reservoir from Dixon Dam north almost 7 miles to Michaud Lane. For rentals, go to **Recycled Cycles,** 4031 S. Mason St. (✆ **970/223-1969;** www.recycled-cycles.com). Adult bikes are $25 to $40 daily.

FLY-FISHING   Guided fly-fishing trips and clinics are available from **Rocky Mountain Adventures,** 1117 N. U.S. 287 (✆ **800/858-6808;** www.shoprma.com). They access the Big Thompson, Cache la Poudre, and North Platte rivers, plus waters on two private ranches and in Rocky Mountain National Park. Full-day guided walk and wade trips cost $290 for two people.

HIKING   The **Comanche Peak Wilderness,** nearly 67,000 acres of pine and spruce-fir forests below expanses of alpine tundra, offers scenic hiking trails along the north and east sides of Rocky Mountain National Park. Contact **Arapaho & Roosevelt National Forests and Pawnee Grasslands** (✆ **970/295-6600**).

There are 29 miles of trails at the 2,700-acre **Horsetooth Mountain Open Space** that are shared by hikers, mountain bikers, and horseback riders. Finally, **Lory State Park** has 26 miles of hiking trails, where the top of Arthur's Rock—a hike of 2 miles—offers a marvelous view across Fort Collins and the northeastern Colorado plains.

RIVER RAFTING   River-rafting enthusiasts have ample opportunities for boating the Cache la Poudre, a nationally designated wild-and-scenic river. **Rocky Mountain Adventures** (✆ **800/858-6808;** www.shoprma.com) offers half-day and full-day trips on the Cache la Poudre and four other regional rivers. Costs range from $55 to $75 for a half-day and $105 for a full day.

Where to Eat

CooperSmith's Pub & Brewing Co. ★ BREWPUB   Just the spot for a meal in beer-loving Fort Collins, CooperSmith's is something of a local institution, located in the heart of Old Town. Beer-wise, the brick-laden place has produced about different 150 beers since it opened in 1989. Food-wise, there are Pubside and Poolside (meaning billiards, not swimming) menus; the former is meatier, with beef medallions and wild game sausage, and the latter a tad less expensive, with burgers, pizzas, and calzones.

5 Old Town Sq. ✆ **970/498-0483.** www.coopersmithspub.com. Main courses and pizzas $8–$18. Sun–Thurs 11am–10pm; Fri–Sat 11am–11pm. Bar open later with limited menu.

Jay's Bistro ★★ NEW AMERICAN   Jay and Jacki Witlen have been Fort Collins' culinary pacesetters for more than 30 years. Serving creative spins on classic dishes like beef tournedos, pork chops, and stuffed quail, the kitchen starts with French influences but brings in ideas from all over the food map for such dishes as Asian-inspired short ribs and linguini and clams spiced with serrano peppers. Lunch includes burgers, big salads, and dishes like lobster mac and cheese.

135 W. Oak St. ✆ **970/482-1876.** www.jaysbistro.net. Main courses $10–$15 lunch, $16–$38 dinner. Mon–Wed 11am–9pm; Thurs 11am–9:30pm; Fri 11am–10pm; Sat 5–10pm; Sun 5–8:30pm.

moose HAVEN

State Forest State Park, about 75 miles west of Fort Collins via Colo. 14 (✆ **970/ 723-8366;** http://cpw.state.co.us), covers more than 70,000 acres with 90 miles of hiking trail, spectacular mountain scenery, alpine lakes, and over 600 resident moose. Day-use fees are $7 per vehicle, camping runs $10 to $20, and there are a number of cabins and yurts are available for $60 to $110 a night.

Silver Grill Cafe ★ AMERICAN   This classic diner in Old Town has been the best breakfast spot in Fort Collins for 80 years. The menu includes all the standards, as well as a few more exotic options like trout and eggs. Come lunchtime, you can also get hot and cold sandwiches, burgers, and salads. But the place is best known for its enormous, delectable cinnamon rolls. It sells more than 10,000 a month, offering them alone and as part of breakfast combos, or battered up and grilled as French toast, or buried under ice cream in a sundae.

218 Walnut St. ✆ **970/484-4656.** www.silvergrill.com. Most dishes $6–$11. Daily 6:30am–2pm.

THE NORTHERN ROCKIES

7

Literally and figuratively, this is the mother lode. It's where scrappy silver and gold miners struck it rich time and time again in the late 19th century, yet it's also where Colorado's rugged beauty is shown off to its fullest effect.

The Northern Rockies begin just outside of Denver and extend on either side of the meandering Continental Divide down saw-toothed ridgelines, through precipitous river canyons, and across broad alpine plains. Here snowfall is measured in feet, not inches; it's where you'll find Colorado's hottest ski resorts—including Aspen, Vail, Breckenridge, and Steamboat—as well as several smaller resorts.

When spring's sun finally melts away the walls of white, a whole new world opens up amid the brilliantly colored alpine wildflowers. You can head to any of the area's ski resorts to shop their stores and hike or cycle their trails. Also here is one of the West's premier mountain vacation spots—Rocky Mountain National Park. Here you can enjoy some of the most spectacular high-elevation scenery in America, as well as outdoor activities from hiking to wildlife viewing to cross-country skiing.

ROCKY MOUNTAIN NATIONAL PARK ★★★

42 miles NW of Denver, 29 miles NW of Boulder

Snow-covered peaks—17 mountains above 13,000 feet—stand over lush valleys and shimmering alpine lakes in the 415 square miles (265,600 acres) of Rocky Mountain National Park. The highest, at 14,259 feet, is Longs Peak. As you rise and descend in altitude, the landscape of the park changes dramatically. Above 11,500 feet, the trees become increasingly gnarled and stunted, until they disappear altogether and alpine tundra predominates. Fully one-third of the park is at this altitude; in this bleak, rocky world, many of the plants are identical to those found in the Arctic.

Colorado has more elk than any other state, and this is their home turf: Look for large herds of elk in meadows and on mountainsides. Park visitors also often see mule deer, beavers, coyotes, and river otters. Watch for moose among the willows on the west side of the park. You also have a chance of seeing bighorn sheep, marmots, and ptarmigan along Trail Ridge Road.

A hiking paradise, Rocky Mountain National Park contains over 350 miles of hiking trails, ranging from short, easy walks to extremely strenuous hikes that require climbing skills. Overnight treks are also popular, as is fishing. In winter, when the park is shrouded in snow and Trail Ridge Road is closed, it's a perfect time for cross-country skiing and snowshoeing.

Essentials

ENTRY POINTS   Entry into the park is from either the east (through the town of Estes Park) or the west (through the town of Grand Lake). The east and west sides of the park are connected by Trail Ridge Road, open during summer and early fall, but closed to all motor vehicle traffic by snow the rest of the year. Most visitors enter the park from the Estes Park side. The **Beaver Meadows Entrance,** west of Estes Park via U.S. 36, leads to the Beaver Meadows Visitor Center and park headquarters, and is the most direct route to Trail Ridge Road. U.S. 34 west from Estes Park takes you into the park via the **Fall River Entrance,** which is north of the Beaver Meadows Entrance. From there you can access Old Fall River Road or Trail Ridge Road. Those entering the park from the west side should take U.S. 40 to Granby and then follow U.S. 34 north to the **Grand Lake Entrance.**

GETTING AROUND   Trail Ridge Road, the park's primary east-west roadway, is one of America's great alpine highways. It cuts west through the middle of the park from Estes Park, then south down its western boundary to Grand Lake. Climbing to 12,183 feet near Fall River Pass, it's the highest continuous paved highway in the United States. The road is usually open from Memorial Day into October, depending on snowfall. The 48-mile scenic drive from Estes Park to Grand Lake takes about 3 hours, allowing for stops at numerous scenic outlooks.

Fall River Road, the original park road, leads to Fall River Pass from Estes Park via Horseshoe Park. West of the Endovalley picnic area, the road is one-way uphill and is closed to trailers and motor homes. As you negotiate its gravelly switchbacks, you get a clear idea of what early auto travel was like in the West. It, too, is closed in winter. One of the few paved roads in the Rockies that leads into a high mountain basin is **Bear Lake Road;** it is kept open year-round, with occasional half-day closings to clear snow. Numerous trails converge at Bear Lake, southwest of the visitor center.

In summer, a free national park **shuttle bus** runs from Moraine Park Campground, Moraine Park Museum, and the Glacier Basin parking area to Bear Lake, with departures every 10 to 30 minutes. Free shuttle buses also run throughout the business district of Estes Park and from Estes Park into Rocky Mountain National Park. The buses run daily from July through Labor Day; schedules are available at the Estes Park Visitor Center (p. 125).

FEES & REGULATIONS   Park admission for up to a week costs $20 per vehicle or $10 per person for motorcyclists, bicyclists, and pedestrians.

As is true for most of the national parks, wilderness permits are required for all overnight backpacking trips, and camping is allowed only in specified campsites. Pets must be leashed, aren't permitted on trails or in the backcountry, and may not be left unattended anywhere, including vehicles and campsites. Both motor vehicles and bicycles must remain on roads or in parking areas. Do not feed or touch any park animals, and do not pick any wildflowers.

VISITOR CENTERS & INFORMATION   Entering the park from Estes Park, the **Beaver Meadows Visitor Center** on U.S. 36 has knowledgeable people to answer questions and give advice, a wide choice of books and maps for sale, and interpretive exhibits, including a relief model of the park. It's open daily from 8am to 4:30pm.

Outside the park, just east of the Fall River entrance, is the **Fall River Visitor Center.** Located in a beautiful mountain lodge–style building, it was built with private funds but is staffed by park rangers and volunteers from the Rocky Mountain Nature Association from 9am to 5pm daily. It contains kid-friendly exhibits on the park and its wildlife, plus an information desk, and a bookstore. Next door is a large souvenir-and-clothing shop plus a cafeteria-style restaurant with snacks and sandwiches.

Near the park's west side entrance is the **Kawuneeche Visitor Center,** open daily from 8am to 4:30pm. Located high in the mountains (11,796 ft. above sea level) is the **Alpine Visitor Center,** at Fall River Pass, open from late spring through early fall, daily from 10:30am to 4:30pm; exhibits here explain life on the alpine tundra.

For more information, contact **Rocky Mountain National Park** (© **970/586-1206** or 970/586-1222 for a recording; www.nps.gov/romo). You can also get detailed information from the **Rocky Mountain Conservancy** (© **970/586-0108;** www.rm conservancy.org), which sells a variety of maps, books, and videos and conducts field seminars in the park.

SEASONS Even though the park is technically open daily year-round, Trail Ridge Road, the main east-west thoroughfare through the park, is almost always closed in winter. The road is usually open by late May (after the snow has been cleared) and closes between mid- and late October. However, it is not uncommon for snowstorms to close the road for several hours or even a full day at any time, especially in early June and October. The high country is open during the summer and as snow conditions permit in winter.

AVOIDING THE CROWDS Because large portions of the park are closed in winter, most people visit the park from late spring through early fall. The busiest period, though, is from mid-June to mid-August. In order to avoid the largest crowds, try to visit just before or just after that period. For those who don't mind chilly evenings, late September and early October are less crowded and can be beautiful, although there's always the chance of an early winter storm. Regardless of when you visit, the absolute best way to avoid crowds is by putting on a backpack or climbing onto a horse. Rocky Mountain has some 350 miles of trails leading into all corners of the park (see "Hiking & Backpacking," p. 121).

RANGER PROGRAMS Evening programs take place at campground amphitheaters, and additional talks and programs are offered at visitor centers between June and September. Consult the park's free newspaper for scheduled activities, which vary from photo walks to fly-fishing and orienteering.

Exploring the Park

Although Rocky Mountain National Park is generally considered the domain of hikers and climbers, it's surprisingly easy to thoroughly enjoy this park without working up a sweat. For that we can thank **Trail Ridge Road.** Built in 1932 and undoubtedly one of America's most scenic highways, it provides expansive and sometimes dizzying views in all directions. The drive from Estes Park to Grand Lake covers some 48 miles through the park, rising above 12,000 feet in elevation and crossing the Continental Divide. It offers spectacular vistas of snowcapped peaks, deep forests, and meadows of wildflowers, where bighorn sheep, elk, and deer graze. Allow at least 3 hours for the drive, and more if you'd like to take a short hike from one of the many vista points.

To get a close look at the tundra, pull off Trail Ridge Road into the **Rock Cut** parking area (elevation 12,110 ft.), about halfway along the scenic drive. The views of glacially carved peaks along the Continental Divide are spectacular, and signs on the half-mile Tundra Nature Trail identify the hardy plants and animals that inhabit the region and explain how they have adapted to the harsh environment.

Outdoor Activities

Rocky Mountain National Park is a fantastic area for a variety of outdoor activities, and many activities also take place just outside the park in the 1,240-square-mile Roosevelt National Forest. In Estes Park, a **Forest Service Information Center** is located at 161 Second St. (© **970/586-3440**); it's usually open daily from 9am to 5pm in summer.

BICYCLING Bicyclists will have to share the roadways with motor vehicles along narrow roads with 5 percent to 7 percent grades. As in most national parks, bikes are not permitted off established roads. However, bicyclists still enjoy the challenge and scenery. One popular 16-mile ride is the **Horseshoe Park/Estes Park Loop,** which goes from Estes Park west on U.S. 34 past Aspenglen Campground and the park's Fall River entrance, and then heads east at the Deer Ridge Junction, following U.S. 36 through the Beaver Meadows park entrance. There are plenty of beautiful mountain views; allow 1 to 3 hours. A free park brochure provides information on safety, regulations, and other suggested routes. **New Venture Cycling** (© **970/231-2736;** www. newventurecycling.com) offers guided downhill and off-road tours in and around the park for $75 to $150 per person. Rentals are available for $39 to $55 daily from **Estes Park Mountain Shop,** 2050 Big Thompson Ave. (© **866/303-6548** or 970/586-6548; www.estesparkmountainshop.com).

CLIMBING & MOUNTAINEERING **Colorado Mountain School,** 341 Moraine Ave., Estes Park (© **800/836-4008,** ext. 3; www.coloradomountainschool.com), is an AMGA accredited year-round guide service, and the sole concessionaire for technical climbing and instruction in Rocky Mountain National Park. The school offers a wide range of programs, including a 2-day mountaineering class for $475 and the guided group hike up Longs Peak starting at $275 per person. The school also offers lodging in a hostel-type setting for $25 per person per night, with closures in fall and spring. Be sure to stop at the ranger station at the Longs Peak trailhead for current trail and weather information before attempting to ascend Longs Peak.

EDUCATIONAL PROGRAMS The **Rocky Mountain Conservancy** (p. 120) offers a wide variety of seminars and workshops, ranging from 1 full day to several days. Subjects vary but might include songbirds, flower identification, edible and medicinal herbs, painting, wildlife photography, tracking park animals, and edible mushrooms. Rates are $35 to $125 for half- and full-day programs and $175 and up for multiday programs.

FISHING Four species of trout are fished in national park and national forest streams and lakes: brown, rainbow, brook, and cutthroat. (Only the cutthroat are natives.) A state fishing license is required (nonresidents: $9 for 1 day or $26 for a year, plus a $10 habitat stamp), and only artificial lures or flies are permitted in the park. A number of lakes and streams in the national park are closed to fishing, including Bear Lake. A free park brochure that's available at visitor centers lists open and closed bodies of water, plus regulations and other information.

HIKING & BACKPACKING Park visitor centers sell U.S. Geological Survey topographic maps and guidebooks, and rangers can direct you to lesser-used trails.

Keep in mind that all trails here start at over—sometimes well over—7,000 feet elevation, and even the easiest and flattest walks will likely be tiring for those accustomed to lower elevations.

One particularly enjoyable (and easy) hike is the **Alberta Falls Trail** from the Glacier Gorge Parking Area (.6 mile one-way), which rises in elevation only 160 feet as it follows Glacier Creek to pretty Alberta Falls.

Starting at Bear Lake, the trail up to **Emerald Lake** offers spectacular scenery en route, past Nymph and Dream lakes. The .5-mile hike to Nymph Lake is easy, climbing 225 feet; from there the trail is rated moderate to Dream Lake (another .6 mile) and then on to Emerald Lake (another .7 mile), which is 605 feet higher than the starting point at Bear Lake.

Among my favorite moderate hikes here is the **Mills Lake Trail,** a 2.8-mile (one-way) hike, with a rise in elevation of about 700 feet. Starting from Glacier Gorge Junction, the trail goes up to a picturesque mountain lake, nestled in a valley among towering mountain peaks. This lake is an excellent spot for photographing dramatic Longs Peak, especially in late afternoon or early evening.

In the Wild Basin unit near Allenspark, the **Ouzel Falls Trail,** 2.7 miles one-way, is a great moderate hike as well; floods took out a bridge in 2013, so continuing to Ouzel Lake might be impossible. **Cascade Falls,** near Grand Lake, is a 3.5-mile waterfall hike that is also highly recommended, especially in fall. From Grand Lake, the East Inlet Trailhead will get you on a 0.6-mile round trip to **Adams Falls,** or further along, the picturesque hike to **Lone Pine Lake,** 5.5 miles one-way.

If you prefer a more strenuous adventure, tackle the 8-mile (one-way) **Longs Peak Trail,** which climbs some 4,855 feet along steep ledges and through narrows to the top of Longs Peak.

Backcountry permits (required for all overnight hikes) can be obtained at Park Headquarters and ranger stations (in summer) for $20 from May to October, free from November to April. For information, call © **970/586-1242.** There is a 7-night backcountry camping limit from June to September, with no more than 3 nights at any one spot.

HORSEBACK RIDING   Many of the national park's trails are open to horseback riders. Several outfitters provide guided rides inside and outside the park, including 2-hour rides (about $50). There are also all-day rides ($120–$150, bring your own lunch) plus breakfast and dinner rides and multiday pack trips. Recommended companies include **SK Horses** (www.cowpokecornercorral.com), which operates **National Park Gateway Stables,** at the Fall River entrance of the national park on U.S. 34 (© **970/586-5269**); and the **Cowpoke Corner Corral,** at Glacier Lodge, 3 miles west of town, 2166 Colo. 66 (© **970/586-5890**). Sombrero Ranches (© **970/586-4577;** www.sombrero.com) operates two stables inside park boundaries, **Moraine Park Stables** (© **970/586-2327**) and **Glacier Creek Stables** (© **970/586-3244**), as well as stables in Estes Park, Grand Lake, and Allenspark.

SKIING & SNOWSHOEING   Much of the park is closed to vehicular travel during the winter, when deep snow covers roads and trails. Snow is usually best January through March. A popular spot for cross-country skiing and snowshoeing in the park is Bear Lake, south of the Beaver Meadows entrance. A lesser-known area of the park is Wild Basin, south of the park's east entrances off Colo. 7, about a mile north of the community of Allenspark. A 2-mile road, closed to motor vehicles for the last mile in winter, winds through a subalpine forest to the Wild Basin Trailhead, which follows a creek to a waterfall, a rustic bridge, and eventually another waterfall. Total distance to the second falls is 2.8 miles. Along the trail, your chances are good for spotting birds such as Clark's nutcrackers, Steller's jays, and the American dipper. On winter weekends, the Colorado Mountain Club often opens a warming hut at the Wild Basin Ranger Station.

Before you set forth, stop by a visitor center for maps, information on where the snow is best, and a permit if you plan to stay out overnight. Rangers often lead guided snowshoe walks on winter weekends. Among shops that rent snowshoes and skis is **Estes Park Mountain Shop,** 2050 Big Thompson Ave. (© **866/303-6548** or 970/586-6548; www.estesparkmountainshop.com). Daily rental costs $5 per pair of snowshoes or $15 for cross-country skis.

WILDLIFE VIEWING & BIRD-WATCHING   Rocky Mountain National Park is a premier wildlife-viewing area; fall, winter, and spring are the best times, although I saw plenty of elk and squirrels, plus a few deer, a marmot, and a coyote, during a mid-July visit. Large herds of elk and bighorn sheep can often be seen in the meadows and on mountainsides. In addition, you may spot mule deer, beavers, coyotes, and river otters. Watch for moose among the willows on the west side of the park. In the forests are lots of songbirds and small mammals; particularly plentiful are gray and Steller's jays, Clark's nutcrackers, chipmunks, and golden-mantled ground squirrels. There's a good chance of seeing bighorn sheep, marmots, pikas, and ptarmigan along Trail Ridge Road. For detailed and current wildlife-viewing information, stop by one of the park's visitor centers, and check on the many interpretive programs, including bird walks. Rangers stress that it is both illegal and foolish to feed any wildlife.

Camping

The best place to camp for those visiting the national park is in the park itself. Although you won't have the modern conveniences of commercial campgrounds (see "Camping," in the Estes Park section), you will have plenty of trees, an abundance of wildlife scurrying by your tent or RV, and a true national park experience. The park has five campgrounds with a total of almost 600 sites. There are 245 sites at **Moraine Park;** another 150 are at **Glacier Basin.** Moraine Park, **Timber Creek** (98 sites), and **Longs Peak** (26 tent sites) are open year-round; Glacier Basin and **Aspenglen** (54 sites) are seasonal. Camping in summer is limited to 3 days at Longs Peak and 7 days at other campgrounds; the limit is 14 days at all the park's campgrounds in winter. Arrive early in summer if you hope to snare one of these first-come, first-served campsites. Reservations for Moraine Park and Glacier Basin are accepted from Memorial Day to early September and are usually completely booked well in advance. However, any sites not reserved—as well as sites at Timber Creek, Longs Peak, and Aspenglen—are available on a first-come, first-served basis. Make reservations with the **National Park Reservation Service** (© **877/444-6777,** or 518/885-3639 for international callers; www.recreation.gov). Campsites cost $20 per night during the summer, $14 in the off-season when water is turned off. No showers or RV hookups are available.

ESTES PARK & GRAND LAKE ★

71 miles NW of Denver, 42 miles SW of Fort Collins, 34 miles NW of Boulder

Estes Park is the eastern gateway to Rocky Mountain National Park, and Grand Lake is the closest town to the park's western entrance. Of the two, Estes Park is more developed. It has more lodging and dining choices, as well as a few noteworthy sights that are worth a visit. If you're driving to Rocky Mountain National Park via Boulder or Denver, you'll want to make Estes Park your base camp.

Estes Park

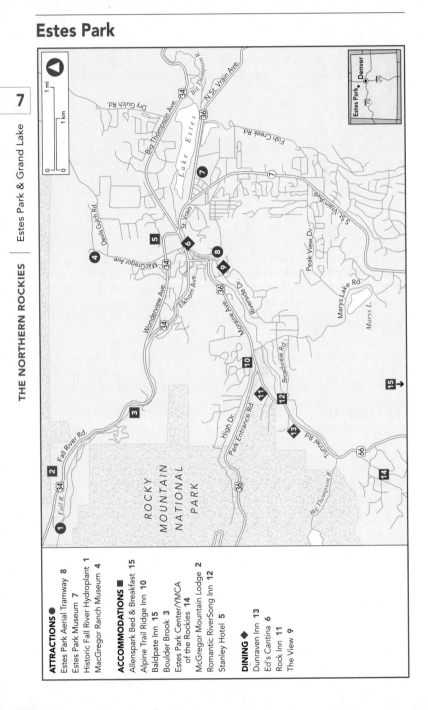

ATTRACTIONS ●
Estes Park Aerial Tramway **8**
Estes Park Museum **7**
Historic Fall River Hydroplant **1**
MacGregor Ranch Museum **4**

ACCOMMODATIONS ■
Allenspark Bed & Breakfast **15**
Alpine Trail Ridge Inn **10**
Baldpate Inn **15**
Boulder Brook **3**
Estes Park Center/YMCA
   of the Rockies **14**
McGregor Mountain Lodge **2**
Romantic RiverSong Inn **12**
Stanley Hotel **5**

DINING ◆
Dunraven Inn **13**
Ed's Cantina **6**
Rock Inn **11**
The View **9**

Grand Lake is a more rustic spot, with plenty of places to camp, a number of motels, and a few guest ranches. If you're coming from Steamboat Springs or Glenwood Springs, Grand Lake is a more convenient base. At any time of year, you can get there via U.S. 34. In summer, you can also get to Grand Lake by taking the Trail Ridge Road through Rocky Mountain National Park from Estes Park (closed in winter).

Estes Park

Unlike most Colorado mountain communities where mining was the economic bedrock before tourism emerged, Estes Park (elevation 7,522 ft.) has always been a resort town. Long known by Utes and Arapahos, it was "discovered" in 1859 by rancher Joel Estes. He soon sold his homestead and it later fell into the hands of Griff Evans, who built it into a lodging operation. One of Evans's guests, the Irish Earl of Dunraven, was so taken by the region that he purchased most of the valley and operated it as his private game reserve, until thwarted by such settlers as Alexander MacGregor, a lawyer and rancher, and W. E. James, who built Elkhorn Lodge.

The growth of Estes Park, however, is inextricably linked with two individuals: Freelan Stanley and Enos Mills. Stanley invented the steam-powered Stanley Steamer automobile in 1899 with his brother Francis, and then he settled in Estes Park, launched a Stanley Steamer shuttle service from Denver, and built the landmark Stanley Hotel in 1909. Mills was one of the prime advocates for the establishment of Rocky Mountain National Park. Although less well known than John Muir, Mills is an equally important figure in the history of the U.S. conservation movement. His efforts resulted in President Woodrow Wilson signing a bill to set aside 400 square miles for Rocky Mountain National Park in 1915. Today the park attracts 3 million visitors annually. Estes Park, meanwhile, has a year-round population of about 6,000.

ESSENTIALS

GETTING THERE   By Car   The most direct route is U.S. 36 from Denver and Boulder. At Estes Park, U.S. 36 joins U.S. 34, which runs up the Big Thompson Canyon from I-25 and Loveland, and continues through Rocky Mountain National Park to Grand Lake and Granby. An alternative scenic route to Estes Park is Colo. 7, the "Peak-to-Peak Scenic Byway" that traverses Central City (Colo. 119), Nederland (Colo. 72), and Allenspark (Colo. 7) under different designations. *Note:* U.S. 34 and U.S. 36 were damaged by the 2013 floods; 34 reopened but crews were hadn't finished 36 by the time we went to press in the fall of 2014. Visit **www.coloradodot.info** for current information.

By Plane   The closest airport is Denver International Airport, 75 miles away. The **Estes Park Shuttle** (✆ **970/586-5151;** www.estesparkshuttle.com) connects DIA with Estes Park. Rates are $45 one-way and $85 round-trip.

GETTING AROUND   Shuttle buses also operate throughout Estes Park and into Rocky Mountain National Park. The buses run daily from July through Labor Day; schedules are available at the Estes Park Visitor Center (see "Visitor Information," below). Local cab service is provided by **Peak-to-Peak Taxi** (✆ **970/586-6111**).

VISITOR INFORMATION   **Estes Park Visitor Center** on U.S. 34, just east of its junction with U.S. 36 at 500 Big Thompson Ave. (✆ **800/443-7837** or 970/577-9900; www.estesparkcvb.com), is open daily year-round.

FAST FACTS   The **Estes Park Medical Center,** with a 24-hour emergency room, is at 555 Prospect Ave. (✆ **970/586-2317;** www.epmedcenter.com). The **post office** is at

215 W. Riverside Dr. Call the U.S. Postal Service (© **800/275-8777;** www.usps.com) for hours and locations of other post offices. For statewide **road conditions,** call © **303/639-1111** or check **www.cotrip.org.**

Where to Stay
EXPENSIVE

Boulder Brook ★★ Low-key, romantic, and nestled in a gorgeous woodland on Fall River, this is a smart pick for couples that want a bit of privacy and good access to the trails in Rocky Mountain National Park. Accommodations have an understated Western vibe and plenty of room. Spa suites have jetted tubs; many rooms are built right on the river. In-room massages are available.

1900 Fall River Rd., Estes Park. © **800/238-0910** or 970/586-0910. www.boulderbrook.com. 19 units. $169–$269 double (3-night minimum stay). **Amenities:** Year-round outdoor hot tub; free Wi-Fi.

Romantic RiverSong Inn ★★★ All sorts of romance are on offer at this nifty B&B, located at the serene dead end of a dirt road. Rooms in the historic Craftsman-style home and adjacent cottages might feature a log-cabin theme (with a bed made of Paul Bunyan–size logs and a rock fireplace—ask for the "Meadow Bright" room), pretty Victorian decor, or a "Little House on the Prairie"–style nook bed covered by colorful quilts. The B&B is one of the best in the Rockies. Hearty breakfasts are cooked with hikers in mind, including potato pancakes and French toast.

1765 Lower Broadview Rd., Estes Park. © **970/586-4666.** www.romanticriversong.com. 10 units. $175–$350 double. Rates include full breakfast. Not suitable for small children. **Amenities:** Free Wi-Fi.

Stanley Hotel ★★ One event shaped the modern reputation of this fabled hotel: Horror writer Stephen King's checking in to room 217 in 1974. The experience served as the inspiration for "The Shining," and this, in tandem with ghost stories galore, makes a stay an absolute must for horror (and King) fans. Nighttime ghost tours ($20–$25) are hugely popular with guests and nonguests alike. Although Stanley Kubrick did not film his 1980 adaptation here, you can just imagine Jack Nicholson bellying up to the ethereal-looking Whiskey Bar, a relatively new addition with the largest selection of whiskeys in Colorado. Standard rooms can be quite small (people were smaller when the hotel was built), but they feature very comfy beds and stylish furnishings; king rooms and suites are significantly larger (as are the one- to three-bedroom condos located on hotel grounds), and you will pay a serious premium for the privilege of sleeping in no. 217 or another allegedly haunted room. Next door is the recently renovated **Lodge at the Stanley,** a smaller replica of the hotel built in 1911 and now offering a luxurious, B&B-like atmosphere. The hotel was opened by F. O. Stanley, the Stanley Steamer tycoon, in 1909.

333 Wonderview Ave., Estes Park. © **800/976-1377** or 970/577-4000. www.stanleyhotel.com. 140 units. $149–$399 double; $300–$700 suite or presidential cottage. Lodge rates include continental breakfast. **Amenities:** Restaurant; lounge; fitness center; spa; free Wi-Fi.

INEXPENSIVE TO MODERATE
In addition to the properties that follow, the best value in town is the **Alpine Trail Ridge Inn,** 927 Moraine Ave. (© **800/233-5023** or 970/586-4585; www.alpinetrail-ridgeinn.com), with summer rates $97 to $150 double, or $147 to $250 for a suite or family unit. Just outside the Fall River Entrance to Rocky Mountain National Park, **McGregor Mountain Lodge,** 815 Fall River Rd. (© **970/586-3457;** www.

mcgregormountainlodge.com), is another good mid-priced option, with summer rates of $135 to $155 double and $165 to $395 for a cottage or a suite. There are also cabins and cottages available at several area campgrounds (see "Camping," below).

Allenspark Lodge Bed & Breakfast ★★ This historic three-story lodge was built in 1933 and is my pick for those looking to focus on the Wild Basin unit of Rocky Mountain National Park. Woodsy to the nines, the property captures the national-park vibe better than its peers in Estes Park proper. The Great Room is one for the ages, and the upstairs guest rooms are small and historic with no shortage of creaky charm. There is a good family room with a queen bed and twin bunks, as well as a full kitchen.

184 Main St. (15 miles south of Estes Park), Allenspark. ℂ **303/747-2552.** www.allensparklodge. com. 13 units, 7 with bathroom. $105–$150 double. Rates include full breakfast. Children 13 and under not accepted. **Amenities:** Bar; indoor Jacuzzi; free Wi-Fi.

Baldpate Inn ★★ Pure Colorado and full of quirks, the Baldpate Inn has long stood under the watchful gaze of the Twin Sisters, aptly named peaks waiting to be summited by trails right out of the front door. Named after the 1913 mystery novel, "The Seven Keys to Baldpate," the key room here has 20,000 keys hanging from the ceiling and walls, donated by guests over the years. Rooms are basic, with quilts and shared or private baths but they have undeniable charm; there are also a quartet of cabins here that can accommodate up to six guests. The restaurant is known for its tasty soup-and-salad buffets.

4900 S. Colo. 7 (7 miles south of Estes Park), Estes Park. ℂ **866/577-5397** or 970/586-6151. www. baldpateinn.com. 12 units (2 with private bathroom), 4 cabins. $130 double with shared bathroom; $150 double with private bathroom; $230 cabin per double ($15 per additional person). Rates include full breakfast. Closed Nov–Apr. **Amenities:** Restaurant; free Wi-Fi.

Estes Park Center/YMCA of the Rockies ★★ The family-friendliest lodging in family-friendly Estes Park, this massive complex backs right up to the boundary of Rocky Mountain National Park. Perfect for weekend getaways as well as family reunions, the overnight options range from lodge rooms to yurts to sizable cabins (the largest sleep 10 people)—more than 700 units in all—and four pay-as-you-go restaurants. None of the digs is upscale or trendy, but that's beside the point here (and they *are* well-maintained and comfortable). The list of activities is mind-boggling: Guests can ride horses, tackle a challenge course, make crafts, hike, bike, play a round of minigolf, and—after dark—roast marshmallows on a campfire.

2515 Tunnel Rd., Estes Park. ℂ **970/586-3341** or 303/448-1616. www.ymcarockies.org. 510 lodge rooms, 205 cabins. Summer $94–$164 double, $139–$429 cabin; lower rates fall to spring. YMCA members get $15 discount. Pets accepted in cabins but not in lodge rooms. **Amenities:** 4 restaurants; bike rentals; children's program; indoor heated pool; tennis courts (3 outdoor); free Wi-Fi.

CAMPING

There are a number of commercial campgrounds in Estes Park. All offer RV hookups and clean bathhouses, and are open from late spring to early fall only. They include **Estes Park KOA,** 2051 Big Thompson Ave. (ℂ **800/562-1887** for reservations, or 970/586-2888; www.estesparkkoa.com), with RV rates for two of $38 to $58, tent sites for $27 to $45, and cabins for $59 to $146; three county-owned facilities in the **Estes Park Campground at Mary's Lake,** 2120 Mary's Lake Rd., **Estes Park Campground at East Portal,** 3420 Tunnel Rd., and **Hermit Park Campground,** 17 Hermit Park Rd. (ℂ **800/397-7795;** www.larimercamping.com), all with rates of $15 to $37 for tent and RV sites as well as cabins at Hermit Park for $80; the family-oriented **Yogi Bear's Jellystone Park of Estes,** 5495 U.S. 36 (ℂ **970/658-2536;** www.jellystoneofestes.com), with campsites for $32 to $72 and cabins for about $60 to $400; and **Spruce Lake R.V.**

Resort, 1050 Mary's Lake Rd. (📞 **800/536-1050** or 970/586-2889; www.sprucelakerv. com), charging $53 to $64 for an RV site and $150 to $200 for a cabin.

Where to Eat
EXPENSIVE

Dunraven Inn ★★ ITALIAN   The place to go for an upscale Italian dinner for a generation, the Dunraven Inn is tucked away in the trees on Colo. 66, halfway before it dead-ends. Countless renditions of the Mona Lisa hang on the walls and more than $16,000 worth of dollar bills wallpaper the bar. The Italian dishes are uniformly good, from lobster ziti to chicken parmesan, and there are also steaks and seafood specialties. I'm a particular fan of the gorgonzola-stuffed filet mignon and the namesake dish, the Lord Dunraven, a center-cut charbroiled sirloin steak.

2470 Colo. 66. 📞 **970/586-6409.** www.dunraveninn.com. Main courses $13–$45. Daily 4–9pm.

The View ★★ FRENCH/AMERICAN   For a romantic spot, look no further than the resident fine-dining restaurant at Crags Lodge, perched above downtown. The menu primarily offers beef and Colorado lamb dishes with inventive preparations—think blackened sirloin and blue cheese rib-eye—as well as a nice selection of poultry and pasta.

At Historic Crags Lodge, 300 Riverside Dr. 📞 **970/586-6066.** www.view-restaurant.com. Main courses $11–$33 dinner. Daily 5–9pm. Closed mid-Oct to mid-May.

INEXPENSIVE TO MODERATE

Beyond the restaurants that follow, **Bob & Tony's Pizza,** 124 W. Elkhorn Ave. (📞 **970/586-2044**), is a touristy pizzeria downtown with redbrick walls covered with chalk signatures. Big breakfasts are the specialty of the **Egg & I,** 393 E. Elkhorn Ave. (📞 **970/586-1173**). South of town, the quirky **Baldpate Inn** (p. 127) has a locally beloved soup-and-salad buffet.

Ed's Cantina ★ MEXICAN   Fronted by a convivial bar and featuring a riverside patio out back, this colorful, kid-friendly bar and grill has been in business since 1985, offering an eclectic Mexican menu. The expected tacos and burritos are complemented by squash-stuffed poblano peppers, bison tacos, and spinach enchiladas, plus a number of gluten-free options. Any description of Ed's without a mention of the margaritas would be remiss—make mine an "avocado".

390 E. Elkhorn Ave. 📞 **970/586-2919.** www.edscantina.com. Main courses $7–$15. Daily 11am–9pm. Bar open later with a limited menu.

Rock Inn ★★★ AMERICAN   Built in 1937 as a big-band dance hall, this is my favorite spot in Estes Park. It is not just the woodsy atmosphere, which has the best national-park-lodge feel in the area, from the stuffed animal heads to the log beams. It's also that the patio has great views, the beer is cold, and the food is first-rate, from roasted beets for starters to the steaks, pastas, burgers, and pizzas for the main event. Brunch includes "Biscuit Burgers," and egg dishes on Sundays. Expect live music and a bit of a wait in peak season.

1675 Colo. 66, south of the intersection with U.S. 36. 📞 **970/586-4116.** www.rockinnestes.com. Main courses $9–$33. Summer Mon–Wed 4–9pm; Thurs–Sat 4–10pm; Sun 10am–9pm. Shorter winter hours. Bar open later.

Exploring Estes Park

Estes Park Aerial Tramway ★   This tram, which climbs 1,100 vertical feet in less than 5 minutes, offers a ride up the side of Prospect Mountain and provides panoramic views of Longs Peak, the Continental Divide, and Estes Park itself. You'll find a gift shop, a snack bar, and an observation deck at the upper terminal, and several trails converge atop the mountain. Allow at least 1 hour.

420 E. Riverside Dr. (✆) **970/586-3675.** www.estestram.com. Admission $12 adults, $11 seniors 60 and older, $8 children 6–11, free for children under 6. Late May to mid-Sept daily 9am–6pm.

Estes Park Museum ★★ The exploits and challenges of pioneers are chronicled at this intriguing museum. Exhibits cover the last 10,000 years of the area's history, from the depths of the Ice Age to the 20th century. Nearby, the Knoll-Willows Open Space holds the ruins of a cabin and other long-abandoned structures Allow about an hour. The museum also manages the **Historic Fall River Hydroplant,** at 1754 Fish Hatchery Rd. Summer hours are Tuesday through Sunday from 1 to 4pm.

200 Fourth St. (at U.S. 36). (✆) **970/586-6256.** www.estesparkmuseumfriends.org. Free admission; donations accepted. May–Oct Mon–Sat 10am–5pm, Sun 1–5pm. Closed Mon–Thurs in winter.

MacGregor Ranch Museum ★ This living-history attraction offers a look back at the ranching heritage of Estes Park with a number of perfectly preserved structures, including the 1896 ranch house, now a museum. But this is still a working cattle ranch, allowing visitors an up-close look at the hard work that comes along with ranching in the high country of Colorado. Allow 1 hour.

180 MacGregor Lane. (✆) **970/586-3749.** www.macgregorranch.org. Admission $5 adults, free for those 17 and under. Summer Tues–Sat 10am–4pm. Closed rest of year.

Shopping

Elkhorn Avenue is the main shopping area in Estes Park. Established in 1917, **Eagle Plume's,** south of town at 9853 S. Colo. 7 (✆ **303/747-2861;** www.eagleplume.com), is a one-of-a-kind museum/gallery that hocks a few souvenirs but mainly focuses on fine art and jewelry. Plenty of contemporary Native American arts, crafts, and jewelry are on display, many of them part of the collection of the store's namesake, the late Charles Eagle Plume.

Nightlife

Estes Park boasts a nice outdoor entertainment venue, **Performance Park,** on West Elkhorn Avenue on the west side of town. A free concert series is held Wednesday and Thursday nights June through August. For details on what's going on when you plan to be in town, contact the **Estes Park Visitor Center,** 500 Big Thompson Ave. (✆ **800/443-7837** or 970/577-9900; www.estesparkcvb.com), or check the website's comprehensive calendar.

The **Estes Park Music Festival** (✆ **970/586-9519;** www.estesparkmusicfestival.org) presents a series of classical music concerts on summer Mondays; and the **Estes Park Repertoire Theatre Company** (www.estesparkreptheatre.org) stages two plays a year.

Of local watering holes, the **Wheel Bar,** 132 E. Elkhorn Ave. (✆ **970/586-9381;** www.thewheelbar.com), which has been operated by the Nagl family since the 1940s, is the best. It's open every day but Christmas, serving as a community hub in more ways than one. The quirky joint has plenty of wheel decor, including a slowly rotating specimen behind the bar. There is also local beer at the **Estes Park Brewery,** 470 Prospect Village Dr. (✆ **970/586-5421**), and the **Rock Inn** (p. 128) has live music most nights.

Grand Lake

The western entrance to Rocky Mountain National Park is at the picturesque little town of Grand Lake, in the shade of Shadow Mountain at the park's southwestern corner.

Here, in the crisp mountain air at 8,370 feet above sea level, you can stroll down an old-fashioned boardwalk as one of the locals rides by on horseback. In fact, take away the automobiles and electric lights, and this town looks and feels like the late 1800s. Located in the Arapaho National Recreation Area, Grand Lake is surrounded by three lakes—Grand Lake itself, Shadow Mountain Reservoir, and Lake Granby—each with a marina offering boating, fishing, and other watersports. In the recreation area, you'll find miles of trails for hiking, horseback riding, four-wheeling, and mountain biking, which become cross-country skiing and snowmobiling trails in winter. You'll also see plenty of dead lodgepole pines: This is the epicenter of the state's mountain pine beetle infestation that has decimated over 1 million acres in recent years.

For further information on what to do in this area, stop at the **Visitor Information Center** on U.S. 34 at the turnoff into town, or contact the **Grand Lake Area Chamber of Commerce** (✆ **970/627-3402;** www.grandlakechamber.com). Information is also available from the Arapaho National Forest's **Sulphur Ranger District office,** 9 Ten Mile Dr., off U.S. 40 about a half-mile south of Granby (✆ **970/887-4100**), open daily in summer.

Where to Stay

MODERATE

Grand Lake Lodge ★★ This 1920 gem reopened in 2011 after a 5-year shutdown, with new ownership immediately bringing it back up to speed. Perched above Grand Lake, the remodeled and modernized cabins are mostly duplexes, offering several bed combinations in one room with a small bathroom, and there are also a couple of larger units that sleep up to 25 people. The lodge, fronted by the swings of "Colorado's Favorite Front Porch," is a classic, with a good restaurant (see "Where to Eat," below), gift shop, taxidermy galore, and plenty of places to sit and play antique pin-games or just while away the time around the colossal fireplace.

15500 U.S. 34, Grand Lake. ✆ 855/585-0004 or 970/627-3967. www.grandlakelodge.com. 70 units, including 2-, 3-, and 8-bedroom cabins. $135–$150 double; $225–$925 2-bedroom cabin or larger. Pets accepted ($10 per night). Closed Oct–May. **Amenities:** Restaurant; lounge; free Wi-Fi.

Where to Eat

Grand Lake Lodge (see "Where to Stay," above) also has an excellent restaurant with the best view on this side of the park. Open for three meals a day in peak season, the menu offers sandwiches and entrees like buffalo burgers, rainbow trout, and honey pepper salmon ($10–$24). In town, the **Backstreet Steakhouse and Pub** at Daven Haven Lodge, 604 Marina Dr. (✆ **970/627-8144;** www.backstreetsteakhouse.com), serves dinner nightly in summer, and the patio is picture-perfect. The house specialty, Jack Daniel's pork chops. Also on the menu are steaks, burgers, pasta, chicken, and fish. Main courses are $10 to $30.

MODERATE

Sagebrush BBQ & Grill ★ AMERICAN   I love the atmosphere at this old-fashioned place and so do others—it always draws a crowd. The appeal is understandable. The barbecue is excellent (especially the pulled pork and sausage with mustard barbecue sauce), you can throw your nutshells on the floor, and the full bar pours draft microbrew. Also on offer: burgers, steaks and game, and seafood, plus pasta, pizza, and burritos for good measure, as well as hearty breakfasts, such as huevos rancheros and biscuits and gravy.

1101 Grand Ave. ✆ **970/627-1404.** www.sagebrushbbq.com. Main courses $7–$15 breakfast; $8–$26 lunch and dinner. Daily 7am–10pm.

STEAMBOAT SPRINGS ★★

158 miles NW of Denver, 194 miles E of Grand Junction, 335 miles E of Salt Lake City, Utah

One of my favorite Colorado resort towns, Steamboat Springs fuses two very different worlds—a state-of-the-art ski village with a genuine Western ranching town. This historic town, with a population of about 15,000, is a pleasant laid-back community where ranchers still go about their business in cowboy boots and Stetsons, seemingly unaware of the fashion statement they are making to city-slicker visitors.

At an elevation of 6,695 feet, Steamboat Springs's numerous mineral springs and abundant wild game made this a summer retreat for Utes centuries before the arrival of white settlers. The bubbling mineral springs also caused many a mid-19th-century trapper to swear he heard the chugging sound of "a steamboat comin' round the bend"—hence the name. But prospectors never thrived here as they did elsewhere in the Rockies, though coal mining has proven profitable. Ranching and farming were the economic mainstays until tourism arrived, and agriculture remains key today.

Cowboys aside, this area is perhaps best known as the birthplace of organized skiing in Colorado. Although miners, ranchers, and mail carriers used primitive skis for transportation as early as the 1880s, it wasn't until Norwegian ski-jumping and cross-country champion Carl Howelsen built Howelsen Hill ski jump here in 1914 that skiing was considered a recreational sport in Colorado. In 1963, Storm Mountain was developed for skiing, and Steamboat's future as a modern ski resort was ensured. The mountain was renamed Mount Werner after the 1964 avalanche death of Olympic skier Buddy Werner, a Steamboat Springs native. Today the mountain is, more often than not, simply called Steamboat. Howelsen Hill, owned by the city of Steamboat Springs, continues to operate as a facility for ski jumpers, as well as a fun little downtown ski area.

Essentials

GETTING THERE   By Car   The most direct route to Steamboat Springs from Denver is via I-70 west to Silverthorne, Colo. 9 north to Kremmling, and U.S. 40 west to Steamboat. (*Note:* Rabbit Ears Pass, 25 miles east of Steamboat, often closes during winter storms.) If you're traveling east on I-70, exit at Rifle, proceed on Colo. 13 to Craig, then take U.S. 40 east to Steamboat. For statewide **road condition reports,** call 𝄞 303/639-1111 or visit **www.cotrip.org**.

By Plane   The **Yampa Valley Regional Airport (HDN),** 22 miles west of Steamboat Springs near Hayden (𝄞 **970/276-5001;** www.co.routt.co.us), is served by **United** year-round, plus **Alaska, American,** and **Delta** in ski season.

Ground transportation from Yampa Valley Regional Airport is provided by Go **Alpine Shuttle** (𝄞 **800/343-7433** or 970/879-2800; www.goalpine.com); the cost is about $60 per adult and $30 per child round-trip. The company also offers shuttle service between Steamboat and Denver International Airport for $180 per adult and $90 per child. **Avis, Hertz,** and **Budget** maintain locations at the airport.

GETTING AROUND   There are really two Steamboats. The ski resort, known as Steamboat Village, is about 2 miles southeast of the historic Steamboat Springs. If you're coming from Denver, U.S. 40 approaches Steamboat from the south and parallels the Yampa River through town. Mount Werner Road, which turns east off U.S. 40, leads directly to the ski resort, centered on Mount Werner Circle and Ski Time Square. U.S. 40 is known as Lincoln Avenue through the town of Steamboat, where it is crossed by Third through 13th streets. **Steamboat Springs Transit** (𝄞 **970/879-3717**)

Steamboat Springs

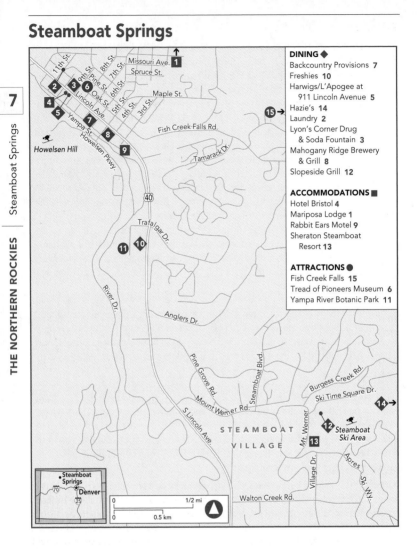

DINING ◆
Backcountry Provisions **7**
Freshies **10**
Harwigs/L'Apogee at
   911 Lincoln Avenue **5**
Hazie's **14**
Laundry **2**
Lyon's Corner Drug
   & Soda Fountain **3**
Mahogany Ridge Brewery
   & Grill **8**
Slopeside Grill **12**

ACCOMMODATIONS ■
Hotel Bristol **4**
Mariposa Lodge **1**
Rabbit Ears Motel **9**
Sheraton Steamboat
   Resort **13**

ATTRACTIONS ●
Fish Creek Falls **15**
Tread of Pioneers Museum **6**
Yampa River Botanic Park **11**

provides free rides throughout the area. Buses run approximately every 20 to 30 minutes during peak hours, less frequently at other times. **Go Alpine** (⟨ **970/879-2800**) provides local taxi service.

VISITOR INFORMATION   The **Steamboat Springs Chamber Resort Association,** 125 Anglers Dr. (⟨ **970/879-0880;** www.steamboat-chamber.com), operates a visitor center just east of downtown, open daily in summer.

FAST FACTS   The **Yampa Valley Medical Center,** 1024 Central Park Dr. (⟨ **970/879-1322;** www.yvmc.org), provides 24-hour medical service. The **post office** is at 200 Lincoln Ave. For hours and other information, contact the U.S. Postal Service (⟨ **800/275-8777;** www.usps.com).

Where to Stay

As at all Colorado ski resorts, rates get progressively higher the closer you get to the slopes. You'll pay the highest rates during the Christmas holiday season (mid-Dec to New Year's Day). Next highest are the rates charged during February and March. Value season is usually January, and the low season runs from Thanksgiving to mid-December and from April until the ski areas close. Rates are normally much lower during the summer, from Memorial Day to mid-October. *Note:* Because vacancy rates are so high during shoulder seasons—April to May and October to November—many accommodations close at these times.

Steamboat Central Reservations (© 877/783-2628; www.steamboat.com) can book your lodging and make virtually all of your travel arrangements. Be sure to ask about special packages and programs. **Steamboat Resorts by Wyndham Vacation Rentals** (© 800/276-6719 or 970/879-8000; www.wvrsteamboat.com) manages numerous properties, offering a variety of possibilities, from small lodge rooms for two to six-bedroom condos that will accommodate up to 14.

EXPENSIVE

Sheraton Steamboat Resort ★★ This is the definitive ski-in, ski-out resort hotel in Steamboat, home to the Nordic skiing center in winter and a top-rated golf course after the snow melts. A good pick for couples and families alike, the property is one of the few on the mountain with traditional hotel rooms, as well as the more common condos. The design of the former eschews Western motifs for contemporary ones, while the condos are woodsier, and the long list of modern amenities will please even the tech-savviest guests. New for the 2014-15 ski season are 56 luxury suites with kitchens, upgraded furnishings and amenities, and a new pool area with cabanas and fireplaces.

2200 Village Inn Court, Steamboat Springs. © **970/879-2220.** www.sheratonsteamboatresort. com. 285 units, including 20 condos, 56 suites, and 21 villas. Ski season $229–$539 double, $349–$1,700 condo, villa, or suite; summer/fall $149–$279 double, $189–$700 condo, villa, or suite. Higher holiday rates; lower rates in spring. Resort fee $20/day. Underground parking. Closed 6 weeks in spring. **Amenities:** 4 restaurants; bar; children's programs; concierge; 18-hole golf course; health club; 4 Jacuzzis; outdoor heated pool; room service; spa; free Wi-Fi.

MODERATE

Hotel Bristol ★ Built in the 1940s by the former police chief, the Bristol is the one of the few lodgings in downtown Steamboat Springs, and offers a much different experience than the condo-heavy complexes at the ski area. With an authentic historic ambiance, Hotel Bristol ratchets up the Old West quotient with black-and-white photos and Native American blankets in the rooms, and offers smallish standard rooms with two twins or one queen along with family rooms (two rooms connected by a shared bath) and more contemporary suites (converted from the former caretaker's unit) with a bit more elbow room.

917 Lincoln Ave., Steamboat Springs. © **800/851-0872** or 970/879-3083. www.steamboathotel bristol.com. 18 units, including suites. Summer and ski season $129–$159 double; $169–$229 family unit or suite. Higher holiday rates; lower rates fall. Resort fee 5 percent. Free off-street parking. Closed mid-Apr to late May. **Amenities:** Restaurant (Italian); 6-person indoor whirlpool; free Wi-Fi.

INEXPENSIVE

Mariposa Lodge ★★ Striking the perfect balance between convenience and privacy in a beautiful setting, the Mariposa has access to both downtown and the slopes with an in-town location that feels like anything but: It's located on the fringes of a residential area, with its own private pond and Soda Creek flowing through the premises. Rooms feature handmade quilts, log bed frames, and other rustic touches that nicely complement the views.

855 Grand St., Steamboat Springs. © **800/578-1467** or 970/879-1467. www.steamboatmariposa. com. 4 units. $159–$189 double. Rates include full breakfast. **Amenities:** Free Wi-Fi.

Rabbit Ears Motel ★ You can't miss the Rabbit Ears Motel—just look for the adorable vintage sign with its pink neon rabbit. The family-run roadside motel behind it is better than most, with reliably maintained rooms and a nifty location on the Yampa River just east of downtown. You will pay a bit more for a room with a view, but all of them have a nice array of in-room perks like fridges and coffeemakers.

201 Lincoln Ave., Steamboat Springs. © **800/828-7702** or 970/879-1150. www.rabbitearsmotel. com. 65 units. Summer and ski season $99–$169 double. Higher holiday rates; lower rates fall and spring. Children 11 and under stay free in parent's room. Rates include continental breakfast. Pets accepted ($20 one-time fee). **Amenities:** Free Wi-Fi.

Where to Eat

Many of the restaurants in Steamboat Springs cut back their hours or close completely in the slow seasons—primarily spring and fall.

EXPENSIVE

Harwigs/L'Apogée at 911 Lincoln Avenue ★★★ FRENCH Jamie and Sandy Jenny have expertly operated this downtown French eatery since 1985. Before that, it was Harwigs Saddlery and Western Wear for the better part of a century, and previous owners insisted that the Jennys keep the name, at least in part. That they have, but they've changed most everything else in the past decades, remodeling, installing an upstairs gallery and downstairs wine cellar, and planting an herb and vegetable garden out back from which they source much of what ends up on the plate in summer. Jamie is the chef, turning out such Gallic classics as rabbit and chestnut sausage and crispy duck breast as well as more Colorado-centric dishes, including local lamb chops and five-spice venison. The bar serves a lighter menu, and service is first-rate.

911 Lincoln Ave. © **970/879-1919.** www.lapogee.com. Main courses $29–$45; steaks $8 per ounce. Daily 5–10pm.

Hazie's ★★★ NEW AMERICAN Take the Silver Bullet Gondola 2,000 feet up to this on-mountain restaurant, at Steamboat Ski resort where three-course, prix-fixe dinners are paired with a spectacular view. The menu changes seasonally, but you will almost always find expertly prepared Colorado lamb, as well as fish, chicken, beef, and pasta selections for the main course. Reservations are recommended for lunch or brunch, but they are required for dinner.

Steamboat Ski Area, 2305 Mt. Werner Circle, Thunderbird Terminal, top of the Silver Bullet Gondola. © **970/871-5150.** www.steamboat.com. Main courses $12–$30 lunch; $24–$49 dinner 3-course meal $52 winter. Mid-Dec to early Apr daily 11:30am–2:30pm and 6–10pm; mid-June to Labor Day Thurs–Sat 7–10pm. Closed spring and fall.

MODERATE

Mahogany Ridge Brewery & Grill ★★ INTERNATIONAL This is one of the best brewpubs in the Rockies, and it owes as much as its appeal to its creative menu and stylish decor as it does to the beer. The menu ranges the globe from burgers to Thai-style baby-back ribs, as well as a number of "dipping entrees." Order up Yucatan pork tenderloin, citrus sea scallops, or Vietnamese tofu and your pick of sauce—options range from mango salsa to wasabi cream to smoked tomato demi-glace. Of the house beers, I'll get the Alpenglow, a rich amber ale that goes down especially smoothly after a day on the slopes.

435 Lincoln Ave. (at Fifth St.). ℭ **970/879-3773.** www.mahoganyridgesteamboat.com. Sandwiches and main courses $11–$19; dipping entrees $17–$31. Daily 4–11pm. Bar open later.

Laundry ★★ NEW AMERICAN   Located in the historic Steamboat Laundry building, this slick eatery opened in 2012, keeping a few of the rough edges for an industrial-chic vibe. The menu focuses on sharable small plates, such as pig-ear lettuce wraps (a creative touch), shrimp and grits, and salt cod fritters; the large plates emphasize local game and trout. The bar mixes up some great craft cocktails, often using historic and mighty strong recipes with such names as "Satan's Whiskers" and "El Diablo."

127 Eleventh St. ℭ **970/870-0681.** www.thelaundryrestaurant.com. Small plates $6–$15; main courses $20–$30. Mon and Wed–Fri 3–9pm; Tues 4–9pm; Sat 4–10pm; Sun 11am–9pm.

Slopeside Grill ★ AMERICAN/ITALIAN   Locals love this casual eatery at the ski area for its social atmosphere and terrific food. The extensive menu ranges from hummus to pizzas to burgers to main dishes as diverse as skirt steak alfredo, fish tacos, and meatloaf. The patio is just the place to be when it is not a blizzard out there, and the location—right off the Preview run—is ideal for a mid-ski snack or après-ski drink.

1855 Ski Time Sq. ℭ **970/879-2916.** www.slopesidegrill.com. Pizza $11–$14; main courses $9–$20. Daily 11am–10pm; pizza oven open until midnight (11pm in summer). Bar open later.

INEXPENSIVE

For a good sandwich to eat on the premises or in the woods, **Backcountry Provisions,** 635 Lincoln Ave. (ℭ **970/879-3617**), is the place, with creative offerings like the Sherpa (Asiago cheese, roasted eggplant, tomato, red peppers, and more) and the Timberline (peanut butter, banana, and local honey). Midway between the slopes and downtown, **Freshies,** 595 S. Lincoln Ave. (ℭ **970/879-8099**), is the local favorite for breakfast and lunch, with omelets, eggs "Benny," and a wide range of sandwiches and wraps. **Lyon's Corner Drug & Soda Fountain,** 840 Lincoln Ave. (ℭ **970/879-1114**), has an old-time soda fountain where you can get real malts, ice-cream sodas, egg creams, phosphates, sundaes, and fresh-squeezed lemonade.

Exploring Steamboat Springs

Downhill skiing is the prime attraction to most winter visitors, and summer brings a wide variety of recreational opportunities.

Skiing & Other Winter Activities

STEAMBOAT ★★★   When devoted skiers talk about Steamboat, they invent new adjectives to describe its incredibly light powder, of which about 350 inches a year falls on the place. The vertical drop here is one of the highest in Colorado: 3,668 feet from the 10,568-foot summit.

Six peaks compose the 2,965-acre ski area: Mount Werner, Christie, Storm, Sunshine, Pioneer Ridge, and Thunderhead. Christie Peak, the lower mountain area, is ideal for beginners. Thunderhead Peak, served by a high-speed detachable quad chairlift called the Thunderhead Express and the gondola, is great for intermediate and advanced skiers and riders. The Morningside Park lift accesses expert and extreme diamond terrain—chutes, advanced mogul runs, powder bowls, and one-of-a-kind tree skiing, all from the top of Mount Werner. Buddy's Run, one of the Rockies' great intermediate cruisers, is located on Storm Peak. The most famous tree runs—Shadows,

Closet, and Twilight—are on Sunshine Peak. The longest run is Why Not, at over 3 miles. Steamboat is a great mountain for snowboarders, who love Mavericks Superpipe, which is 56 feet wide and 450 feet long.

Regular-season lift tickets (2013–14 prices) cost $115 per day for adults, $95 for youth 13 to 17, $81 for seniors 70 and older, and $69 for children under 13. Kids under 13 ski free when their parents buy the same number of days. Night skiing is offered Wednesday through Sunday for $29 adults and $19 kids. Rates are lowest at the beginning of the season, highest during the Christmas and New Year's holidays, and a bit lower the rest of the season; snow conditions can also affect pricing (making it go up when skiing is good and down when the snow is paltry). Discounts are available for 3 or more days or buying online a week in advance, and the ticket window for 1 day is always most expensive. Lessons and rentals are available.

Steamboat is usually open from the third week in November through mid-April, daily from 8:30am to 4pm. For further information, contact **Steamboat Ski & Resort Corporation** (© **970/879-6111** or 970/879-7300 for snow reports; www.steamboat.com).

HOWELSEN HILL ★   In addition to Steamboat, there's Howelsen Hill (© **970/879-8499;** www.steamboatsprings.net), which has remained open every winter since its first day in 1915, making it the oldest ski area in continuous use in Colorado. The first accredited public-school ski classes in North America were taught on this slope, which is operated by the city of Steamboat Springs, and sees many future Olympians starting off practicing after school. It offers both day and night skiing and snowboarding on 30 acres of terrain.

Tickets (2013–14 prices) are $20 for adults and $15 for children 7 to 18 and seniors 60 and older, $8 for kids under 7, and $10 for everyone for night skiing. It's open from late November through late March Tuesday and Friday 1 to 6pm, Wednesday and Thursday from 1 to 8pm, and Saturday and Sunday 10am to 4pm.

Howelsen Hill has bred more North American skiers for international competition than any other ski resort—primarily because of its ski-jumping complex. The U.S. ski-jumping team trains each year on the 20m, 30m, 50m, 70m, and 90m jumps; there is also a new year-round jump. For more information, contact the **Steamboat Springs Winter Sports Club** (© **970/879-0695;** www.sswsc.org).

CROSS-COUNTRY SKIING   Seasoned cross-country skiers swear by the **Steamboat Ski Touring Center** at the Sheraton Steamboat Resort (© **970/879-8180;** www.nordicski.net). Some 19 miles of groomed cross-country trails are set beside Fish Creek, near the foot of the mountain; there are also 6 miles of snowshoe trails. A full-day adult trail pass costs $18 a day; children 12 and under and seniors 65 and older pay $12. Gear rentals and lessons are available. Trails are open daily during ski season from 9am to 5pm.

There are also cross-country trails at **Howelsen Hill** (see above). Popular cross-country ski trails in nearby national forestland include **Rabbit Ears Pass,** 25 miles east of Steamboat on U.S. 40, and **Dunkley Pass,** 25 miles south on Colo. 131. For trail maps and information, contact **Medicine Bow–Routt National Forest,** 925 Weiss Dr. (© **970/870-2299**).

ICE DRIVING   Okay all you NASCAR fans, you think you're great drivers? Any wimp (well, almost any) can drive on dry pavement, but how good are you when your car's sliding down a sheet of ice? This is the place to find out. Bridgestone Winter Driving School teaches safe winter driving the smartest way possible—hands-on, on a 1-mile circuit packed with frozen water and snow, and guarded by high snow banks.

Classes combine instruction with on-track practice and are available for average drivers as well as professionals. Classes include a half-day introductory course ($280) and the most popular—a full-day course for $495. There are also 2-day performance courses for $2,850. The school is open daily from mid-December to early March, and reservations are recommended. Contact **Bridgestone Winter Driving School** (© **800/949-7543** or 970/879-6104; www.winterdrive.com).

Outdoor Activities

Most outdoor recreation pursuits are enjoyed in 1.1-million-acre **Routt National Forest,** which virtually surrounds Steamboat Springs and offers opportunities for camping, hiking, backpacking, mountain biking, horseback riding, fishing, and hunting. For trail maps and information, contact **Medicine Bow–Routt National Forest,** 925 Weiss Dr. (© **970/870-2299**).

Two wilderness areas in the forest are easily reached from Steamboat. Immediately north of town is the **Mount Zirkel Wilderness Area,** a region of rugged peaks approached through 10,800-foot Buffalo Pass, on Forest Road 60 off Strawberry Park Road via Seventh Street. Southwest of Stillwater Reservoir, some 40 miles south of Steamboat via Colo. 131 through Yampa, is the **Flat Tops Wilderness Area,** with picturesque alpine meadows and sheer volcanic cliffs. No motorized vehicles or mountain bikes are allowed in wilderness areas, although horses and dogs are permitted (dogs must be leashed in some areas).

The **Steamboat Ski Resort** doesn't go into hibernation after the snow melts; it just changes its focus, offering hiking, gondola rides, and a multitude of other activities, including many that are great for kids. There are a wide variety of mountain-biking trails in Steamboat Bike Park ($37 for an adult day pass). For information, check with **Steamboat Ski & Resort Corporation** (© **970/879-6111**).

BIKING & MOUNTAIN BIKING   The 5-mile, dual-surface **Yampa River Trail** connects downtown Steamboat Springs with Steamboat Village, and links area parks and national forest trails. The **Mount Werner Trail** links the river to the ski area, which has numerous slopes open to mountain bikers in summer. **Spring Creek Trail** climbs from Yampa River Park into Routt National Forest. Touring enthusiasts can try their road bikes on the scenic 110-mile loop over Rabbit Ears and Gore passes. Another option, especially for those of us who don't believe that sweating our way up the side of a mountain is fun, is to take the Silver Bullet Gondola into the mountains and then ride the more than 40 upper mountain trails. Mountain bike rentals are available for $93 for 3 hours for an adult bike and slightly less for kids' bikes. Day passes are $37 for adults and $27 for kids 12 and under. Town cruisers are also available, as are repairs, gear, and advice.

CATTLE DRIVES   The **Saddleback Ranch,** on C.R. 179 about 14 miles southwest of Steamboat Springs (© **970/879-3711;** www.saddlebackranch.net), is a working cattle ranch that offers a genuine Old West experience. The ranch has some 1,500 head of cattle on its 8,000 acres, and participants join working cowboys in moving cattle from pasture to pasture and performing other ranching tasks that are still done the old-fashioned way. Horses, gear, and snacks are provided, and cost for a half-day on the trail is $110 for those 10 and older. Children under 10 are not permitted. The cattle drives are held from June through mid-September.

GOLF   The golf season here usually runs May through October, or as long as the snow isn't falling. The 18-hole municipal **Haymaker Golf Course,** at the intersection of U.S. 40 and Colo. 131, east of Steamboat Springs (☎ **970/870-1846;** www.hay makergolf.com), is a challenging links-style course with only 110 of its 233 acres used for fairways and greens. It conforms to the open-space philosophy of the Steamboat community, with native grasses, wetlands, and contours mimicking the surrounding valley and mountains. The nonresident greens fee is $75 to $115 for 18 holes; carts are not included. The **Steamboat Golf Club,** 6 miles west of downtown Steamboat Springs along U.S. 40 (☎ **970/879-4295;** www.steamboatgolfclub.com), is a pictur-esque 9-hole course along the Yampa River, with greens fees of $31 for 9 holes and $45 for 18 holes, carts not included.

GONDOLA RIDES   Summer visitors don't have to work hard to get up into the mountains above Steamboat—simply hop on the **Silver Bullet Gondola** (☎ **877/237-2628** or 970/879-0740; www.steamboat.com), which operates weekends in mid-June and mid-September, and daily from late June through Labor Day weekend. Prices for all-day passes are as follows: adults $22, children 6 to 12 $11 (or $27 for one adult and one child), and free for children 5 and younger. From the top of the gondola, hiking and mountain-biking trails can be accessed.

HIKING, BACKPACKING & MOUNTAINEERING   There are numerous trails in the **Mount Zirkel Wilderness Area,** immediately north of Steamboat, and the **Flat Tops Wilderness Area,** 48 miles southwest. An especially scenic 4-hour hike in the Flat Tops area takes you from Stillwater Reservoir to the Devil's Causeway, with unforgettable views. Contact the U.S. Forest Service (☎ **970/870-2299**) for informa-tion. There are also hiking trails at Steamboat Ski Area, which are easily reached on the Silver Bullet Gondola.

HORSEBACK RIDING   Located behind the rodeo grounds in town (follow Fifth St. south from Lincoln Ave.) is **Sombrero Ranches** (☎ **970/879-2306;** www.sombrero. com), which offers 1- and 2-hour rides, breakfast rides, and special supervised rides for young children. Prices are $35 for an hour, $45 for the 2-hour and breakfast rides, and $20 for a half-hour lead-horse ride for kids.

   Steamboat Lake Outfitters (☎ **970/319-4866;** www.steamboatlakeoutfitters.com) leads guided horseback tours at Steamboat Lake State Park; half- and full-day rides, with lunch, run $150 and $300 per person, respectively. This company also offers pack trips and horseback fishing trips into nearby wilderness areas (call for details) and rents rooms and cabins.

   Dinner rides are offered during the summer by **Saddleback Ranch** (☎ **970/879-3711;** www.saddlebackranch.net), with a choice of New York strip steak, pork tender-loin, salmon, or barbecued chicken, plus all the extras. There's a 35-minute ride to the dinner site (transportation by hay wagon is also available), and the cost is $85 for those over 5. Two-hour trail rides are $65.

HOT SPRINGS   More than 150 mineral springs are located in and around the Steamboat Springs area. Several are located in city parks. Their healing and restorative qualities were recognized for centuries by Utes, and James Crawford, the area's first white settler, regularly bathed in Heart Spring and helped build the first log bathhouse over it in 1884.

   Today Heart Spring is part of **Old Town Hot Springs,** 136 Lincoln Ave. (☎ **970/879-1828;** www.steamboathotsprings.org), in downtown Steamboat Springs. In addition to the attractive soaking pools into which the spring's waters flow, there's a lap pool, a pair of water slides, a spa, a whirlpool, a fitness center, tennis courts, and massage therapy. Pool admission is $16 for adults, $11 seniors 65 and over, $9 for children under 3 to 17, and free for children under 3. Suit and towel rentals are available. The complex is open daily year-round. The slides, in addition to the pool admission, cost $2 for one ride or $6 for unlimited rides.

My personal favorite place to soak in Colorado, the **Strawberry Park Hot Springs,** 44200 C.R. 36 (✆ **970/879-0342;** www.strawberryhotsprings.com), are 7 miles north of downtown (from Seventh St., follow the signs) up a rugged, rocky road navigable by regular cars in summer but it's strongly recommended to ride the shuttle in winter. (In summer, you can drive to the Hot Springs trailhead off of C.R. 129 and hike 3 miles to the park.) The trip is worth the wonderful experience of a moonlit evening in a sandy-bottomed, rock-lined soaking pool. The hot springs are open Sunday through Thursday from 10am to 10:30pm (no entry after 9:30pm except to shuttles) and Friday and Saturday 10am to midnight (no entry after 10:30pm except to shuttles). Admission is $12 to $15 adults, $7 youths 13 to 17, and $5 children 3 to 12. After dark, children 17 and under are not permitted and clothing is optional. Massages are available ($90 for an hour). Rustic cabins ($65–$75 a night), covered wagons without bedding ($60 a night), and tent sites ($55 a night) can be rented year-round, as well as a nifty caboose-turned-kitchenette ($115 a night). Overnighters get the pool all to themselves after hours. There's a picnic area but no restaurant.

RODEO The **Steamboat Springs ProRodeo Series** (✆ **970/879-1818;** www. steamboatprorodeo.com) takes place each year from mid-June through mid-August at the Brent Romick Rodeo Arena in Howelsen Park, at the corner of Fifth Street and Howelsen Parkway. Professional rodeo cowboys and cowgirls compete in bull riding, bareback and saddle bronco riding, steer wrestling, calf roping, team roping, and barrel racing. In the Calf Scramble, children can try to pluck a ribbon from the tail of a calf. The rodeo takes place Friday and Saturday nights starting at 7:30pm. Admission costs $20 for adults, $10 for youths 7 to 15, and is free for kids 6 and under.

More to See & Do

Fish Creek Falls ★★　Just 4 miles from downtown Steamboat in Routt National Forest, a quarter-mile footpath leads to a historic bridge at the base of this breathtaking 283-foot waterfall that inspired the original Coors logo. There's also an overlook with a short .1-mile trail and ramp designed for those with disabilities, as well as a picnic area and hiking trails. From the falls, you can choose to embark on longer day hikes. Allow at least 1 to 2 hours.

Fish Creek Falls Rd. ✆ **970/870-2299.** $5 per vehicle admission. Turn right off Lincoln Ave. onto Third St., go 1 block, and turn right again onto Fish Creek Falls Rd. Daily 24 hr.

Tread of Pioneers Museum ★★　Steamboat Springs has a fascinating history, ranging from Native Americans to outlaws to Olympians. It's all chronicled at this excellent small-town museum in a 1908 Victorian home downtown. There are the expected displays of heirlooms, firearms, and mining and farming tools, as well as some high-tech interactive exhibits, plus a scavenger hunt for kids. Allow about 1 hour.

800 Oak St. ✆ **970/879-2214.** www.treadofpioneers.org. Admission $5 adults, $4 seniors 62 and older, $1 children 6–12, free for kids 5 and under. Tues–Sat 11am–5pm.

Yampa River Botanic Park ★★　For a pleasant and relaxing stroll among lovely gardens, stop at this botanic park along the Yampa River, between the ski mountain and downtown. Several picturesque ponds are set among low rolling hills, surrounded by a wide variety of flowering and nonflowering plants and trees of the Yampa River Basin plus many nonnative plants from many areas. A brochure describes the planted areas,

musical MOUNTAINS

Summer is a musically magical time in Steamboat Springs. **Strings Music Festival ★★★** offers an incredible array of musical programs, including classical, jazz, blues, and family-friendly music, in a beautiful performance hall inspired by the lines of a string instrument.

If **chamber and classical music** is your kick, don't miss the Wednesday and Saturday evening concerts. The choices are diverse: An evening might start with a gentle Chopin nocturne and move to a Schumann piano quartet, then finish off with Brahms. Should **jazz, country, bluegrass,** or **pops** be the music that thrills your soul, Friday night is the night.

Don't forget to pack your lunch for the **free concert series** at Yampa River Botanic Park—an inspiring location, the gardens a stirring backdrop—for a concert each Thursday at 12:15pm in the summer. It's a lovely way to spend your lunchtime—and many locals agree, so get there early to snag one of the free umbrellas to keep the scorching sun off your head.

Kid-oriented concerts on Tuesday mornings, cost $10 for adults and just $1 for those 18 and under. Chamber and most classical music performances cost $33 to $38 ($5 kids). Friday evening programs, which offer a variety of music, have varied prices. There's a cafe that serves light fare and drinks.

For additional information and a complete schedule, contact Strings Music Festival (© **970/879-5056;** www.stringsmusicfestival.com).

with a map to help you navigate the many paths. There are wetlands on each side of the park, and the Yampa River Core trail connects to the park on its west side. The park is not wheelchair accessible, but tours for people with disabilities are offered by appointment. Allow at least an hour.

1000 Pamela Lane. © **970/846-5172.** www.yampariverbotanicpark.org. Free admission, donations welcome. May–Oct dawn–dusk. From U.S. 40, turn west toward the river on Trafalger Dr. (the traffic light north of the Chamber Resort office light), then left on Pamela Lane, and go to the parking lot at the far end.

Nightlife

The **bar scene** in Steamboat, while never dull, comes especially alive in winter. (Like Steamboat's restaurants, its nightlife ranges from quiet to nonexistent in spring.) Downtown, one of the hottest hangouts is the **Ghost Ranch,** 56 Seventh St. (© **970/879-9898**), modeled after the legendary Montana Bar in Miles City, Montana, and featuring local and touring rock acts on its stage. The **Tap House,** 729 Lincoln Ave. (© **970/879-2431**), has dozens of TVs showing just about any sporting event you'd want to see. There are 21 beers on tap, good fajitas and chicken wings, pool tables, and a video arcade. A riverside bar and grill with New Orleans roots, **Sunpie's,** 735 Yampa St. (© **970/870-3360**), attracts the young and restless, specializing in po' boy sandwiches and potent rum "Slurricanes." **Mahogany Ridge Brewery & Grill,** 435 Lincoln Ave. (© **970/879-3773**), brews a nice selection of handcrafted ales. The **Old Town Pub,** 600 Lincoln Ave. (© **970/879-2101**), is a local favorite, a low-key bar in a historic downtown building.

We also recommend a pair of new-in-2014 breweries in town: **Butcherknife Brewing,** with a tap room at 2875 Elk River Rd. (© **970/879-2337;** www.butcherknifebrewing.com); and **Storm Peak Brewing Co.,** 1744 Lincoln Ave. (© **970/879-1999;** www.stormpeakbrewing.com).

WINTER PARK ★★

67 miles NW of Denver

Originally an Arapaho and Ute hunting ground, Winter Park was first settled by whites in the 1850s. The laying of a rail track over Rollins Pass in 1905 and the completion of the 6¼-mile Moffat Tunnel in 1928 opened forests here to logging, which long supported the economy while providing Denver with raw materials for its growth.

The birth of the Winter Park ski area in January 1940, at the west portal of the Moffat Tunnel, helped give impetus to the Colorado ski boom. Although it hasn't yet achieved the celebrity of Vail or Aspen, the tiny town of Winter Park—population around 1,000—still manages to attract about a million skier visits per season. Elevation here is about 9,400 feet.

Essentials

GETTING THERE **By Car** From Denver, take I-70 to exit 232, at Empire, and climb 24 miles north on U.S. 40 over Berthoud Pass to Winter Park. U.S. 40 links Winter Park to Steamboat Springs, 101 miles northwest, and, via U.S. 34 (at Granby) through Rocky Mountain National Park, to Estes Park, 84 miles northeast.

By Plane Visitors fly into Denver International Airport and can continue to Winter Park with **Home James Transportation Services** (© **800/359-7503;** www.home jamestransportation.com); a one-way trip runs $65.

By Train The **Amtrak California Zephyr** (© **800/872-7245;** www.amtrak.com) stops in Fraser, just north of Winter Park, on its Chicago-to-California run. You can catch it in Denver.

GETTING AROUND U.S. 40 (Winter Park Dr.) runs almost directly north-south through the community. Vasquez Road, one of the few side roads with accommodations, is the first major left turn as you arrive from the south. Two miles north on U.S. 40 is Fraser, site of the Amtrak terminal and several condominium developments. **The Lift** (© **970/726-4163**), a free local shuttle service, runs between most accommodations and the ski area during the ski season, and offers in-town service in summer. **Car rentals** are available from **Hertz.**

VISITOR INFORMATION Main sources of visitor information are the **Winter Park and Fraser Valley Chamber of Commerce** (© **800/903-7275** or 970/726-4221; www.playwinterpark.com), and the **Winter Park Resort** (© **970/726-1564;** www. winterparkresort.com). The chamber of commerce's visitor center, on the east side of U.S. 40 in the center of town, is open daily year-round.

FAST FACTS There is a **medical clinic** at Winter Park Resort. The **post office** is in the heart of Winter Park at 78490 U.S. 40.

Where to Stay

There are more than 60 accommodations in the Fraser Valley, including hotels, condominiums, family-style mountain inns (serving breakfast and dinner daily), bed-and-breakfasts, lodges, and motels. Bookings can be made through **Winter Park Central Reservations** (© **800/979-0332;** www.winterparkresort.com). The agency can also book air and rail tickets, rental cars, airport transfers, lift tickets, ski-school lessons, ski rentals, and other activities. Another option, for those interested in renting a private, upscale home, town house, or condo, is to contact **Destinations West**

(© **800/545-9378;** www.mtnlodging.com) or **Winter Park Lodging Company** (© **877/329-1383;** www.winterparklodgingcompany.com).

    Snow Mountain Ranch–YMCA of the Rockies, on U.S. 40 between Winter Park and Grand Lake at 1101 C.R. 53 (© **970/887-2152;** www.ymcarockies.org), offers a wide range of lodging possibilities, from economical lodge rooms to delightful Western-style cabins with up to five bedrooms. Peak summer and winter rates are $94 for yurts, $124 to $164 double for the lodge rooms and $219 to $499 for cabins. There are also campsites for $47 to $51nightly, and a full slate of recreational activities.

    The **Rocky Mountain Chalet,** U.S. 40, Fraser (© **970/726-8256;** www.therocky mountainchalet.com), is a solid budget option, clean and well maintained with a gorgeous valley view, with private rooms from $89 to $129 double and bunks for $30 a night, with higher holiday rates. Taxes add about 10 percent to lodging bills; many properties in the area have resort fees.

MODERATE TO EXPENSIVE

Devil's Thumb Ranch Resort & Spa ★★★

Above Devil's Thumb Ranch is its namesake, jutting from the majestic mountainside (ask about the legend that gave it that name). Unspooling in the idyllic Ranch Creek Valley below this geological formation, the ranch (est. 1938) has become decidedly more upscale in recent years, adding luxurious cabins, two picture-perfect lodges, and a nature-based spa. The Ranch is not only comfortable and stylish, it is green, with geothermal and solar heating, its new additions made from reclaimed materials (from beetle-ravaged trees and rockslides). For budgeteers there's the less expensive Bunkhouse down the road.

    And any description of Devil's Thumb Ranch without the recreation opportunities would be sorely lacking: In winter, it is one of the best cross-country ski and snowshoe resorts in the West. Come summer, you can ride a zip line, fish, hike, bike, raft, paddle, or ride a horse on the 6,000-acre property, and the seemingly boundless public land that surrounds it.

Grand County Rd. 83 (8 miles north of Winter Park), Tabernash. © **970/726-5632.** www.devils thumbranch.com. 111 units, including 15 cabins and 13 Bunkhouse rooms (4 with shared bathroom). $260–$610 double lodge room or suite; $315–$890 cabin; $83–$115 Bunkhouse room. Higher holiday rates. Minimum stay may be required. **Amenities:** 3 restaurants; bar; room service; concierge; fitness center; indoor/outdoor Jacuzzi; indoor/outdoor heated pool; sauna; spa; free Wi-Fi.

Vasquez Creek Inn ★★

If you can't get a room at the Devil's Thumb ranch, no worries: This new-in-2014 inn was opened by the same owners and has a similar design aesthetic (chic) and standard of service (high). More intimate, with only 15 rooms, it sits on Vasquez Street in the heart of the town of Winter Park. Most of the rooms have one king bed, but a few have a queen and a twin. The resident restaurant, **Volario's,** serves Northern Italian fare with Spanish influences.

78746 U.S. 40, Winter Park. © **970/722-1188.** www.vasquezcreekinn.com. 15 units. $179–$259 double. Rates include continental breakfast. **Amenities:** Outdoor Jacuzzi; free Wi-Fi.

Where to Eat

There are numerous restaurants in **Copper Creek Square** (www.coppercreeksquare. com), the outdoor mall at U.S. 40 and Vasquez Road.

EXPENSIVE

Deno's Mountain Bistro ★ ITALIAN/AMERICAN

Deno's has a two-pronged menu: classic Italian fare, with a little bit of Colorado flavor for good measure. That means such dishes as chicken Marsala, linguine and clams, and Rocky Mountain trout with almond butter. At lunch it changes its focus once again with a casual menu of burgers and sandwiches, including Greek standards like gyros and souvlaki. Deno's offers a wide array of libations, including 10 beers on draft and several craft cocktails, and the happy hour deals are a good match for an après-ski appetite.

78911 U.S. 40 (downtown, across from Copper Creek Sq.). ℂ **970/726-5332.** www.denoswp.com. Main courses lunch 10–$12; dinner $15–$38. Daily 11:30am–11pm.

Tabernash Tavern ★★ NEW AMERICAN   Tabernash looks something out of a Western movie, a relic of a structure that has stood for nearly a century. But looks (and names) can be deceiving—this is no mere rustic mountain tavern. The menu changes seasonally, and the culinary inspiration spans the globe. When available, we highly recommend the meatloaf of elk, boar, and buffalo, with a balsamic ketchup glaze, and the knockout green chile paella with a half lobster and saffron rice. To top it off, the Mudslide Pie, with an Oreo crust barely holding in the praline ice cream, bananas, and hot fudge, is one decadent dessert.

72287 U.S. 40, Tabernash. ℂ **970/726-4430.** www.tabernashtavern.com. Main courses $15–$45. Daily 4–9pm. Closed several weeks in spring and fall.

Skiing & Other Winter Activities

Winter Park Resort ★★ is one of those rare, reliably snowy resorts that seems to have something for everyone. Experts rave about the chutes and steep mogul runs on Mary Jane Mountain and the extreme skiing in the Vasquez Cirque, but intermediates and beginners are well served on other slopes. Moreover, Winter Park is noted for wide-ranging programs for children and those with disabilities.

The resort includes three interconnected mountain areas totaling 3,081 acres of skiable terrain, served by 25 lifts. The resort rates its trails as 8 percent beginner, 18 percent intermediate, and 74 percent advanced and expert. The vertical drop is 3,060 feet, from the 12,060-foot summit off North Cone of Parsenn Bowl to the 9,000-foot base.

Daily peak-season lift tickets (2013–14 prices) cost $104 for adults ages 13 to 69, $94 for seniors, $62 for children 6 to 12, and kids 5 and under ski free. You can get discounts by buying multiday packages or buying lift tickets online in advance of your visit. Rentals and lessons are available.

Winter Park is usually open for skiing from mid-November to mid-April. It's open for summer operations daily from early June until early September. For more information, contact **Winter Park Resort** (ℂ **970/726-1564** or 970/726-7669 for snow reports; www.winterparkresort.com).

OTHER SKIING NEARBY   About 15 miles north of Winter Park, **Ski Granby Ranch** (formerly SolVista), near the town of Granby (ℂ **888/850-4615** or 970/887-5123; www.granbyranch.com), is a family favorite for its beginner terrain and affordable prices. The ski area comprises two separate but interconnected mountains comprising 406 acres of skiable terrain. Full-day lift tickets (2013–14 prices) cost $59 for adults, $39 for children 6 to 12, $44 for seniors 61 to 69, $10 for those over 69, and are free for kids under 6. A $20 ticket is good only on the beginner lifts.

CROSS-COUNTRY SKIING & SNOWSHOEING   The outstanding cross-country skiing in the Winter Park area is highlighted by one of the best Nordic resorts in the West. The **Devil's Thumb Nordic Country Center** at Devil's Thumb Ranch (ℂ **970/726-8231** or 970/726-7010 for a trail report; www.devilsthumbranch.com) has more than 62 miles of groomed trails. Full rentals and instruction are available. Day passes are $20 adults, $8 for those 65 and over or 11 and under, and free for guests.

Totally Tubular

The **Historic Fraser Snow Tubing Hill,** 455 C.R. 72 (© **970/726-5954;** www. thefrasertubinghill.com), offers a return to childhood for many adults, as well as a lot of fun for kids (who must be 7 or older to ride alone). A lift pulls you and your big inner tube to the top of a steep hill, and then you zip down, sometimes reaching speeds of 45 mph. Hours are daily from 10am to 10pm, and the tubing hill is open November to April, snow permitting. Rides run $15 to $20 per tuber per hour.

Snow Mountain Ranch–YMCA Nordic Center, on U.S. 40 between Winter Park and Grand Lake (© **888/573-9622;** www.ymcarockies.org), has more than 60 miles of groomed trails for all abilities on 5,200 acres. Trail passes cost $15 for adults, and overnight guests and children 5 and under ski free.

Both of the above provide **snowshoeing** opportunities, with rental equipment and guided tours.

More Outdoor Activities

There are plenty of recreational opportunities in the **Arapaho National Forest** and **Arapaho National Recreation Area.** Maps and brochures on hiking, mountain biking, and other activities are available at the **Sulphur Ranger District office,** 9 Ten Mile Dr., off U.S. 40 just south of Granby (© **970/887-4100**). **Devil's Thumb Ranch** (see "Where to Stay," p. 141) is famous for its numerous recreation packages, including rafting, hiking, and fly-fishing.

ALPINE SLIDE Colorado's longest alpine slide, at 3,030 feet long and with 26 turns, cools summer visitors. Rates Friday through Sunday are $15 for ages 6 and older and $6 for kids 5 and under. For information, contact the Winter Park Resort (© **970/726-1564;** www.winterparkresort.com). There is also a climbing wall, scenic chairlift, human maze, zip line, and other diversions for $6 to $15 per ticket. An "Adventure Pass" that runs $49 for all day ($15 for children 5 and under) includes the alpine slide and other activities.

GOLF Local courses include the 27-hole **Pole Creek Golf Club,** 10 miles northwest of Winter Park on U.S. 40 (© **970/887-9195;** www.polecreekgolf.com), one of the top mountain courses in the state, with greens fees of $48 to $99 for 18 holes; and **Headwaters Golf Course** (© **888/850-4615;** www.granbyranch.com), with fees of $75 to $90 for 18 holes, or $25 for golfers 17 and under.

HIKING & BACKPACKING The nearby Arapaho National Forest and Arapaho National Recreation Area (© **970/887-4100**) offer miles of hiking trails and plenty of backpacking opportunities. Beautiful Rocky Mountain National Park is less than an hour's drive north (see "Rocky Mountain National Park," p. 118).

MOUNTAIN BIKING Winter Park and the Fraser Valley have won national recognition for their expansive trail system and established race program. Many off-road bike trails connect to the more than 600 miles of backcountry roads and trails in the adjacent national forest. The King of the Rockies Off-Road Stage Race and Festival, held each year in August, is one of the top professional mountain-bike races in America; part of it is run on the 30-mile **Tipperary Creek Trail,** one of Colorado's best mountain-bike trails. The Fat Tire Classic in late June is another big mountain-biking event and a big fundraiser for the American Red Cross. Entrants are recommended to be intermediate or advanced bikers or hikers.

Utilizing the Zephyr Express and Olympia Express chairs to access the trails, the **Trestle Bike Park** at the Winter Park Resort (© **970/726-1564;** www.winterpark resort.com) is open daily late June to early August, with adult lift passes running $39 for a full day or $34 for a half-day. Rentals are available, as are combo packages that include a rental and a lift pass.

More to See & Do

Cozens Ranch Museum ★   Pioneer life in the Fraser Valley was difficult, and the exhibits at this history museum allow visitors to understand exactly why. Packed with historic artifacts of all kinds, this former working ranch was also a stagecoach stop, and displays cover this wrinkle in interesting detail. Allow 30 minutes to an hour.

U.S. 40 (btw. Winter Park and Fraser). © **970/726-5488.** www.grandcountymuseum.com. Admission $5 adults, $4 seniors 62 and over, $3 students 6–18, free for children 5 and under. Wed–Sat 10am–4pm. Closed in winter.

BRECKENRIDGE & SUMMIT COUNTY ★★

67 miles W of Denver, 114 miles NW of Colorado Springs, 23 miles E of Vail

Breckenridge, founded in 1859, and its neighbors throughout Summit County comprise a major outdoor recreation center, with skiing in winter and fishing, hiking, and mountain biking in summer. But the area actually offers much more, with a number of historical attractions, good shopping opportunities, fine restaurants, and some interesting places to stay. The town of Breckenridge (elevation 9,603 ft.) is a good place to be your base. Colorfully painted shops and restaurants occupy the old buildings, most dating from the 1880s and 1890s.

Most of the mountain towns that surround the area's excellent ski resorts—Arapahoe Basin, Breckenridge, Copper Mountain, Keystone, and Loveland—were barely on the map in the 1880s, when the rest of the state was laying claim to its stake of history. Breckenridge, however, was a prosperous mining town in 1887 when the largest gold nugget ever found in Colorado, "Tom's Baby," was unearthed here. It weighed all of 13 pounds, 7 ounces. Today these communities are strictly in the tourism business and fill to capacity during peak seasons. Breckenridge, for example, has a year-round population of about 4,500 people, but swells to almost 34,000 during its top tourism times.

Essentials

GETTING THERE   By Car   I-70 runs through the middle of Summit County. For Keystone, exit on U.S. 6 at Dillon; the resort is 6 miles east of the interchange. For Breckenridge, exit on Colo. 9 at Frisco and head south 9 miles to the resort. Copper Mountain is right on I-70 at the Colo. 91 interchange.

By Airport Shuttle   Most visitors fly into Denver International or Colorado Springs and continue to Breckenridge, Frisco, Keystone, and/or Copper Mountain via shuttle. **Colorado Mountain Express** (© **800/525-6363** or 970/754-7433; www.colorado mountainexpress.com) offers shuttles; the cost from Denver is typically $66 per person, one-way ($36 for kids 12 and under).

Breckenridge

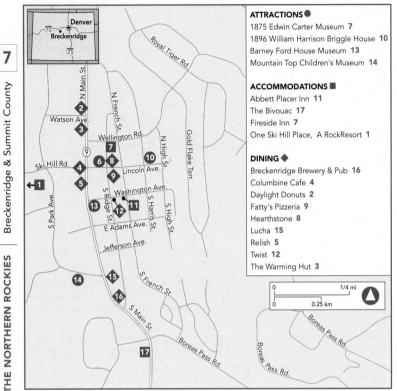

ATTRACTIONS ●
1875 Edwin Carter Museum **7**
1896 William Harrison Briggle House **10**
Barney Ford House Museum **13**
Mountain Top Children's Museum **14**

ACCOMMODATIONS ■
Abbett Placer Inn **11**
The Bivouac **17**
Fireside Inn **7**
One Ski Hill Place, A RockResort **1**

DINING ◆
Breckenridge Brewery & Pub **16**
Columbine Cafe **4**
Daylight Donuts **2**
Fatty's Pizzeria **9**
Hearthstone **8**
Lucha **15**
Relish **5**
Twist **12**
The Warming Hut **3**

GETTING AROUND   Dillon Reservoir is at the heart of Summit County, and I-70 lies along its northwestern shore, with Frisco at its west end, and Dillon and Silverthorne to the east. From Dillon, take U.S. 6 about 5 miles east to Keystone and another 15 miles to Arapahoe. Breckenridge is about 10 miles south of Frisco on Colo. 9, and Copper Mountain is just south of I-70 exit 195 (Colo. 91). Loveland Ski Area is just across the county line at exit 216 on the east side of the Eisenhower Tunnel.

   Summit Stage (⌀ **970/668-0999;** www.summitstage.com) provides free year-round service between Frisco, Dillon, Silverthorne, Keystone, Breckenridge, and Copper Mountain, daily from 6am to after midnight from late November to mid-April and shorter hours the rest of the year. The **Lake County Link** is a Frisco-to-Leadville route that costs $5 one-way. You can get around Breckenridge on the **free bus system** (⌀ **970/547-3140**), and there's also **free shuttle service** at the Keystone Resort (⌀ **970/496-4200**).

VISITOR INFORMATION   For additional information on Breckenridge and other parts of Summit County, contact the **Breckenridge Resort Chamber** (⌀ **888/251-2417** or 970/453-2918; www.gobreck.com) at its welcome center at 203 S. Main St.

FAST FACTS   Medical facilities here include a **medical clinic,** located in the Village at Breckenridge, 555 S. Park Ave. (⌀ **970/453-1010**), and the **Summit Medical**

Center, 340 Peak One Dr., Frisco (✆ **970/668-3300**). **Post offices** are at 305 S. Ridge St., Breckenridge, and 35 W. Main St., Frisco. For **weather** and **road conditions,** call ✆ **303/639-1111** or visit **www.cotrip.org**.

Where to Stay

Thousands of rooms are available here at any given time. Even so, during peak seasons, finding accommodations may be difficult, and rates are dramatically higher from Christmas to New Year's. Throughout the county, condominiums prevail. Local reservation services include **Wildernest Lodging** (✆ **800/554-2212;** www.skierlodging. com), **Breckenridge Central Reservations** (✆ **888/251-2417;** www.gobreck.com or www.gobrecknow.com for last-minute deals); **Breckenridge Accommodations** (✆ **800/872-8789;** www.breckaccommodations.com), with last-minute online auctions; **Ski Country Resorts** (✆ **800/633-8388;** www.skicountry.com); and **Key to the Rockies** (✆ **800/248-1942;** www.keytotherockies.com).

For a hostel bunk or private bed-and-breakfast room, try the lively and eclectic **Fireside Inn,** 114 N. French St. (✆ **970/453-6456;** www.firesideinn.com), with 18 bunks ($33–$49) and private rooms for about $100 to $200. Another great budget option is the quirky **Bivouac,** 9511 Colo. 9 (✆ **970/423-6553;** www.thebivvi.com), featuring private rooms for $80 to $130 and dorm-style bunks for $45 to $60, as well as draft microbrew, recreation referrals, and a 10-person outdoor hot tub.

EXPENSIVE

One Ski Hill Place, A RockResort ★★   One Ski Hill Place pretty much has it all: ski-in, ski-out access at the base of Peak 8, a billiards room, two bowling lanes, a pool outfitted with built-in squirt guns, complimentary GoPro cameras, movie lounges, a limited-service spa (a.k.a. "rejuvenation center"), and oodles of New West style. The condos range from studios to 4-bedroom units, and all have kitchens, washers and dryers, gas fireplaces, and private balconies. Decor is apt for the location, with earth tones and color photos of Breckenridge icons and landmarks. The lobby is set off from public facilities in a base lodge, and features a nice restaurant and ski rental shop.

1521 Ski Hill Rd., Breckenridge. ✆ **877/354-6747.** http://oneskihill.rockresorts.com. 88 condos. Winter $279–$699 studios and 1-bedroom condos; summer $150–$275 studios and 1-bedroom condos. Higher holiday rates; lower rates fall and spring. Resort fee $30/night. Free underground parking. **Amenities:** 3 restaurants; lounge; concierge; exercise room; 1 indoor and 1 outdoor Jacuzzi; 2 indoor heated pools; room service; free Wi-Fi.

MODERATE

Abbett Placer Inn ★★   This 1898 house was converted into ski lodging in the 1970s, and innkeepers Emma and Niels Hagen have taken pains to create a place that balances the intimacy of a B&B with the local, outdoor-centric lifestyle. The hot tub on the inn's back deck features a massive map of the ski area so that guests can relive the day or plan the next one (the slopes are about 5 miles away). Inside, all is pretty and Victorian, with historic photos on the walls and quality reproduction antique furnishings. Our favorite digs: the Peaks Panorama Suite, which boasts a private balcony with stunning mountain views.

205 S. French St., Breckenridge. ✆ **970/453-6489.** www.abbettplacer.com. 5 units, including 2 suites. $119–$209 double; $159–$259 suite. Rates include full breakfast. No children under 13. Closed mid-Apr to Memorial Day and early Nov to early Dec. **Amenities:** Outdoor Jacuzzi; free Wi-Fi.

Where to Eat

Because of the seasonal nature of tourism in Breckenridge, most restaurants shut down for a few weeks in spring and/or fall.

EXPENSIVE

Hearthstone ★★ REGIONAL   This is the best spot for a celebratory dinner in town. Hearthstone, exuding historic ambiance from Breckenridge's Victorian days, is in the Kaiser House, which has stood on Ridge Street since the 1880s. The restaurant has been in business from the 1980s, delivering reliably excellent grub. That includes plenty of creative regional dishes—blackberry elk and locally farmed striped bass—as well as far-flung inspirations like shrimp and grits. The deck, with a splendid mountain view, is perfect for drinks and appetizers.

130 S. Ridge St. *©* **970/453-1148.** www.hearthstonerestaurant.biz. Main courses $26–$42. Daily 5–9pm.

Keystone Ranch ★★★ REGIONAL   Reservations are strongly recommended for this renowned restaurant at Keystone Ranch which serves prix-fixe dinners in a ranching homestead dating back to the 1930s. There is nothing staid or basic about the fare here. The menu changes seasonally, but a recent edition included crispy duck with cherry confit, Wagyu strip steak, and wild boar tenderloin—all were superb. There is always Colorado lamb, and the desserts are as decadent as any in Summit County. The restaurant also targets golfers with traditional American breakfast and lunch in summer only.

1437 C.R. 150, Keystone. *©* **800/354-4386.** www.keystoneresort.com. Main courses $8–$15 breakfast and lunch; 2-course dinner $45, 5-course dinner $75, $18 children 12 and under. Summer daily 7am–3pm; summer and winter daily 6–8:30pm;

Relish ★★ NEW AMERICAN   Chef-owner Matt Fackler—also the proprietor of Twist (see below)—raised the Breckenridge culinary bar when he opened Relish above Blue River Plaza, in the heart of downtown Breck, in 2006. His inventive menus change regularly, but expect surprising and always delish dishes like quail wrapped in bacon and jalapeno and pork tenderloin with a blackberry-barbecue demi-glace.

137 S. Main St. *©* **970/453-0989.** www.relishbreckenridge.com. Main courses $18–$39. Daily 5–9pm. Bar opens 4pm.

INEXPENSIVE TO MODERATE

Fatty's Pizzeria, 106 S. Ridge St. (*©* **970/453-9802**), is a local favorite with burgers, sandwiches, pizzas, pasta dinners, and a boisterous old bar room. My best budget option is **Lucha,** downstairs at 500 S. Main St. (*©* **970/453-1342**), with inexpensive burritos and margaritas. For breakfast, local standbys are **Columbine Cafe,** 109 S. Main St. (*©* **970/547-4474**), and **Daylight Donuts,** 305 N. Main St. (*©* **970/453-2548**).

Breckenridge Brewery and Pub ★ BREWPUB   Ignore the fact that Breckenridge Brewery has such high demand that its bottling operation today is in Denver. Here at the original, brick-laden location (it opened in 1990), the suds are still fab, and the excellent craft beer is complemented by a meat-centric menu that veers from burgers to elk meatloaf to steaks. Lighter fare is available in the form of entree salads and a vegetarian sandwich, and a smattering of Mexican dishes is also available. Truth be told, I come for the great beer: The Vanilla Porter is one of my favorite Colorado microbrews.

600 S. Main St. *©* **970/453-1550.** www.breckbrewpub.com. Main courses $9–$28. Daily 11am–10pm. Bar open later with limited menu.

Twist ★★ NEW AMERICAN   One of the newer entries in the Breck restaurant scene, the casual, fun Twist is so named for its fare, which is a "twist" on comfort food. That means cunning interpretations of burgers, meatloaf, mac and cheese and other American standards, plus comfort foods from north and south of the border in poutine and pork tacos, respectively (think unusual toppings, better-quality ingredients, fab sides). You'll wash it all down with an expertly curated beer and wine list; there's also a full bar.

200 S. Ridge St. ℭ **970/547-7100.** www.twistbreck.com. Main courses $13–$28. Daily 5–9pm. Bar opens at 4pm.

The Warming Hut ★ NEW AMERICAN   In a converted 1898 Queen Anne residence, the Warming Hut offers a comfortable, sunny space and menu that's more interesting than it has to be. It is an especially good pick for lunch, with gourmet sandwiches (the Colorado elk bratwurst is a big hit) and an excellent kale, quinoa, and avocado salad. Dinner brings heartier dishes, like lamb and caprese lasagna, ruby red trout, and bison short ribs. Instead of happy hour, come for "Blissful Hour" and an assortment of craft cocktails.

207 N. Main St. ℭ **970/389-3104.** www.thewarminghutrestaurant.com. Main courses $10–$16 lunch, $14–$26 dinner. Tues–Sat 11:30am–3pm; Tues–Sun 5:30–9pm; Fri–Sat 5:30–10pm. Also lunch Sun in winter. Bar opens at 4pm.

Exploring Breckenridge

Families will like the **Mountain Top Children's Museum,** 605 S. Park Ave. (ℭ **970/453-7878;** www.mtntopmuseum.org), and its hands-on exhibits; it is open Monday to Friday in summer and winter. The **Breckenridge Arts District,** Ridge Street and Washington Avenue, is a reclaimed series of old structures that offers workshops, programs, and a glimpse into working studios of visiting artists. Visit the town website at **www.townofbreckenridge.com** for further information.

Breckenridge National Historic District ★★   The entire Victorian core of this 19th-century mining town has been carefully preserved, and you can see it on your own (pick up a free walking-tour brochure at the Visitor Information Cabin), or during the summer on guided 1½-hour walking tours. Colorfully painted shops and restaurants occupy the old buildings, most dating from the 1880s and 1890s. Most of the historic district focuses on Main Street and extends east on either side of Lincoln Avenue. Among the 254 historic buildings in the district are the **Barney Ford House Museum,** 111 E. Washington Ave., in the house of Ford, a son of a slave who became a successful businessman and activist in Breckenridge; the 1875 **Edwin Carter Museum,** 111 N. Ridge St., the one-time home of a prominent naturalist. The society also leads tours during the summer to the outskirts of town to visit the underground shaft of the hard-rock **Washington Gold Mine** and the gold-panning operation at **Lomax Placer Gulch.** Allow 2 to 4 hours.

Downtown Breckenridge and other locations. ℭ **970/468-2207** or 970/453-9767 for tour reservations. www.breckheritage.com. www.summithistorical.org. Call for currently available guided tours (fees apply). Tour tickets available at the Breckenridge Resort Chamber Welcome Center, 309 N. Main St. Tours available mid-June to Sept Tues–Sat; museums open year-round, call for times.

Country Boy Mine ★★   At this mine that dates to the late 1800s, you can take a guided tour 1,000 feet underground, pan for gold in Eureka Creek, explore the mining exhibit and the five-story 75-year-old mill, and listen to the legends. The mine is a constant 45°F (7°C) year-round, so take a jacket even in August. Burros also roam around, posing for pictures with children; every summer sees the addition of a baby burro. Tours start on the hour. Allow at least an hour.

0542 French Gulch Rd., Breckenridge. © **970/453-4405.** www.countryboymine.com. Mine tour $26 adults, $20 children 4–12, free for kids 3 and under. Gold panning $16. Summer daily 10am–4pm; fall and winter Mon–Fri 11am–1pm.

7 Skiing & Other Winter Activities

Breckenridge and Keystone ski areas are part of Vail Resorts, and any lift ticket purchased at Vail or Beaver Creek is valid without restriction at Breckenridge and Keystone (and Arapahoe Basin). However, only multiday lift tickets for 3 or more days purchased at Breckenridge or Keystone are also valid at Vail and Beaver Creek. Snowboarding is permitted at all local resorts.

ARAPAHOE BASIN ★ Arapahoe Basin, 28194 U.S. 6, between Keystone and Loveland Pass, is one of Colorado's oldest ski areas, having opened in 1946. Several features make "A-Basin" exceptional: Most of its 960 skiable acres are intermediate and expert terrain, much of it above timberline; the wide-open slopes of Montezuma Bowl on the back side of the mountain; and it is frequently one of the last Colorado ski areas to close for the season—often not until mid-June. It usually opens in early November. Arapahoe offers a 2,270-foot vertical drop from its summit at 13,050 feet, the highest skiable terrain in North America.

Lift tickets during regular season (2013–14 rates) cost $82 for adults, $67 for youths 15 to 19, $40 for children 6 to 14, $72 for seniors 60 to 69, $25 per day for seniors 70 and older, and free for children 5 and under. Buy lift tickets in advance online for discounts. For information, including a snow report, contact Arapahoe Basin (© **888/272-7246** or 970/468-0718; www.arapahoebasin.com).

BRECKENRIDGE ★★ Spread across five mountains on the west side of the town of Breckenridge, this area ranks third in size among Colorado's ski resorts and is neck and neck with Vail as the busiest. Known for its wealth of open, groomed beginner and intermediate slopes, Breckenridge has become a favorite of experts with the addition of the Imperial Express Super Chair (the highest chairlift in North America) and some impressively steep terrain.

Peak 8, the original ski mountain, is the highest of the five at 12,998 feet and has the greatest variety. Peak 9, heavily geared to novices and intermediates, rises above the principal base area. Peak 10, served by a single high-speed quad chair, is predominantly expert territory. The vast bowls of Peak 8 and the North Face of Peak 9 are likewise advanced terrain. Peak 7 is predominately intermediate and expert skiing. Featuring 543 acres for intermediate and expert skiers, Peak 6 opened for the 2013-14 season. All told, the resort has 2,908 skiable acres, including Four O'Clock, the longest, at 3½ miles!

The price of lift tickets can change from day to day, and are always least expensive when you buy online 7 to 14 days in advance and most expensive during holiday periods when you buy at the window; packages of 3 days or more also get discounts. Online 2013-14 prices ranged from about $75 to $110 for adults, but the window rate in peak season can hit $130. Online prices were $60 to $100 for seniors, $50 to $60 for children 5 to 12, and free for younger children.

Breckenridge is usually open from mid-November to mid-May daily from 9am to 4pm. For further information, contact **Breckenridge Ski Resort** (© **800/789-7669** or 970/453-5000, or 970/496-4111 for snow conditions; www.breckenridge.com).

COPPER MOUNTAIN ★★ Self-contained but within easy striking distance of all the area attractions, Copper Mountain is an ideal mid-priced mountain with something for just about everyone. Terrain is about half beginner and intermediate, with the rest ranging from advanced to "you'd better be really good." The area has a vertical drop of 2,601 feet from a peak elevation of 12,313 feet. There are 2,465 skiable acres and more than 140 trails. The terrain and corresponding villages are nicely divided by skill level: The East Village connects to the most difficult runs, while the Center Village accesses intermediate terrain, and the West Village is best for beginners.

Also of note is the year-round **Woodward at Copper** (www.woodwardatcopper. com), which the resort dubs "the only year-round, indoor/outdoor ski, snowboard, and action-sport camp on the planet," featuring 20,000 square feet of jumps, foam pits, and other features to practice your moves sans snow.

Lift tickets (2013–14 prices) during the peak season cost $104 for adults, $60 for children 6 to 12, and $89 for seniors 65 and older, and free for children under 6. You can save by buying online in advance and resort lodging guests also save $30 daily.

Copper Mountain is typically open from early November to mid-April, Monday through Friday from 9am to 4pm, Saturday and Sunday from 8:30am to 4pm. For information, contact **Copper Mountain Resort** (✆ **866/841-2481** or 888/219-2441 for reservations; www.coppercolorado.com).

KEYSTONE ★ Keystone is actually three separate mountains, offering a variety of terrain. And the 3,148-acre resort is one of the best spots for night skiing in America, open after dark on Wednesday through Sunday from late November to March, and on other nights at peak times. From its peak elevation of 12,408 feet, vertical drop is 3,128 feet, with runs for all skill levels. For snowboarders, the A51 Terrain Park is one of the country's best.

The price of lift tickets can change from day to day, and are always least expensive when you buy online 7 to 14 days in advance and most expensive during holiday periods when you buy at the window; packages of 3 days or more also get discounts. Peak 2013-14 window rates were about $120 for adults, $100 for seniors, $65 for children 5 to 12, and free for younger children. (Kids 12 and under ski free when 2 or more nights are booked at resort accommodations.) Tickets purchased at Keystone are also valid at Breckenridge or Arapahoe Basin; those valid at Breckenridge are a bit more expensive.

Keystone is usually open from early November through mid-April from 8:30am to 4pm daily and stays open until 8pm on Wednesday through Saturday and 6pm on Sunday. For further information, contact **Keystone Resort** (✆ **800/354-4386** or 970/496-4386; www.keystoneresort.com). For **snow reports,** call ✆ **970/496-4111.**

LOVELAND ★ Just across the Clear Creek County line, on the east side of I-70's Eisenhower Memorial Tunnel, is **Loveland Ski Area,** at I-70, exit 216 (✆ **800/736-3754** or 303/569-3203; www.skiloveland.com). Comprising Loveland Basin and Loveland Valley, it was created in the late 1930s by a Denver ski club wanting to take advantage of the area's heavy snowfall (422 in., or more than 35 ft., annually, making it the snowiest resort off I-70).

There's good beginner and intermediate terrain on the resort's 1,800 skiable acres—13 percent and 41 percent, respectively, leaving 46 percent for advanced skiers. The vertical drop is 2,210 feet from a top elevation of 13,010 feet, and the longest run is 2 miles. The resort usually opens in mid-October and remains open daily through May, although it has been known to rival A-Basin for the state's latest closing.

You can still see the original rope-tow cabins from 1942, when all-day tickets cost $2. Inflation (and the cost of many improvements) has taken a toll, but this is one of the best deals in the area. Tickets during the 2013–14 season cost $49 to $61 for adults,

$36 to $50 for seniors 60 to 69, and $22 to $27 for children 6 to 14; children 5 and under ski free, and seniors 70 and older are offered a season pass for $89.

CROSS-COUNTRY SKIING & SNOWSHOEING The **Frisco Nordic Center,** at 616 Recreation Way, just south of Frisco (© **970/668-0866;** www.frisconordic.com), sits on the shores of Dillon Reservoir. Its trail network includes 27 miles of groomed cross-country ski trails. The lodge has a snack bar and a shop with rentals and retail sales; instruction and backcountry and snowshoe tours are also offered, and there is also a tubing hill here. From the Frisco Nordic Center, you can ski to the **Breckenridge Nordic Center,** 1200 Ski Hill Rd. (© **970/453-6855;** www.breckenridgenordic. com), with its own series of 19 miles of groomed trails. The two operations share several miles of snowshoe trails around Lake Dillon. The **Gold Run Nordic Center** at the Breckenridge Golf Club, 200 Club House Dr. (© **970/547-7889;** www.goldrun nordic.com), features more than 14 miles of groomed trails, from beginner to advanced, in addition to backcountry and snowshoe trails, and also offers rental equipment. One trail pass ($20 for adults, $15 for seniors and children) covers all three Nordic centers, and rental equipment is available. There are also numerous cross-country skiing possibilities in the area's national forests; contact the **Dillon Ranger District** (© **970/468-5400**). If you want to try an overnight trip, **Summit Huts** (© **970/453-8583** or 970/925-5775 for reservations; www.summithuts.org) offers spartan backcountry accommodations for $38 per person; the huts are on cross-country routes and accommodate up to 20 people.

More Outdoor Activities

The **White River National Forest** encompasses the boundaries of Summit County. This recreational playground offers opportunities not only for downhill and cross-country skiing and snowmobiling in winter, but also for hiking and backpacking, horseback riding, boating, fishing, hunting, and bicycling in summer. White River National Forest includes the **Eagles Nest Wilderness Area** and **Green Mountain Reservoir,** both in the northern part of the county.

From Memorial Day weekend to Labor Day at **Breckenridge Ski Resort** (© **800/789-7669**), the slopes are replaced by Breckenridge Fun Park, with a roller coaster, alpine slide, a people maze, and other amusements in operation; and the trails are open to mountain bikers and hikers. Unlimited bike hauls are $30, chairlift rides are $10, and coaster rides are $20 adults and $10 ride-along kids; all-day passes are $75 adults and $39 kids 6 and under.

The **U.S. Forest Service's Dillon Ranger District office,** located in the town of Silverthorne at 680 Blue River Pkwy. (Colo. 9), about half a mile north of I-70 exit 205 (© **970/468-5400**), has an unusually good selection of information on outdoor recreation possibilities, including maps and guides to hiking and mountain-biking trails, jeep roads, cross-country skiing, snowmobiling, fishing, and camping. The unofficial website (**www.dillonrangerdistrict.com**) is a better resource than the official one. You can also get information on a wide variety of outdoor activities from the **Breckenridge Resort Chamber** (© **888/251-2417**).

BICYCLING There are more than 40 miles of paved bicycle paths in the county, including a path from Breckenridge (with a spur from Keystone) to Frisco and Copper Mountain, continuing across Vail Pass to Vail. This spectacularly beautiful two-lane path is off-limits to motorized vehicles. Contact the Breckenridge Resort chamber for maps.

BOATING **Dillon Reservoir,** a beautiful mountain lake along I-70 between Dillon and Frisco, is the place to go. Also called Lake Dillon, the 3,300-acre reservoir, which provides drinking water to Denver, is more than 200 feet deep in spots. At 9,017 feet elevation, it claims to have America's highest-altitude yacht club and holds colorful regattas most summer weekends. Swimming is not permitted. **Dillon Marina,** 150 Marina Dr. (© **970/468-5100;** www.dillonmarina.com), is open from the last weekend of May through the last weekend of October, offering rental boats and sailing instruction.

GOLF Among area golf courses, which all boast wonderful scenery, are the 27-hole **Breckenridge Golf Club,** 200 Clubhouse Dr., Breckenridge (© **970/453-9104;** www. breckenridgegolfclub.com), the only municipal course designed by Jack Nicklaus anywhere, with greens fees of $65 to $114 for 18 holes, cart not included; **Raven at Three Peaks,** 2929 N. Golden Eagle Rd., Silverthorne (© **970/262-3636;** www. ravenatthreepeaks.com), charging $60 to $169 for 18 holes, cart included; **Keystone Ranch Golf Course,** 1239 Keystone Ranch Rd., Keystone (© **800/464-3494**), charging $55 to $125, including a cart, for 18 holes; and the par-71 **River Course at Keystone,** 155 River Course Dr., Keystone (© **800/464-3494**), which charges $55 to $150, including cart, for 18 holes.

HIKING & BACKPACKING The **Colorado Trail** cuts a swath through Summit County. It enters from the east across Kenosha Pass, follows the Swan River to its confluence with the Blue River, then climbs over Ten Mile Mountain to Copper Mountain. The trail then turns south toward Tennessee Pass, north of Leadville. Contact the **Colorado Trail Foundation** (© **303/384-3729;** www.coloradotrail.org). Another option is hiking to one of the **Summit Huts** (© **970/453-8583;** www.summithuts.org) for an overnight hiking trip where you won't need a tent. Consult the U.S. Forest Service or the Breckenridge Resort Chamber Welcome Center for maps and details. Check out **www.breckenridgetrails.org** and **www.dillonrangerdistrict.com** or information about hiking in the area.

HORSEBACK RIDING For some spectacular views of this area from atop a horse, take a ride with **Breckenridge Stables,** located in the Peak 9 base area (© **970/453-4438;** www.breckstables.com). Rides are 90 minutes for $65 per person (children under 7 are $30).

MOUNTAIN BIKING Numerous trails are available for mountain bikers. Energetic fat-tire fans can try the **Devil's Triangle,** a difficult 80-mile loop that begins and ends in Frisco after climbing four mountain passes (including 11,318-ft. Fremont Pass). Check with the U.S. Forest Service or Breckenridge Resort Chamber Welcome Center for directions and tips on other trails. For mountain bikers who prefer not to work so hard, head to the Peak 8 base area of **Breckenridge Ski Resort** (© **800/789-7669**) for chairlift rides that access about a dozen mostly intermediate and advanced trails; a day pass is $30. Among the companies providing bike rentals and information is **Lone Star Sports,** at 200 W. Washington St., Breckenridge (© **800/621-9733** or 970/453-2003; www.skilonestar.com), which charges full-day rates of $32 to $52.

RIVER RAFTING Trips through the white water of the Blue River—which runs through Breckenridge to Frisco—as well as longer journeys on the Colorado and Arkansas rivers, are offered by various companies, including **KODI Rafting** (© **877/747-7238;** www.whitewatercolorado.com), **Good Times Rafting Company** (© **970/402-6081;** www.goodtimesrafting.com), **Performance Tours Rafting** (© **800/328-7238;** www.performancetours.com), and the **Adventure Company** (© **800/497-7238;** www.theadventurecompany.com). Rates for half-day trips on the Blue River cost about $55 to $65 for adults and a bit less for children. Full-day trips on other area rivers are about $80 to $110 for adults and $70 to $85 for kids.

Nightlife

In the Arts District of Breckenridge, the **Backstage Theatre,** 121 S. Ridge St., Breckenridge (© **970/453-0199;** www.backstagetheatre.org), has been presenting a variety of live theater since 1974.

Popular bars in usually rowdy Breckenridge include the **Breckenridge Brewery and Pub,** 600 S. Main St. (© **970/453-1550**), where the microbrews include Avalanche Ale, Vanilla Porter, and the ultra-hoppy 471 Double IPA. Also see "Where to Eat" (p. 148). For everything from live blues to reggae, try **three20south,** 320 S. Main St. (© **970/368-3204**). **Downstairs at Eric's,** 111 S. Main St. (© **970/453-1401**), is popular with locals and the après-ski crowd alike and boasts 120 brands of beer, including 22 on tap. **Motherloaded Tavern,** 103 S. Main St. (© **970/453-2572**), is a quirky place and a favorite of the young and wasted. The bar at **Ember,** 106 E. Adams Ave. (© **970/547-9595**), is arguably the most romantic spot for a glass of wine in town. Established in the 1870s and said to be the longest continually operating bar west of the Mississippi (local lawmen were afraid to shut it down during Prohibition), the **Gold Pan Saloon,** 103 N. Main St. (© **970/453-5499**), is a rough-and-tumble, ornery place that's hard not to like. Makers of small-batch whiskey and vodka, **Breckenridge Distillery,** 1925 Airport Rd. (© **970/547-9759**), has a tasting room downtown on Blue River Plaza and a store at the distillery itself (touted as the highest in the world); tours are available.

The Festival Scene

The **Breckenridge Music Festival** (© 970/453-9142; www.breckenridgemusic festival.com) presents concerts in the Riverwalk Center throughout the summer; and the **Breckenridge Festival of Film** (www.breckfilmfest.com) held in mid-June, attracts Hollywood directors and actors to discuss some two dozen films in all genres.

But my favorite Breck festival is undoubtedly **Ullr Fest,** a week in mid-January devoted to the Norse god of snow, Ullr, the stepson of Thor. There are such events as the wacky Ullympics, concerts, dating games, and other events, culminating in one of the best (and strangest) winter parades in the Rockies. The events are family-friendly, although the bar scene afterward is anything but. Contact the **Breckenridge Resort Chamber** (© **888/251-2417**) for more information.

VAIL & BEAVER CREEK ★★

109 miles W of Denver, 150 miles E of Grand Junction

Consistently ranked the country's most popular ski resort by skiers and ski magazines almost since its inception, Vail is the big one. It's hard to imagine a more celebrated spot to schuss. Off the slopes, Vail is an incredibly compact replica of a Tyrolean village, full of restaurants, hotels, and shops frequented by almost as many Europeans as Americans. But the size of the mountain and the difficulty and excitement of many of its trails still draw the faithful. Beware weekends and holidays, however: This is also the busiest resort on the continent, which can translate into serpentine lift lines. Posh Beaver Creek, just 10 miles west, is also a terrific resort.

Historically speaking, there is very little in the town's past to indicate that Vail would become the megadestination it is. Until U.S. 6 was built through Vail Pass in 1939, the only inhabitants were a handful of sheep ranchers. Dropping farther back into history, it's worth noting that the resort could never have been possible if it weren't for severe droughts in the mid-1800s that resulted in numerous forest fires. The

Vail

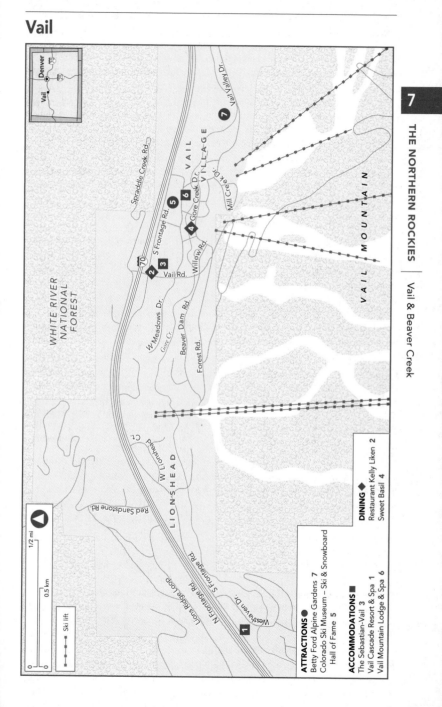

WHITE RIVER NATIONAL FOREST

VAIL VILLAGE

VAIL MOUNTAIN

LIONSHEAD

Denver

Vail

Spraddle Creek Rd.

Vail Valley Dr.

Mill Creek

S Frontage Rd.

Gore Creek Dr.

Vail Rd.

Willow Rd.

W Meadows Dr.

Gore Ck.

Beaver Dam Rd.

Forest Rd.

W Lionshead Ct.

Red Sandstone Rd.

Lions Ridge Loop

N Frontage Rd.

S Frontage Rd.

Westhaven Dr.

ATTRACTIONS ●
Betty Ford Alpine Gardens 7
Colorado Ski Museum – Ski & Snowboard
Hall of Fame 5

ACCOMMODATIONS ■
The Sebastian–Vail 3
Vail Cascade Resort & Spa 1
Vail Mountain Lodge & Spa 6

DINING ◆
Restaurant Kelly Liken 2
Sweet Basil 4

Ski lift

0   1/2 mi
0   0.5 km

burnings created the wide-open ridges and back bowls that make skiers and snowboarders the world over quiver in their boots.

It was only when veterans of the 10th Mountain Division, who trained during World War II at Camp Hale, 23 miles south of the valley, returned in the 1950s that the reality of skiing was realized. One of them, Pete Siebert, urged development of this mountain in the White River National Forest, and Vail opened to skiers in December 1962, and it became America's largest ski resort by 1964.

The Vail area has some of the most stunning natural scenery in the Rockies, with the majestic Gore Range providing an apt backdrop for the Blue and Eagle rivers, the White River National Forest, and local wildlife such as elk and black bears.

The only real complaint about Vail (aside from the expense) is that it didn't exist before it became a ski resort, and so it lacks the historical ambience and Old West downtown area that you'll find in Aspen, Steamboat Springs, Telluride, Crested Butte, and a number of other Western ski centers.

Essentials

GETTING THERE **By Car** Vail is right on the I-70 corridor, so it's exceedingly easy to find. Just take exit 176, whether you're coming from the east (Denver) or the west (Grand Junction). A more direct route from the south is U.S. 24 through Leadville; this Tennessee Pass road joins I-70 5 miles west of Vail. Beaver Creek is located about 10 miles west of Vail, off I-70 exit 167.

By Plane Year-round, visitors can fly directly into **Eagle County Airport (EGE),** 35 miles west of Vail via I-70 (*C* **970/328-2680;** www.flyvail.com), which is served by **American, Delta,** and **United** as well as **Air Canada.**

By Airport Shuttle Many visitors fly into Denver International Airport and continue to Vail and Beaver Creek aboard a shuttle service such as **Colorado Mountain Express** (*C* **800/525-6363** or 970/754-7433; www.coloradomountainexpress.com), with one-way rates running $69 to $93 per adult. There are also shuttle services from the Eagle County Airport to Vail and Beaver Creek. **High Mountain Taxi** (*C* **970/524-5555;** www.hmtaxi.com) charges roughly $150 for up to six passengers in a van.

GETTING AROUND Vail is one of only a few Colorado communities where you really don't need a car. The town of Vail runs the nation's largest **free shuttle-bus service** between 6am and 2am daily, although hours may be shorter in shoulder seasons. Shuttles in the Vail Village–Lionshead area run every 10 minutes, and there are regularly scheduled trips to West Vail and East Vail (*C* **970/477-3456;** www.vailgov.com). **ECO Transit** (*C* **970/328-3520;** www.eaglecounty.us/transit) runs shuttles between Vail and Beaver Creek, a 12-mile trip, plus regional bus service to Avon, Edwards, Minturn, Leadville, and the Eagle County Airport daily ($4–$7 each way, or $8–$14 for a day pass). **Car rentals** are available at the Eagle County Airport from **Alamo, Avis, Budget, Dollar, Hertz, National,** or **Thrifty.**

VISITOR INFORMATION For information or reservations in the Vail Valley, contact the **Vail Valley Partnership** (*C* **970/476-1000;** www.visitvailvalley.com), **Vail** (*C* **970/754-8245;** www.vail.com), or **Beaver Creek Resort** (*C* **970/754-4636;** www.beavercreek.com). Information centers are located at the parking structures in Vail and the Lionshead area on South Frontage Road.

FAST FACTS The hospital, **Vail Valley Medical Center,** with 24-hour emergency care, is at 181 W. Meadow Dr., between Vail Road and East Lionshead Circle

(✆ **970/476-2451;** www.vvmc.com). The **post office** is at 1300 N. Frontage Rd. W. For **road conditions,** call ✆ **303/639-1111** or 511 (in-state) or visit **www.cotrip.org**.

Where to Stay

Like most of Colorado's ski resorts, Vail has an abundance of condominiums. Many are individually owned and available for rent when the owners aren't in town; you'll find that they have more individuality and homey touches than you'd often find in a hotel. As in most ski areas, rates are highest during peak ski season, particularly Christmas, and can sometimes be halved after the lifts close. During ski season, you'll find the lowest rates at the very beginning, from opening to about December 20. Skiers on a tight budget can save a few dollars by staying in the town of Eagle, just south of I-70 exit 147, about 18 miles west of Beaver Creek and 29 miles west of Vail.

IN VAIL
Expensive

The Sebastian-Vail—A Timbers Resort ★★★   An architectural and artistic marvel, The Sebastian-Vail is among the best luxury hotels in the West. It eschews Bavarian and New West motifs for a more contemporary look, featuring world-class abstract works by Manuel Felguérez and a design that maximizes the available real estate with a pair of cantilevered rectangles. Rooms include hotel-style units with one king or two queen beds and a few palatial suites with private balconies and full kitchens. The facilities are extensive, including a swank outdoor year-round pool, a library with the works of Felguérez, a sleek bar, **Frost,** and an excellent eatery in **Leonora.**

16 Vail Rd., Vail. ✆ **800/354-6908** or 970/477-8000. www.thesebastianvail.com. 107 units, including 7 suites. Winter $389–$970 double, $1,240–$5,850 suite; summer $239–$669 double, $1,000–$2,900 suite. Higher holiday rates; lower rates spring and fall. Resort fee $25/night. **Amenities:** Restaurant; lounge; bike rentals ($40/day); concierge; fitness center; outdoor Jacuzzi; outdoor heated year-round pool; sauna; free Wi-Fi.

Vail Cascade Resort ★★   Managed by Destination Hotels & Resorts, Vail Cascade is one of the biggest and best lodging properties in Vail, featuring its own chairlift and an enviable location on the western fringe of town on Gore Creek. Rooms got a slick renovation for spring 2013, with a "contemporary mountain" bent including earth tones, impressionist art, and sleek lighting. With the **Aria Athletic Club & Spa** (the largest fitness center in the valley) and great dining in Atwater on Gore Creek, the facilities here are excellent.

1300 Westhaven Dr., Vail. ✆ **800/282-4183** or 970/476-7111. www.vailcascade.com. 292 rooms and suites, including 80 condos and private residences. Winter $259–$659 double, $879–$1,400 suite; summer $129–$299 double, $750 suite. Higher holiday rates; lower rates spring and fall. Resort fee $27/night. Self-parking $18 ski season, free in summer (7-ft. height limit); valet parking $25 year-round. **Amenities:** 2 restaurants; lounge; concierge; fitness center; 5 Jacuzzis (3 outdoor, 2 indoor); 2 heated outdoor pools; room service; sauna; spa; tennis courts; free Wi-Fi.

Vail Mountain Lodge & Spa ★★   On the east side of Vail Village, this small boutique property has a romantic vibe. Each featuring a gas fireplace and separate shower and soaking tub, guest rooms and condos are comfortable, with a classic look that spurns "New West" motifs. Free for guests, the in-house **Vail Vitality Center** (www.vailvitalitycenter.com) is known for getting skiers ready for the season, and there is a climbing wall and in-house guide service as well. We also must give kudos to the renowned spa here and terrific resident eatery, **Terra Bistro.**

352 E. Meadow Dr. ✆ **888/794-0410** or 970/476-0700. www.vailmountainlodge.com. 27 units, including 7 condos. Winter $219–$559 double, $600–$1,900 condo; rest of year $149–$299 double,

$235–$600 condo. Higher holiday rates. Minimum stays required in ski season. Rates include continental breakfast. **Amenities:** Restaurant; lounge; health club; indoor Jacuzzi; spa; free Wi-Fi.

BEAVER CREEK
Expensive
Park Hyatt Beaver Creek Resort and Spa ★★★   Undergoing a $4 million room renovation in 2014, this landmark lodging is the flagship of Beaver Creek Village, with very European architecture and sensibility. Built in the 1980s and perpetually updated and meticulously maintained ever since, the majestic resort is a fitting cornerstone of the base village, with sumptuous, oversized rooms (standard: 400 sq. ft.) featuring private balconies and Western-tinged modern design. Then there are the little details, like nightly s'mores at the outdoor fire pit, and the big ones, like the massive antler chandelier hanging above the majestic (and aptly named) Antler Hall.

136 E. Thomas Pl., Avon. ✆ **800/778-7477** or 970/949-1234. www.parkhyattbeavercreek.com. 90 units. Winter $479–$1,179 double, $1,250–$4,500 suite; rest of year $139–$439 double, $350–$2,100 suite; higher holiday rates. Resort fee $20–$25/night. Valet parking $24. **Amenities:** 2 restaurants; lounge; children's program; concierge; health club; 5 outdoor Jacuzzis; indoor/outdoor heated pool; room service; spa; sauna; free Wi-Fi.

Westin Riverfront Resort & Spa at Beaver Creek Mountain ★★   This is one of the best ski hotels in the country, featuring a postcard-perfect riverside location, a lavish year-round pool, and its own gondola up to the slopes of Beaver Creek. The large, full-service hotel matches convenience with service, from helpful ski valets to an attentive bell staff, and there is style to spare. Take the rooms, with stately decor, plenty of dark wood, and stunning views, as one example, and Maya, the contemporary Mexican restaurant from Chef Richard Sandoval, as another. Spa Anjali offers mountain-inspired treatments, and there is a kids' program in winter and summer.

126 Riverfront Lane, Avon. ✆ **970/790-6000.** www.westinriverfrontbeavercreek.com. 357 units. Winter $319–$889 double, $399–$1,099 suite; summer $189–$429 double, $259–$499 suite. Higher holiday rates; lower rates spring and fall. Resort fee $25/night. Pets accepted ($25/night). **Amenities:** Restaurant; lounge; exercise room; outdoor Jacuzzi; outdoor heated year-round pool; spa; free Wi-Fi.

Inexpensive
Inn & Suites at Riverwalk ★   You can save significantly if you bypass the base villages in favor of this hotel in Edwards, home of Beaver Creek's Arrowhead area. It offers king and double queen rooms as well as suites and condos, and some have terrific Eagle River views. None are fancy, but they're neat as a pin and comfy. The hotel is located in the Riverwalk development, with shopping and dining within walking distance.

27 Main St., Edwards. ✆ **888/926-0606** or 970/926-0606. www.innandsuitesatriverwalk.com. 75 units, including 16 condos. Winter $130–$180 double, $225–$600 condo; rest of year $100–$130 double, $135–$380 condo. Rates include full breakfast. Pets accepted ($25 the first night, $5 thereafter). **Amenities:** Exercise room; outdoor Jacuzzi; outdoor heated pool; free Wi-Fi.

Where to Eat
You will find most restaurants in Vail and Beaver Creek villages shut down for a few weeks in the spring and/or fall; year-round options are easily found in Edwards, Avon, and Eagle.

EXPENSIVE
Beano's Cabin ★★★ CONTINENTAL/GAME   Named for Frank "Beano" Bienkowski, an early Beaver Creek homesteader, this on-mountain restaurant has both

views and stellar food. Depending on the season, guests arrive by horse, sleigh, shuttle, or tractor-pulled wagon, and then are treated to a fantastic five-course dinner at the rustic but elegant mid-mountain cabin. The food draws from influences near and far—local fish and elk chili, chops, or tartare might represent the former, with dishes like potato dumplings, whiskey-glazed porterhouses, and oysters with tequila, lime, and cucumber being examples of more far-flung fare. Reservations are required.

Near Larkspur Bowl, Beaver Creek Resort. ⓒ **970/754-3463.** www.beanoscabinbeavercreek.com. Fixed-price meal $98–$135. Departures from Beaver Creek ChopHouse (at Centennial Lift) winter daily 4:30–9:30pm; summer Thurs–Sun 4:30–9:30pm. Closed several months in spring and fall.

Restaurant Kelly Liken ★★★ NEW AMERICAN   Kelly Liken is one of the most celebrated chefs in Colorado—with appearances on shows like "Iron Chef" and "Top Chef"—and a meal at her eponymous Vail eatery makes it crystal-clear why her profile is so high. The seasonally shifting menu is cutting edge, and the wine pairings are pitch-perfect. Liken emphasizes a farm-to-table menu with local ingredients like lamb and striped bass, but expect inventive preparations that let the fresh flavors shine: potato-crusted trout with cherry tomatoes and lemon *beurre blanc,* for instance, or an asparagus and spring onion salad with a slow-cooked egg.

In the Gateway Building, 12 Vail Rd., Ste. 100. ⓒ **970/479-0175.** www.kellyliken.com. Main courses $42; 3-course dinner $45–$75. Daily 6–10pm. Bar open later.

Sweet Basil ★★★ NEW AMERICAN   A standby in Vail since it opened in 1977, Sweet Basil is not only reliable but reliably terrific. Serving in a refined dining room with picture windows showcasing the surrounding scenic beauty, the kitchen plates up a regularly changing menu using a high proportion of local ingredients like Olathe sweet corn and Palisade peaches. If they're on the menu, the Colorado lamb T-bones with charred eggplant, and Chilean salmon with cultured cream and dill are both stellar. Lunch dishes are similar, and include a build-your-own Angus burger with premium toppings.

193 E. Gore Creek Dr. ⓒ **970/476-0125.** www.sweetbasil-vail.com. Main courses $14–$21 lunch, $30–$45 dinner. Daily 11:30am–10pm. The bar remains open throughout the day.

Exploring Vail

Betty Ford Alpine Gardens ★★   At 8,250 feet, these are the highest public botanical gardens in North America. The alpine display, perennial garden, and mountain meditation garden together represent about 2,000 varieties of plants, demonstrating the wide range of choices to be grown at high altitudes. Named for the late first lady for her many local contributions, the gardens attract a variety of birds, and there is also a rock garden with a stunning 120-foot waterfall. Allow 1 to 3 hours.

Ford Park (east of Vail Village), Vail. ⓒ **970/476-0103.** www.bettyfordalpinegardens.org. Free admission. Daily dawn–dusk.

Colorado Ski Museum—Ski & Snowboard Hall of Fame ★   This museum is dedicated to the history of the sport most associated with Colorado, as well as honoring snowsports greats past and present. From the inaugural 1977 class with Carl Howelsen (the godfather of Colorado skiing) to recent inductees like Jake Burton and Jeremy Bloom, the Hall of Fame is a who's who of athletes, gear-makers, resort owners, and others. Museum exhibits run the gamut from the history of Vail to the "Colorado Snowboard Archive," showing the evolution of the gear. Allow 1 hour.

Vail Transportation Center, Level 3. ⓒ **970/476-1876.** www.skimuseum.net. Free admission; suggested donation $2. Daily 10am–6pm (until 4pm in spring and fall).

Skiing & Other Winter Activities

VAIL ★★★ America's top ski resort by practically any standard, Vail is something that all serious skiers must experience at least once. It has fantastic snow and great runs, and everything is so convenient that skiers can concentrate solely on skiing.

Ski area boundaries stretch 7 miles from east to west along the ridge top, from Outer Mongolia to Game Creek Bowl, and the skiable terrain is measured at 5,289 acres, the most on one mountain in North America. (It also attracts the most skier visits: 1.75 million in recent years.) Virtually every lift on the front side of the mountain has runs for every level of skier, with 18 percent beginner terrain, 29 percent intermediate, and the remaining 53 percent expert and advanced. The seven legendary Back Bowls are primarily for advanced and expert skiers; there are some beginner and intermediate routes. One trip down the Slot or Rasputin's Revenge will give you a fair idea of just how good you are. Blue Sky Basin, on the next mountain south of Vail, has three high-speed quad chairlifts and both intermediate to advanced backcountry-like terrain.

Vail has a vertical drop of 3,450 feet; average annual snowfall is 346 inches (nearly 29 ft.). All told, there are 193 conventional trails served by 33 lifts. The big news for 2012-13 was the replacement of the Vista Bahn Express quad with a state-of-the-art gondola. There are also three terrain parks, a superpipe, and a half-pipe for snowboarders of all skill levels.

The price of lift tickets can change from day to day, and are always least expensive when you buy online 7 to 14 days in advance and most expensive during holiday periods when you buy at the window; packages of 3 days or more also get discounts. Online 2013-14 prices typically ranged from about $75 to $115 for adults for a full-day lift ticket, but the window rate in peak seasons can hit $130. Online prices were $70 to $105 for seniors, $50 to $80 for children 5 to 12, and free for younger children. Any lift ticket purchased at Vail is also valid at Beaver Creek. Vail is usually open from mid-November to late April daily from 9am to 3:30pm. For further information, contact **Vail** (*©* **800/805-2457** for reservations or 970/754-8245 for information, snow report 970/754-4888; www.vail.com).

BEAVER CREEK ★★★ Built in 1980 and now owned by Vail Resorts, Beaver Creek is an outstanding resort in its own right, one with a more secluded atmosphere and maybe even more luxury than its better-known neighbor. Located in a valley 1½ miles off the I-70 corridor, Beaver Creek combines European château–style elegance in its base village. The Grouse Mountain, Birds of Prey, and Cinch Express lifts reach expert terrain. For the hardy of heart, the Stone Creek Chutes is an expert terrain area with chutes up to 550 vertical feet long, with pitches up to 44 degrees.

But at Beaver Creek, there's a trail for everyone. Experts are challenged but beginners aren't left out—they, too, can head straight to the top and then ski all the way down on a trail that matches their skill level. The vertical drop is 3,488 feet from the 11,440-foot summit, and there are 1,832 skiable acres in all.

The price of lift tickets can change from day to day, and are always least expensive when you buy online 7 to 14 days in advance and most expensive during holiday periods when you buy at the window; packages of 3 days or more also get discounts. Online 2013-14 prices ranged from $80 to $115 for adults for a full-day lift ticket, but the window rate in peak seasons can hit $130. Online prices were $75 to $105 for seniors, $50 to $80 for children 5 to 12, and free for younger children. Any lift ticket purchased at Beaver Creek is also valid at Vail. Instruction is available. Families will also get a kick out of the lift-served **Haymaker Tubing Hill** ($32 per hour; *©* **970/754-5368**).

Beaver Creek is open from mid-November to late April daily from 9am to 4pm, conditions permitting. For more information, contact **Beaver Creek Resort** (© **800/226-0355** or 970/754-4636, or 970/754-4888 for snow reports; www.beavercreek.com).

BACKCOUNTRY SKI TOURS **Paragon Guides** (© **970/926-5299;** www.paragonguides.com) is one of the country's premier winter guide services, offering backcountry ski trips on the 10th Mountain Trail and Hut System between Vail and Aspen (see "Cross-Country Skiing," below). A variety of trips are available, lasting from 1 to 6 days and designed for all ability levels. Costs start around $400 for two people for the day trip and $1,000 to $1,400 per person for a 3-day expedition.

CROSS-COUNTRY SKIING Cross-country skiers won't feel left out here, with trails at both resorts as well as a system of trails through the surrounding mountains. **Vail Nordic Center** (© **970/476-8366;** www.vailnordiccenter.com) has 21 miles of trails, part of them on the Vail Golf Course, and offers guided tours, lessons, and snowshoeing. A day pass is $8. The **Beaver Creek Nordic Center** (© **970/845-5313**), at Beaver Creek Resort, has a 20-mile mountaintop track system with a skating lane in 9,840-foot McCoy Park. Most of the high-altitude terrain here is intermediate, though there's some space for both beginner and advanced skiers; lessons are available. A day pass is $32 for adults, $20 for seniors and kids 12 and under.

For general information on the network of backcountry trails in the Vail area, contact the **White River National Forest,** at 24747 U.S. 24, 2 miles north of Minturn, off I-70 exit 171 (© **970/827-5715**).

Of particular note is the system of trails known as the **10th Mountain Division Hut System** (© **970/925-5775;** www.huts.org). Generally following the World War II training network of the Camp Hale militia, the trails cover 350 miles and link Vail with Leadville and Aspen, with 29 huts along the way where cross-country skiers and hikers can find shelter for the night. Huts are basic, with bunk beds, but do have woodstoves, propane burners, photovoltaic lighting, kitchen equipment, mattresses, and pillows. A one-person bed in one of the huts owned by the 10th Mountain Division Hut Association costs $33 per night for adults; huts owned by others but booked through the association cost a little more, and some require the entire unit to be rented for around $300.

More Outdoor Activities

Vail doesn't shut down once the skiers go home. Instead, visitors and locals alike trade their skis for mountain bikes and hiking boots, and hit the trails again. The resort closes parts of the mountain from early May to late June to protect elk-calving habitats, but other than that, warm-weather activities cover the mountains.

The Epic Pass

If you are planning on skiing multiple days, you can always do better than the single-day, nondiscounted prices listed in this book with multiday packages, but if you are planning on skiing a week or more in the area, for about $750 the **Epic Pass** (www.epicpass.com) might be your best bet: It gets you unlimited access at Vail, Beaver Creek, Breckenridge, Keystone, Arapahoe Basin, and Eldora in Colorado, Canyons in Utah, Heavenly, Northstar, and Kirkwood in California, for the entire season, as well as resorts in the Midwest, Japan, France, and Switzerland. More limited passes are less expensive, as are passes for kids.

Paragon Guides (© 970/926-5299; www.paragonguides.com) offers llama trekking, mountaineering, climbing, and other guide services in summer. **Nova Guides,** in Vail (© 719/486-2656; www.novaguides.com), offers guided fishing, mountain-bike and off-road tours, plus paintball and white-water rafting. The **10th Mountain Division Hut System** (© 970/925-5775; www.huts.org) is open to hikers and mountain-bikers in the summer months.

On Vail Mountain, the ski resort is significantly expanding its summer activities and facilities. For **Epic Discovery** (www.epicdiscovery.com), Vail Resorts has partnered with the nonprofit Nature Conservancy for education and is installing a roller coaster, a waterless tubing track, zip lines, a wildlife observation platform, a ropes course, and a kids adventure park, as well as expanding its biking and hiking trails. Call the resort (© 970/754-8245) for information.

For maps and information on the numerous activities in the White River National Forest, consult the **Holy Cross Ranger District Office** in Minturn (© 970/827-5715).

GOLF Courses here are usually open from mid-May to mid-October. The **Vail Golf Club,** 1778 Vail Valley Dr., Vail (© 970/479-2260; www.vailgolfclub.net), has greens fees of $45 to $90, cart not included; the **Eagle-Vail Golf Course,** 6 miles west of Vail at 431 Eagle Dr., Avon (© 970/949-5267; www.eaglevailgolfclub.com), charges $50 to $99 for 18 holes, cart included.

HIKING & BACKPACKING The surrounding White River National Forest has a plethora of trails leading to pristine lakes and spectacular panoramic views. The Holy Cross Wilderness Area, southwest of Vail, encompasses 14,005-foot Mount of the Holy Cross and is an awesome region with over 100 miles of trails. Eagle's Nest Wilderness Area lies to the north, in the impressive Gore Range. For information and maps for these and other hiking areas, consult the **Holy Cross Ranger District Office** in Minturn (© 970/827-5715).

HORSEBACK RIDING & CATTLE ROUNDUPS One of the best ways to explore this beautiful and rugged mountain country is on the back of a horse. **Vail Stables,** 915ASpraddle Creek Rd. (© 970/476-6941; www.vailstables.com), is open mid-May through September and is especially geared to families, with rides for beginners to experts. A 1½-hour ride costs $79. Also providing guided horseback rides is **Triple G Outfitters,** at 4 Eagle Ranch, 4 miles north of I-70 exit 157 (© 970/926-1234; www.tripleg.net), charging $60 and up for horseback rides, and also offering cattle roundups for $120 (experts only).

LLAMA TREKKING **Paragon Guides** (© 970/926-5299; www.paragonguides.com) offers llama-trekking trips that last from 3 to 6 days from July through September. They are limited to eight persons for camping, or slightly larger groups for hut trips, and start around $1,000 per person for 3 days. Pricier custom treks are also available, from overnight to 1 week. There are also llama-supported lunch hikes for about $100 per person.

MOUNTAIN BIKING Summer visitors can take their bikes up the Eagle Bahn Gondola on Vail Mountain (all-day passes are $31) and cruise downhill on a series of trails. There are many other choices for avid bikers, on both backcountry trails and road tours. A popular trip is the 10-mile route along Red Sandstone Road to Piney Lake. The 30-mile Vail Pass Bikeway goes to Frisco, with a climb from 8,460 feet up to 10,600 feet. Pick up a trail list (with map) at an information center. Guided trips are available. Mountain-bike repairs and rentals are available at a number of shops, including **Wheel Base,** 610 W. Lionshead Circle (℗ **970/476-5799;** www. vailwheelbase.com), also offering guided and unguided Vail Pass tours. Rental rates are $40 to $65 for a full day.

RIVER RAFTING The Eagle River, just a few miles west of Vail, offers thrilling white water, especially during the May-to-June thaw. Families can enjoy the relatively gentle (Class II–IV) lower Eagle, west of Minturn; the upper Eagle, above Minturn, is significantly rougher (Class IV–V rapids). Area rafting companies also take trips on the Colorado River, which they access about 35 miles northwest via Colo. 131, at State Bridge. Rafting companies here include **Timberline Tours** (℗ **800/831-1414;** www. timberlinetours.com), **Nova Guides** (℗ **719/486-2656;** www.novaguides.com), and **Lakota River Guides** (℗ **970/845-7238;** www.lakotariver.com). Rates run $80 to $120 per adult for a half-day trip, with slightly lower rates for youths. (Young children aren't usually permitted.)

Nightlife

Vail's greatest concentration of late-night haunts can be found in a 1½-block stretch of Bridge Street from Hanson Ranch Road north to the covered bridge over Gore Creek. They include **Vendetta's,** 291 Bridge St. (℗ **970/476-5070**), reportedly the hangout for Vail's ski patrollers, the **Tap Room,** 333 Bridge St. (℗ **970/479-0500**), with an extensive selection of beers on tap, plus good pub grub and martinis, and **Samana Lounge,** 228 Bridge St. (℗ **970/476-3433**), a small, sophisticated dance club with a candlelit ambience and world-class DJs. **Garfinkel's,** 536 E. Lionshead Circle (℗ **970/476-3789**), keeps sports fans busy with tons of TVs, and everybody else happy with a great deck at the foot of the Eagle Bahn gondola. In nearby Minturn, the happy hour at the historic **Minturn Saloon,** 146 N. Main St. (℗ **970/827-5954**), attracts a party-hearty horde for Vail Valley's best margaritas, plus those who just skied the "Minturn Mile."

The Festival Scene

The summer season's big cultural event is the **Bravo! Vail Music Festival** (℗ **877/812-5700** or 970/827-5700; www.vailmusicfestival.org), held from late June through early August. Established in 1988, the festival features a variety of classical music, from orchestral to chamber music to vocal, with performers such as the New York Philharmonic, the Philadelphia Orchestra, and the Dallas Symphony.

The **Vail International Dance Festival** (℗ **888/920-2787;** www.vaildance.org) features both classes and performances. The World Masters Ballet Academy at Vail teaches the Russian style of artistic expression and other techniques, and presents a series of performances each summer.

The Vail Valley Foundation also hosts **Hot Summer Nights** (℗ **970/777-2015**), free concerts of contemporary rock, jazz, or blues, on Tuesday evenings from mid-June through early August at the Gerald R. Ford Amphitheatre near Betty Ford Alpine Gardens.

LEADVILLE ★

38 miles S of Vail, 59 miles E of Aspen, 113 miles W of Denver

Not much more than a century ago, Leadville was the most important city between St. Louis and San Francisco. It was the stopping point for Easterners with nothing to lose and everything to gain from the promise of gold and silver. Today Leadville is one of the best places to rediscover the West's mining heritage.

A float ON THE WILD SIDE

Rancho Del Rio is a former hippie commune that's now one of the last remaining river-rat communities of its kind. The slow waters of the Upper Colorado River in this area are perfect for beginner rafters and families; even first-timers will be comfortable paddling the river solo. The **Colorado River Center** (☎ **888/888-7238** or 970/653-7238; www.colorado rivercenter.com) offers rentals, shuttles, lessons, and guided rafting trips. I recommend renting a duckie (an inflatable kayak) for about $50 and paddling it to State Bridge, and then getting a shuttle back to Rancho.

After a river trip and a shuttle ride back, it's time for a bite and a beer at **K.K.'s BBQ,** also known as the "Center of the Universe." An outdoor bar and grill with jars of homemade pickles and pots of homemade sauce and slices of homemade pies, this is the most fun you can have at a meal in the vicinity. Eponymous proprietor K. K. is quite the character and a one-woman act, cooking burgers, ringing bells, telling jokes, and generally entertaining everyone within earshot. She is open on weekends only.

For more information, contact **Rancho Del Rio,** 4199 Trough Rd., Bond, CO 80423 (☎ **970/653-4431;** www.rancho delrio.com). There is a campground ($3 per person per night), rental cabins ($50–$80 a night), shuttles ($25–$80), and fly-fishing guides. The day-use fee is $1 per person and $2 per vehicle.

Founded in 1860 on the gold that glimmered in prospectors' pans, Leadville and nearby Oro City quickly attracted 10,000 miners who dug $5 million in gold out of a 3-mile stretch of the California Gulch by 1865. Then in 1875, two prospectors located the California Gulch's first paying silver lode. Over the next 2 decades, Leadville grew to an estimated 30,000 residents—among them "the Unsinkable" Molly Brown, whose husband made his fortune here before moving to Denver.

Now an isolated mountain town (elevation 10,152 ft., making it the highest incorporated municipality in the country) of about 2,600 residents, Leadville has managed to maintain its historic character. Many buildings of the silver boom, which produced $136 million in 1879–89, have been preserved in Leadville's National Historic Landmark District. It has also emerged as a hotspot for endurance sports (and the athletes training for such sports) with dual 100-mile hike and bike races every August.

Essentials

GETTING THERE   By Car   Coming from Denver, leave I-70 at exit 195 (Copper Mountain) and proceed south 24 miles on Colo. 91. From the west, depart I-70 at exit 171 (Minturn) and continue south 33 miles on U.S. 24. From Aspen, in the summer take Colo. 82 east 44 miles over Independence Pass (closed winter), then go north on U.S. 24 for 15 miles. There's also easy access from the south via U.S. 24.

By Plane   The nearest airport with commercial service is the **Eagle County Regional Airport,** which offers car rentals and bus service to Leadville (p. 156).

GETTING AROUND   U.S. 24 is Leadville's main street. Entering Leadville from the north, it's named Poplar Street; then it turns west on Ninth Street for a block and then south on Harrison Avenue. The next 7 blocks south, to Second Street, are the heart of this historic town. A block north, Seventh Street climbs east to the historic train depot and 13,186-foot Mosquito Pass, among America's highest, open to four-wheel-drive vehicles. **Dee Hive Tours** (☎ **719/486-2339**) offers **taxi and shuttle** service.

VISITOR INFORMATION   Contact the **Leadville/Lake County Chamber of Commerce** (*ℂ* **719/486-3900;** www.visitleadvilleco.com).

FAST FACTS   There's a 24-hour emergency room at **St. Vincent's General Hospital,** 822 W. Fourth St. (*ℂ* **719/486-0230;** www.svghd.org). The **post office** is at 130 W. Fifth St.

Where to Stay
MODERATE
Delaware Hotel ★   The Delaware opened in 1886 as a rival to the Tabor Grand Hotel across the street (now apartments), and saw a long period of decline after silver crashed in 1893. ("Baby Doe" Tabor would come here to warm her newspaper-wrapped feet when she was penniless.) New ownership came in and restored the old hotel in the 1990s and today it is the most historic lodging in what is arguably Colorado's most historic town. The lobby is lined with taxidermy and antiques; guest rooms likewise have period antiques as well as many original features. The lobby and upstairs halls double as an antiques store, plus guests can choose a getup from a vintage costume collection and pose for photos ($3 per person). Free tours are available to guests and non-guests alike.

700 Harrison Ave., Leadville. *ℂ* **800/748-2004** or 719/486-1418. www.delawarehotel.com. 36 units, including 4 suites. $65–$160 double; $140–$245 family room or suite. Children 10 and younger stay free in parent's room. Rates include continental breakfast. **Amenities:** Restaurant; free Wi-Fi.

INEXPENSIVE
Leadville Hostel & Inn ★★   This hostel is the best in the Rockies, thanks to the detail-oriented owners, "Wild Bill" Clower and Cathy Hacking. A converted house just up Seventh Street from the main drag, it's popular with travelers of all kinds, from college-age ramblers to retirees to endurance athletes. The services are a la carte—laundry or walk-in showers are $3, breakfasts are $7, and carb-heavy dinners are $13—and Clower and Hacking are terrific hosts. Besides men's and women's dorm rooms, there are three small rooms for couples and a pair of larger private rooms (the only ones with private baths). The hostel has a social vibe, exemplified by the nightly movies in the comfy living room.

500 E. Seventh Ave., Leadville. *ℂ* **719/486-9334.** www.leadvillehostel.com. 32 dorm beds, 7 private rooms (4 with private bathroom). $23–$30 dorm bed; $35–$60 private room. Dogs accepted ($5 per stay). **Amenities:** Wi-Fi ($1 per day).

Where to Eat
INEXPENSIVE
The Golden Burro Café ★ AMERICAN   They don't make restaurants like the Golden Burro anymore. Fronted by one of the most photogenic vintage signs in the state, the restaurant started serving in 1938, targeting miners coming off their shifts at the local molybdenum mine. Now you'll find a mix of Leadville residents and tourists and one of the longest menus around. (It is in a binder and is a full 24 pages long.) You can get greasy-spoon standards like egg plates and biscuits and gravy, plus burgers, steaks, and Mexican food. The pie alone is worth a stop.

710 Harrison Ave. *ℂ* **719/486-1239.** www.goldenburro.com. Main courses $5–$20. Daily 6:30am–9pm (until 8pm fall to spring).

Quincy's Steakhouse ★ STEAKS   If you like steak but don't care for spending, this is the spot for you. You get filet mignon on weekdays, Prime rib on weekends, and there is also salmon and vegetarian lasagna for good measure. There are also locations in Salida and Buena Vista.

416 Harrison St. ℂ **719/486-9765.** www.quincystavern.com. Main courses $9–$20. Daily 5–9pm.

Experiencing Leadville's Past

A great many residences of successful mining operators, engineers, and financiers are preserved within the **Leadville National Historic Landmark District,** which stretches along 7 blocks of Harrison Avenue and part of Chestnut Street, where it intersects Harrison at the south end of downtown. A self-guided walking tour of this district, with map, is available free at the chamber.

Leadville has numerous historic buildings open to the public; allow 30 minutes to an hour for each of the following.

You'll discover Leadville's colorful past at the **Heritage Museum,** corner of Ninth Street and Harrison Avenue (ℂ **719/486-1878;** www.leadvilleheritagemuseum.com), where the displays include a miniature replica of the Leadville Ice Palace that fell prey to an early spring in 1896. Admission costs $6 for adults, $3 for students 6 to 16, and free for children 5 and under. It's open May to September daily from 10am to 5pm.

The **National Mining Hall of Fame and Museum,** 120 W. Ninth St. (ℂ **719/486-1229;** www.mininghalloffame.org), covers the rich history of mineral extraction in Colorado with antique tools and machinery and several faux mines representative of different eras, as well as telling the stories of the industry luminaries who are enshrined in the National Mining Hall of Fame. Admission is $9 for adults, $7 for seniors 62 and older, $7 for teens, $4 for children 6 to 12, and it's free for younger children. The museum is open daily from 9am to 5pm.

Peer into mining magnate's Horace Tabor's **Matchless Mine,** 1¼ miles east up Seventh Street, and tour the **Baby Doe Tabor Museum** (ℂ **719/486-1229**), where you'll see how Tabor's widow, Baby Doe, spent the final 36 years of her life hoping to strike it rich once more. Admission is the same as the mining museum (see above). It's open Memorial Day to Labor Day daily from 10am to 5pm, with the last tour leaving at 4:30pm. Combination mining museum/mine tickets run $13 adults, $11 seniors and teens, and $7 kids 6 to 12.

To get an up-close look at where a few fortunate miners were able to escape the rough-and-tumble atmosphere of the mines, if only for an evening, visit **Healy House and Dexter Cabin,** 912 Harrison Ave. (ℂ **719/486-0487;** www.historycolorado.org). Healy House was built by smelter owner August Meyer in 1878 and later converted into a lavish boardinghouse by Daniel Healy. The adjacent rough-hewn log cabin was built by James Dexter and furnished in an elegant style. Admission is $6 for adults, $5.50 for seniors 65 and older, $4.50 for children 6 to 16, and free for younger children. It is open Memorial Day weekend through September daily from 10am to 4:30pm, with the last tour at 3:45pm.

The **Tabor Opera House,** 308 Harrison Ave. (ℂ **719/486-8409;** www.taboropera house.net), is where Leadville's mining magnates and their wives kept up with cultural happenings back East. Opened in 1879, it has hosted everything from the Ziegfeld Follies and the Metropolitan Opera to prizefighter Jack Dempsey (a Colorado native) and magician Harry Houdini (whose vanishing square is still evident on the stage floor). Visitors can explore the 880-seat theater, backstage, and the dressing rooms, or attend one of the musical or theater performances still held here. (Check the website for the current schedule and prices.) Admission to tour the opera house is $5 for adults, $4 for seniors 65 and older, and $2.50 for children under 13. There is also a tour of the second floor of the opera house, with exhibits on Baby Doe and the area's mining heritage, for the same admission prices. (Both admissions are separate, however.) The building is open Memorial Day to Labor Day Monday to Saturday from 10am to 5pm.

More to See & Do

Leadville, Colorado & Southern Railroad ★ This spectacularly scenic ride, in a 1955 diesel train, departs the 1893 C&S Depot, 3 blocks east of U.S. 24, and follows the old "high line" along the headwaters of the Arkansas River to a splendid view of Fremont Pass. The return takes you to the French Gulch water tower for a dramatic look at Mount Elbert, Colorado's tallest mountain (14,433 ft.). The ride lasts about 2½ hours, and because of the high elevations, jackets or sweaters are recommended even on the hottest summer days.

326 E. Seventh St. (at Hazel St.). ✆ **866/386-3936** or 719/486-3936. www.leadville-train.com. Admission $35 adults, $20 children 4–12, free for children under 4. Caboose or engine seating $30–$40 extra, Daily Memorial Day to late Sept or early Oct, with 1 or 2 departures daily from 10am–2pm.

Leadville National Fish Hatchery ★ Established in 1889, this is the second-oldest hatchery operated by the U.S. Fish and Wildlife Service that's in existence today. Rainbow, brown, and cutthroat trout are raised here, at an elevation of 10,000 feet on the east side of Mount Massive—you can view the fish and feed them. Visitors can also enjoy self-guided nature trails, with breathtaking views of the surrounding mountains and occasionally deer and elk. One trail passes by the remains of the Evergreen Hotel, a late-1800s resort, and several trails connect to the Colorado Trail. In winter, take cross-country skis or snowshoes. Allow 30 to 45 minutes.

2844 Colo. 300 (6 miles southwest of Leadville, off U.S. 24). ✆ **719/486-0189.** www.fws.gov/leadville. Free admission. Daily 7am–3:30pm. Guided tours available by appointment.

Outdoor Activities

Much of the outdoor recreation in this area takes place in nearby national forestlands, and you can get information at the **San Isabel National Forest** office, 810 Front St. (✆ **719/486-0749**). **Bill's Sport Shop,** 225 Harrison Ave. (✆ **719/486-1497;** www. billsrentals.com), is a good source for gear (to rent or buy) and advice.

Adventurous **hikers** can attempt an ascent of Mount Elbert (14,440 ft., the highest peak in the Rockies), Mount Sherman (14,035 ft.), or Mount Massive (14,428 ft.); all three can be climbed in a day without technical equipment, though altitude and abruptly changing weather conditions are factors that should be weighed. One popular trail for hiking, walking, and mountain biking is the **Mineral Belt Trail,** a 12-mile loop that circles Leadville, passing through the mining district and the mountains in the process.

If snowsports are more to your liking, **Ski Cooper** (✆ **800/707-6114** or 719/486-3684, 719/486-2277 for snow reports; www.skicooper.com) is a small mom-and-pop-style resort, with 400 acres of lift-served skiable terrain and another 2,400 acres accessible by snowcat. It began as a training center for 10th Mountain Division troops from Camp Hale during World War II. Located 10 miles north of Leadville on U.S. 24 near Tennessee Pass, it offers numerous intermediate and novice runs, and backcountry snowcat tours of Chicago Ridge for experts ($299 a day). Five lifts serve 400 skiable acres—rated 31 percent beginner, 35 percent intermediate, and 34 percent expert—and the mountain has a 1,200-foot vertical drop from the peak of 11,700 feet. Full-day tickets (2013–14) cost $47 for adults, $27 for children 6 to 14, $39 for seniors 60 to 69, $24 for seniors 70 and older, and are free for kids 5 and under. The **Tennessee Pass**

Nordic Center (✆ **719/486-1750;** www.tennesseepass.com), at the foot of the mountain, has 15 miles of groomed cross-country skiing trails and a highly regarded restaurant, the **Tennessee Pass Cookhouse** (✆ **719/486-8114** for reservations; prix-fixe dinners run $75–$80). Trail passes cost $14 for adults and $10 for children and seniors. Lessons and rentals are available.

Shopping

Pick up locally made fleece goods at **Melanzana,** 716 Harrison Ave. (✆ **719/486-3245**), funky vintage clothing at **Mule Kick,** 721 Harrison Ave. (✆ **719/293-2039**), and antiques at the **Delaware Hotel,** 700 Harrison Ave. (✆ **719/486-1418**).

Nightlife

There's occasional entertainment at the **Tabor Opera House** (p. 166), and a handful of historic watering holes. My picks are the 1878 **Pastime Bar,** 120 W. 2nd St. (✆ **719/486-9434**), and the 1879 **Silver Dollar Saloon,** 315 Harrison Ave. (✆ **719/486-9914**), both one-time haunts of Doc Holliday.

ASPEN ★★★

172 miles W of Denver, 130 miles E of Grand Junction

If you take the time to dig beneath the Hollywood hype, you may be surprised. Aspen, at an elevation of 7,908 feet, is a real town with a fascinating history and spectacular mountain scenery.

Long a Ute tribal hub, Aspen was "discovered" by silver miners in the 1870s. When the Smuggler Mine produced the world's largest silver nugget (1,840 lb.), the boom began. The city soon had 12,000 citizens, but the population dwindled after the 1893 silver crash. It took almost 50 years for Aspen to begin its comeback, which came as a result of another natural resource—snow. The original vision of the resort was not exclusively commercial, but also intellectual and artistic.

Essentials

GETTING THERE   By Car   Aspen is located on Colo. 82, halfway between I-70 at Glenwood Springs (42 miles northwest) and U.S. 24 south of Leadville (44 miles east). In summer, it's a scenic 3½-hour drive from Denver: Leave I-70 West at exit 195 (Copper Mountain); follow Colo. 91 south to Leadville, where you pick up U.S. 24; turn west on Colo. 82 through Twin Lakes and over 12,095-foot Independence Pass. In winter, the Independence Pass road is closed, so you'll have to take I-70 to Glenwood Springs and head southeast on Colo. 82. In optimal driving conditions, it'll take 4 hours from Denver by this route.

By Plane   Visitors who wish to fly directly into Aspen can arrange to land at **Aspen/Pitkin County Airport (ASE),** 5 miles northwest of Aspen on Colo. 82 (✆ **970/920-5384;** www.aspenairport.com), served year-round by **Delta, United,** and **American.** Another option is the **Eagle County Regional Airport (EGE;** p. 156).

By Airport Shuttle   Colorado Mountain Express (✆ **800/525-6363** or 970/754-7433; www.coloradomountainexpress.com) offers shuttle service from Denver International Airport starting at $120 per person, one-way.

By Train   Coming from San Francisco or Chicago, **Amtrak** (✆ **800/872-7245;** www.amtrak.com) stops in Glenwood Springs, 42 miles northwest of Aspen.

GETTING AROUND   Entering town from the northwest on Colo. 82, the artery jogs right (south) 2 blocks on Seventh Street, then left (east) at Main Street. East and west street numbers are separated by Garmisch Street, the next cross street after First Street. Mill Street is the town's main north-south street. There are several pedestrian malls downtown, which throw a curve into the downtown traffic flow, but Aspen is small enough that it's fairly hard to get lost.

By Shuttle Bus   Free bus service is available within the Aspen city limits and between Aspen and Snowmass Village, beyond which you can get connections as near as Woody Creek and as far west as Rifle, at reasonable rates: Aspen to Glenwood Springs is just $7. Exact fare is required. Information can be obtained from the Roaring Fork Transportation Authority's **Rubey Park Transit Center,** Durant Avenue between Mill and Galena streets, in Aspen (℡ **970/925-8484;** www.rfta.com). Schedules, frequency, and routes vary with the seasons; services include free ski shuttles in winter between all four mountains, shuttles to the Aspen Music Festival, and tours to the Maroon Bells in summer. Free shuttle transportation within Snowmass Village is offered daily during ski season and on a limited schedule in summer, by the **Snowmass Transportation Department** (℡ **970/923-2543;** www.snowmasstransit.com).

By Taxi   Call **High Mountain Taxi** (℡ **970/925-8294;** www.hmtaxi.com). For a more distinctive (and bizarre) experience, hail the **Ultimate Taxi** (see below).

By Rental Car   Car-rental agencies at Aspen/Pitkin County Airport include **Alamo/National, Avis, Budget, Dollar,** and **Hertz.** Also of note is **Go Rentals** (℡ **800/464-8267;** www.gorentals.com), specializing in luxury cars and electric vehicles.

VISITOR INFORMATION   For information, contact the **Aspen Chamber of Commerce and Resort Association** (℡ **800/670-0792** or 970/925-1940; www.aspenchamber.org), which operates a **visitor center** at 425 Rio Grande Place and another at the Wheeler Opera House, located at Hyman Avenue and Mill Street. You can also get information from the **Snowmass Village Resort Association** (℡ **800/766-9627;** www.snowmassvillage.com).

FAST FACTS   The **Aspen Valley Hospital,** 0401 Castle Creek Rd., near Aspen Highlands (℡ **970/925-1120;** www.aspenhospital.org), has a 24-hour emergency room. The **post office** is at 235 Puppy Smith St., off Mill Street north of Main. For **road reports,** call ℡ **970/920-5454** or 511 in-state or visit **www.cotrip.org**.

Riding in Style: The Ultimate Taxi

Known in the Aspen Valley as the **Ultimate Taxi,** Jon Barnes's yellow cab is one of the most unusual vehicles on the planet: There's a rainbow of luminescent fiber optics and LED lights on the ceiling, laser projectors, a webcam, a recording studio complete with keyboards and drum machines, a mirror ball, a roller-coaster simulator, and much more. Barnes has worked as a cabbie in Aspen since 1984, but started modifying his taxi in the early '90s. A 40-minute ride is $200. Barnes even takes your picture and posts it on his website (www.ultimatetaxi.com) for posterity. Call Jon for reservations or a ride at ℡ **970/927-9239.**

Aspen

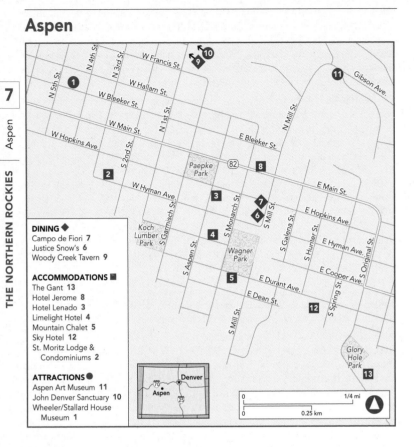

DINING ◆
Campo de Fiori **7**
Justice Snow's **6**
Woody Creek Tavern **9**

ACCOMMODATIONS ■
The Gant **13**
Hotel Jerome **8**
Hotel Lenado **3**
Limelight Hotel **4**
Mountain Chalet **5**
Sky Hotel **12**
St. Moritz Lodge & Condominiums **2**

ATTRACTIONS ●
Aspen Art Museum **11**
John Denver Sanctuary **10**
Wheeler/Stallard House Museum **1**

Where to Stay

Occupancy rates run 90 percent or higher during peak winter and summer seasons, so it's essential to make reservations as early as possible (or avoid peak seasons, as I try to do). The easiest way to book your lodgings is to call **Stay Aspen Snowmass** central reservations (© **888/649-5982;** www.stayaspensnowmass.com).

EXPENSIVE

The Gant ★★ This '70s-era condo resort underwent a stunning renovation in 2014. Today, it's one of the most fashion-forward hotels in the Rockies, with neo-mid-century-modern furnishings (done in cheerful colors), distressed plank walls, fireplaces, and fun shag rugs. The beds are downright sumptuous, and all the units are oversized, making them a great pick for families. Set on 5 acres, The Gant is one of the few condo properties in town with full kitchens and washer/dryers along with a long list of amenities.

610 S.W. End St., Aspen. © **800/549-0530** or 970/925-5000. www.gantaspen.com. 120 units. $400–$900 1-bedroom condo, $550–$1,995 2- or 4-bedroom condo. Higher holiday rates Resort fee 5 percent. **Amenities:** 2 heated outdoor pools; 3 outdoor Jacuzzis; access to nearby health club; bike rentals; 5 outdoor tennis courts (3 clay); free Wi-Fi.

Hotel Jerome ★★★ Historic hotels don't get any more luxurious than the Jerome, but don't expect Victorian frills: The 1889 hotel's redbrick facade belies the contemporary decor inside. Unlike many historic lodgings, the rooms here are spacious, often created from melding two or more of the originals into one, with plenty of nods to the Rocky Mountain locale, including log-inspired bed frames. The age of the hotel also has proven no impediment to modern technology; flatscreen TVs, iPads, and humidifiers are standard.

330 E. Main St., Aspen. ✆ **800/331-7213** or 970/920-1000. www.hoteljerome.com. 91 units. Summer and ski season $495–$675 double, $700–$1,700 suite; spring and fall $225–$420 double, $375–$520 suite. Higher holiday rates Resort fee $30/night. Pets permitted ($100 fee). **Amenities:** 2 restaurants; 2 bars; concierge; exercise room; 2 outdoor Jacuzzis; outdoor heated pool; room service; Wi-Fi (included w/resort fee).

Viceroy Snowmass ★★ Snowmass is dominated by condominium complexes, making this full-service hotel a much needed change of pace when it opened here in 2009. The modern, lodgelike look is perfect for the setting at the base of the slopes, and the motif carries over to the rooms and suites, sleek visions of contrasting colors and inspired design by Jean-Michel Gathy. The year-round pool terrace, complete with plush chaise lounges and cabanas, is the best in the area, and the ski-in, ski-out access to the slopes is as good as it gets in wintertime.

130 Wood Rd., Snowmass Village. ✆ **888/622-4567** or 970/923-8000. www.viceroyhotelsand resorts.com. 173 condos. Ski season $225–$695 studios and $535–$1,785 1- to 4-bedroom condos. Higher holiday rates; lower rates spring to fall. Rates include continental breakfast. Resort fee 15 percent summer, 30 percent winter. Pets accepted ($100 one-time fee). **Amenities:** 2 restaurants; lounge; concierge; exercise room; 2 outdoor Jacuzzis; outdoor heated pool; spa; free Wi-Fi.

MODERATE

Hotel Lenado ★★ Tucked away from the hustle, bustle, and glitz in a quiet neighborhood, the Hotel Lenado is also not going to induce sticker shock; the rates are quite reasonable for Aspen. The lodging melds the intimacy and style of a boutique hotel with the comfort and service of a B&B, and the results are inviting. Accommodations are bright and cheery, with light woods and checkered comforters, including the larger Smuggler rooms and the slightly smaller Larkspur rooms. The vibe is sociable, and the rooftop hot tub is one of the best places to see Aspen while not being seen yourself.

200 S. Aspen St., Aspen. ✆ **800/321-3457** or 970/925-6246. www.hotellenado.com. 19 units. Ski season and summer $225–$425. Higher holiday rates; lower rates spring and fall. Rates include full breakfast. Pets accepted (free). **Amenities:** Bar; concierge; outdoor Jacuzzi; free Wi-Fi.

Limelight Hotel ★★ There is lot to like at the Limelight, from the sustainably minded architecture to the resident Lounge and its terrific happy hour. Rooms range from standard hotel quarters to 1,000-square-foot suites, all with a contemporary mountain style and a long list of amenities. Other perks include a free "First Tracks" program at Aspen Mountain and complimentary snowshoes.

228 E. Cooper Ave. (at Monarch St.), Aspen. ✆ **855/925-3025** or 970/925-3025. www.limelight hotel.com. 126 units. Summer $235–$595 double, $705 suite; ski season $330–$690 double, $850 suite. Higher holiday rates; lower rates spring and fall. Resort fee 6 percent. Rates include continental breakfast. Pets accepted. **Amenities:** Airport shuttle; restaurant (American); lounge; bikes (complimentary); concierge; fitness center; 2 outdoor Jacuzzis; outdoor heated pool; free Wi-Fi.

Sky Hotel ★★ Right on the base of Aspen Mountain, this Kimpton has personality and color to spare. The small rooms were redecorated in 2012 with a nod to the

1969 Robert Redford ski-racing flick "Downhill Racer." The headboards resemble retro ski sweaters, furnishings are colorful and quirky, and the carpet pattern was inspired by fresh ski tracks. Off the lobby are the standout outdoor pool—a vision of rock and mountain views, perfect for real and would-be celebrities alike—and the popular bar, **39 Degrees** (p. 177).

709 E. Durant Ave., Aspen. © **800/882-2582** or 970/925-6760. www.theskyhotel.com. 90 units, including 6 suites. Summer $185–$499 double, $299–$649 suite; winter $209–$629 double, $329–$779 suite. Higher holiday rates; lower rates spring and fall. Valet parking $26. Pets accepted (free). **Amenities:** Lounge; exercise room; outdoor Jacuzzi; outdoor heated pool; Wi-Fi (free for members of Kimpton loyalty program).

INEXPENSIVE

In addition to the property discussed below, those on a budget might want to consider the **St. Moritz Lodge & Condominiums,** 334 W. Hyman Ave., Aspen (© **800/817-2069** or 970/925-3220; www.stmoritzlodge.com), which is one of the best deals in town; small double rooms with shared bathrooms start at $185 in summer and $119 in ski season. There are also hostel beds ($36–$75 per person), plus pricier rooms with private bathrooms, kitchenettes, and condos.

The Mountain Chalet ★　This is the best value in Aspen. Harking back to 1954, before the luxury boom, this slopeside motel has great access to Aspen Mountain, and comfortable, if standard motel rooms, as well as a pair of larger apartments with kitchens. There is also a winter-only bunk room for ski bums who don't mind sharing space ($59–$79).

333 E. Durant Ave., Aspen. © **888/925-7797** or 970/925-7797. www.mountainchaletaspen.com. 59 units. Winter $109–$415 double, $319–$609 apt; summer $109–$299 double, $229–$499 apt. Higher holiday rates; lower rates spring and fall. Rates include full breakfast in winter, continental breakfast in summer. Free underground parking. **Amenities:** Exercise room; large indoor Jacuzzi; outdoor heated pool; sauna and steam room; free Wi-Fi.

Where to Eat

Most restaurants in the Aspen-Snowmass area are open during the ski season (Thanksgiving to early Apr) and summer (mid-June to mid-Sept) seasons. Between seasons, however, some close their doors or limit hours.

EXPENSIVE

Campo de Fiori ★★★ ITALIAN　Since 1994, this has been the place to see and be seen—and *mangia, mangia, mangia!*—in Aspen. The food is first-rate, with the kitchen plating up authentic Italian fare like fettuccine Bolognese, shrimp and zucchini risotto, and fusilli pesto, plus steaks and seafood with preparations from "the Boot". A bar menu offers smaller and less expensive variations of these dishes. In summer, there is no better place to dine than the courtyard here, set on the main level of a gallery-laden shopping complex.

205 S. Mill St. © **970/920-7717.** www.campodefiori.net. Dinner main courses $19–$30 pasta, $28–$44 entrees. Daily 5:30–10:30pm; closed Sun–Mon or Mon–Tues in fall and spring.

INEXPENSIVE TO MODERATE

Justice Snow's ★★ GASTROPUB　Replacing the venerable Bentley's as the resident eatery and watering hole at the historic Wheeler Opera House, Justice Snow's is one of the best new restaurants and cocktail bars in the in the West. Named for the local justice of the peace in the late 1800s, the copper-topped bar and rough, ornate woodwork prove a nice backdrop for the inventive fare. The kitchen takes both regional and

Mediterranean cues with small plates like chickpea fritters and main courses such as Colorado lamb French dips and grilled Norwegian salmon. But the thick, leather-bound cocktail list with 100-plus offerings organized by liquor, including a bit of history on each drink, is a showstopper, as is the cocktail-making, verging on performance art.

In the Wheeler Opera House, 328 E. Hyman Ave. *C* **970/429-8192.** www.justicesnows.com. Main courses $10–$27. Daily 11am–10pm. Bar open later.

Woody Creek Tavern ★★ AMERICAN/MEXICAN   No establishment is more associated with late local legend Hunter S. Thompson. Fans learned the "Fear and Loathing in Las Vegas" author would hang out here, leading Thompson to call the bar to keep it open late for him—and him alone. Today you will still find many nods to the gonzo journalist in the photos and posters plastering the walls, but the connection is not the only reason to come. The Mexican food is the best in the valley—the tamales have attained near-mythic status—and the strong, blue agave margaritas are the best in the Aspen area. Neither credit cards nor reservations are accepted.

2858 Upper River Rd., Woody Creek (8 miles northwest of Aspen via Colo. 82). *C* **970/923-4585.** www.woodycreektavern.com. Main courses $11–$20 lunch; $11–$28 dinner. Daily 11am–10pm.

Exploring Aspen

The **Aspen Historical Society,** 620 W. Bleeker St. (*C* **970/925-3721;** www.aspen history.org), offers a variety of guided tours of Aspen and the surrounding mining camps during the summer. One walking tour of Aspen explores the West End residential area, another delves into the historic **Hotel Jerome** (p. 171), and a third involves a demo of steam and early gasoline engines. A bicycle tour is also offered (bring your own bike). The cost of a tour is $15 adult, $12 seniors, and free for kids under 13. The **History Coach** is a motorized electric vehicle that takes six guests at a time on 2-hour tours of town. Tours are offered Tuesday through Saturday for $25 per adult, $20 seniors, and free for kids under 13. Additionally, guided tours of Ashcroft and Independence **ghost towns** are available daily in summer for $3 adults. Call for reservations. Self-guided tour brochures are also available.

Also recommended are the forays into Aspen's past led by Dean Weiler of **Aspen Walking Tours** (*C* **970/948-4349;** www.aspenwalkingtours.com). Weiler is an engaging storyteller who offers a variety of walking tours at select times and dates in the summer and fall. His DarkSide tour is especially recommended: It hits Aspen's seamy side, detailing everything from Ute curses to serial killer Ted Bundy. The tours last 60 to 90 minutes and cost $20 per person.

Aspen Art Museum ★★   Aspen has a long legacy as an arts hub, and nowhere is it more apparent than this top-flight museum that moved into a new state-of-the-art building in 2014. Recent exhibitions included work by Brazilian installation artist Ernesto Neto and the annual open exhibition in October. The museum also stages exhibitions at various facilities in Aspen and at the local ski areas. Allow 1 to 2 hours.

633 S. Spring St. *C* **970/925-8050.** www.aspenartmuseum.org. Free admission. Tues–Sat 10am–6pm (until 7pm Thurs); Sun noon–6pm.

John Denver Sanctuary ★   This memorial on the bank of the Roaring Fork River is one of the more peaceful spots in Aspen. A series of cut stones were carved with the lyrics of the late singer-songwriter and longtime Aspen-area resident, including, naturally, "Rocky Mountain High," now an official state song of Colorado.

North side of Rio Grande Park. *C* **970/920-5120.** Free admission. Daily 24 hr.

Wheeler/Stallard House Museum ★   Jerome B. Wheeler made his money in the local silver business, building this beautiful Queen Anne-style home 5 years before the market collapsed in 1893. But Wheeler never actually lived here—his wife would not leave Manitou Springs—thus the Stallard name, from a family who resided here for 40 years. Today it is a museum that offers a glimpse into the heyday of the Colorado silver boom as well as a changing series of temporary exhibits covering local history. For one admission, visitors can also tour the **Holden/Marolt Mining and Ranching Museum,** 40180 Colo. 82 (© **970/544-0820**). The one-time silver mill became a ranch in 1940. Allow 1 or 2 hours.

620 W. Bleeker St. © **970/925-3721.** www.aspenhistory.org. Admission $6 adults, $5 seniors, free for children under 13. Summer Tues–Sat 10:30am–4:30pm; rest of year Tues–Sat 1–5pm.

Skiing & Other Winter Activities

Shortly before World War II, a small ski area was established on Ajax, a.k.a. Aspen Mountain. During the war, 10th Mountain Division ski-soldiers training near Leadville spent weekends in Aspen and were enthralled with its possibilities. An infusion of money in 1945 by Chicago industrialist Walter Paepcke, who moved to Aspen with his wife, Elizabeth, resulted in the construction of what was then the world's longest chairlift. The Aspen Skiing Company was founded the following year, and in 1950 Aspen hosted the alpine world skiing championships. Then came the opening in 1958 of Buttermilk Mountain and Highlands, and in 1967, the birth of Snowmass.

Skiing Aspen today means skiing all four Aspen-area resorts—Aspen Mountain, Aspen Highlands, Buttermilk, and Snowmass. All are managed by Aspen Skiing Company, and one ticket gives access to all. Daily lift ticket prices (2013–14 prices) during peak season cost $117 for adults 18 to 64, $108 for youths 13 to 17 and seniors 65 and older, and $82 for children 7 to 12. Children 6 and under ski free. There is a refundable $5 fee for the RFID card that doubles as a lift ticket. You can get substantial savings by buying tickets by phone or online a week or more in advance, or buying for 3 days or more. For more information, contact **Aspen Skiing Company** (© **800/525-6200** or 970/923-1227; www.aspensnowmass.com).

ASPEN MOUNTAIN ★★   Named for an old miner's claim, Aspen Mountain is not for the timid. This is the American West's original hard-core ski mountain, with no fewer than 23 of its runs named double diamond—for experts only. One-third of the mountain's runs are left forever ungroomed—sheer ecstasy for bump runners. There are mountain-long runs for intermediates as well as advanced skiers, but beginners should look to one of the other Aspen/Snowmass mountains.

From the **Sundeck** restaurant at the mountain's 11,212-foot summit, numerous intermediate runs extend on either side of Bell Mountain—through Copper Bowl and down Spar Gulch. To the east of the gulch, the knob of Bell offers a mecca for mogul mashers, with bump runs down its ridge and its east and west faces. To the west of the gulch, the face of Ruthie's is wonderful for intermediate cruisers, while more mogul runs drop off International. Ruthie's Run extends for over 2 miles down the west ridge of the mountain, with an extension via Magnifico Cut Off and Little Nell to the base, and is accessed by the unique Ruthie's high-speed double chair.

Aspen Mountain has a 3,267-foot vertical drop, with 76 trails on 675 skiable acres. The resort rates its trails as follows: none easiest, 48 percent more difficult, 26 percent most difficult, and 26 percent expert. Aspen Mountain is usually open from late November to mid-April from 9am to 3:30pm.

ASPEN HIGHLANDS ★★★   A favorite of locals for its expert and adventure terrain—Highland Bowl—Aspen Highlands has the feel of a small resort. It also has a good mix of terrain, from novice to expert, with lots of intermediate slopes on its 1,040 acres. It also offers absolutely splendid views of the famed Maroon Bells.

It takes two lifts to reach the 11,675-foot Loge Peak summit, where most of the advanced expert runs are found in the Steeplechase area and 199 acres of glades in the Olympic Bowl. Several blue trails give the intermediate skier a long run from top to bottom, and novices are best served midmountain on trails like Red Onion and Apple Strudel. There are also some fantastic opportunities for experts at Highland Bowl, which is a short walk from the top of the Loge Peak lift. Highlands is usually open from mid-December to early April, with lifts operating from 9am to 3:30pm.

BUTTERMILK MOUNTAIN ★   Buttermilk is a premier beginners' mountain, one of the best places in America to learn how to ski. The smallest of Aspen's four mountains with 470 skiable acres, it has 44 trails, which the resort rates at 35 percent easiest, 39 percent more difficult, 26 percent most difficult, and none expert, plus a great terrain park. Buttermilk is usually open from mid-December to early April, its lifts running from 9am to 3:30pm.

SNOWMASS ★★★   A huge, mostly intermediate mountain with something for everyone, Snowmass has 33 percent more skiable acreage than the other three Aspen areas combined! Actually four distinct self-contained areas, each with its own lift system, its terrain varies from easy beginner runs to the pitches of the Cirque and the Hanging Valley Wall, the steepest in the Aspen area.

Big Burn, site of a 19th-century forest fire, boasts wide-open advanced and intermediate slopes and the expert drops of the Cirque. Atop the intermediate Alpine Springs trails is the advanced High Alpine Lift, from which experts can traverse to the formidable Hanging Valley Wall. Elk Camp is ideal for early intermediates that prefer long cruising runs. Sam's Knob has advanced upper trails diving through trees, and a variety of intermediate and novice runs around its northeast face and base. All areas meet in the base village. All told, there are 3,332 skiable acres at Snowmass, with a state-best 4,406-foot vertical drop from the 12,510-foot summit. The mountain has 94 trails, rated 6 percent easiest, 47 percent more difficult, 17 percent most difficult, and 30 percent expert. The longest run is one of the longest in the ski world: more than 5 miles long. Snowmass is usually open late November to mid-April from 8:30am to 3:30pm.

CROSS-COUNTRY SKIING   The Aspen/Snowmass Nordic Council operates a free Nordic trail system with about 40 miles of groomed double track extending throughout the Aspen-Snowmass area, and incorporating summer bicycle paths. Instruction, guided tours, and rentals are offered along the trail at the **Aspen Cross-Country Center,** Colo. 82 between Aspen and Buttermilk (𝄫 **970/925-2145;** www.aspennordic. com), and the **Snowmass Cross-Country Center,** Snowmass Village (𝄫 **970/923-5700;** www.aspennordic.com). Independent backcountry skiers should consult **White River National Forest,** 806 W. Hallam St. (𝄫 **970/925-3445**), where two hut systems provide shelter on multiday trips.

More Outdoor Activities

Your best source for information on outdoor activities in the mountains around Aspen, including hiking, mountain biking, horseback riding, four-wheeling, fishing, and camping, is the **White River National Forest** (𝄫 **970/925-3445**). There's no lack of guides, outfitters, and sporting-goods shops in Aspen. Among the best one-stop outfitters is **Blazing Adventures** (📞 **800/282-7238;** www.blazingadventures.com), which offers rafting, stand-up paddleboarding, kayaking, mountain-biking, hiking, four-wheeling, hot-air ballooning, and horseback-riding excursions.

BICYCLING   There are two bike paths of note. One connects Aspen with Snowmass Village; it covers 13 miles and begins at Seventh Street south of Hopkins Avenue, cuts through the forest to Colo. 82, then follows Owl Creek Road and Brush Creek Road to the Snowmass Mall. Extensions link it with Aspen High School and the Aspen Business Park. The Rio Grande Trail follows the Roaring Fork River from near the Aspen Post Office, on Puppy Smith Street, 2 miles west to Cemetery Lane, and ultimately 40 miles to Glenwood Springs via Woody Creek. **Ajax Bike and Sport,** 400 E. Cooper Ave. (📞 **970/925-7662;** www.ajaxbikeandsport.com), rents road bikes, hybrid bikes, kids' bikes, and cruisers for $45 to $80 daily.

GOLF   Public 18-hole courses include **Aspen Golf Course,** 9461 Colo. 82, 1 mile west of Aspen (📞 **970/429-1949;** www.aspengolf.com), one of the longer courses in Colorado at 7,156 yards, charging about $40 to $160 for 18 holes, cart included.

HIKING & MOUNTAINEERING   Among the best ways to see the spectacular scenery here is on foot. You can get maps and tips on where to go from **White River National Forest** office in Aspen (📞 **970/925-3445**). One popular trail is the route past the Maroon Bells to Gothic, near Crested Butte; it would be 175 miles by mountain road, but it's only about 30 miles by foot—and just 14 miles from the end of Aspen's Maroon Creek Road.

Hikers can make use of two hut systems for multiday trips—the 12-hut **10th Mountain Trail Association**'s system toward Vail, and the six-hut **Alfred A. Braun and Friends Hut System** (📞 **970/925-5775;** www.huts.org) toward Crested Butte. Huts are basic, with bunk beds, wood stoves, propane burners, photovoltaic lighting, and equipped kitchens. A bed in one of the huts costs $33 per night; some only can be rented out in their entirety for about $300 a night.

Those who would like a hiking guide should contact **Aspen Expeditions,** 414 E. Cooper Ave. (📞 **970/925-7625;** www.aspenexpeditions.com), which offers guided trips around the Maroon Bells and up other mountains (about $250–$500 per person per day, depending on the size of the group), as well as less strenuous days of high-alpine trekking (about $100–$200 per person). Aspen Expeditions also offers guided rock climbing and backcountry skiing trips in winter.

HORSEBACK RIDING   Several stables in the Aspen valley offer a variety of rides, and some outfitters package gourmet meals and country-and-western serenades with their expeditions. Rates run about $75 to $125 per person for a 2-hour ride or $140 to $175 for a half-day. Inquire at **Aspen Wilderness Outfitters** (📞 **970/928-0723;** www.aspenwilderness.com) or **Blazing Adventures** (📞 **800/282-7238**).

MOUNTAIN BIKING   There are hundreds of miles of trails through the White River National Forest that are perfect for mountain bikers, offering splendid views of the mountains, meadows, and valleys. Check with the Forest Service (📞 **970/925-3445**) and local bike shops for tips on the best trails. **Snowmass** (📞 **800/525-6200;** www.aspensnowmass.com) has opened the Elk Camp Gondola to mountain bikers, offering access to over 40 miles of trails on the mountain. A day pass costs $29 to $39 for adults, less for kids 17 and under. Rentals and lessons are also available. In Aspen, rentals are available at **Ajax Bike and Sport,** 400 E. Cooper Ave. (📞 **970/925-7662;** www.ajaxbikeandsport.com). A 24-hour rental is $90.

RIVER RAFTING   Rafting trips are offered on the Roaring Fork and other rivers with several companies, including **Up Tha Creek Expeditions** (✆ **877/982-7335** or 970/947-0030; www.upthacreek.com). Rates are $50 to $90 for a half-day.

Shopping

Curious George Collectibles, 426 E. Hyman Ave. (✆ **970/925-3315**), has silver buckles, belts, and Western artifacts. For high-end Western clothing, try **Kemo Sabe,** 434 E. Cooper Ave. (✆ **970/925-7878;** www.kemosabe.com). For books, head over to **Explore Booksellers,** 221 E. Main St. (✆ **970/925-5336;** www.explorebooksellers.com).

Nightlife

Aspen's major performing arts venue is the 1889 **Wheeler Opera House,** 320 E. Hyman Ave., at Mill Street (✆ **970/920-5770** box office; www.wheeleroperahouse. com). Built at the peak of the mining boom by silver baron Jerome B. Wheeler, this meticulously restored stage hosts a year-round program of music, theater, dance, film, and lectures. The resident bar and eatery, **Justice Snow's** (p. 172Σ), makes more than 100 specialty cocktails.

My favorite Aspen bar is the storied **J-Bar,** in the Hotel Jerome at Main and Mill streets (✆ **970/920-7674**). The rich, hip, and wasted flock to **39 Degrees,** in the Sky Hotel, at 709 E. Durant Ave. (✆ **970/925-6760**), for outer-limits specialty cocktails and the unbeatable slopeside pool, which you can use even if you're not a hotel guest. **Syzygy,** 308 E. Hopkins Ave. (✆ **970/925-3700**), also ranks high with those who live for the "Aspen scene." Live rock, folk, and country concerts are the hallmark of **Belly Up,** 405 S. Galena St. (✆ **970/544-9800**). And don't miss the **Red Onion** at 420 E. Cooper Ave. (✆ **970/925-9955**), which first opened its doors in 1892.

ASPEN music

The **Aspen Music Festival and School** originated in 1949 and is now considered one of America's top summer music programs. Lasting 9 weeks from mid-June to late August, it offers more than 350 events, including symphonic and chamber music, opera, choral, and children's programs. Most concerts take place in the state-of-the-art, 2,050-seat Benedict Music Tent and 500-seat Joan and Irving Harris Concert Hall, both at Third and Gillespie streets. The acoustics in the tent are very good, but in Harris Hall they're amazing.

Atop Aspen Mountain—you'll have to buy a ticket and ride the gondola—student groups perform free 1-hour **Music on the Mountain** concerts each Saturday at 1pm. **Family concerts** include several programs geared to youngsters under 10, such as storytelling and music (free admission; various times and locations). Certain **dress rehearsals** of the Aspen Chamber Symphony and Aspen Festival Orchestra are open to the public, giving visitors an inside look at how a concert is put together. Open rehearsals typically cost under $20, and most concert tickets run $50 to $80. For additional information, contact **Aspen Music Festival and School** (✆ **970/925-9042** for the box office and 970/925-3254 for the office; www.aspenmusicfestival.com).

THE WESTERN SLOPE

S eparated from Colorado's major cities by the mighty Rocky Mountains, the communities along the state's western edge are not only miles but also years away from the hustle and bustle of Denver. Even Grand Junction, the region's largest city, is an overgrown Western town, and the rugged canyons and stark rocky terrain make you feel like you've stepped into a John Ford movie.

The lifeblood of this semidesert land is its rivers: The Colorado, Gunnison, and Yampa have not only brought water to the region, but over tens of thousands of years, their ceaseless energy has also gouged out stunning canyons that lure visitors from around the world. Colorado National Monument, west of Grand Junction, is remarkable for its landforms and prehistoric petroglyphs; Dinosaur National Monument, in the state's northwestern corner, preserves a wealth of dinosaur remains; and the Black Canyon of the Gunnison is a dark, narrow, and almost impenetrable chasm east of Montrose.

GRAND JUNCTION & PALISADE ★

251 miles W of Denver, 169 miles N of Durango

Grand Junction is an excellent jumping-off point for those who want to explore the awe-inspiring red-rock canyons and sandstone monoliths of Colorado National Monument, or sip and savor in the wine country of Palisade, just a short drive east.

Located at the confluence of the Gunnison and Colorado rivers at an elevation of 4,586 feet, the city was founded in 1882 where the spike was driven to connect Denver and Salt Lake City by rail. It quickly became the primary trade and distribution center between the two state capitals, and its mild climate, together with the fertile soil and irrigation potential of the river valleys, helped it grow into an important agricultural area. The city was the center of a uranium boom in the 1950s and an oil-shale boom in the 1970s. Today it is a trade center for much of western Colorado and eastern Utah.

Essentials

GETTING THERE   By Car   Grand Junction is located on I-70. U.S. 50 is the main artery from the south, connecting with Montrose and Durango.

By Plane   On the north side of Grand Junction, **Grand Junction Regional Airport (GJT),** 2828 Walker Field Dr. (✆ **970/244-9100;** www.

gjairport.com), is accessed via I-70's Horizon Drive exit and served by **Allegiant, American, Delta, United,** and **US Airways.**

By Train   Amtrak (📞 **800/872-7245** or 970/241-2733; www.amtrak.com) has a passenger station at 339 S. First St. The California Zephyr stops here on its main route from the San Francisco area to Denver and Chicago.

GETTING AROUND   Main Street and named avenues run east-west, and numbered streets and roads run north-south. Downtown Grand Junction lies south of I-70 and north of the Colorado River, encompassing 1 block on each side of Main Street between First and Seventh streets. There is metered street parking (free 2-hr. parking on Main St. btw. First and Seventh sts.), plus several public parking lots.

Car-rental agencies in the airport area include **Alamo, Avis, Enterprise, Hertz,** and **National. Sunshine Taxi** (📞 **970/245-8294**) offers cab service, and **Grand Valley Transit** (📞 **970/256-7433;** www.gvt.mesacounty.us) operates buses in the Grand Junction area, including a shuttle service to and from the airport.

VISITOR INFORMATION   Contact the **Grand Junction Visitor & Convention Bureau** (📞 **970/244-1480;** www.visitgrandjunction.com). There's a visitor center on Horizon Drive at I-70 exit 31, open daily; and a **Colorado Welcome Center** at I-70 exit 19 for Fruita and Colorado National Monument (📞 **970/858-9335**), 12 miles west of Grand Junction, which is open daily as well.

FAST FACTS   There's a 24-hour emergency room at **St. Mary's Hospital,** 2635 N. 7th St. (📞 **970/244-2273;** www.stmarygj.com). The main **post office** is at 241 N. Fourth St. For **weather conditions,** call 📞 **970/243-0914;** for **road conditions,** call 📞 **303/639-1111** or 511 (in-state), or visit **www.cotrip.org**.

Where to Stay

Major chains offering reasonably priced lodging are lined up along Horizon Drive near I-70. Downtown, you'll find a very nice **Fairfield Inn & Suites** at 225 Main St. (📞 **970/242-2525**), with double rates of $109 to $159 and suites for $159 to $209.

In the high county atop Grand Mesa to the southeast of Grand Junction, there are several **Forest Service cabins** (📞 **877/444-6777;** www.recreation.gov) for $120 to $180 nightly. Contact the **Grand Valley Ranger District office** (📞 **970/242-8211**) for more information. You will also find spartan rooms ($55–$65 double) and cabins ($80–$160) at **Grand Mesa Lodge,** Colo. 65, 16 miles north of Cedaredge (📞 **970/856-3250;** www.grandmesalodge.com).

Wine Country Inn ★★   More hotel than inn, this full-service property is convenient to I-70, surrounded by farmland, and offers an upscale alternative to the properties near the interstate in Grand Junction. The romantic vibe extends from the accommodations—which include richly furnished rooms (plush bedding, heavy drapes, lots of wood) as well as premium patio rooms and suites—to the outdoor pool and its stunning views—to the fine dining at the in-house eatery, **Caroline's.**

777 Grande River Dr., Palisade. 📞 **888/855-8330** or 970/464-5777. www.coloradowinecountryinn. com. 81 units. $153–$173 double, $269–$289 suite. Rates include full breakfast and daily wine reception. Pets accepted ($35 one-time fee). **Amenities:** Restaurant; lounge; exercise room; outdoor Jacuzzi; outdoor heated pool; free Wi-Fi.

Where to Eat

Most of the top restaurants in Grand Junction are on Main Street downtown.

MODERATE TO EXPENSIVE

Rockslide Brewery ★ BREWPUB   This friendly neighborhood brewpub is the finest on the Western Slope. The Baja-tinged menu includes fish and shrimp tacos alongside pub fare like burgers and fish and chips, not to mention a nice selection of steaks. But it's the brews that keep me coming—especially the Horsethief IPA and Big Bear Stout. The dining room is family-friendly, and there is also bar seating.

401 Main St. ✆ **970/245-2111.** www.rockslidebrewpub.com. Main courses $11–$24. Mon–Sat 11am–10pm; Sun 8am–10pm. Bar open later with limited menu.

The Winery Restaurant ★★ STEAK/SEAFOOD   Long the best restaurant for a splurge in Grand Junction, The Winery balances an intimate ambiance with time-tested cuisine. The menu doesn't veer too far from the traditional, but the kitchen expertly handles staples like seafood bisque, filet Oscar, and prime rib. From the gas-lit entrance in a vine-clad alleyway to the dimly lit dining room, the atmosphere is refined, and romantic.

642 Main St. ✆ **970/242-4100.** www.winery-restaurant.com. Main courses $24–$80. Sun–Thurs 5–9pm; Fri–Sat 5–10pm. Bar opens at 4:30pm and serves a limited menu until 10:30pm.

INEXPENSIVE

Palisade Cafe ★ AMERICAN/MEXICAN   With brick walls, hardwood floors, and a smattering of sports memorabilia, this local institution looks the part of a beloved, small-town cafe. It tastes like it, too, with red chili, green chile, big salads, great burgers (including the $5 Lincoln Burger), and a few Mexican dishes. Weekends bring hearty breakfasts like pancakes, breakfast burritos, and biscuits and gravy. There is local wine and beer at the bar, but no liquor.

113 W. 3rd St. ✆ **970/464-0657.** www.palisadecafe.com. Main courses $5–$10. Mon–Wed 11am–3pm; Thurs 11am–8pm; Fri 11am–9pm; Sat 8am–8pm Sun 8am–2pm.

Exploring Grand Junction & Palisade

Grand Junction is not a tourist destination but has a number of good museums.

The Art Center ★   Home to working artists in the studios on-site, this is the best art museum on the Western Slope, with 25 different exhibitions annually and an emphasis on works by regional artists. Most exhibitions are up for about a month, with recent shows covering art made of recyclables and clay works. First Fridays and the annual summer open studio show are the big events. Allow at least an hour.

1803 N. Seventh St. ✆ **970/243-7337.** www.gjartcenter.org. Admission $3 adults, free for children under 12. Tues–Sat 9am–4pm.

Art on the Corner ★★   This outdoor sculpture exhibit, with more than 100 works, helps make Grand Junction's downtown area a feast for the eyes. About half of the sculptures are on loan by the artists for a year, during which time they are for sale, and the rest are on permanent display. Keep an eye out for fat frog "Puffed Up Prince," bronze pig "Sir," and "Greg La Rex," a steel dinosaur skeleton atop a bicycle.

Main St., from Second to Seventh sts. ✆ **970/245-9697.** www.downtowngj.org. Free admission. Daily 24 hr., with shops and restaurants open usual business hours.

Cross Orchards Historic Site ★   With over 22,000 trees on 243 acres, Cross Orchards was one of the largest apple orchards in western Colorado in the early 1900s. Today the remaining 24 acres of the historic site preserve the feel of a real working farm and orchard. Costumed guides lead tours through the original barn and other buildings. Allow 2 hours.

3073 F Rd. ☏ **970/434-9814** or 970/242-0971 (for event schedule). www.museumofwesternco. com. Admission $5 adults, $4 seniors 60 and over, $3.50 children 12 and under; immediate family rate $12. May–Oct Thurs–Sat 9am–4pm. Closed Nov–Apr except for special events.

Dinosaur Journey ★   There is a lot to see here, between the robotic triceratops, velociraptor skeletons, and kid-sized dig site where young patrons can uncover bones themselves. The museum also organizes digs in fossil-rich Utah and the Western Slope. Exhibits allow you to get a sense of scale—how humans and dinosaurs stack up to Amphicoelias, the largest known vertebrate, sometimes measuring in at 200 feet. Allow about an hour, more if you have a big fan of dinosaurs in your party.

550 Jurassic Ct., Fruita (just south of I-70 exit 19). ☏ **970/858-7282.** www.dinosaurjourney.org. Admission $8.50 adults, $6.50 seniors 60 and over, $5.25 children 12 and under; family rate $25. May–Sept daily 9am–5pm; Oct–Apr Mon–Sat 10am–4pm; Sun noon–4pm.

John McConnell Math & Science Center of Western Colorado ★   The eponymous founder of this museum was a retired physicist who focused on education after moving to Grand Junction in 1990. His facility opened in 2000, and features exhibits on everything from beekeeping to hydrogen fuel cells. Allow about 2 hours.

2660 Unaweep Ave. ☏ **970/254-1626.** www.mathandsciencecenter.org. Admission $4; $12 family. Tues–Sat 10am–5pm.

Museum of the West ★   The high point of the museum, literally, is the observation tower, offering a stunning view of the local landscape, and the low point is a replica of an underground uranium mine. In between are a wide range of other displays: firearm, a unique fire truck with chain-driven wheels, and a great pottery collection. The museum got a nice update in 2013, with an exhibit covering early Colorado baseball, upgraded galleries, and more. Allow 2 hours.

462 Ute Ave. ☏ **970/242-0971.** www.museumofwesternco.com. Admission $6.50 adults, $5.50 seniors 60 and over, $3.50 children 12 and under; family rate $20. May–Sept Mon–Sat 9am–5pm and Sun noon–4pm; Oct–Apr Tues–Sat 10am–3pm.

Western Colorado Botanical Gardens ★   This botanical garden along the Colorado River offers a delightful escape into the natural world. Located on 15 acres, the facility s home to more than 600 exotic tropical plants, both indoors and outside. In the butterfly house, visitors stroll through a lush forest of flowering plants and ferns. The adjacent greenhouse has orchids and other colorful tropical varieties, as well as sculptures and a fish pond. Walkways connect the botanical gardens with trails on the Colorado River (discussed under "Hiking" on p. 183). Allow 1 or 2 hours.

641 Struthers Ave. ☏ **970/245-3288.** www.wcbotanic.org. Admission $5 adults, $4 students and seniors, $3 children 5–12, free for kids 4 and under, free for all Tues. Tues–Sun 10am–5pm. Located at the south end of Seventh St

Outdoor Activities

In addition to activities in Colorado and Dinosaur national monuments (p. 184 and 185), there are numerous opportunities for hiking, camping, mountain biking, off-roading, horseback riding, cross-country skiing, snowmobiling, and snowshoeing on other public lands administered by the federal government. Contact the **Bureau of Land Management** (☏ **970/244-3000**; www.blm.gov/co), and the **Grand Valley Ranger District of Grand Mesa National Forest** (☏ **970/242-8211**). Grand Mesa offers a particularly scenic drive from the Collbran exit of I-70 (exit 49) to Delta on the Grand Mesa Scenic and Historic Byway, with plenty of trailheads and overlooks.

PALISADE: wine & spirits AMID THE CANYONS

Colorado may not be the first place that comes to mind for wine, but it is a growing industry here, and the heart of it lies in the fertile Grand Valley. Most wineries are located in the community of **Palisade,** about 12 miles east of Grand Junction (I-70 exit 42). About 20 wineries—plus a standout distillery and brewery—are located in this little fruit-growing town of approximately 2,700 people.

Here are a few to wet your whistle: **Colorado Cellars Winery,** 3553 E Rd. (© **970/464-7921;** www.coloradocellars. com), produces an award-winning selection of chardonnays, merlots, Rieslings, fruit wines, and port. **Carlson Vineyards,** 461 35 Rd. (© **888/464-5554;** www.carlsonvineyards.com), produces a variety of easy-drinking reds and whites. Other Palisade wineries include **Plum Creek Cellars,** 3708 G Rd. (© **970/464-7586;** www.plumcreekwinery.com), with its unique "Chardonnay Chicken" sculpture standing sentry out front; **Garfield Estates Winery,** located on a 100-year-old homestead at 3572 G Rd. (© **970/464-0941;** www.garfieldestates.com); and **Maison La Belle Vie Winery,** 3575 G Rd. (© **970/464-4959;** www.maisonlabellevie.com), with a slick tasting room and courtyard.

But Palisade isn't just about wine. **Peach Street Distillers,** 144 Kluge Ave., Bldg. 2 (© **970/464-1128;** www.peachstreetdistillers.com), is giving the local winemakers a run for their money with its award-winning craft spirits, including bourbon, vodka, gin, and brandy. Serving a diverse menu of creative cocktails, the tasting room is a social spot with a large outdoor area. Next door is the **Palisade Brewing Company,** 200 Peach Ave. (© **970/464-1462;** www.palisadebrewingcompany.com), known for its Dirty Hippie Dark Wheat, good barbecue, and live music.

Most of the wineries in Palisade are located along a 10-mile loop that is perfect for bicycling. Rent a cruiser ($35) at **Rapid Creek Cycles,** 237 Main St. (© **970/464-9266;** www.rapidcreekcycles.com), and ask for its map covering the suggested route with no fewer than 11 wineries (plus the brewery and distillery).

Palisade is just as famous for its fruit orchards as it is for its vineyards and wineries. Most fruit is picked between late June and mid-September, when it's available at roadside fruit stands. For more information, contact the **Palisade Chamber of Commerce** (© **970/464-7458;** www.palisadecoc.com).

You'll also find plenty to do at **James M. Robb–Colorado River State Park** (© **970/434-3388;** www.parks.state.co.us), which has two main sections, both with campgrounds. **Island Acres,** on the east side of Grand Junction at I-70 exit 47, also offers hiking, picnicking, fishing, and just gazing out at the river. The **Fruita** section, located in the community of Fruita about ½ mile south of I-70 exit 19, covers 81 acres and has all of the above, plus boating and a swimming lagoon. Day-use fee at both sections is $7 per vehicle; camping is $16 to $24 nightly.

The Grand Junction **Parks and Recreation Department** (© **970/254-3866;** www.gjcity.org) manages more than 30 parks and other facilities. A busy local shop where you can get gear and information on the best spots for outdoor recreation is **Summit Canyon Mountaineering,** 461 Main St. (© **970/243-2847;** www.summitcanyon.com).

GOLF Grand Junction is known for its long golf season and challenging courses. My favorite course here, in large part because of the views—it's like golfing in the

Grand Canyon—is the 18-hole **Golf Club at Redlands Mesa,** 2325 W. Ridges Blvd. (℅ **970/263-9270;** www.redlandsmesa.com), with nonresident greens fees of $51 for 9 holes and $89 for 18 holes, cart not included. You'll also find great golfing and views at the 18-hole **Tiara Rado Golf Course,** 2057 S. Broadway (℅ **970/254-3830;** www. golfgrandjunction.net), at the base of the Colorado National Monument canyons. Greens fees are $19 to $21 for 9 holes and $35 to $38 for 18 holes, cart not included.

HIKING   Hikers and walkers who want to stay close to town can explore the trails in the Colorado Riverfront Project. Collectively known as the **Colorado River Trails,** the system includes about 20 miles of paved trails that meander along the Colorado and Gunnison rivers, offering the chance to see ducks, geese, blue heron, deer, and rabbits.

The best hiking in the area is in **Colorado National Monument** (p. 184) and in the high country on Grand Mesa southeast of the city. On the latter, the **Crag Crest National Recreation Trail** is a good choice. The 10.3-mile moderately difficult loop has trailheads near Island Lake off Colo. 65 and Eggleston Lake off Forest Rd. 121, offering vistas to red-rock country and surrounding mountain ranges, as well as plenty of crystalline alpine lakes perfect for a picnic lunch. Contact the Forest Service's **Grand Mesa Visitor Center** (℅ **970/856-4153**) for additional information.

HORSEBACK RIDING   Trail rides near the west entrance of Colorado National Monument are available through **Rimrock Adventures** (℅ **888/712-9555** or 970/858-9555; www.rradventures.com). The stables are about a mile south of Fruita on Colo. 340. Rates for a 1-hour ride are $35 for adults and $25 for kids 5 to 12, and a half-day ride into the wilderness of Devil's Canyon costs $80 for adults and $70 for children. Kids' pony rides, running 15 minutes, cost $10.

MOUNTAIN BIKING   Grand Junction has become important to mountain bikers as the eastern terminus of **Kokopelli's Trail** to Moab, Utah. Winding for 142 miles through sandstone and shale canyons, it has an elevation differential of about 4,200 feet. There are primitive campsites at intervals along the trail. The Colorado gateway is at the Loma Boat Launch, 15 miles west of Grand Junction off I-70.

There's also a bike route through and around **Colorado National Monument** (p. 184). Covering 33 miles, it follows Rim Rock Drive through the park and 10 additional miles on rural South Camp Road and South Broadway at the base of the canyons. Rim Rock Drive does not have a separate bike lane or shoulders, so be alert for motor traffic. The national monument publishes a free brochure.

Fruita, 9 miles west of Grand Junction, and Palisade, 12 miles to the east, are also both mountain-biking hubs. For more information on Kokopelli's Trail and other area trails, contact the **Colorado Plateau Mountain-Bike Trail Association** (℅ **970/244-8877;** www.copmoba.com).

You can also get information on area biking; rent mountain, road, and tandem bikes; and see some antique and unique bikes at **Brown Cycles,** 549 Main St. (℅ **970/245-7939;** www.browncycles.com). Bikes rent for $40 to $70 per day, and the shop's bicycle museum includes an 1885 high-wheeler, Schwinns from the 1920s and 1930s, and the tallest unicycle on Earth (it is 40 ft. from seat to tire). In Fruita, contact **Over The Edge Sports,** 202 E. Aspen Ave. (℅ **970/858-7220;** www.otesports.com); and in Palisade, head to **Rapid Creek Cycles,** 237 Main St. (℅ **970/464-9266;** www.rapid creekcycles.com). Rental rates are similar to those at Brown Cycles.

RIVER RAFTING   For my money, one of the best ways to see this area's beautiful red sandstone canyons is from the river, in a big old rubber raft. Colorado River–rafting trips are provided by **Rimrock Adventures** in Fruita (℅ **888/712-9555;** www.

rradventures.com). Cost for a 3-hour trip about 9 miles down the Colorado is $45 for adults and $35 for children 12 and under; a 25-mile full-day float trip costs $100 per adult and $70 per child 13 and under. An exciting 17-mile white-water trip through Westwater Canyon costs $150 per person. The company also rents rafts and offers shuttles for those who want to explore the river on their own.

Adventure Bound River Expeditions, in Grand Junction (© **800/423-4668** or 970/245-5428; www.adventureboundusa.com), offers multiday trips. Two-day trips on the Colorado River cost $325 per adult and $250 for children 17 and under.

In Palisade, try **Palisade River Trips,** 317 Main St. (© **970/260-5848;** www.palisaderivertrips.com), offering guided 2-hour float trips for $50 with a two-person minimum, rentals, and combo bike-float trips.

SKIING & SNOWBOARDING Powderhorn Mountain Resort, Colo. 65, 7 miles south of Mesa (© **970/268-5700;** www.powderhorn.com), is located 35 miles east of Grand Junction on the north face of the Grand Mesa. A favorite among local skiers and snowboarders of all ability levels, this pleasant resort offers 1,600 acres of skiable terrain with a nice mix of terrain for all skill levels. Lift-ticket prices (2013–14) cost $59 adults 18 to 64, $51 for youth 13 to 17 and seniors 65 to 74, $30 for those 7 to 12, $32 for 75 and older, and $15 for children under 7. The resort has a ski school, a rental shop, and a repair center. It is usually open from mid-December through late March. There is also a ski-in, ski-out lodge, the **Slopeside Ski Club** (© **855/754-3866;** www.slopesideskiclub.com), with double rates in winter from $149 to $179 and a 2-bedroom condo from $300 to $350.

SNOWMOBILING A trail connects Powderhorn Mountain Resort to Sunlight Mountain Resort, near Glenwood Springs, at 120 miles the longest multiuse winter recreational trail in Colorado. It is fully marked and continuously groomed. Other trails are accessed from parking areas along Colo. 65 on Grand Mesa.

A NEARBY NATIONAL MONUMENT

Colorado National Monument ★★

Just minutes west of Grand Junction, this relatively undiscovered national monument is a delight, offering a colorful maze of steep-walled canyons filled with an array of naturally sculpted spires, pinnacles, and other impressive sandstone rock formations. Easy to get to and easy to see, in many ways it's a miniature Grand Canyon, only without the crowds. You can see much of the monument from your car on the 23-mile Rim Rock Drive, but there are ample opportunities to hike, ride, and cross-country-ski the monument's many trails as well. Bighorn sheep, mountain lions, golden eagles, mule deer, and lizards are among the monument's residents.

Carved by water and wind over millions of years, Colorado National Monument encompasses 32 square miles of red-rock canyons and sandstone monoliths, more than 1,000 feet above the Colorado River. The east entrance is only 5 miles west of Grand Junction, off Monument Road, but the best way to explore the monument is to follow the signs off I-70 from Fruita to the west entrance, 15 miles west of Grand Junction. It's here that **Rim Rock Drive,** built during the Great Depression, begins. Snaking up dramatic Fruita Canyon, it offers panoramic views of fanciful and bizarre natural stone monuments, as well as the cliffs and mesas beyond. At 4 miles, it reaches the national monument headquarters and **visitor center.**

From Rim Rock Drive, many short, easy trails lead to spectacular canyon overlooks, while the longer backcountry trails head out across the mesas or down into the canyons. Strange formations such as Window Rock, the massive rounded Coke Ovens, the boulder-strewn Devils Kitchen, and the free-standing Independence Monument—all of which can be viewed from the road—are easily reached by foot.

If you're looking for a quick hike, try the 1-mile (round-trip) **Canyon Rim Trail,** which follows the edge of a cliff to spectacular views of the colorful rock formations in Wedding Canyon. Allow about an hour.

While the monument is worth visiting at any time of year, the best time to go is fall, when the air is crisp but not cold, the cottonwood trees turn a brilliant gold, and the summer crowds have departed. Those visiting in May and June should carry insect repellent to combat the clouds of gnats that invade at this time.

The **Saddlehorn Campground,** located in a piñon-juniper forest near the visitor center, has 80 first-come, first-served sites and restrooms but no showers or RV hookups. Sites are $20 per night. Pets must be leashed and are not allowed on trails or in the backcountry.

dinosaur NATIONAL MONUMENT

This national monument, about 100 miles north of Grand Junction, is really two separate parks divided by the Utah-Colorado border. One side takes a close-up look at the world of dinosaurs, while the other opens onto a wonderland of colorful rock, deep river canyons, and a forest of Douglas firs.

About 150 million years ago, a river and sufficient vegetation made this region a suitable habitat for dinosaurs. Most of their skeletons decayed and disappeared, but in at least one spot they were preserved under a layer of sediment, when the river dried up and they died of thirst.

On the Utah side, the **Quarry Exhibit Hall** here is the big attraction, featuring a view of over 1,500 dinosaur fossils encased in stone. This is the only place in the monument to see dinosaur bones.

There is plenty to do outdoors here, especially on the Colorado side. Your first stop should be the **Canyon Visitor Center,** just east of the town of Dinosaur, Colorado, at the intersection of U.S. 40 and Harpers Corner Drive. Allow about 4 hours for the scenic **Harpers Corner Drive,** more if you want to hike

one of the trails it accesses. Another noteworthy spot is the **Gates of Lodore,** the scenic entry to Lodore Canyon at the northern tip of the park.

Rafters often put in to the Green River here; one of the best companies running the Yampa and Green rivers through the monument is **Don Hatch River Expeditions** of Vernal, Utah (✆ 800/342-8243 or 435/789-4316; www.donhatchrivertrips.com). Prices start at $99 for adults, $76 for kids ages 6 through 14 for a 1-day trip spring to fall. The rivers here are not safe for swimming or wading.

There are **campgrounds** in both sections of the monument, but no showers or RV hookups, and camping fees range from $8 to $12 per night; backcountry camping is free, but a permit is required.

The national monument entrance near Dinosaur, Colorado, is about 110 miles north of Grand Junction. Admission, charged only during summers on the Utah side, is $10 per vehicle and $5 per person for those on foot, motorcycles, or bicycles. For information, contact **Dinosaur National Monument** ✆ 970/374-3000 or 435/781-7700; www.nps.gov/dino).

The national monument is open year-round. The fee for a week of access is $10 per vehicle or $5 per person for motorcyclists, bicyclists, and pedestrians. The visitor center is open daily from 9am to 6pm, with shorter hours fall to spring. To obtain a brochure and other information, contact **Colorado National Monument** (ℂ **970/858-3617,** ext. 360; www.nps.gov/colm).

GLENWOOD SPRINGS ★★

90 miles E of Grand Junction, 41 miles NW of Aspen, 169 miles W of Denver

Scenic beauty and hot mineral water are the big lures here. Members of the Ute tribe visited the Yampah mineral springs on the banks of the Colorado River for centuries. Calling it "big medicine," they came from miles around to heal their wounds or use nearby vapor caves as natural saunas. But it wasn't until the 1880s that the springs were commercially developed. The three Devereux brothers, who made a small fortune in silver at Aspen, built the largest hot-springs pool in the world. Soon everyone from European royalty to movie stars to President Theodore Roosevelt had stayed in Glenwood Springs.

Today this city of about 8,500, at an elevation of 5,746 feet, is a popular recreational center. The hot-springs complex underwent a total renovation in the 1970s, and additional improvements have been made in more recent years: In 2008, the Spa of the Rockies opened here.

In 1993, workers finished a 12-year, $490-million project to build a four-lane interstate through the 18-mile Glenwood Canyon. One of the most expensive roadways ever built—as well as one of the most beautiful interstate highway drives in America—the road offers a number of trail heads and raft-launching areas, as well as viewpoints from which travelers can safely gaze at the Colorado River and its spectacular canyon.

Essentials

GETTING THERE   **By Car**   I-70 follows the Colorado River through Glenwood Springs. Colo. 82 (the Aspen Hwy.) links the city with Aspen, 42 miles southeast.

By Plane   The nearest airport is in Eagle County (p. 156).

By Bus   **Roaring Fork Transportation Authority** (ℂ **970/925-8484;** www.rfta. com) offers service between Glenwood Springs and Aspen, with numerous stops along the route daily, at a cost of $7 each way, less for intermediate stops.

By Shuttle Van   Transportation from Denver to Glenwood Springs is provided by **Colorado Mountain Express** (ℂ **800/525-6363** or 970/754-7433; www.colorado mountainexpress.com), at $93 per person one-way.

By Train   There's **Amtrak** service (ℂ **800/USA-RAIL** [872-7245]; www.amtrak. com) to Glenwood Springs daily aboard the California Zephyr, direct from Denver and Salt Lake City. The depot is at Seventh Street and Cooper Avenue.

GETTING AROUND   The confluence of the Roaring Fork and Colorado rivers forms a T in the heart of Glenwood Springs; downtown is south of the Colorado and east of the Roaring Fork. **Ride Glenwood Springs** (ℂ **970/384-6400;** www. ci.glenwood-springs.co.us) operates buses; fare is $1 and kids under 6 ride free.

VISITOR INFORMATION   The **Glenwood Springs Chamber Resort Association** (ℂ **970/945-6589;** www.visitglenwood.com) maintains a visitor center on the southeast corner of 8th and Grand that is open daily.

FAST FACTS   **Valley View Hospital,** providing 24-hour emergency care, is at 1906 Blake Ave. (ℂ **970/945-6535;** www.vvh.org). The post office is at 113 Ninth St. For

Glenwood Springs

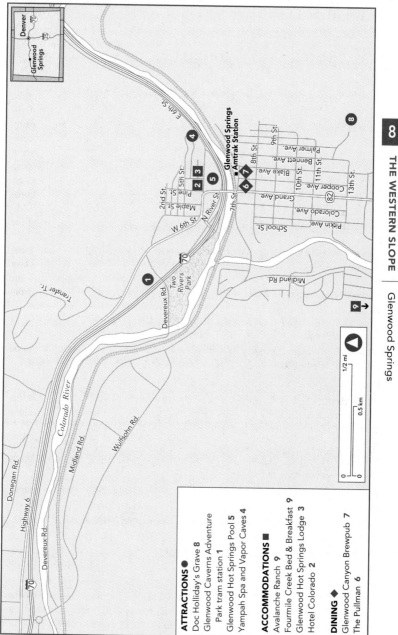

ATTRACTIONS ●
Doc Holliday's Grave **8**
Glenwood Caverns Adventure
Park tram station **1**
Glenwood Hot Springs Pool **5**
Yampah Spa and Vapor Caves **4**

ACCOMMODATIONS ■
Avalanche Ranch **9**
Fourmile Creek Bed & Breakfast **9**
Glenwood Hot Springs Lodge **3**
Hotel Colorado **2**

DINING ◆
Glenwood Canyon Brewpub **7**
The Pullman **6**

weather conditions, call ℂ **970/243-0914;** for **road conditions,** call ℂ **303/639-1111** or 511 (in-state), or visit **www.cotrip.org**.

Where to Stay

The tidiest, best-serviced budget motel in Glenwood Springs is the **Caravan Inn,** 1826 Grand Ave. (ℂ **800/945-5495** or 970/945-7451; www.caravaninn.com), with high-season rates of $69 to $109 for double rooms and suites for $99 to $149. There is a seasonal outdoor pool and year-round hot tub.

Four Mile Creek Bed & Breakfast ★ From its location 5 miles up Four Mile Creek from Glenwood Springs—thus the name—this 1885 homestead has one of the prettiest locations of any B&B in Colorado. The country-style furnishings are a nice match for the setting, nestled in the gardens and aspen groves, below a verdant mountainside. Two rooms are in the main house, and there are two cabins and a suite in the old red barn, the site of guitar-picking jam sessions and movie nights. The innkeepers also manage a nearby guesthouse that sleeps up to 18 people.

6471 C.R. 117, Glenwood Springs. ℂ **970/945-4004.** www.fourmilecreek.com. 5 units, 3 with private bathroom, including 3 cabins and suites. $95 double with shared bathroom; $130 double with private bathroom; $145–$155 cabin or suite (up to 4 people); $750–$1,000 guesthouse. Rates include full breakfast and evening refreshments. **Amenities:** Free Wi-Fi.

Glenwood Hot Springs Lodge ★★ Location is everything, and if you are in Glenwood Springs to soak in the renowned hot springs pools, there is no better location than this lodge, which replaced the old lodge in the 1980s. The rooms were nicely updated in recent years, and now feature mellow earth tones that contrast nicely with the white bedding, as well as energy-efficient lighting, microwaves, and fridges, and high-tech perks like iPod docks and flatscreen TVs. Guest also enjoy unlimited access to the **Glenwood Hot Springs Pool** (p. 190).

415 Sixth St., Glenwood Springs. ℂ **800/537-7946** or 970/945-6571. www.hotspringspool.com. 107 units. $159–$209 double, $249–$299 suite. Rates include full breakfast. **Amenities:** Health club; 2 hot springs pools; spa; free Wi-Fi.

Hotel Colorado ★★ There are few more storied historic hotels in the West, let alone Colorado. This stunning 1893 example of Italianate architecture awash in legends: It is the alleged birthplace of the teddy bear—supposedly crafted by maids for the visiting Theodore "Teddy" Roosevelt in 1905—and served as a favored getaway for Chicago mobsters during Prohibition. Today it is a beautifully restored hotel, with a shady green courtyard that is just the spot for a sunset cocktail. Standard rooms have a king bed or two doubles and are decorated with reproduction antiques; there are several larger suites, including a pair in the iconic bell towers.

526 Pine St., Glenwood Springs. ℂ **800/544-3998** or 970/945-6511. www.hotelcolorado.com. 130 units. $119–$169 double; $159–$749 suite. Lower rates fall to spring. Pets accepted ($15 per night). **Amenities:** Restaurant; lounge; exercise room (fee); spa; free Wi-Fi.

A NEARBY HOT SPRINGS RESORT

Avalanche Ranch ★★ Set on 36 acres with jaw-dropping mountain views, this iconic cabin complex, 30 miles south of Glenwood Springs, is home to a picture-perfect new hot springs pool (free for guests, but $15–$18 for nonguests; reservations recommended). The historic cabins, woodsy with red trim and quirky character, are nicely maintained and comfortable, and range from studios to 2-bedroom units. There are also barns full of antiques for sale, big green lawns for kids to romp around, and funky details like wagon wheels and hand-painted signs. There is also a budget option: three covered wagons with beds and shared facilities for $85 a night.

12863 Colo. 133, Redstone. ⓒ **970/963-2846.** www.avalancheranch.com. 15 units, including 1 apt. and 1 guest house. Late May–early Sept $150–$230 cabin or apt. double, $465 house; early Sept–late May $135–$189 cabin or apt. double, $385 house. 2- to 3-night minimum. Pets accepted ($25 per stay). **Amenities:** Free Wi-Fi.

Where to Eat

Most of the restaurants are downtown, just south of the Colorado River.

Glenwood Canyon Brewpub ★ BREWPUB   For a casual meal complemented by locally made craft beer, look no further than this brewpub on the south side of the Colorado River in the historic Hotel Denver. Brewing since 1996, the beers—including a swell red ale—are a nice match for the food, burgers and sandwiches, plus steaks, tacos, and pasta.

In the Hotel Denver, 402 Seventh St. ⓒ **970/945-1276.** www.glenwoodcanyon.com. Main courses $10–$23. Daily 11am–10pm. Bar usually open until 11pm or midnight.

The Pullman ★★ NEW AMERICAN   Chef-owner Mark Fischer has won numerous national accolades for The Pullman, which he opened in downtown Glenwood Springs in 2011. In a restored railroad diner with spare industrial chic look and a big bronze pig, the emphasis is on the savvy, inventive cuisine. The menus change on a near-monthly basis and use largely local ingredients. Expect a terrific grass-fed burger and hearty salads for lunch, and unique and delectable dinner dishes like duck meatloaf, goat tostadas, and Colorado bass.

330 7th St. ⓒ **970/230-9234.** www.thepullmangws.com. Main courses $9–$20. Mon–Sat 11–10pm; Sun 10–10pm.

Exploring Glenwood Springs

Glenwood Springs is a fun place to explore for a day or two, with the renowned hot springs and a historic attraction of note.

Doc Holliday's Grave ★   After the famous shootout at the OK Corral, Doc Holliday began a final search for relief from his advanced tuberculosis. But even the mineral-rich waters of Glenwood Springs could not dissipate the ravages of hard drinking and disease, and Doc died in 1887 at the Hotel Glenwood. Although the exact location of Doc's grave is not known, it is believed he was buried in or near the Linwood Cemetery, on Lookout Mountain overlooking the city. Also in the cemetery are the graves of other early citizens of Glenwood. The trail is a half-mile uphill hike, and you'll have a grand view of the city along the way. Allow a half-hour.

Linwood Cemetery, trailhead on Bennett and 11th sts. No phone. Free admission. Dawn–dusk.

Glenwood Caverns Adventure Park ★★ This park is not in Glenwood proper, but rather above it: Gondolas rise 1,400 feet from the valley floor up the side of Iron Mountain, where visitors can not only tour a cave, but also ride the **Cliffhanger,** the highest-elevation roller coaster in the U.S., and other amusements. The centerpiece of this park is the historic **Fairy Caves,** which were first visited by tourists in the late 1890s. The standard cave tours offer handrails and stair cases, but most of the caves have been left in as natural a state as possible for the **Wild Tour** ($60), which is for individuals who don't mind crawling through dirty narrow passages wearing knee pads and helmet lights. Allow several hours.

51000 Two Rivers Plaza Rd. ☎ **800/530-1635** or 970/945-4228. www.glenwoodcaverns.com. Day passes $48 adults, $43 children 3–12, free for children 2 and under. Park entrance and cavern tour only $25 adults, and $20 children 3–12. Summer hours 9am–9pm; shorter hours rest of year.

Glenwood Hot Springs Pool ★★ Named Yampah Springs—meaning "Big Medicine"—by the Utes, this pool was created in 1888 when enterprising developers diverted the course of the Colorado River and built a stone bathhouse. The springs flow at a rate of more than three million gallons per day, and, with a temperature of 122°F (50°C), they're one of the world's hottest springs. The two open-air pools together are nearly 2 city blocks in length. The larger pool, 405 feet by 100 feet, holds more than a million gallons of water and is maintained at 90°F (32°C). The smaller pool, 100 feet long, is kept at 104°F (40°C). There's also a kiddie pool, two waterslides, plus a restaurant, sport shop, and mini golf course. Suit and towel rentals and coin-operated lockers available. The **Spa of the Rockies** offers a full menu of treatments.

401 N. River St. ☎ **970/947-2955.** www.hotspringspool.com. Admission summer $19–$21 adults, $12–$13 children 3–12; rest of year $16 adults, $11 children 3–12; free for children 2 and under year-round. Reduced evening rates. Extra for waterslide and mini golf. Summer daily 7:30am–10pm; rest of year daily 9am–10pm.

Yampah Spa and Vapor Caves ★ The hot Yampah Spring water flows through the floor of nearby caves, creating natural underground steam baths. Once used by Utes for their curative powers, the cave has an adjacent spa where such treatments as massages, facials, and wraps are offered. Allow at least 1 hour.

709 E. Sixth St. ☎ **970/945-0667.** www.yampahspa.com. Admission to caves $12; spa treatments vary. Daily 9am–9pm.

Outdoor Activities

There are plenty of outdoor recreation opportunities in and around Glenwood Springs. Contact the **White River National Forest** (☎ 970/945-2521 or 970/319-2670; www.fs.usda.gov/whiteriver) or the **Bureau of Land Management** (☎ **970/876-9000;** www.blm.gov/co) for maps and other information.

A busy local shop where you can get info on the best spots for hiking, mountain climbing, rock climbing, kayaking, camping, and cross-country skiing is **Summit Canyon Mountaineering,** 732 Grand Ave. (☎ **970/945-6994;** www.summitcanyon.com); it sells and rents ski and camping gear.

BICYCLING Biking options abound here. The 44-mile **Rio Grande Trail** connects Glenwood Springs and Aspen, a paved bike trail runs from the Yampah Vapor Caves into Glenwood Canyon, and trails and four-wheel-drive roads in the adjacent White River National Forest are ideal for mountain bikers. You'll find bike rentals ($25–$65 per day) in town at **Canyon Bikes,** 319 6th St. (☎ **970/945-8904;** www.canyonbikes.com).

FISHING Brown and rainbow trout are caught in the Roaring Fork and Colorado rivers, and fishing for rainbow and brook trout is often good in the Crystal River above the community of Redstone. Get licenses, equipment, and advice from **Roaring Fork Anglers,** 2205 Grand Ave. (☎ **800/781-8120** or 970/945-0180; www.rfanglers.com), who have offered guided fly-fishing trips since 1975.

HIKING Hikers will also find numerous trailheads along the **Glenwood Canyon Recreation Trail** ★ in Glenwood Canyon, with some of the best scenery in the area. Among them, **Hanging Lake Trail,** 9 miles east of Glenwood Springs off I-70, is especially popular. The trailhead is accessible from eastbound I-70; westbound travelers must make a U-turn and backtrack a few miles to reach the parking area. The trail climbs 1,000 feet in 1 mile; allow several hours for the round-trip. (Try to go in the evening if you can—the trail can be quite busy in the morning and afternoon.) **Grizzly Creek Trail** is in the Grizzly Creek Rest Area, along I-70 in Glenwood Canyon, where there is also a launching area for rafts and kayaks. The trail climbs along the creek, past wildflowers and dogwood trees.

RIVER RAFTING   Bouncing down the rapids through magnificent **Glenwood Canyon** is certainly one of the best ways to see this spectacular country. Companies offering raft trips include **Blue Sky Adventures,** at the Hotel Colorado at 319 Sixth St. ($ 877/945-6605 or 970/945-6605; www.blueskyadventure.com), which offers rafting on the Colorado and Roaring Fork rivers. A popular full-day trip through the whitewater of Shoshone Rapids costs $88 for adults and $68 for kids, including a hot barbecue lunch. Half-day trips are also available.

SKIING & SNOWBOARDING   Sunlight Mountain Resort ($ 800/445-7931 or 970/945-7491; www.sunlightmtn.com) is located 10 miles south of Glenwood Springs. Geared toward families, Sunlight has 680 skiable acres and a 2,010-foot vertical drop from its 9,895-foot summit; it's served by one triple and two double chairlifts and a ski-school surface lift. There are 67 runs, rated 20 percent beginner, 55 percent intermediate, 20 percent advanced, and 5 percent expert. The ski area is open from early December to early April daily from 9am to 4pm. A full-day lift ticket cost $57 for adults, $45 for children 6 to 12 and seniors 65 to 79, and free for seniors 80 and over and kids 5 and under. There is also a terrain park. Rentals are available on the mountain or **Sunlight Mountain Ski & Bike Shop,** 309 Ninth St. in downtown Glenwood Springs ($ 970/945-9425).

THE BLACK CANYON OF THE GUNNISON NATIONAL PARK ★★

The **Black Canyon of the Gunnison,** which had been a national monument since 1933, became a national park on October 21, 1999. In a statement issued after the bill-signing ceremony, President Bill Clinton called the Black Canyon a "true natural treasure" and added, "Its nearly vertical walls, rising a half-mile high, harbor one of the most spectacular stretches of wild river in America."

The canyon was avoided by early American Indians and later Utes and Anglo explorers, who believed that no human could survive a trip to its depths. The entire thing measures 48 miles long, and the 14 miles that are included in the national park (which, at 30,385 acres, is among America's smallest) range in depth from 1,730 to 2,700 feet. Its width at the narrowest point (a.k.a. "the Narrows") is only 40 feet. This deep slash in the earth was created by 2 million years of erosion, a process that's still going on—albeit slowed by the damming of the Gunnison River above the park.

Most visitors view the canyon from the South Rim Road, site of the visitor center, or the lesser-used North Rim Road. Short paths branching off both roads lead to splendid viewpoints with signs explaining the canyon's unique geology.

The park has hiking trails along both rims, backcountry-hiking routes down into the canyon, and excellent fishing for ambitious anglers willing to make the trek to the canyon floor. It also provides an abundance of thrills for the experienced rock climbers who challenge its sheer walls. In winter, much of the park is closed to motor vehicles, but that only makes for a peaceful delight for cross-country skiers and snowshoers.

The Black Canyon shares a portion of its south boundary with **Curecanti National Recreation Area** (p. 231), which offers boating and fishing on three reservoirs, as well as hiking and camping.

Essentials

ENTRY POINTS   The park is located northeast of Montrose. To reach the south rim, head east on U.S. 50 for 8 miles to the well-marked turnoff to the entrance, where you will turn north (left) onto Colo. 347 for 6 miles. To reach the north rim from Montrose, drive north 21 miles on U.S. 50 to Delta, east 31 miles on Colo. 92 to Crawford, then south on the 11-mile access road.

FEES & REGULATIONS   Admission for up to 7 days costs $15 per vehicle or $7 for those on foot or two wheels. Required backcountry permits are free. Visitors are warned not to throw anything from the rim into the canyon, since even a single small stone thrown or kicked from the rim could be fatal to people below; and to supervise children very carefully because many sections of the rim have no guardrails or fences. Unlike most national parks, leashed pets are permitted on several trails (check with rangers), but they are specifically prohibited from wilderness areas.

VISITOR CENTERS & INFORMATION   The **South Rim Visitor Center** is open daily year-round, except major holidays, with hours from 8am to 6pm in summer and from 8:30am to 4pm the rest of the year. For information, contact **Black Canyon of the Gunnison National Park** (© **970/641-2337;** www.nps.gov/blca).

RANGER PROGRAMS   Ranger-conducted **nature walks, geology talks,** and **astronomy programs** are presented daily from Memorial Day through late September on the South Rim. During the winter, guided **snowshoe walks** and **cross-country ski tours** are offered on the South Rim.

FAST FACTS   There are no post offices or medical facilities in the park.

Where to Stay & Eat

There are campgrounds on both rims, with pit toilets and no showers, but there are electric hookups available on Loop B of the South Rim Campground. Cost per site is $12, $18 with electric hookups. The **South Rim Campground,** which is open year-round and is rarely full, has 88 sites; the **North Rim Campground** is open from spring through fall and occasionally fills up; it has only 13 sites. Reservations can be made for some sites in the South Rim Campground from late May through early September through the park website or **www.recreation.gov,** or by phone (© **877/444-6777**). There is no dining in the park.

The nearest restaurants and motels are in **Montrose,** about 15 miles southwest of the park. Contact the **Office of Business and Tourism** (© **970/497-8558;** www.visit montrose.com) for information.

Exploring the Park

It's fairly easy to see a great deal here in a short amount of time, especially if you stick to the South Rim. First stop at the visitor center to see the exhibits and get an understanding of how this phenomenal canyon was created. Then drive the 7-mile (one-way) **South Rim Drive,** stopping at the overlooks. There are about a dozen overlooks along the drive, and in most cases you'll be walking from 140 feet to about 700 feet to reach the viewpoints from your vehicle. Among the not-to-be-missed overlooks are **Gunnison Point,** behind the visitor center, which offers stunning views of the seemingly endless walls of dark rock, and the **Pulpit Rock Overlook,** which provides a splendid view of the rock walls and the Gunnison River, some 1,770 feet down. Farther along the drive is **Chasm View,** where you can see the incredible power of water, which here cuts through over 1,800 feet of solid rock. Near the end of the drive, stop at **Sunset View,** where there's a picnic area and viewpoint, which offers distant views beyond the canyon, as well as of the river, now 2,430 feet below your feet. If your timing is right, you might be treated to a classic Western sunset, in all its red and orange glory.

Outdoor Activities

CLIMBING   The sheer vertical walls and scenic beauty of the Black Canyon make it an ideal destination for rock climbers, but this is no place for novices. These cliffs, known for crumbling rock, dizzying heights, and very few places to put protective gear, require a great deal of experience and the best equipment. Free permits are required; prospective climbers should discuss their plans first with park rangers.

HIKING & BACKPACKING   Trails on the park's rims range from short, easy walks to moderate-to-strenuous hikes of several miles. Hiking below the rim is mostly difficult and not recommended for those with a fear of heights. Permits are not needed for hiking rim trails, but are required for all treks below the rim.

Trails along the **South Rim** include the easy **Cedar Point Nature Trail.** From the Cedar Point trail head, along South Rim Road, this .7-mile round-trip walk has signs along the way describing the plants you'll see and provides breathtaking views of the Gunnison River, 2,000 feet down, at the end. The moderate **Warner Point Nature Trail** begins at High Point Overlook at the end of South Rim Road. It's 1.5 miles round-trip and offers a multitude of things to see, from flora such as mountain mahogany, piñon pine, and Utah juniper, to distant mountains and valleys, as well as the Black Canyon and its creator, the Gunnison River. The trailhead for the 2-mile round-trip **Oak Flat Loop Trail,** rated moderate to strenuous, is near the visitor center. Dropping slightly below the rim, this trail offers excellent views into the canyon. Be aware that the trail is narrow in spots and a bit close to steep drop-offs.

Trails along the **North Rim** include the moderate **Chasm View Nature Trail** (.3 miles, round-trip), with a trailhead at the end of the North Rim campground loop. Beginning in a piñon-juniper forest, this trail heads to the rim for good views of the canyon and the river; you'll also have a good chance of seeing swallows, swifts, and raptors here. The 7-mile **North Vista Trail,** which begins at the North Rim Ranger Station, is moderate to strenuous. It offers some of the best views into the Black Canyon and also rewards hikers with a good chance of seeing such birds as red-tailed hawks, white-throated swifts, Clark's nutcrackers, and ravens.

Experienced **backcountry hikers** in good physical condition may want to hike down into the canyon. Although there are no maintained or marked trails, there are several routes that rangers can help you find. Free permits are required, and there are a limited number of campsites for backpackers. The most popular inner canyon hike is the strenuous **Gunnison Route,** branching off the South Rim's Oak Flat Trail en route to the river. An 80-foot length of chain helps keep you from falling on a stretch about a third of the way down. This hike drops 1,800 feet and takes about 5 hours.

WATERSPORTS   Although the river may look tempting, my advice for watersports enthusiasts is: **Don't do it!** The Gunnison River through the park is **extremely dangerous,** for both swimmers and rafters. (It's considered **unraftable.**)

WILDLIFE VIEWING   The park is home to plenty of chipmunks, ground squirrels, badgers, marmots, and mule deer. Although not frequently seen, there are also black bears, cougars, and bobcats, and you'll probably hear coyotes at night. Peregrine falcons can sometimes be spotted along the cliffs, and you may also see red-tailed hawks, turkey vultures, golden eagles, and white-throated swifts.

WINTER SPORTS When South Rim Road is closed by snow, the park service plows to the visitor center and leaves the rest of the road a perfect cross-country ski trail. For snowshoeing trails, get directions at the visitor center.

PAONIA ★

69 miles SE of Grand Junction, 51 miles NE of Montrose

Named by founder Samuel Wade for the Latin spelling of the peony flower, Paonia has an enviable location in a fertile valley surrounded by rugged mountains. Lined with trees and surrounded by orchards in the picturesque North Fork Valley, Paonia was settled by white pioneers who pushed out the Ute Indians in 1881. The economy has long been based almost exclusively on agriculture and coal mining, but it has grown increasingly diverse as young people priced out of the exclusive real-estate markets in the nearby resort towns have made Paonia their home in recent years. Today downtown Paonia is a vibrant place, with a number of unique retailers, and access to outdoor recreation and a mild climate continue to attract newcomers.

Essentials

GETTING THERE **By Car** Paonia is a 1½-hour drive southeast of Grand Junction via U.S. 50 and Colo. 92 and Colo. 133.

By Plane The closest airports are in Montrose and Grand Junction.

GETTING AROUND Paonia is situated on Colorado's shortest state highway, Colo. 187, which becomes Grand Avenue downtown, just south of Colo. 133 between Hotchkiss and Somerset. The 2-block downtown is centered on Second Street and Grand Avenue.

VISITOR INFORMATION Contact the **Paonia Chamber of Commerce** (*Ⓒ* **970/527-3886;** www.paoniachamber.com). **Delta County Tourism** (*Ⓒ* **970/874-2100;** www.deltacountycolorado.org) is another good resource.

FAST FACTS **Delta County Memorial Hospital,** with a 24-hour emergency room, is at 1501 E. Third St. in Delta, 30 miles west of Paonia (*Ⓒ* **970/874-7681;** www.deltahospital.org). The **post office** is at 125 Grand Ave.

Where to Stay

Upstairs at the downtown **Living Farm Café,** 120 Grand Ave. (*Ⓒ* **970/527-3779;** www.thelivingfarmcafe.com), there are five B&B-like rooms, for $90 to $115.

MODERATE

Fresh & Wyld Farmhouse Inn ★★ This funky, colorful, 4-acre property on the pastoral outskirts of Paonia is part B&B and part organic farm. That means fab farm-to-table breakfasts and an opportunity to work in the gardens. Rooms are in a renovated farmhouse that dates to the early 1900s, with an appropriately rustic feel (quilts, hardwoods, and spare decor). Proprietor and expert chef Dava Parr teaches cooking classes; come summertime, the inn hosts terrific Friday night dinners and Sunday brunches with local musicians

1978 Harding Rd., Paonia. © **970/527-4374.** www.freshandwyld.com. 6 units. $110–$170 double. Rates include full breakfast. **Amenities:** Free Wi-Fi.

Where to Eat

For a pizza and a beer, it's hard to beat **Louie's,** 202 Grand Ave. (© **970/527-3265;** www.paoniapizza.com). The **Living Farm Café,** 120 Grand Ave. (© **970/527-3779;** www.thelivingfarmcafe.com), gets ingredients from its own farm and local suppliers.

MODERATE

Flying Fork Cafe and Bakery ★★ ITALIAN   Superlative baked goods in the morning give way to a creative list of sandwiches for lunch, but dinner is a more involved affair. Main courses include homemade pasta dishes, braised Colorado lamb shank, and polenta with local heirloom tomatoes. There is also a selection of Neapolitan-style pizzas.

Third and Main sts. © **970/527-3203.** www.flyingforkcafe.com. Main courses $6–$9 lunch, $9–$23 dinner. Daily 11:30am–2:30pm and Tues–Sun 5:30–9pm.

Exploring Paonia

There are three big draws for tourists to Paonia: farming, wineries, and the outdoors. A good first stop is **Delicious Orchards,** 39130 Colo. 133 west of Paonia (© **970/527-1110;** www.deliciousorchardstore.com), a combination market/farm with 16 acres of orchards where visitors can go out and pick their own fruit (apricots, pears, and apples), or shop for locally grown produce, wine, and other regional products. The store is the retail face of a locally produced brand of juice and cider, Big B's, and the best place to try some. There's also a cafe and campground ($10–$20 nightly). For more info on the valley's farms—a good many of which welcome visitors—the **Valley Organic Growers Association Directory** (www.vogaco.org) is a useful resource.

As far as the vino, there are about 10 wineries in Paonia and Hotchkiss, including **Terror Creek Winery,** 17445 Garvin Mesa Rd., Paonia (© **970/527-3484;** www. terrorcreekwinery.com); and **Stone Cottage Cellars,** 41716 Reds Rd., Paonia (© **970/527-3444;** www.stonecottagecellars.com). In Hotchkiss, check out the organic, biodynamic winery/distillery at **Jack Rabbit Hill,** 26567 North Rd. (© **970/835-3677;** www.jackrabbithill.com).

Outdoor Activities

Located 16 miles north of Paonia via Colo. 133, **Paonia State Park** (© 970/921-5721; http://cpw.state.co.us) offers boating, biking, and hiking as well as a campground ($10 nightly). Contact the **Gunnison National Forest,** 423 N. Rio Grande Ave. (© **970/527-4131**), for advice and information.

BIKING   There are numerous biking routes in the vicinity. The 5-mile **German Creek Loop** starts and ends in downtown Paonia and traverses Mt. Lamborn.

HIKING   A good trail for a day hike is the **Inter-Ocean Pass Trail,** a moderate to strenuous 8-mile round-trip hike that gains 2,500 feet in altitude. Contact the Paonia Ranger District (© **970/527-4131**) for directions.

SOUTHWESTERN COLORADO

A land apart from the rest of the state, southwestern Colorado is set off by the spectacularly rugged wall of the San Juan Mountains. The Ancestral Puebloans (also known as the Anasazi) who once lived here created cliff dwellings that withstood the tests of time and weather, and remain in excellent condition today, a thousand years or more after their making. The ancient cliff dwellings of Mesa Verde National Park are a case in point, and there are similar but less well-known sites throughout the area, primarily around Cortez.

Durango is the area's major city. Its vintage downtown and narrow-gauge railroad harks back to the Old West days of the late 1800s, when it boomed as a hub for the region's mining industry. Telluride, at the end of a box canyon surrounded by 14,000-foot peaks, has capitalized on its still-evident mining heritage in its evolution into an increasingly posh ski and summer resort. And those who drive the Million Dollar Highway—down U.S. 550 from Ouray, over 11,008-foot Red Mountain Pass through Silverton, and on to Durango—can't miss the remains of turn-of-the-20th-century mines scattered over the mountainsides.

DURANGO ★★★

332 miles SW of Denver, 169 miles S of Grand Junction, 50 miles N of Farmington, New Mexico

Born as a railroad town more than a century ago, Durango remains a railroad town to this day, as thousands of visitors take a journey back in time aboard the Durango & Silverton Narrow Gauge Railroad. Durango was founded in 1880 when the Denver & Rio Grande Railroad line was extended to Silverton to haul precious metals from high-country mines. Within a year, 2,000 new residents had turned the town into a smelting and transportation center. Although more than $300 million worth of silver, gold, and other minerals rode along the route over the years, the unstable nature of the mining business gave the town many ups and downs.

Durango remained a center for ranching and mining into the 1960s. In 1965, with the opening of the Purgatory ski area, 25 miles north of town, a tourism boom began. When the railroad abandoned its tracks from Antonito, Colorado, to Durango in the late 1960s, leaving only the Durango-Silverton spur, the locals panicked. But from that potential economic disaster blossomed a savior: The Durango & Silverton Narrow Gauge Railroad is now Durango's biggest attraction, hauling more than 200,000 passengers each year. The area also attracts mountain bikers from all over the country, and opportunities abound for outdoor activities of all kinds.

Durango

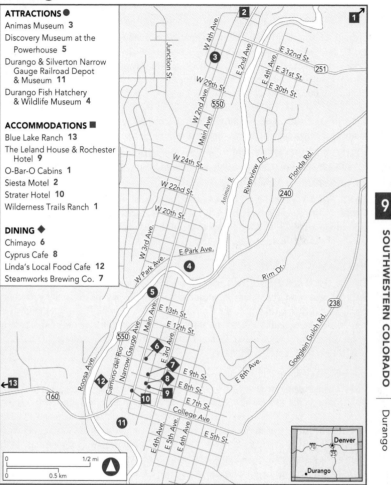

ATTRACTIONS ●

Animas Museum **3**

Discovery Museum at the
 Powerhouse **5**

Durango & Silverton Narrow
 Gauge Railroad Depot
 & Museum **11**

Durango Fish Hatchery
 & Wildlife Museum **4**

ACCOMMODATIONS ■

Blue Lake Ranch **13**

The Leland House & Rochester
 Hotel **9**

O-Bar-O Cabins **1**

Siesta Motel **2**

Strater Hotel **10**

Wilderness Trails Ranch **1**

DINING ◆

Chimayo **6**

Cyprus Cafe **8**

Linda's Local Food Cafe **12**

Steamworks Brewing Co. **7**

9

SOUTHWESTERN COLORADO | Durango

Essentials

GETTING THERE   By Car   Durango is located at the crossroads of east-west U.S. 160 and north-south U.S. 550. It is 222 miles west of I-25 at Walsenburg and 56 miles north of Farmington, New Mexico.

By Plane   Durango-La Plata County Airport (DRO), 14 miles southeast of Durango off Colo. 172 (© **970/382-6050;** www.flydurango.com), is served by **American, Frontier, United,** and **US Airways.**

GETTING AROUND   The city is on the banks of the Animas River. U.S. 160 lies along the southern edge and is joined by U.S. 550 just east of Durango. Just before U.S. 160 crosses the river, U.S. 550 branches north as Camino del Rio and rejoins with

Main Avenue at 14th Street. Downtown Durango is built around Main Avenue from 14th Street south to Fifth Street. College Drive (Sixth St.) is the principal cross street.

Transportation throughout Durango is provided by the **Durango T** (© 970/259-5438; www.getarounddurango.com). The **city bus** has three fixed-route loops that operate weekdays, from about 7am to 7pm, year-round (but not on major public holidays), and there are also some evening schedules, including late-night transportation Friday and Saturday. The fare is $1 per ride one-way, and $5 for the late-night bus. Also part of the Durango Lift is the **free downtown trolley,** running along Main Avenue. **Taxi service** is provided 24 hours a day by **Durango Transportation** (© 970/259-4818). Car rentals are available at the airport are from **Avis, Budget, Enterprise, Hertz,** and **National.** Central Durango is walkable and bikeable, but many of the regional attractions require a car.

VISITOR INFORMATION Contact the **Durango Area Tourism Office** (© 800/525-8855 or 970/247-3500; www.durango.org). The **Durango Welcome Center** is downtown at 802 Main Ave., open daily.

FAST FACTS There's a 24-hour emergency room at **Mercy Regional Medical Center,** 1010 Three Springs Blvd. (© 970/247-4311; www.mercydurango.org). The **post office** is at 222 W. 8th St. For **road conditions,** call © 303/639-1111 or 511, or browse **www.cotrip.org.**

Where to Stay

Durango has a definite lodging season. When the Durango & Silverton Narrow Gauge Railroad runs most of its trains in midsummer, expect to pay top dollar for your room, and expect higher rates during the Christmas holidays as well. But go in the low season—early spring and fall—and you'll find much more reasonable rates. An easy way to book accommodations is to contact **Durango Central Reservations** (© 866/294-5187; www.durangoreservations.org).

EXPENSIVE

Blue Lake Ranch ★★★   This is Colorado's first B&B, operating since 1974, and for my money, it's also the best. Featuring over 10,000 irises in full summer bloom, the perfectly sculpted 200 acres here are a spectacular tableau of wildflowers and greenery, with a turtle- and trout-laden lake, sweeping views, and a secluded location about 10 miles southwest of Durango. Stylishly adorned with Southwestern art, rooms are in the main house and standalone structures nestled in the surrounding woodland, ranging from the cozy and colorful La Plata Vista Room (with a king bed swathed in a deep orange, hand-woven throw and a majestic view) to various casitas (with gas fireplaces, kitchens, and whirlpool tubs) to the Cabin on the Lake (sleeping up to eight in a rustic log cabin). There is also four miles of river access for anglers, fall hunting packages, and the perfect setting for unadulterated relaxation—this is just the place to unwind and do nothing.

16919 Colo. 140, Hesperus. © **888/258-3525** or 970/385-4537. www.bluelakeranch.com. 16 units, including 4 cabins and cottages. $199–$219 double; $269–$419 suite, cabin, or cottage. Lower rates fall to spring. Rates include full breakfast. **Amenities:** Free Wi-Fi.

Strater Hotel ★★★   Opened in 1887, the redbrick-and-limestone Strater has long been the landmark piece of architecture in Durango. In the subsequent century and a quarter, the hotel has weathered all of the local booms and busts quite nicely, and today is the toniest place in town. Guest rooms are unique, each furnished with period antiques. Most requested is room 222, the favored accommodation for legendary Western writer, Louis L'Amour, who was inspired by the piano music and carousing at the

Diamond Belle Saloon just below. The resident restaurant, the Mahogany Grille, won the Wine Spectator Award of Excellence in 2013.

699 Main Ave., Durango. ✆ **800/247-4431** or 970/247-4431. www.strater.com. 93 units. Early May to mid-Oct and Christmas holidays $175–$300 double; mid-Oct to early May $100–$150 double. **Amenities:** Restaurant; 2 bars; concierge; hot tub; limited room service; free Wi-Fi.

Wilderness Trails Ranch ★★ Operated by the Roberts family since 1970, this aptly named ranch, bounded by the Weminuche Wilderness Area 35 miles northeast of Durango, is just the place for a family getaway in the increasingly elusive Colorado where cowboys and mountain scenery abound. Most cabins have two bedrooms, one with a king or queen bed and the other with a pair of twins for the kids, and the list of activities is long and comprehensive. Horseback riding is the primary pursuit, and the wranglers here are topnotch and able to work with people of all ability levels. Guests can also go mountain biking, fishing, and hiking, or even go on a cattle drive. The food (three meals a day are provided) is varied and delicious.

24386 C.R. 501, Bayfield. ✆ **800/527-2624** or 970/247-0722. www.wildernesstrails.com. 9 cabins. $2,695–$2,895 per adult per 6-day stay; $2,195 per child 3–17; free for children 2 and under. Rates include all meals and most activities. Shorter stays available when capacity allows. Closed early Oct to late May. **Amenities:** Restaurant; bar; children's program; outdoor Jacuzzi; outdoor heated pool (seasonal); free Wi-Fi.

MODERATE

The Leland House & Rochester Hotel ★★ Under the same ownership and across Second Avenue from one another, these historic sister properties share a staff, and what can only be called a "breakfast experience" (yes, it's that good). The 1927 Leland House has a more traditional B&B look, while 1892 Rochester Hotel's rooms sport movie themes based on Westerns filmed in and around Durango. Perks include free cruiser bikes to ride around town and an unbeatable courtyard at the Rochester that hosts concerts in the summertime.

721 and 726 E. Second Ave., Durango. ✆ **970/385-1920.** www.rochesterhotel.com. 27 units. $129–$229 double; $179–$229 1-bedroom suite; $359–$399 2-bedroom suite. Rates include full breakfast. Pets accepted ($20 per night). **Amenities:** Bar; complimentary cruiser bikes; free Wi-Fi.

O-Bar-O Cabins ★★ Just 12 miles northeast of Durango on the bank of the Florida River, the O-Bar-O is a world away. The recently restored cabins here balance rugged and comfortable, ranging in size from the petite Birdsnest studio for two to the summer-only Hummingbird, a two-story duplex that sleeps six. Most have fireplaces and decks, but the best feature is undoubtedly the idyllic setting, a perfect match to most people's mental image of a Colorado cabin resort.

11998 C.R. 240, Durango. ✆ **970/259-3649.** www.durango-colorado-cabins.com. 9 cabins. $159–$289 double, plus about $20 per additional person. Pets accepted ($50 one-time fee). **Amenities:** Outdoor hot tub; free Wi-Fi.

INEXPENSIVE

Siesta Motel ★ Fronted by a vintage sign, the family-owned Siesta Motel is the most reliable budget lodging in Durango. With a location on the north side of the city and rooms that are clean and comfortable, sporting a mild Southwestern motif, this is a good pick for families who need a bit of elbow room—the central courtyard offers just that. Many of the rooms have kitchenettes; some have tub-showers and others have showers only.

3475 Main Ave., Durango. ✆ **877/314-0741** or 970/247-0741. www.durangosiestamotel.com. 22 units, including 2 suites. $72–$156 double; $88–$165 suite. Pets accepted ($10–$20 per night). **Amenities:** Free Wi-Fi.

Where to Eat

Durango is full of terrific restaurants, with an emphasis on New American, Mexican and pub fare.

EXPENSIVE

Chimayo ★★ NEW AMERICAN   Opening in 2012, the chefs at Chimayo prepare almost everything in a stone-fired oven, including pizzas, wood plank salmon, and steaks. (The kitchen does not even have a fryer.) Served in a contemporary setting with garage doors in lieu of front windows that open on to Main Avenue, the results are uniformly excellent, with Southwestern-style small plates like stuffed poblano chiles and queso fundido for starters and a superlative banana tart for dessert. We also approve heartily of the expert mixology going on here; if you're not a cocktail type, note that there's a well-curated list of wines and craft beers.

862 Main Ave. ℰ **970/259-2749.** www.chimayodurango.com. Main courses $10–$16 lunch, $10–$27 dinner. Mon–Fri 11:30am–9pm; Sat–Sun 10:30am–9pm.

Cyprus Cafe ★★ MEDITERRANEAN   Featuring live jazz and great views, the outdoor patio here is home to Durango's most in-demand restaurant seating in the summer, but it's not just the picture-perfect atmosphere—it's the first rate food that draws the crowds. The culinary inspirations are pan-Mediterranean, reflected in small plates like falafel with curried yogurt and pan-seared calamari as well as main dishes like *spanakopita* (pastry stuffed with spinach and feta) and angel hair puttanesca. You won't forget you're in Colorado though: Elk, trout, and local lamb often appear on the menu. Lunch is more casual: pita pizzas, burgers, pasta, and terrific salads.

725 E. Second Ave. ℰ **970/385-6884.** www.cypruscafe.com. Lunch $10–$18; dinner $15–$34. Mid-May to Sept daily 11:30am–3pm and 5–10pm; Oct to mid-May Mon–Sat 11:30am–2:30pm and 5–9pm.

MODERATE

Steamworks Brewing Co. ★ BREWPUB   This is the best brewpub in the Four Corners area. The social, family-friendly vibe is nicely complemented by good food—there are burgers, small gourmet pizza, steaks, and some Cajun dishes—and great beer. Try a pint of the Third Eye PA or Colorado Kolsch.

801 E. Second Ave. (at Eighth St.). ℰ **970/259-9200.** www.steamworksbrewing.com. Main courses $10–$25; pizza $10–$18. Daily 11am–11pm. Bar open later with a limited menu.

INEXPENSIVE

Linda's Local Food Cafe ★★ MEXICAN   Proprietor Linda Illsley trained at the Culinary Institute of America and worked all over Europe before opening her eponymous eatery in 2003. With chalkboard menus, a sunny patio, and food from local suppliers—the restaurant sources as much as 75 percent of ingredients from Durango-area farms and ranches—Linda's makes authentic Mexican dishes like tamales, chile rellenos, and burritos. The tamales are the specialty: Illsley and company grind the corn in house and stuff them with pork, chicken, or zucchini and corn. Local beer and craft cocktails are available. Highly recommended: the homemade limeade with fresh basil.

309 W. College Dr. (in the Albertsons parking lot). ℰ **970/259-6729.** www.lindaslocalfoodcafe.com. Most items $8–$14. Tues–Sat 8am–3pm.

Exploring Durango

While taking a steam-train trip on the Durango & Silverton Narrow Gauge Railroad is undeniably the area's top attraction, there are other things to do here. Those interested in a close-up view of the city's numerous historic buildings will want to pick up free copies of several **walking-tour** brochures from the visitor center at Eighth and Main.

Animas Museum ★ Durango's history comes to life at this century-old schoolhouse on the north side of town. Beyond the impressive collection of archival photographs, visitors can get a look at displays covering the pioneer and mining eras, including the classroom outfitted like it was in 1904 and the "Law and Disorder" focused on the outlaws who ruled the roost in the Four Corners area. Allow a minimum of 1 hour.

31st St. and W. Second Ave. ℓ **970/259-2402.** www.animasmuseum.org. Admission $4 adults, $3 seniors, $2 children 7–12, free for children 6 and under. May–Oct Mon–Sat 10am–5pm; Nov–Apr Tues–Sat 10am–4pm.

Durango Discovery Museum ★ The former Children's Museum of Durango moved to the historic powerhouse on the Animas River. The result is a great kids' museum nicknamed "The Pow," with a multistory indoor playground, science exhibits including a 3-D printer and an Earth simulator, and plenty of fun activities

1333 Camino Del Rio. ℓ **970/259-9234.** www.durangodiscovery.org. Admission $7.50 adults, $6.75 seniors and students, $6 children 3 to 10, free for children under 3. Tues–Sat 10am–5pm; Sun noon–5pm. Closed Mon and major holidays.

The Durango & Silverton Narrow Gauge Railroad ★★★ Colorado's most famous train has been in continual operation since 1881. In all that time, its route has never varied: up the Río de las Animas Perdidas (River of Lost Souls), through 45 miles of mountain and San Juan National Forest wilderness to the historic mining town of Silverton, and back. The coal-fired steam locomotives pull strings of gold-colored Victorian coaches on the 3,000-foot climb, past relics of mining and railroad activity from the last century. Summer trips take 3½ hours each way, with a 2¼-hour stopover in the picturesque town of Silverton before the return trip. You can also overnight in Silverton and return to Durango the following day. Stops are made for water, and also at remote trailheads inaccessible by road. Refreshments and snacks are available on all trains. There are also first-class cars and cars available for charter. The ticket price includes entry to the depot museum, covering railroad history in Durango and the San Juan Mountains.

479 Main Ave., Durango. ℓ **877/872-4607** or 970/247-2733. www.durangotrain.com. Advance reservations advised. Summer round-trip fare $85 adults, $51 children 4–11. Numerous other tickets and passes available; lower rates in winter. Parking $7 per day per car, $9 for RVs and buses; $4 in winter for any vehicle.

Durango Fish Hatchery and Wildlife Museum ★ The rainbow trout that hatch here are released to stock a number of rivers and lakes in southwestern Colorado, and the outdoor tanks that hold thousands of fish are the prime attraction. The facility produces more than 1.3 million fish a year, and visitors can feed the fish via coin-operated dispensers. Inside, the museum has displays covering the area's wildlife. Allow 30 minutes.

151 E. 16th St. ℓ **970/247-4755.** Free admission. Hatchery year-round 8am–4pm; museum mid-May to mid-Sept daily 10am–4:30pm.

Southern Ute Cultural Center & Museum ★★ Visitors get firsthand experience with Ute culture and tradition at this 52,000-square-foot facility that celebrates the living history of Colorado's longest continuous residents. Dynamic multi-sensory and interactive exhibitions, along with rare artifact collections, are presented. These include texts, photographs, video presentations, and recorded oral histories tell the compelling story of the Southern Ute people. It is located next to a casino. Expect to spend about an hour seeing (and hearing) it all.

77 C.R. 517, Ignacio (25 miles southeast of Durango). (✆ **970/563-9583.** www.succm.org. Admission $7 adults, $4 seniors, $3 children, free for children under 4. Memorial Day to Labor Day Tues–Fri 9am–4:30pm, Sat 10am–4pm, Sun noon–4pm; shorter hours rest of year.

Outdoor Activities

Durango is surrounded by public land, with numerous opportunities for hiking, mountain biking, fishing, and winter sports. For information, contact the **San Juan Public Lands Center,** at 15 Burnett Ct. (✆ 970/247-4874), off U.S. 160 in the Durango Tech Center, offering information from the **San Juan National Forest** (www.fs.fusda.gov/sanjuan) and the **Bureau of Land Management** (www.blm.gov/co). The center is open Monday through Friday from 8am to 4:30pm.

The **Durango Parks and Recreation Department** (✆ 970/375-7321; www.durangogov.org) operates about 20 parks throughout the city, where you'll find picnic areas, free tennis courts, swimming pools, and other facilities.

Purgatory at Durango Mountain Resort, some 25 miles north of Durango on U.S. 550 (✆ 970/247-9000; www.durangomountainresort.com), doesn't close down—or even slow down—after the winter's snows are gone. Summer activities here include running on water in a human-sized hamster ball, a zip line, scenic chairlift rides, a climbing wall, miniature golf, disc golf, and bungee trampolines. Individual activities cost from $7 for a round of mini golf to $15 for the zip line, alpine slide, or bungee trampoline, but the best deal is the Total Adventure Ticket—a 5-ride pass for $45. Purgatory at Durango Mountain Resort also offers free guided naturalist hikes; call ✆ 970/385-1210 for times and registration.

FISHING Six-mile-long **Vallecito Lake,** 23 miles northeast of Durango via C.R. 240 and C.R. 501, is a prime spot for rainbow trout, brown trout, kokanee salmon, and northern pike; for information, contact the **Vallecito Lake Chamber of Commerce** (✆ 970/247-1573; www.vallecitolakechamber.com). There are also numerous rivers and streams in the Durango area. For licenses, supplies, and advice, or to arrange for a guided fly-fishing trip, stop in at **Duranglers,** 923 Main Ave. (✆ 888/347-4346 or 970/385-4081; www.duranglers.com). Full-day float trips for two people cost $375 to $475; wading trips for two cost $375.

GOLF Two public 18-hole golf courses open in spring, weather permitting. There's **Hillcrest Golf Club,** 2300 Rim Dr., adjacent to Fort Lewis College (✆ 970/247-1499; www.golfhillcrest.com), with fees of $39 for 18 holes, not including cart; and **Dalton Ranch Golf Club,** 589 Trimble Lane (C.R. 252), north of Durango via U.S. 550 (✆ 970/247-8774; www.daltonranch.com), charging $65 to $105 for 18 holes, cart included.

HIKING & BACKPACKING The **Animas Mountain Trail** is a 5-mile loop with terrific views of the entire valley, accessible via a trail head in the northwest corner of town near 32nd Street and Fourth Avenue. Durango is at the western end of the 500-mile **Colorado Trail** (www.coloradotrail.org) to Denver. The trail head is 3½ miles up Junction Creek Road, an extension of 25th Street west of Main Avenue. There are numerous other trails in the Durango area, including several that delve into the Weminuche Wilderness Area via the Durango & Silverton railroad or trailheads near Vallecito Lake. For information on area trails, contact the San Juan Public Lands Center (✆ 970/247-4874).

HORSEBACK RIDING   My choice for a licensed outfitter here is **Rapp Corral,** located on the east side of U.S. 550 about 20 miles north of Durango at 51 Haviland Lake Rd. (𝄐 **970/247-8454;** www.rappcorral.com). Riders go into the San Juan National Forest, and rides start at $48 for a 1-hour ride. A 2-hour ride to a natural cave costs $80, and a 4- to 5-hour trip into southern Colorado's high country costs $175 to $200. Overnight trips and winter sleigh rides are also available.

LLAMA TREKKING   Guided llama trips, overnight pack trips, and llama leasing are the specialty of **Buckhorn Llama Co.** (𝄐 **970/667-7411;** www.llamapack.com). Guided pack trips in the Weminuche Wilderness Area for one to three people cost $400 per person per day and include all meals and equipment, except sleeping bags.

MOUNTAIN BIKING   The varied terrain and myriad trails of San Juan National Forest have made Durango a nationally known mountain-biking center. The Hermosa Creek Trail (11 miles north of Durango off U.S. 550) and the La Plata Canyon Road (11 miles west of Durango off U.S. 160) are among my favorites. For information, contact the Public Lands Center (𝄐 **970/247-4874**). You can also get information and rent mountain bikes at **Hassle Free Sports,** 2615 Main Ave. (𝄐 **970/259-3874;** www. hasslefreesports.com), which rents full suspension mountain bikes for about $50 per day. Bikers can also take their rig up a chairlift at **Purgatory at Durango Mountain Resort** (𝄐 **970/247-9000;** www.durangomountainresort.com) for $10 a trip or $25 all day. Rentals at the resort run $50 a day.

MOUNTAINEERING & ROCK CLIMBING   A variety of terrain offers mountaineering and rock-climbing opportunities for beginners as well as advanced climbers. **San Juan Mountain Guides** (𝄐 **800/642-5389;** www.mtnguide.net) offers guided climbs in the La Plata and San Juan mountain ranges ($150 and up for 1 day) and instruction ($295 for a 2-day introductory class).

RIVER RAFTING   The three stages of the Animas River provide excitement for rafters of all abilities The churning Class IV and V rapids of the upper Animas mark its rapid descent from the San Juans. The 6 miles from Trimble Hot Springs into downtown Durango are an easy, gently rolling rush. Downstream from Durango, the river is mainly Classes II and III—more relaxing than thrilling. Most outfitters in Durango offer a wide variety of rafting excursions, such as 2- to 4-hour raft trips that cost $30 to $50 for adults and $25 to $40 for kids, and full-day river trips, which include lunch, costing $80 to $110 for adults and $60 to $75 for kids. Recommended outfitters include **Durango Rivertrippers** (𝄐 **970/259-0289;** www.durangorivertrippers.com) and **Mild to Wild Rafting** (𝄐 **970/247-4789;** www.mild2wildrafting.com).

SWIMMING & SOAKING   **Trimble Hot Springs** ★, 7 miles north of Durango just off U.S. 550 (𝄐 **970/247-0111;** www.trimblehotsprings.com), at the junction of C.R. 203 and Trimble Lane, is a National Historic Site more than 100 years old, where you'll often find mom and dad relaxing in the soothing mineral pools or getting a massage while the kids have fun in the adjacent swimming pool. Facilities include two natural hot-springs therapy pools, a separate Olympic-size swimming pool (heated by the hot springs but not containing hot-springs water), massage and therapy rooms, a snack bar, a picnic area, and gardens. The complex is open daily, and day passes cost $18 for adults and $12 for children 5 to 12, and free for children 4 and under, and cover use of the therapy mineral pools and the swimming pool. There is a spa onsite, and lodging is available for $150 to $195 a night.

SOARING TREETOP ADVENTURES:
A bird's-eye view OF THE FOREST

Dubbed a "Canopy Tour," **Soaring Tree Top Adventures** offers visitors a chance to ride a one-of-a-kind zip-line course through the trees north of Durango. The course is accessible only by the Durango & Silverton train and consists of over a mile of zip line spans ranging in length from 50 feet to 1,400 feet, many of them crossing over the Animas River. The zip lines connect a number of stainless-steel platforms that grip their host trees without harming them, some of them 100 feet above the forest floor.

After an exhilarating day confronting acrophobia and learning to keep facing forward, I found it to be worth the high price ($479 per person for the full day, lunch and train included) and a great time for all ages. You have to just take a step and let gravity and technology do the rest—the harnesses are state of the art and the staff make sure you're connected properly every span of the way—and you're literally flying through the treetops at speeds pushing 30 mph, gliding to a stop thanks to the resort's patented braking system.

The season runs from mid-May to mid-October. For more information, contact Soaring Tree Top Adventures (© **970/ 769-2357;** www.soaringcolorado.com).

SOUTHWESTERN COLORADO

WINTER SPORTS Some 25 miles north of Durango on U.S. 550, **Purgatory at Durango Mountain Resort** (© **800/982-6103** or 970/247-9000; www.durangomountainresort.com) has bragging rights to more sunshine than any other Colorado resort. Surprisingly, the sun doesn't come at the expense of snow—average annual snowfall is 260 inches—so you really get the best of both snow and sun. The resort contains 1,360 acres of skiable terrain, with runs for every skill level. The nearby **Durango Nordic Center** (© **970/385-2114;** www.durangonordic.org) has more than 10 miles of trails, and charges $15 for a trail pass ($8 for kids and seniors).

The village includes lodging, several restaurants and taverns, shops, a ski school, and equipment rentals. All-day lift tickets (2013–14 rates) cost $77 for adults, $66 for seniors, $60 for teenagers up to 17, $46 for children 6 to 12, and free for children 5 and under. The resort is usually open from late November or early December to early April, daily from 9am to 4pm.

There's also dinky **Ski Hesperus,** 13 miles west of Durango (© **970/259-3711;** www.ski-hesperus.com): one lift, one rope tow, night skiing, and $39 adult lift tickets or $26 for children 12 and under ($29 and $18 for night skiing, respectively).

Nightlife

During summer, the acclaimed **Durango Melodrama & Vaudeville,** at the Strater Hotel, 699 Main Ave. (© **970/375-7160;** www.durangomelodrama.com), presents authentic late-1800s melodrama—hiss the evil villain and cheer the beautiful heroine—plus a vaudeville review of singing, dancing, and comedy. Tickets are $18 to $30.

You'll get a tasty meal and a live Western stage show at **Bar D Chuckwagon Suppers,** 8080 C.R. 250 (© **970/247-5753;** www.bardchuckwagon.com), north of Durango via U.S. 550 and Trimble Lane (C.R. 252). Open Memorial Day to Labor Day, Bar D offers a choice of roast beef, chicken, or steak, with all of the fixings. After dinner comes the show: Western music with fiddle, guitar, mandolin, bass, and great singers, plus some really hokey comedy. Reservations are required. Cost includes supper and show, and is $24 to $34 for those 9 and older and $10 for kids 8 and under.

In July and August, the long-running **Music in the Mountains** brings virtuosos from all over the world for a series of chamber and orchestra concerts at Durango Mountain Resort, Fort Lewis College, and other venues. Some performances are free; tickets for others run $10 to $54. For the schedule and other information, contact **Music in the Mountains** (✆ **970/385-6820;** www.musicinthemountains.com).

As Durango is both a college and tourist town, the bar scene is especially lively. Stalwarts include **El Rancho Tavern,** 975 Main Ave. (✆ **970/259-8111**), a historic local favorite with pool tables and TVs; the very authentic **Irish Embassy Pub,** 900 Main Ave. (✆ **970/403-1200**); and **Lady Falconburgh's Barley Exchange,** 640 Main Ave. (✆ **970/382-9664**), with more than 140 beers on tap; as well as **Steamworks Brewing Co.** (p. 200) and the **Diamond Belle Saloon** at the Strater Hotel (p. 198).

Just south of downtown at 225 Girard St. is the world headquarters of **Ska Brewing** (✆ **970/247-5792;** www.skabrewing.com), a commercial brewery with a lively taproom open Monday through Saturday until 7 or 8pm. The beer is excellent and there is live music on Thursdays.

SILVERTON ★

For a look at the real Old West without the need for a time machine, head north 48 miles to the town of Silverton. At an elevation of 9,318 feet at the northern terminus of the Durango & Silverton Narrow Gauge Railroad, the town has a year-round population of about 500 and plenty to see and do for the more than 250,000 people who visit each year.

Founded on silver production in 1871, today the entire town is a National Historic Landmark District. In its heyday, Blair Street was such a notorious area of saloons and brothels that no less a character than Bat Masterson, fresh from taming Dodge City, Kansas, was imported to subdue the criminal elements. Today the original false-fronted buildings remain—some in better shape than others—but they now house restaurants and galleries, and are occasionally used as Old West movie sets. There are some fascinating shops and galleries here, along with stagecoach rides and plenty of places to buy tacky T-shirts. I strongly recommend that you spend at least an hour just wandering around.

You can get walking-tour maps of the historic downtown area; information on local shops, restaurants, and lodgings; plus details on the numerous outdoor activities in the surrounding mountains from the **Silverton Chamber of Commerce,** at 414 Greene St. (✆ **800/752-4494** or 970/387-5654; www.silvertoncolorado.com).

For a step back into Silverton's Wild West days, head for the **San Juan County Historical Society Museum,** in the 1902 county jail at Greene and 15th streets (✆ **970/387-5838** or 970/387-5609 in winter; www.silvertonhistoricsociety.org). Here you'll see memorabilia of Silverton's boom days, including lots of railroad stuff and a collection of Derringer handguns. Altogether, there are three floors of historic displays, including the most popular stop—the original jail cells, a good place to snap a photo of that would-be convict you're traveling with. From this building, a tunnel leads to the mining museum next door, which re-creates the feeling of being deep in a mine, with displays of mining machinery, ore cars, and other mining memorabilia. There's also a shop that sells books on area history. The museum is open daily Memorial Day weekend to September from 10am to 5pm and from 10am to 3pm in the first part of October.

Admission is $7 for adults, $3 for kids 5 to 12, and free for children under 5. The adjacent **San Juan County Courthouse** has a gold-domed clock tower, and the restoration of the **Town Hall,** at 14th and Greene streets, after a devastating 1993 fire, has won national recognition.

The **Old Hundred Gold Mine** (✆ **800/872-3009** or 970/387-5444; www.minetour.com) is located about 5 miles east of Silverton via Colo. 110, offering an underground guided tour that takes 45 to 50 minutes and starts with a ride 1,500 feet underground in an electric mine train. The tour continues with a walk through lighted tunnels, where you see drilling and mucking demonstrations. There's gold panning above the surface, plus a gift shop, snack bar, and picnic area. Cost is $18 for adults 13 to 59, $9 for children 5 to 12 (children 4 and under held on a lap are free), and $16 for seniors 60 and older. Reservations are not necessary; a sweater or jacket is recommended. The mine is open from early May through mid-October daily from 10am to 4pm, with tours on the hour in peak summer season.

Expert and advanced skiers and snowboarders have discovered Silverton's newest attraction, **Silverton Mountain Ski Area,** which opened in early 2002 and has been booked solid ever since. Located almost 7 miles north of Silverton, the ski area has one double chairlift that accesses more powder than most skiers have ever seen. The base is at 10,400 feet, with a peak lift-served elevation of 12,300 feet and a fairly easy hike to the summit at 13,487 feet. This area is for experts only; intermediates will be outclassed by every run. Both guided and unguided skiing is available (guided-only skiing from mid-Jan through Mar), and the season usually runs from Thanksgiving through April. The day rate for unguided skiing is $49, and rates for guided group skiing are $99 to $139 a day. Single guided runs are $35. Private guided skiing is also available. For current hours, required equipment, and other details, contact **Silverton Mountain** (✆ **970/387-5706;** www.silvertonmountain.com).

WHERE TO EAT

For lunch or dinner, I like the **Stellar Bakery & Pizzeria,** 1260 Blair St. (✆ **970/387-9940**), with addictive cheesy rolls, big salads, and tasty pizzas, served inside or on the sunny patio. Most lunch and dinner entrees run $7 to $10. For a tasty rum cocktail, stop in at the tasting room at **Montanya Distillers,** 1309 Greene St. (✆ **970/387-9904;** www.montanyarum.com), crowned by a rooftop deck with unbeatable views.

THE SAN JUAN SKYWAY ★★

The **San Juan Skyway,** a 233-mile circuit, crosses five mountain passes and takes in the magnificent San Juan Mountains, as well as the cities and towns of the region. It can be accomplished in a single all-day drive from Durango or divided into several days, incorporating stops in Cortez, Telluride, and Ouray—all of which are discussed in this chapter. Check for closed passes in winter and early spring. The route can be driven either clockwise (heading west from Durango on U.S. 160) or counterclockwise (heading north from Durango on U.S. 550). I'll describe the clockwise route.

Eleven miles west of Durango you'll pass through the village of Hesperus, from which a county road runs 10 miles north into **La Plata Canyon,** with its mining ruins and ghost towns. Farther west, U.S. 160 passes the entrance road to **Mesa Verde National Park** (p. 209). About 45 miles west of Durango, just before Cortez, turn north on Colo. 145, which traverses the historic town of Dolores, site of the **Anasazi Heritage Center** (p. 212), then proceeds up the **Dolores River Valley,** a favorite of trout fishermen. Sixty miles from Cortez, the route crosses 10,222-foot **Lizard Head**

Pass, named for a startling rock spire looming above the roadside alpine meadows. It then descends 13 miles to the resort town of **Telluride,** set in a beautiful box canyon 4 miles off the main road.

Follow Colo. 145 west from Telluride down the San Miguel River valley to **Placerville.** Then turn north on Colo. 62, across 8,970-foot Dallas Divide, to Ridgway, a historic railroad town and home of **Ridgway State Park** (𝄐 **970/626-5822;** www. parks.state.co.us), with a sparkling mountain reservoir, trout fishing, boating (there's a marina), swimming, hiking, mountain biking, horseback riding, and camping ($16–$26). There are also three yurts available for overnight rentals ($70, plus a $10 reservation fee). The day-use fee is $7.

From Ridgway, turn south and follow U.S. 550 to the scenic and historic town of **Ouray** (p. 220). Here begins the remarkable **Million Dollar Highway,** so named for all the mineral wealth that passed over it. The 23-mile drive from Ouray over 11,008-foot **Red Mountain Pass** to Silverton is unforgettable. It shimmies up the sheer sides of the Uncompahgre Gorge, through tunnels and past cascading waterfalls, then follows a historic toll road built in the 19th century. Long-abandoned mining equipment and log cabins are in evidence on the slopes of the iron-colored mountains, many of them over 14,000 feet in elevation. Along this route you'll pass a monument to snowplow operators who died trying to keep the road open during winter storms.

From Silverton, U.S. 550 climbs over the Molas Divide (elevation 10,910 ft.), then more or less parallels the track of the Durango & Silverton Narrow Gauge Railroad as it follows the Animas River south to Durango, passing **Purgatory at Durango Mountain Resort** (p. 202) en route.

CORTEZ ★

45 miles W of Durango, 203 miles S of Grand Junction

An important archaeological center, Cortez is surrounded by a vast complex of ancient villages that dominated the Four Corners region—where the Colorado, New Mexico, Arizona, and Utah borders meet—1,000 years ago. Mesa Verde National Park, 10 miles east, is certainly the most prominent nearby attraction, drawing hundreds of thousands of visitors annually (p. 209). In addition, archaeological sites such as those at Canyons of the Ancients and Hovenweep national monuments, as well as Ute Mountain Tribal Park, are an easy drive from the city. San Juan National Forest, just to the north, offers a wide variety of recreational opportunities. The community of Cortez provides lodging, food, and supplies, making it the best spot to use as a home base when visiting these sites. Elevation is 6,200 feet.

Essentials

GETTING THERE   By Car   Cortez is located at the junction of north-south U.S. 491 and east-west U.S. 160. As it enters Cortez from the east, U.S. 160 crosses Dolores Road (Colo. 145, which goes north to Telluride and Grand Junction), then runs due west through town for about 2 miles as Main Street. The city's main thoroughfare, Main Street, intersects U.S. 491 (Broadway) at the west end of town.

By Plane   **Cortez Airport (CEZ),** off U.S. 160 and 491, southwest of town (𝄐 **970/565-7458;** www.cityofcortez.com), is served by **Great Lakes Airlines** with daily flights to Denver. **Budget** and **Hertz** provide car rentals at the airport. Call **Cortez Cab** (𝄐 **970/565-6911**) for a taxi, which will take you all the way to Telluride.

Getting Around   You will want a rental car in Cortez (see above).

VISITOR INFORMATION   Stop at the **Colorado Welcome Center at Cortez/ Cortez Area Chamber of Commerce,** 928 E. Main St. (*C* **970/565-3414;** www. cortezchamber.com), open daily year-round, or contact the **Mesa Verde Country Visitor Information Bureau** (*C* **970/565-8227;** www.mesaverdecountry.com).

FAST FACTS   **Southwest Memorial Hospital,** 1311 N. Mildred Rd. (*C* **970/565-6666;** www.swhealth.org), has a 24-hour emergency room. The **post office** is at 35 S. Beech St.

Where to Stay

MODERATE

Canyon of the Ancients Guest Ranch ★★   Located deep in scenic McElmo Canyon, southwest of Cortez, this remote and unique property consists of four cabins and houses that are a perfect fit for the surroundings—a 2,000-acre working sheep and cattle ranch, complete with dogs, chickens, and fruit trees. The most extravagant lodging, the slick Mokee House, features authentic Pueblo-style architecture and commanding views and can sleep up to five (there is a 1-week minimum). The property also offers the historic Elden Stone House, the charming Cowboy Log Cabin, and the largest, the Pioneer House, sleeping up to seven. The decor is eclectic and fascinating—relics from the ranch that are more than a century old are displayed next to contemporary Southwestern pieces, Mexican masks, and model trains.

7950 C.R. G, Cortez. *C* **970/565-4288.** www.canyonoftheancients.com. 4 units. $165–$310 double with a 2-night minimum; $875–$3,000 per week. **Amenities:** Free Wi-Fi.

Where to Eat

MODERATE

The Farm Bistro ★★ NEW AMERICAN   Owned and supplied in large part by the local Seven Meadows Farm, the Farm Bistro takes a, you guessed it!, farm-to-table

---

THE four corners MONUMENT

In addition to the area's excellent archaeological sites, discussed later in this chapter, attractions here include the **Four Corners Monument,** touted as the only place in the United States where you can stand in four states at once. Operated by the **Navajo Parks and Recreation Department** (*C* **928/871-6647;** www.navajonationparks.org), there's a flat monument marking where Utah, Colorado, New Mexico, and Arizona were thought to meet, and where visitors have perched for photos for generations. However, the marker was incorrectly placed in 1912, and now—thanks to modern GPS technology—work is underway on a new marker that's in the right spot. Until then, the official seals of the four states are displayed, along with the motto "Four states here meet in freedom under God." Surrounding the monument are the states' flags, flags of the Navajo Nation and Ute tribe, and the U.S. flag.

A visitor center has crafts demonstrations by Navajo artisans, and jewelry, pottery, sand paintings, and other crafts are for sale. In addition, traditional Navajo food, such as fry bread, is available. The monument is located half a mile northwest of U.S. 160, about 40 miles southwest of Cortez. It's open daily from 8am to 7pm in summer and 8am to 5pm the rest of the year. Admission costs $5 per person over age 6, and only cash is accepted.

approach. That translates to plenty of vegetable soups and salads, terrific paninis and pizzas with lots of healthy toppings. Dinner, served Thursdays to Saturday only, includes local trout, vegetable risotto, and burgers made from grass-fed local beef. The space is in a historic hardwood storefront, with a pressed tin ceiling, pastoral photos, and a pleasant atmosphere.

34 W. Main St. ℰ **970/565-3834.** www.thefarmbistrocortez.com. Main courses $7–$10, $11–18 dinner. Mon–Sat 11am–3pm; Thurs–Sat 5–9pm.

Stonefish Sushi & More ★★ SUSHI   With an opera-singing proprietor and an unexpectedly creative take on sushi, Stonefish is the best place in Cortez for a celebratory dinner. There are all sorts of sushi rolls, as well as nigiri, sashimi, and noodle dishes. Kids will like the PBJ roll, while parents will dig the long sake list, specialty cocktails, and hip sensibility.

16 W. Main St. ℰ **970/565-9244.** Main courses $9–$12 lunch, $9–26 dinner. Tues–Fri 11am–2pm; Mon–Thurs 4:30–9pm; Fri–Sat 4:30–10pm.

Exploring Cortez

Cortez is home to a pair of wineries in scenic and sunny McElmo Canyon just west of town. My favorite winery in Colorado, award-winning **Sutcliffe Vineyards,** 12174 Rd. G (ℰ **970/565-0825;** www.sutcliffewines.com), is open for tastings by appointment. Gregarious owner John Sutcliffe has been growing grapes in this arid landscape since 1989, and can spin quite the tale if you have the time. **Guy Drew Vineyards,** 19891 Rd. G (ℰ **970/565-4958;** www.guydrewvineyards.com), is also notable, with a tasting room open daily from noon to 5pm.

MESA VERDE NATIONAL PARK ★★★

Mesa Verde is the largest archaeological preserve in the United States, with some 4,000 known sites dating from A.D. 600 to 1300, including the most impressive cliff dwellings in the Southwest.

The earliest known inhabitants of Mesa Verde (Spanish for "green table") built subterranean pit houses on the mesa tops. During the 13th century, they moved into shallow caves and constructed complex cliff dwellings. Although a massive construction project, these homes were only occupied for about a century; their residents left in about 1300 for reasons as yet undetermined.

The area was little known until ranchers Charles and Richard Wetherill chanced upon it in 1888. Looting of artifacts followed their discovery until a Denver newspaper reporter's stories aroused national interest in protecting the site. The 52,000-acre site was declared a national park in 1906—it's the only U.S. national park devoted entirely to the works of humans.

Essentials

ENTRY   The park entrance is located on U.S. 160, 10 miles east of Cortez and 6 miles west of Mancos.

FEES & REGULATIONS   Admission to the park for up to 1 week costs $15 per vehicle in spring and summer, $10 in fall, and winter is free. Motorcyclists, bicyclists, and pedestrians must pay $8 in spring and summer, $5 in fall, and winter is free. Tours of Cliff Palace, Balcony House, and Long House are $4; ranger-guided tours of other areas are free. To protect the many archaeological sites, the Park Service has outlawed backcountry camping and off-trail hiking. It's also illegal to enter cliff dwellings without a ranger present. The Wetherill Mesa Road cannot accommodate vehicles longer than 25 feet. Cyclists must have lights to pedal through the tunnel on the entrance road.

VISITOR CENTERS & INFORMATION Chapin Mesa, site of the park headquarters, museum, and a post office, is 20 miles from the park entrance on U.S. 160. The **Mesa Verde Visitor Center,** the site of Far View Lodge, a restaurant, gift shop, and other facilities, is 15 miles off U.S. 160. For a park brochure, contact Mesa Verde National Park (© **970/529-4465;** www.nps.gov/meve).

HOURS & SEASONS The park is open daily year-round, but full interpretive services are available only from mid-June to Labor Day. In winter, the Mesa Top Road and museum remain open, but many other facilities are closed. The **Mesa Verde Visitor Center** is open daily year-round, peaking at 7:30am to 7pm for most of the summer. The **Chapin Mesa Archeological Museum** is open daily from 8am to 6:30pm from early April through early October, and daily the rest of the year.

AVOIDING THE CROWDS With more than a half a million visitors annually, Mesa Verde seems packed at times, but the numbers are much lower just before and after the summer rush, usually from June 15 to August 15. Another way to beat the crowds is to make the 12-mile drive to Wetherill Mesa, which attracts only a small percentage of park visitors.

Seeing the Highlights in a Day

If you have only a day to spend at the park, stop first at the Far View Visitor Center to buy tickets ($4) for a late-afternoon tour of either Cliff House or Balcony House—visitors are not allowed to tour both on the same day. Then travel to the Chapin Mesa archaeological museum for a look at the history behind the sites you're about to see. From there, walk down the trail behind the museum to Spruce Tree House. Then drive the Mesa Top Loop Road. Cap your day with the guided tour.

Where to Stay & Eat in the Park
MODERATE

Far View Lodge ★ Open since 1972, this lodge looks the part, but its Anasazi-inspired architecture belies the fairly basic, albeit well-maintained, rooms inside. Located in more than 10 different structures in the heart of the park, guest rooms come in two varieties: standard and the premium Kiva. All have private balconies and none have TVs, but the latter feature upgraded "New West" furnishings (it's mostly fancier bedding) and a king or two double beds, while the Standard rooms have queens and no A/C.

1 Navajo Hill, Mesa Verde National Park. © **800/449-2288** or 970/529-4421. www.visitmesaverde. com. 150 units. $134–$188 double. Closed mid-Oct to mid-Apr. Pets accepted ($10 per night with a $50 deposit). **Amenities:** 2 restaurants; free Wi-Fi.

Exploring the Park

The **Cliff Palace,** the park's largest and best-known site, is a four-story apartment complex with stepped-back roofs forming porches for the dwellings above. Accessible by guided tour only, it is reached by a quarter-mile downhill path. Its towers, walls, and kivas (large circular rooms used for ceremonies) are all set back beneath the rim of a cliff. Another ranger-led tour takes visitors up a 32-foot ladder to explore the interior of **Balcony House.** Each of these tours is given only in summer and into fall (call for exact dates).

Two other important sites—**Step House** and **Long House,** both on Wetherill Mesa—can be visited in summer only. Rangers lead free tours to **Spruce Tree House,** another of the major cliff-dwelling complexes, only in winter, when other park facilities are closed. There are also special summer hikes to backcountry archaeological sites for $5 to $40 per person.

Although the trails to the sites are not strenuous, the 7,000-foot elevation can make the treks tiring for visitors who aren't used to the altitude. For those who want to avoid hiking and climbing, the 12-mile **Mesa Top Road** makes a number of pit houses and cliff-side overlooks easily accessible by car. **Chapin Mesa Archeological Museum** houses artifacts and specimens related to the history of the area, including other nearby sites.

Outdoor Activities

Although this isn't an outdoor recreation park, per se—the reason to come here is to see the cliff dwellings and other archaeological sites—you'll find yourself hiking and climbing to get to the sites. Several longer hikes into scenic Spruce Canyon let you stretch your legs and get away from the crowds. Hikers must register at the ranger's office before setting out.

CAMPING   Open from early May to early October, **Morefield Campground** (✆ **800/449-2288** or 970/529-4421; www.visitmesaverde.com), 4 miles south of the park entrance, has 267 sites, including 15 with full RV hookups. The campground is set in a wooded canyon that's rich in wildlife. The attractive sites are fairly well spaced and are mostly separated by trees and other foliage. There's a gas station, RV facilities, hot showers, a restaurant, and a grocery store. Ranger programs on the area's human and natural history and other subjects are presented nightly at the campground amphitheater from Memorial Day weekend through Labor Day weekend. Campsites start at $27; RV hookups cost $37.

Nearby Archaeological Sites
CORTEZ CULTURAL CENTER ★

The **Cortez Cultural Center,** 25 N. Market St., Cortez (✆ **970/565-1151;** www.cortezculturalcenter.org), includes a museum with exhibits on both prehistoric and modern American Indians, an art gallery with displays of regional art, a good gift shop offering crafts by local tribal members, and a variety of programs including American Indian dances during the summer at 7pm every day but Sunday. It is open Monday through Saturday from 10am to 9pm or 10pm (5pm or 6pm in winter). Admission is free and you should plan to spend at least an hour. Call or check the website for the schedule of Indian dances and other programs, which are also free.

What's in a Name?

The prehistoric inhabitants of the Four Corners area have long been known as the Anasazi. That word is being phased out in favor of Ancestral Puebloans, because modern descendants consider Anasazi demeaning. In Navajo, it means "enemy of my people," as the Navajo people saw the Ancestral Puebloans as their enemies.

UTE MOUNTAIN TRIBAL PARK ★★★

If you liked Mesa Verde but would have enjoyed it more without the company of so many fellow tourists, you'll *love* the **Ute Mountain Tribal Park** in Towaoc (② **970/565-9653** or 970/565-3751, ext. 330; www.utemountaintribalpark.info). Set aside by the Ute Mountain tribe to preserve its heritage, the 125,000-acre park—which abuts Mesa Verde National Park—includes ancient pictographs and petroglyphs as well as hundreds of surface sites and cliff dwellings that are similar in size and complexity to those in Mesa Verde.

Access to the park is strictly limited to guided tours. Full- and half-day tours begin at the Ute Mountain Museum and Visitor Center at the junction of U.S. 491 and U.S. 160, 20 miles south of Cortez. Mountain-biking and backpacking trips are also offered. No food, water, lodging, gasoline, or other services are available within the park. Some climbing of ladders is necessary on the full-day tour. There's one primitive **campground** ($12 per vehicle; permits required), with a few plain cabins ($10 extra).

Charges for tours in your vehicle start at $29 per person for a half-day, $49 for a full day; it's $12 per person extra to go in the tour guide's vehicle, and reservations are required.

CANYONS OF THE ANCIENTS NATIONAL MONUMENT ★★

Among the country's newest national monuments, Canyons of the Ancients was created by a proclamation by President Bill Clinton in June 2000. The 164,000-acre national monument, located west of Cortez, contains over 6,000 archaeological sites—what some claim is the highest density of archaeological sites in the United States—including the remains of villages, cliff dwellings, sweat lodges, and petroglyphs at least 700 years old, and possibly as much as 10,000 years old.

Canyons of the Ancients includes **Lowry Pueblo,** an excavated 12th-century village that is located 26 miles north of Cortez via U.S. 491, on C.R. CC, 9 miles west of Pleasant View. This pueblo, which was likely abandoned by 1200, is believed to have housed about 100 people. It has standing walls from 40 rooms plus nine kivas (circular underground ceremonial chambers). A short, self-guided interpretive trail leads past a kiva and continues to the remains of a great kiva, which, at 54 feet in diameter, is among the largest ever found. There are also a picnic area, drinking water, and toilets.

There is also excellent hiking on the **Sand Canyon Trail** off C.R. G, southwest of Cortez off U.S. 160, a moderate trail that passes by a number of ruins and breathtaking vistas, and connects with several loops; bring a hat, sunscreen, and plenty of water.

Canyons of the Ancients is managed by the Bureau of Land Management. Those wishing to explore the monument are strongly advised to contact or, preferably, stop first at the visitor center located at **Anasazi Heritage Center,** located at 27501 Colo. 184, Dolores (② **970/882-5600;** www.co.blm.gov/ahc), for information, especially current road conditions and directions.

A little background on the Anasazi Heritage Center: When the Dolores River was dammed and the McPhee Reservoir was created in 1985, some 1,600 ancient archaeological sites were threatened. Four percent of the project costs were set aside for archaeological work, and over two million artifacts were rescued. Most are displayed in the center 10 miles north of Cortez. It's open March through October daily from 9am to 5pm, and 10am to 4pm the rest of the year. Admission is $3 for adults and free for those 17 and under. Allow at least 2 hours.

HOVENWEEP NATIONAL MONUMENT ★★★

Preserving some of the most striking and isolated archaeological sites in the Four Corners area, this national monument straddles the Colorado-Utah border, 40 miles west of Cortez. Hovenweep is the Ute word for "deserted valley," appropriate because its inhabitants apparently left around 1300. The monument contains six separate sites and is noted for mysterious 20-foot-high sandstone towers, some square, others oval, circular, or D-shaped. Archaeologists have suggested possible functions: everything from guard or signal towers, celestial observatories, and ceremonial structures to water towers or granaries.

A ranger station, with exhibits, restrooms, and drinking water, is located at the **Square Tower Site,** in the Utah section of the monument, the most impressive and best preserved of the sites. The **Hovenweep Campground,** with 30 sites, is open year-round. The campground has flush toilets, drinking water, picnic tables, and fire pits, but no showers or RV hookups. Cost is $10 per night; reservations are not accepted, but the campground rarely fills.

From Cortez, take U.S. 160 south to C.R. G (McElmo Canyon Rd.) and follow signs into Utah and the monument. The other five sites are difficult to find, and you'll need to obtain detailed driving directions and check on current road conditions before setting out. Summer temperatures can reach over 100°F (38°C), and water supplies are limited—so take your own and carry a canteen, even on short walks. Bug repellent is advised, as gnats can be a nuisance in late spring.

The visitor center is open daily from 8am to 6pm from April through September and 8am to 5pm the rest of the year; it's closed major holidays. Trails are open from sunrise to sunset. Admission for up to a week costs $6 per vehicle or $3 per person on bike or foot. For advance information, contact Hovenweep National Monument (✆ **970/562-4282,** ext. 10; www.nps.gov/hove).

CROW CANYON ARCHAEOLOGICAL CENTER ★★

The Crow Canyon Archaeological Center focuses on the rich history of the Anasazi. Crow Canyon's campus-based programs allow visitors to participate in actual research in both the field and laboratory. Offerings open to the public include digs with pro archaeologists, family programs that cover a gamut of archaeological skills, and summer camps for teens. Programs have been developed with help from American Indians. The 170-acre campus—complete with labs, classrooms, a dormitory, and 10 rustic cabins inspired by Navajo hogans—is located just a few miles north of Cortez at 23390 County Rd. K. Classes range from a $60 day tour to programs that last a week or more starting at about $1,700 a student. Contact the Center (✆ **800/422-8975** or 970/565-8975; www.crowcanyon.org) for more information.

TELLURIDE ★★★

126 miles NW of Durango, 127 miles S of Grand Junction

This was one seriously rowdy town a century ago—in fact, this is where Butch Cassidy robbed his first bank, in 1889. Incorporated with the boring name of Columbia in 1878, the mining town assumed its present name the following decade. Some say the name came from tellurium, a gold-bearing ore, while others insist the name really means "to hell you ride," referring to the town's boisterous nature.

Telluride became a National Historic District in 1964. The Telluride Ski Company opened its first runs in 1972, and Telluride was a boomtown again. Telluride's first summer festivals (bluegrass in June, film in Sept) were celebrated the following year. Today the resort, at 8,745 feet elevation, is a year-round destination for mountain bikers, skiers, anglers, and hikers. Funky has mostly given way to chic these days, but the surrounding natural beauty remains unforgettable.

Essentials

GETTING THERE **By Car** Telluride is located on Colo. 145. From Cortez, follow Colo. 145 northeast for 73 miles. From the north (Montrose), turn west off U.S. 550 at Ridgway, onto Colo. 62. Proceed 25 miles to Placerville and turn left (southeast) onto Colo. 145. Thirteen miles ahead is a junction—a right turn will take you to Cortez, but for Telluride, continue straight ahead 4 miles to the end of a box canyon. From Durango, in summer take U.S. 550 north to Colo. 62 and follow the directions above; in winter it can be best to take the route through Cortez.

By Plane **Telluride Regional Airport (TEX;** ✆ **970/728-5313;** www.telluride airport.com), 5 miles west of Telluride atop a plateau at 9,078 feet (making it the highest airport in North America), is served year-round by **Frontier** and **Great Lakes/ United.** It's also good to check the flights into **Montrose Regional Airport (MTJ),** 68 miles north of Telluride (✆ **970/249-3203;** www.montroseairport.com), with service from **United, Delta, American, Allegiant,** and **Republic;** you can save money by driving or shuttling to the resort. For a ride from either airport, contact **Telluride Express** (✆ **970/728-6000;** www.tellurideexpress.com), about $100 round-trip for an adult, $60 for kids 2 to 11.

GETTING AROUND The city is located on the San Miguel River, where it flows out of a box canyon formed by the 14,000-foot peaks of the San Juan Mountains. Colo. 145 enters town from the west and becomes Colorado Avenue, the main street.

With restaurants, shops, and attractions within easy walking distance of most lodging facilities, many visitors leave their cars parked and use their feet. However, if you do want to ride, there's a free town shuttle in winter and summer. Telluride Mountain Village, at 9,500 feet, can be reached in winter and summer by a free gondola, operating daily from 7am to midnight. Motorists can take Mountain Village Boulevard off Colo. 145, a mile south of the Telluride junction.

Hertz and **National** provide car rentals, including vans and four-wheel-drive vehicles, at the airport. **Budget** has an outlet between Telluride and the airport on Colo. 145. The Montrose airport has the same companies as well as **Avis** and **Enterprise.**

VISITOR INFORMATION Contact **Telluride Tourism Board** (✆ **888/605-2578** or 970/728-3041; www.visittelluride.com). The **Telluride Visitor Information Center,** open daily year-round, can be found at 700 W. Colorado Ave.

FAST FACTS The hospital, **Telluride Medical Center,** with a 24-hour emergency room, is at 500 W. Pacific Ave. (✆ **970/728-3848;** www.tellmed.org). The **post office** is at 150 S. Willow St.

Where to Stay

Telluride's lodging rates probably have more different "seasons" than anywhere else in Colorado. Generally speaking, you'll pay top dollar for a room over the Christmas holidays, during the film and bluegrass festivals, and at certain other peak times. Non-holiday skiing is a bit cheaper, summertime lodging (except for festival times) is cheaper yet, and you may find some real bargains in spring and fall.

Regardless of the season, there are a wide variety of B&Bs, hotels, private homes, and condominiums. Many are managed by **Telluride Alpine Lodging** (𝄢 970/728-3388; www.telluridelodging.com). **Telluride Central Reservations** (𝄢 888/605-2578; www.visittelluride.com) is another good resource, as is **Telluride Ski Resort Lodging** (𝄢 800/778-8581).

IN TELLURIDE
Expensive
Hotel Columbia ★★   If you want good access to the slopes and the historic core, it is difficult to top this boutique hotel located a stone's throw from the gondola station in downtown Telluride. Behind the attractive redbrick exterior, the rooms and suites are at once classic and contemporary, with dark woods, white bedding, and eye-catching art and photos on the walls. The restaurant, **Cosmopolitan,** is a good pick for dinner or a handcrafted cocktail at the bar.

301 W. San Juan Ave., Telluride. 𝄢 **800/201-9505** or 970/728-0660. www.columbiatelluride.com. 21 units. Ski season $195–$465 double, $335–$1,795 suite; summer $175–$385 double, $325–$735 suite. Lower off-season rates. Rates include continental breakfast. Self-parking $20/night. Closed mid-Apr to late May and mid-Oct to late Nov. Dogs accepted ($25 per night). **Amenities:** Restaurant; free Wi-Fi.

New Sheridan Hotel ★★★   With historic cachet to spare, the New Sheridan has been the place to bed down in Telluride for a dozen decades running. The New Sheridan first opened in 1895—a year after the old Sheridan Hotel burned down—and has seen it all in the time since, from mudslides overwhelming the lobby in the early 1900s to a luxurious renovation in the early 2000s. Now the hotel is contemporary in its niceties (plump mattresses, good shower pressure, excellent maintenance), but its brightly painted wainscoting and adorable print armchairs give a hat tip to the past. The hotel's bar and **New Sheridan Chop House** (p. 216) are among the best spots to imbibe and dine in town.

231 W. Colorado Ave., Telluride. 𝄢 **800/200-1891** or 970/728-4351. www.newsheridan.com. 26 units. $159–$259 double; $279–$349 suite. Closed mid-Apr to mid-May and mid-Oct to late Nov. **Amenities:** 2 restaurants; bar; concierge; outdoor Jacuzzi; free Wi-Fi.

IN MOUNTAIN VILLAGE
Expensive
Bear Creek Lodge ★★   Tucked away in a quiet forested area just above a gondola station, Bear Creek Lodge is a good pick for those looking for a little more space and easy access to the slopes. The former comes in the form of spacious and downright chic condominium units (they're done in several different styles and layouts), ranging from one to four bedrooms. Easy access comes via the trainlike funicular that picks guests up at the lodge and drops them off on a run below, and vice versa. Bear Creek offers a handy menu of services, from shopping to in-house massage to local shuttle rides.

135 San Joaquin Rd., Telluride. 𝄢 **888/893-0158** or 970/728-3388. www.bearcreeklodgetelluride. com. 40 condominiums. Winter and summer $149–$399 1-bedroom condo, $199–$979 2- to 4-bedroom condo. Higher holiday and festival rates; lower rates spring and fall. Resort fee 8 percent. **Amenities:** Concierge; outdoor Jacuzzi; outdoor year-round pool; free Wi-Fi.

The Peaks ★★★   The mothership of Mountain Village, this ski-in/ski-out, golf-in/golf-out property is one of the best mountain resorts in the state. From the regal Great Room to the standout restaurant **Palmyra,** the Peaks has all of the requisite amenities and facilities and then some, including the area's only indoor waterslide, a squash court, and even a spa for dogs. Rooms are sizable, with a king or two queen beds, private balconies, and subdued but swank New West style. The spa is especially impressive, filling 42,000 square feet with everything from Pilates studios to state-of-the-art fitness equipment. Powder fiends take note: This is the site of the helipad for **Telluride Helitrax** (p. 219).

136 Country Club Dr., Telluride. ✆ **800/789-2220** or 970/728-6800. www.thepeaksresort.com. 159 units, including 32 suites. Winter $189–$450 double, $299–$799 suite; summer $189–$320 double, $299–$499 suite. Higher holiday and festival rates; lower rates spring and fall. Resort fee $25/night. Dogs accepted (one-time fee of $75) **Amenities:** 3 restaurants; 2 bars; concierge; exercise room; indoor and outdoor Jacuzzis; 1 indoor/outdoor pool; 1 indoor lap pool; spa; free Wi-Fi.

Where to Eat

Telluride lives by its seasons, and some eateries temporarily close in spring and fall. Hardcore foodies should jump on a walking tour with **Telluride Food Tours** (✆ **800/979-3370**; www.telluridefoodtours.com). Tours run 3 hours and cost $75.

EXPENSIVE

New Sheridan Chop House ★★ STEAKS/SEAFOOD Refined and intimate, the Chop House is a "special night on the town" pick. The kitchen dishes up remarkable presentations of beef, game, and seafood; trout and elk are almost always on the menu. For dessert, try the transcendent chocolate mousse with black pepper and balsamic, which seemingly stimulates every taste bud at once. With plenty of candlelight, white tablecloths, and privacy-enhancing booths, we'd say there are few better places in the West to get engaged (and many have here before you).

In the New Sheridan Hotel, 231 W. Colorado Ave. ✆ **970/728-9100**. www.newsheridan.com. Main courses $10–$22 breakfast and lunch, $21–$65 dinner. Daily 8am–2pm and 5:30–9pm.

Rustico Ristorante ★★ ITALIAN Proprietors Paolo Canclini and Carmela Sanna brought their restaurant experience in Italy to Telluride in the late 1990s and have been packing the house here ever since. Located in a historic storefront, Rustico is indeed rustic, with a casual atmosphere that is a nice fit for active vacationers, and a time-tested menu. Pizzas come from the only authentic Italian pizza oven in town, and pasta dishes include staples like spaghetti, ravioli, and gnocchi. Dinner also brings steaks and seafood dishes, as well as local lamb. When the weather agrees, the deck here is one of the loveliest outdoor dining areas in the state.

114 E. Colorado Ave. ✆ **970/728-4046**. www.rusticoristorante.com. Main courses $13–$26 lunch, $14–$49 dinner. Daily 11:30am–2:30pm and 5:30–9:30pm. No lunch fall and spring.

MODERATE & INEXPENSIVE

Start (or end) your day right at **Baked in Telluride,** 127 S. Fir St. (✆ **970/728-4775**), offering donuts, bagels, breakfast burritos in the morning, sandwiches for lunch, and pizza and Mexican food for dinner, plus Thanksgiving every Thursday. For superlative sandwiches, head to **The Butcher & The Baker,** 217 E. Colorado Ave. (✆ **970/728-2899**; www.butcherandbakercafe.com), with a build-your-own menu with above-and-beyond ingredients like chèvre, Napa slaw, and gluten-free rolls. Another good value: the Mexican fare at **La Cocina de Luz,** 123 E. Colorado Ave. (✆ **970/728-9355**; www.lacocina telluride.com). In Mountain Village, **Tracks,** 670 Mountain Village Blvd. (✆ **970/728-6077**), has tasty sandwiches and a full bar that packs them in when the lifts stop turning.

there. ★★ ASIAN/NEW AMERICAN This funky little eatery, hidden away on the southwest side of town, is a great place to start or end an evening in Telluride….or you can just stay all night. There is character to spare: a tin ceiling over graffiti, a world map and jackalopes on the walls, and cocktail lists slipped into repurposed novels. You get a bag of world-class popcorn when you sit down, and the menu includes some very tasty small plates (the sashimi tostadas stand out), as well as more substantial (and often sharable) entrees like octopus, lamb, and ramen bowls. The bar is lively, serving an array of beer, wine, and cocktails, with the back bar made from an upcycled dresser.

627 W. Pacific Ave. ℰ **970/728-1213.** www.therebars.com. Small plates $4–$8, main courses $15–$30. Daily 6–11pm and Sat–Sun 10am–3pm. Bar open later.

Exploring Telluride

The best way to see the Telluride National Historic District, examine its hundreds of historic buildings, and get a feel for the West of the late 1800s is to take to the streets.

Among the buildings you'll see are the **San Miguel County Courthouse,** Colorado Avenue at Oak Street, built in 1887 and still in use today. Two blocks east of Fir Street, on Galena Avenue at Spruce Street, is **St. Patrick's Catholic Church,** built in 1895, whose wooden Stations of the Cross figures were carved in Austria's Tyrol region. Perhaps Telluride's most famous landmark is the 1895 **New Sheridan Hotel** (p. 215), opposite the county courthouse at Colorado and Oak. And don't miss a living testament to Telluride's hippie heritage on Pine Street just south of Colorado Avenue: the **Telluride Free Box,** where locals leave books, clothes, and other odds and ends for whoever might want to take them.

Colorado's longest continuous waterfall (365 ft.) can be seen from the east end of Colorado Avenue. **Bridal Veil Falls** freezes in winter, and then slowly melts in early spring, creating a dramatic effect. Perched at the top edge of the falls is a National Historic Landmark, a hydroelectric power plant that served area mines in the late 1800s and is the second oldest such plant on the planet. (The oldest is in nearby Ophir.) Recently restored and once again supplying power to the community, it's accessible by hiking or driving a switchback, four-wheel-drive road.

Telluride Historical Museum ★★   The compelling local history is expertly told at this top-flight museum, where kid-friendly exhibits detail the stories of the Ute natives, the mining boom, the subsequent bust, and the ski industry that arrived in the 1970s. Hands-on displays allow visitors to pan for gold and delve into the inner workings of the first industrial-grade alternating current (AC) power line on the planet, installed here by Nikola Tesla and George Westinghouse in 1891. Allow 1 to 2 hours.

201 W. Gregory Ave. (at the top of Fir St.). ℰ **970/728-3344.** www.telluridemuseum.com. Admission $5 adults, $3 seniors and students 6–17, free for children 5 and under. Tues–Sat 11am–5pm. Open until 7pm Thurs. Closed spring and fall.

Outdoor Activities

Telluride isn't just a ski town—there's a wide variety of year-round outdoor activities. **Town Park** is home to the community's various festivals. It also has a public outdoor pool, open in summer, plus tennis courts, sand volleyball courts, a small outdoor basketball court, a skateboarding ramp, picnic area, and fishing pond. A first-come, first-served **campground** for tent and car campers, open from mid-May to mid-October, has 33 sites and hot showers ($3 in quarters only; cold showers are free), but no RV hookups, and costs $17 to $23 per night. Call ℰ **970/728-2173** for more information.

There are a number of outfitting companies in the Telluride area, including **Telluride Outside,** 121 W. Colorado Ave. (ℰ **800/831-6230** or 970/728-3895; www.tellurideoutside.com), with a wide range of guided adventures. Equipment rentals are available throughout Telluride and Mountain Village. You'll find mountain bikes, fishing gear, camping equipment, and inflatable kayaks at **Telluride Sports,** 150 W. Colorado Ave. (ℰ **970/728-4477;** www.telluridesports.com), and other locations.

FISHING   There's excellent fishing in the San Miguel River in Telluride, but it's even better in nearby alpine lakes, including Silver Lake, reached by foot in Bridal Veil Basin, and Trout and Priest lakes, about 12 miles south via Colo. 145. At Town Park there's a stocked fishing pond for children 12 and under. Recommended guides include **San Miguel Anglers** (C 970/728-4477; www.sanmiguelanglers.com), with prices of $450 for a full-day wade trip for two people on the San Miguel or Upper Dolores.

FOUR-WHEELING   To see old ghost towns, mining camps, and spectacular mountain scenery from the relative comfort of a bouncing four-wheel-drive vehicle, join **Telluride Outside** (C 800/831-6230) or **Dave's Mountain Tours** (C 970/728-9749; www.telluridetours.com). A variety of trips is offered, including rides over the 13,000-foot Imogene Pass jeep road, with prices for full-day trips about $150 for adults and $100 for children. Half-day trips run $85 to $110 and $65 to $90, respectively.

GOLF   The 18-hole par-71 **Telluride Golf Course** is located at Telluride Mountain Village (C 970/728-2606; www.tellurideskiresort.com). Peak-time greens fees with the required cart are $190 from July through Labor Day, lower at other times.

HIKING & MOUNTAINEERING   The mountains around Telluride offer innumerable opportunities for hiking, mountaineering, and backpacking. Sporting goods stores and the visitor center have maps of trails in the Telluride area. Especially popular are the easy 4-mile (round-trip) **Bear Creek Canyon Trail,** which starts at the end of South Pine Street and leads to a picturesque waterfall; the **Jud Wiebe Trail** that begins at the north end of Aspen Street and does a 2.7-mile loop above the town, offering views of Bridal Veil Falls, the town, and ski area; and the 1.8-mile (one-way) hike to the top of **Bridal Veil Falls,** which starts at the east end of Telluride Canyon. There are also numerous opportunities for hikes in the national forests and wilderness areas in all directions. For hikers who want to overnight in the backcountry but don't want to carry a huge pack, the backcountry huts in the **San Juan Hut System** (C 970/626-3033; www.sanjuanhuts.com) are a civilized alternative.

HORSEBACK RIDING   One of the best ways to see this spectacular country is by horse. **Telluride Horseback Adventures** (C 970/728-9611; www.ridewithroudy.com) has "gentle horses for gentle people and fast horses for fast people, and for people who don't like to ride, horses that don't like to be rode." Rates are $90 for a 2-hour ride. There are winter sleigh rides.

MOUNTAIN BIKING   Telluride is a major mountain-biking center. The **San Juan Hut System** links Telluride with Moab, Utah, via a 206-mile-long network of backcountry dirt roads. Every 35 miles is a primitive cabin, with bunks, a woodstove, propane cooking stove, and cooking gear. The route, open to mountain bikers and hikers from June through September (and cross-country skiers and snowshoers in snow season), is appropriate for intermediate-level riders in good physical condition. Cost for riders who plan to make the whole trip is about $900, which includes use of the six huts, three meals daily, sleeping bags at each hut, and maps and trail descriptions. Shorter trips, guide services, and vehicle shuttles are also available. For information, contact San Juan Hut System (C 970/626-3033; www.sanjuanhuts.com). Mountain bike rentals are available from **Telluride Sports** (C 970/728-4477) for $45 to $80 per day.

Skiing & Snowboarding: Telluride Ski Resort ★★★

The elegant European-style Mountain Village, built in 1987, offers a fascinating contrast to the laid-back community of artists, shopkeepers, and dropouts in the 1870s

Victorian mining town of Telluride below. Located midmountain at an elevation of 9,540 feet, the Mountain Village offers ski-in/ski-out accommodations, a variety of slopeside restaurants, and great skiing all the way into Telluride proper.

The mountain's **North Face,** which drops sharply from the summit to the town of Telluride, is characterized by steep moguls, tree-and-glade skiing, and challenging groomed pitches for experts and advanced intermediates. The broad, gentle slopes of the **Meadows** features long trails devoted entirely to novice skiers, is served by a high-speed quad chair. The gently rolling slopes of **Ute Park** serve as another beginner training area, while the **Prospect Express** lift accesses beginner, intermediate, and expert terrain and offers everyone the chance to see the views from the top of the mountain with a comfortable route down. **Revelation Bowl** is a perfectly powdery depression beloved by advanced skiers.

In all, Telluride offers more than 2,000 acres of skiable terrain. The lift-served vertical drop is an impressive 3,845 feet from the 12,570-foot lift-served summit. (Those willing to hike can get all the way up to 13,150 ft. above sea level for 4,425 vertical ft. of skiing.) Average annual snowfall is 309 inches (more than 25 ft.). The mountain has 128 trails served by 18 lifts (two high-speed gondolas, seven high-speed quads, one fixed-grip quad, two triples, two doubles, two surface lifts, and two Magic Carpets). Of the trails, 23 percent are rated for beginners, 36 percent for intermediates, and 41 percent for experts. The longest run here, at just over 4½ miles, is **Galloping Goose,** but for some of the most spectacular views in Colorado, ski **See Forever.** Telluride also has one of the top **snowboarding parks** in Colorado, offering more than 13 acres of terrain.

Full-day lift tickets during the peak season (2013–14 rates) cost $109 for adults and teens, $65 for children 6 to 12, $96 for seniors 65 and older, and are free for children 5 and under. You can save as much as 25 percent by booking multiday packages online in advance. Rates over the Christmas holidays are highest and rates at the very beginning of the season are lower. Ski and snowboarding lessons are offered, along with childcare. The resort is usually open daily from 9am to 4pm from Thanksgiving to early April. For additional information, contact **Telluride Ski Resort** (✆ **970/728-6900;** www.tellurideskiresort.com).

Other Winter Activities

In addition to skiing at Telluride Ski Resort, there are plenty of opportunities for other cold-weather adventures in the Telluride area. Many of them take place at **Town Park,** at the east end of town (✆ **970/728-2173** [year-round] or 970/728-1144 for the Nordic Center in winter only; www.telluride-co.gov), where there are groomed cross-country trails, daytime sledding and tubing at Firecracker Hill, and free ice-skating.

The **River Corridor Trail** follows the San Miguel River from Town Park to the valley floor. There are about 8 miles of **Nordic trails** in Mountain Village, which connect with the groomed trails at Town Park and River Corridor Trail.

Those who want to (and can afford to) take a helicopter to some of the best powder skiing anywhere should contact **Telluride Helitrax** (✆ **877/500-8377;** www.helitrax.com), with day rates (six ski runs) for $1,199 to $1,249 per person.

Nightlife

The **Palm Theatre,** 721 W. Colorado Ave. (✆ **970/369-5669;** www.telluridepalm.com), has emerged as a centerpiece venue for the area, with regular touring shows of all kinds. If you're in luck, the **Telluride Theatre** (✆ **970/369-5675;** www.

telluridetheatre.org) will be staging a production during your visit. The gorgeous **Sheridan Opera House,** 110 N. Oak St. (✆ **970/728-6363;** www.sheridanoperahouse. com), hosts music, comedy, and theatrical productions.

On the other side of the cultural spectrum is the **Last Dollar Saloon,** 100 W. Colorado Ave. (✆ **970/728-4800**), a lively watering hole that's about as close to a dive as Telluride gets. For good burgers and cold draft beer, stop at local favorite the **Cornerhouse Grille,** 131 N. Fir St. (✆ **970/728-6207**). In Mountain Village, you'll find good grub, beer, and conversation at **Poachers Pub,** 113 Lost Creek Lane (✆ **970/728-9647**).

The Festival Scene

Telluride must be the most festival-happy town in America, and visitors come from around the world to see the finest new films, hear the best musicians, and even pick the most exotic mushrooms.

The **Telluride Film Festival** (✆ **510/665-9494;** www.telluridefilmfestival.org), an influential festival within the film industry that takes place over Labor Day weekend, has premiered some of the finest films produced in recent years ("Brokeback Mountain," "The King's Speech," and "Blue Velvet" are just a few examples). What sets it apart, however, is the casual interaction between stars and attendees. While passes that grant broad access start around $400, four open-air premieres, numerous seminars, and other events are free to all.

Mountainfilm (✆ **970/728-4123;** www.mountainfilm.org), which takes place every Memorial Day weekend, brings together filmmakers, writers, and outdoor enthusiasts to celebrate mountains, adventure, and the environment. Four days are filled with films, seminars, and presentations

The **Telluride Bluegrass Festival** (✆ **800/624-2422;** www.bluegrass.com/telluride) is one of the most intense and renowned bluegrass, folk, and country jam sessions in the United States. Held in mid- to late June in conjunction with the Bluegrass Academy, recent lineups have featured Alison Krauss, Leftover Salmon, and Steve Martin.

The **Telluride Jazz Celebration** (✆ **970/728-7009;** www.telluridejazz.org) in early August is marked by day concerts in Town Park and evening happenings in downtown saloons. Recent performers have included Dianne Reeves, Grupo Fantasma, and Poncho Sanchez.

Held over a weekend in late June, the **Telluride Wine Festival** (✆ **970/728-9790;** www.telluridewinefestival.com) is another popular event, featuring dinners and tastings at multiple venues, including "the highest grand tasting in North America" on Saturday evening.

OURAY ★★

73 miles N of Durango, 96 miles S of Grand Junction

Named for the greatest chief of the southern Ute tribe, whose homeland was in this area, Ouray, at an elevation of 7,760 feet, got its start in 1876 as a gold- and silver-mining camp. Within 10 years it had 1,200 residents, a school, a hospital, dozens of saloons and brothels, and even a few churches. Today Ouray, nicknamed "the Switzerland of America" for its sheer scenery, retains much of its 19th-century charm, with two-thirds of its original buildings still standing. It offers visitors a quiet getaway as a base for exploring the untamed wilds of the San Juans, and has emerged as a destination for hot-potters, Jeepers, and ice climbers.

Essentials

GETTING THERE **By Car** U.S. 550 runs through the heart of Ouray, paralleling the Uncompahgre River and connecting it with Durango to the south and Montrose to the north. As you enter town from the north, the highway becomes Main Street. Above Third Avenue, U.S. 550 begins its climb up switchbacks to Red Mountain Pass and the Million Dollar Highway.

By Plane The nearest airport is in Montrose (p. 214).

VISITOR INFORMATION Stop at the **Ouray Visitor Center,** 1230 Main St., or contact the **Ouray Chamber Resort Association** (⌀ **800/228-1876** or 970/325-4746; www.ouraycolorado.com).

FAST FACTS The nearest extensive medical facilities are in Montrose. The post office is at 620 Main St.

Where to Stay

There are B&Bs, lodges, and motels, as well as historic hotels. Many properties have their own private hot springs.

EXPENSIVE

Beaumont Hotel ★★ With storybook looks inside and out, this historic hotel is the most extravagant lodging in Ouray. It originally opened during the halcyon mining days of the 1880s, and saw a long list of luminaries sleep in its beds (Theodore Roosevelt to King Leopold of Belgium) before inevitably going downhill in the mid–20th century. Restored for the new millennium, the rooms and suites hold a canny mix of antiques and period reproductions, with exceedingly romantic results. Every room has one king or queen bed.

505 Main St., Ouray. ⌀ **888/447-3255** or 970/325-7000. www.beaumonthotel.com. 12 units. Summer $194–$244 double; $294–$305 suite. Lower rates fall to spring. Children 16 and under not accepted. **Amenities:** 2 restaurants; bar; spa; free Wi-Fi.

MODERATE

Box Canyon Lodge and Hot Springs ★ While the rooms here are reliable but unremarkable, the surroundings are anything but. Take a stroll from your room up the stairs on the hillside behind the motel—it's also the southern fringe of development in Ouray—and you will encounter four redwood tubs fed by natural hot springs. (The water is also used to heat the motel in winter.) The standard rooms have one or two queen or king beds, and large suites have two queen beds and a queen-sized futon. There is also a 2-bedroom apartment with a kitchen.

45 Third Ave., Ouray. ⌀ **800/327-5080** or 970/325-4981. www.boxcanyonouray.com. 39 units, including 5 suites. $110–$165 double; $169–$190 suite or apt. Lower rates fall to spring. Rates include continental breakfast. **Amenities:** Outdoor hot springs; free Wi-Fi.

Wiesbaden Hot Springs ★★ Few lodgings have their own hot springs, and even fewer yet are built on top of a vapor cave, but you will find both of these rare amenities at this charming property. Originally a bathhouse in 1879, and a medical facility for much of the subsequent century, Wiesbaden started a new chapter as a small resort in the 1970s. Accommodations come in the form of rooms in the main building and adjacent homes and cottages. Guests have unlimited use of the pool and vapor cave, plus discounts at the spa and the private soaking pool named Lorelei.

Sixth Ave. and Fifth St., Ouray. © **970/325-4347.** www.wiesbadenhotsprings.com. 21 units, including 4 cottages and houses. $132–$189 double; $189–$349 cottage or house. Lower winter weekday rates. Pets accepted ($25 one-time fee). **Amenities:** Outdoor hot-springs pools; underground vapor cave; spa; free Wi-Fi.

Where to Eat

Almost all of Ouray's restaurants are on Main Street. There are no chains here.

EXPENSIVE

Bon Ton Restaurant ★★ STEAK/ITALIAN   The original Bon Ton opened in Ouray in the 1880s, and the St. Elmo Hotel named its very Victorian in-house eatery after the legendary spot. There is a regal air to the basement establishment, and a menu that veers between classic Continental and Italian. Main courses include steaks, pasta, and fresh fish, and there are a number of poultry dishes (Tuscan garlic chicken and chicken piccata, to name two) as well. Desserts are highlighted by the Black Nasty, a fudge pie with a graham-cracker crust.

In the St. Elmo Hotel, 426 Main St. © **970/325-4951.** www.stelmohotel.com. Main courses $15–$45 dinner, $10–$18 brunch. Daily 5:30–9:30pm; Sun also 9:30am–1pm.

INEXPENSIVE

Ouray Brewery ★ BREWPUB   With swings for barstools on the ground floor and a great rooftop patio, Ouray is fun and family-friendly, and the food is good as well. Options for lunch and dinner include burgers, wraps, barbecued ribs, and bratwurst. Beers are top-notch, especially the Box Canyon Brown and San Juan IPA.

607 Main St. © **970/325-7388.** www.ouraybrewery.com. Main courses $9–$13. Daily 11am–9pm.

Exploring Ouray

The main summertime outdoor activity here is exploring the spectacularly beautiful mountains and forests by foot, mountain bike, horse, or four-wheel-drive vehicle. Call **Switzerland of America,** 226 Seventh Ave. (© **866/990-5337** or 970/325-4484; www.soajeep.com), which rents Jeeps for about $160 per day. The company leads jeep tours into the high country (about $70 adult for a half-day, $130 for a full day) and arranges horseback rides, raft rides, and balloon rides.

At the southwest corner of Ouray, at Oak Street above Third Avenue, the **Box Canyon Falls & Park** (© **970/325-4464;** www.ci.ouray.co.us) features some of the most impressive waterfalls in the Rockies. The Uncompahgre River tumbles 285 feet through—not over, through—a cliff: It's easy to get a feeling of vertigo as you study the spectacle. The trail to the bottom of the falls is easy; to the top it is moderate to strenuous. Admission to the area is $4 for adults, $3 for seniors 62 and older, and $2 for children 6 to 12 (younger kids are free). From June to October, it's open daily 8am to 8pm or dark, whichever comes first (9am–5pm in May).

If you have 3 or 4 hours and some energy, the moderately difficult **Perimeter Trail** circumnavigates town and provides viewing opportunities of Box Canyon Falls and Cascade Falls, as well as great views of the San Juans and Ouray. The trail is moderately difficult and about 4.2 miles long. Pick up a map at the Ouray Visitor Center; the stairs across the street are the beginning of the trail.

Ouray's main claim to wintertime fame is the **Ouray Ice Park,** located in the southwest corner of town off U.S. 550 (© **970/325-4288;** www.ourayicepark.com). Climbing is free in the park, and it's open daily in winter. Ice-climbing guiding and instruction is offered by **San Juan Mountain Guides** (© **800/642-5389;** www.ouray climbing.com).

Bachelor-Syracuse Mine Tour ★★   I heartily recommend this fun and educational trip into the underworld. A mine train takes visitors 1,800 feet inside Gold Hill, to see where some $8 million in gold, $90 million in silver, and $5 million in other minerals have been mined since silver was discovered here in 1884. Guides, many of them former miners, explain the mining process and equipment and recount the various legends of the mine. Jackets are recommended, even in summer. Allow about 1½ hours.

2 miles from Ouray via C.R. 14. © **970/325-0220.** www.bachelorsyracusemine.com. Admission $15 adults, $8 children 6–12, free for children 5 and under. Tours Mid-May to mid-Sept 9am–4pm; shorter hours at the beginning and end of this period. Closed July 4 and mid-Sept to mid-May.

Ouray County Museum ★   A better-than-average small-town history museum, this former hospital (1884) houses a wide variety of artifacts from Ouray's past. The collection focuses on mining history in the form of antique tools and archival photos, but it also covers ranching, railroading, and medical history, as well as telling the story of the town's namesake, Chief Ouray. Allow about an hour, and inquire about a walking-tour map.

420 Sixth Ave. © **970/325-4576.** www.ouraycountyhistoricalsociety.org. Admission $6 adults, $1 children 12 and under. Summer Mon–Sat 10am–4:30pm, Sun noon–4:30pm; shorter hours spring and fall. Closed mid-Nov to Apr.

Ouray Hot Springs Pool & Fitness Center ★   Open since 1926, this oval outdoor pool measures 120 feet by 150 feet and holds nearly a million gallons of odorless mineral water. Spring water is cooled from 150°F (66°C), and there are three separate soaking sections, with temperatures ranging from 80° to 106°F (29°–42°C). Also here: waterslides, inflatables for kids to scale, and a fitness center. Towels and swimsuits are available for rent. Allow 1 to 2 hours.

U.S. 550, at the north end of Ouray. © **970/325-7073.** www.ci.ouray.co.us. Pool only $12 adults, $10 seniors 62 and over, $8 children 4–12 and seniors 62 and over, free for children 5 and under and seniors over 74. Memorial Day to Labor Day daily 10am–10pm (waterslides noon–6pm, weather permitting); the rest of the year Mon–Fri noon–9pm and Sat–Sun 11am–9pm.

Especially for Kids

The waterslides at the **Ouray Hot Springs Pool** (see above) are the main event, but Ouray has plenty for the younger set, The **Gator Emporium,** 608 Main St. (© **970/325-4557**), has one of the most offbeat inventories in the Rockies, including masks, toys, taxidermy, beads, and more. **Mouse's Chocolates & Coffee,** 520 Main St. (© **970/325-7285**), has a mouthwatering selection of truffles, plus ice cream, fudge, and "Scrap Cookies" made from all of their leftovers.

PAGOSA SPRINGS & WOLF CREEK SKI AREA ★★

Sixty miles east of Durango, Pagosa (meaning "healing waters" in the Ute tongue) Springs is best known for its hot springs, but the former lumber hub is also an excellent base for outdoor recreation and also has a vibrant downtown on the San Juan River. Population is about 1,500.

Exploring Pagosa Springs & Wolf Creek Ski Area

About 15 miles east atop the pass of the same name, Wolf Creek Ski Area is famous throughout Colorado as the area that consistently has the most natural snow in the state—an annual average of 430 inches (almost 40 ft.)! One of the state's oldest ski areas, Wolf Creek has terrain for skiers and snowboarders of all ability levels. Expert skiers often leave the lift-served slopes to dive down the powder of the Water Fall area. Alberta Peak offers expert skiing through a perfectly spaced forest and one of the most spectacular views of the peaks and pristine wilderness. Slopes are rated 20 percent beginner, 35 percent intermediate, 25 percent advanced, and 20 percent expert.

In all, the area has 1,600 acres of terrain with a vertical drop of 1,604 feet from the 11,904-foot summit. The mountain has seven lifts—one quad, one detachable quad, two triple chairs, one double, a high-speed Poma, and a Magic Carpet. There is a day lodge with a restaurant and bar, as well as ski sales, rentals, and lessons. Lift tickets (2013–14 rates) cost $58 for adults, $31 for children 12 and under and seniors 65 and over, and $6 for kids 5 and under The resort is usually open from early November through mid-April daily from 8:30am to 4pm. Contact **Wolf Creek Ski Area** (ⓒ **970/264-5639** or 800/754-9653 for the snow report; www.wolfcreekski.com).

The other big area attraction is **Chimney Rock National Monument** about 20 miles west of Pagosa Springs via U.S. 160 and Colo. 151 (ⓒ **970/883-5359;** www. chimneyrockco.org). The 4,100-acre site was an Ancestral Puebloan stronghold a millennia ago, with over 200 structures below the iconic rock pinnacles. Guided tours are available daily from 9:30am to 2:30pm mid-May through September; a self-guided option is available from 10:30am to 2:30pm. Admission is $12 adults, $5 kids 5 to 16, and free for kids 4 and under.

For more information on the area, consult the **Pagosa Springs Area Chamber of Commerce** (ⓒ **800/252-2204** or 970/264-2360; www.pagosachamber.com).

Where to Stay & Eat

It is hard not to like the Baja-style Mexican grub at **Kip's Grill & Cantina,** 121 Pagosa St. (ⓒ **970/264-3663;** www.kipsgrill.com), with fish, chicken, and tacos as well as American-style sandwiches.

EXPENSIVE

The Springs Resort & Spa ★★ This long-standing hot-springs resort got all gussied up with a Gold LEED-certified lodge that opened here in 2009. Attractive, subtly decorated rooms range from comfortable doubles and kings to palatial suites that sleep six. At the center of it all are the riverside hot springs that fill 23 soaking pool with water that tops out at an extreme 114°F (45°C)—by far the hottest water I have ever personally soaked. The source of the springs is more than 1,000 feet below ground, making them the deepest measured hot springs in the world. Guests get unlimited access to the pools, but you can experience them even if you aren't staying the night for $25, or $14 for those 13 and under.

165 Hot Springs Blvd., Pagosa Springs. ⓒ **800/225-0934** or 970/264-4168. www.pagosa hotsprings.com. 79 units. $199–$279 double; $309–$619 suite. Lower rates fall and spring. **Amenities:** Lounge; outdoor hot-springs pools; spa; free Wi-Fi.

THE SOUTHERN ROCKIES

I f Colorado is the rooftop of America, then the Southern Rockies are the peak of that roof. Some 30 of Colorado's fourteeners—more than half of the state's 14,000-plus-foot peaks—ring the area, and from Monarch Pass, at 11,312 feet, rivers flow in three directions.

Isolated from the rest of Colorado by mountains and canyons, this area saw settlers come north from Taos, New Mexico, in the 1700s and build some striking structures that still stand today. Today these mountain and river towns are renowned as recreational capitals: Crested Butte for skiing and mountain biking, Gunnison for fishing and hunting, and Salida and Buena Vista for white-water rafting. Alamosa is within easy reach of numerous attractions, including the remarkable Great Sand Dunes National Park and Preserve. In the foothills of the San Juan Range are the historic mining towns of Creede and Lake City, and in the tiny community of Antonito you can hop a narrow-gauge steam train for a trip back to a simpler (though smokier) time. This is rugged and sparsely populated land, with numerous opportunities for seeing the wilds of mountain America at their best.

10

CRESTED BUTTE ★★★

28 miles N of Gunnison, 224 miles SW of Denver

A delightful little gem of a town, Crested Butte is a year-round destination resort, with wonderful skiing in winter, and hiking, mountain biking, and other outdoor recreational activities in warmer weather. In fact, Crested Butte has the best mountain biking in the state, and boasts of having some of the most colorful displays of wildflowers you'll see anywhere. To this end, the town was dubbed the official "Wildflower Capital of Colorado" by the state legislature in 1990.

The town of Crested Butte was born in 1880 as the Denver & Rio Grande line laid a narrow-gauge rail track from Gunnison to serve the gold and silver mines in the area. But it was coal, not the more precious minerals, which sustained the town from the late 1880s until 1952, when the last of the mines closed. The economy languished until Mt. Crested Butte ski area was developed in 1961.

An influx of newcomers began renovating the old buildings in the 1970s, and in 1974 the town was designated a National Historic District—one of the largest in Colorado. In 1976, local riders were integral in the birth of the sport of mountain biking. Crested Butte is quite different from many of Colorado's resorts in that it's not overdeveloped and its funky personality still outshines the Western chic.

Essentials

GETTING THERE By Car   Crested Butte is 28 miles north of Gunnison on Colo. 135, the only year-round access. In summer, the gravel-surface Kebler Pass Road links Crested Butte with Colo. 133 at Paonia Reservoir, to the west.

By Plane   The **Gunnison–Crested Butte Regional Airport,** 711 Rio Grande Ave. (© **970/641-2304**), is just off U.S. 50, a few blocks south of downtown Gunnison. **American** provides air service during ski season and **United** provides daily year-round service from Denver. **Dolly's Mountain Shuttle** (© **970/349-2620;** www. crestedbutteshuttle.com) and **Alpine Express** (© **800/822-4844** or 970/641-5074; www.alpineexpressshuttle.com) provide shuttle service from the airport.

GETTING AROUND   There are actually two separate communities here: the old mining town of Crested Butte and the modern resort village of Mt. Crested Butte, 3 miles away. Colo. 135 enters Crested Butte from the south and is intersected by Elk Avenue, which runs east-west as the town's main street. Free transportation throughout Crested Butte and the ski resort is provided by **Mountain Express** (© **970/349-5616;** www.mtnexp.org) in hand-painted buses from 7 or 7:30am until about midnight.

VISITOR INFORMATION   Consult the **Gunnison/Crested Butte Tourism Association** (© **877/448-1410;** www.gunnisoncrestedbutte.com). An **information center** is located downtown at 601 Elk Ave., as well as at the base area at the ski resort and in Gunnison, 28 miles south.

FAST FACTS   The **Town Clinic of Crested Butte,** 214 6th St., #1 (© **970/349-6749;** www.towncliniccb.com), can handle most health needs. The **post office** is at 217 Elk Ave.

Where to Stay

Contact **Crested Butte Mountain Resort** (© **800/810-7669**) for lodging options in Mt. Crested Butte. The best value in town is the **Crested Butte International Lodge and Hostel,** 615 Teocalli Ave. (© **888/389-0588;** www.cbhostel.com), with bunks for $25 to $35 per night and private rooms and apartments for $75 to $200.

Visitors can also save by staying in Gunnison, 28 miles south of Crested Butte. The **Water Wheel Inn,** 37478 W. U.S. 50 (© **800/642-1650** or 970/641-1650; www.water wheelinnatgunnison.com), is a good pick, with rates of $69 to $109 double and $120 to $155 suite. Just east of town, the **Inn at Tomichi Village,** 41883 U.S. 50 (© **970/641-1131;** www.theinnattomichivillage.com), recently saw a major renovation, and it features a quiet location and upscale furnishings. Rates are $89 to $159 double.

EXPENSIVE

The Nordic Inn ★★   Built when the resort opened in 1961, the Nordic Inn snatched up the very best on-mountain positioning. The property was recently updated for the new millennium, and now its slick decor (with a few quirky touches—think faux fur and license-plate art) matches its spectacular perch. The rooms feature historic photos of the area and an atmosphere meshing that of a ski lodge and a country inn. It is a short walk to the base area and the lifts, as well as the shuttle stop downtown.

14 Treasury Rd., Mt. Crested Butte. © **800/542-7669** or 970/349-5542. www.nordicinncb.com. 30 units, including 1 suite and 1 chalet. $249–$269 double; $329–$429 suite or chalet. Lower rates spring and fall. Rates include continental breakfast. Pets accepted ($25 per night). **Amenities:** Outdoor Jacuzzi; free Wi-Fi.

The Ruby of Crested Butte ★★   No detail is left to chance at this modern B&B, for my money the nicest in Crested Butte. Built in the 1990s and operated by Chris and Andrea Greene since 2005, the Ruby is not named for its red hue, but Andrea's late grandmother. Decorated with classic Colorado-centric antiques, rooms have one king or queen bed, and the two-story suite sleeps six. This is as pet-friendly a property as you will find, as the Greenes can arrange walks, daycare, and even "doggie spa treatments." They collect a voluntary donation to local pet shelters in lieu of a nightly fee for your pooch's stay.

624 Gothic Ave., Crested Butte. ℓ **800/390-1338** for reservations or 970/349-1338. www. therubyofcrestedbutte.com. 6 units, including 1 suite. $199–$279 double; $229–$399 suite. Lower rates spring and fall. Rates include full breakfast. Pets accepted ($10 donation per night). **Amenities:** Complimentary bikes; concierge; indoor/outdoor Jacuzzi; pet friendly; free Wi-Fi.

MODERATE

Elk Mountain Lodge ★   Miners were the primary lodgers when this place opened in 1919, but the market has since shifted towards thrifty outdoor lovers looking to stay within walking distance of the historic core of Crested Butte proper. Historic rooms are basic but reliable, with private baths, ceiling fans, and TVs, and the hotel does have a wonderfully convivial vibe.

Second St. and Gothic Ave., Crested Butte. ℓ **800/374-6521** or 970/349-7533. www.elkmountain lodge.com. 19 units. $119–$199 double. Rates include full breakfast. **Amenities:** Bar; complimentary bikes; indoor Jacuzzi; free Wi-Fi.

Pioneer Guest Cabins ★   Isolated, but only 15 minutes by car to Crested Butte, these historic cabins are located in the picturesque Elk Mountains along Cement Creek, within walking distance of a number of terrific hiking trails. The cabins originally served as lodging for the defunct Gunnison-Pioneer Winter Sports Area, but have seen plenty of modernization in recent years; all feature kitchens and comfortable beds but thankfully lack TVs.

2094 Cement Creek Rd., Crested Butte. ℓ **970/349-5517.** www.pioneerguestcabins.com. 8 units. $131–$189 double. Most dogs accepted for $20 per dog per night fee (maximum 2 dogs per unit) at management discretion. **Amenities:** Free Wi-Fi.

Where to Eat

EXPENSIVE

Soupçon ★★★ FRENCH   Never judge a book by its cover—or a restaurant by its location in a converted back-alley cabin. Because if you do, you would probably pass on one of the top eateries in the Rockies. Soupçon—pronounced "soup's on" but meaning "a slight trace of a seasoning"—cooks up exquisite French fare with a contemporary American spin. The seasonally changing menu includes Gallic classics like escargot and bouillabaisse alongside Western specialties like lamb and elk.

127 Elk Ave. (at Second St.), in the alley behind Kochevar's Saloon. ℓ **970/349-5448.** www. soupconcrestedbutte.com. Main courses $35–$62. Daily seatings at 6pm and 8:15pm.

MODERATE

Django's ★★ TAPAS/NEW AMERICAN   Named for gypsy jazz legend Django Reinhardt, this is the best eatery in the base village at Mt. Crested Butte, and worth the trip up the hill even if you are overnighting in Crested Butte proper. With a circular bar, intimate booths, and an outdoor patio where live jazz is the norm, Django's specializes in small plates that owe inspiration to Mediterranean cuisine—you might have venison and duck pastrami, parsnip gnocchi, or summer-squash ravioli on the constantly changing menu, as well as a few larger dishes like steak frites or slow-roasted duck. The excellent wine list features Italian, French, and Spanish vintages.

Mountaineer Sq., Mt. Crested Butte. ⓒ **970/349-7574.** www.djangosrestaurantcrestedbutte.com. Small plates $5–$10; main courses $10–$21. Tues–Sun 5–10pm. Bar opens at 4pm in ski season. Located at the Mountain Express bus stop at Mountaineer Square.

Slogar ★ AMERICAN   Families cannot top the chicken and steak dinners at this longstanding eatery located in the historic building of the same name. The fixed-price menu features those two selections (and only those selections) with mashed potatoes, creamed corn, and delectable biscuits with gravy, honey, or jam, and homemade ice cream for a crowd-pleasing finish.

517 Second St., at Whiterock Ave. ⓒ **970/349-5765.** Fixed-price dinner $20–$30. Daily 5–9pm.

INEXPENSIVE

Secret Stash ★★ PIZZA   This local landmark moved from a small converted house to more spacious quarters in 2013, and it immediately filled out the space with all sorts of wacky details, from Hindu art to kitsch, as well as an ornate wooden bar and a wall made of books downstairs. The pizzas are similarly eclectic, from fig and prosciutto to BBQ (featuring pulled pork, corn, and beans) to the KGB, with chipotle sauce and bleu and feta cheese. Stop in for an appetizer or drink even if you are not staying for dinner—this is Crested Butte.

303 Elk Ave. ⓒ **970/349-6245.** www.stashpizza.com. Pizzas $17–$32. Daily 11am–10pm. Bar open later.

Exploring Crested Butte

The Crested Butte Heritage Museum provides a free brochure on a **self-guided walking tour** of more than three dozen historic buildings in Crested Butte, including the picturesque 1883 Town Hall, 1881 railroad depot, numerous saloons and homes, and a unique two-story outhouse.

Crested Butte Mountain Heritage Museum ★★   This museum has a compelling story to tell, from the town's 19th-century mining days to the opening of the ski resort in the 1960s. But the most captivating tale to be told might be the (arguable) invention of mountain biking here when a ragtag crew took single-speed cruisers over Pearl Pass to Aspen in 1976. (*Note:* The Mountain Bike Hall of Fame moved to California from the museum in late 2013.)

331 Elk Ave. ⓒ **970/349-1880.** www.crestedbuttemuseum.com. Admission $4, free for children 12 and under. Winter daily noon–6pm; summer daily 10am–6pm; by appointment spring and fall.

Skiing & Other Winter Activities

CRESTED BUTTE MOUNTAIN RESORT ★★★   This may well be Colorado's best-kept secret. Situated at the intersection of two overlapping winter storm tracks, it's almost guaranteed to have outstanding snow. There are plenty of runs for beginners and intermediate skiers, but Crested Butte also has what many experts consider the most challenging runs in the Rockies. Then you have what is arguably the best ski town in the West below the slopes.

   The resort has 1,547 acres of skiable terrain. Altogether, trails are rated 27 percent beginner, 57 percent intermediate, and 16 percent advanced and expert. The vertical drop is 3,062 feet from a summit of 12,162 feet. There are 121 trails served by 15 lifts (including four high-speed quads, two fixed-grip quads, two triples, three doubles, one surface lift, and two conveyors). Average annual snowfall is 300 inches, and there's snowmaking on trails served by all but two of the resort's lifts. The resort also has an easily accessible snowboard terrain park and superpipe, and offers lessons for skiers and snowboarders.

For more information or lodging reservations, contact **Crested Butte Mountain Resort** (✆ **800/810-7669** or 970/349-2222, or 970/349-2323 for snow reports; www.skicb.com). Full-day regular-season lift tickets (2013–14 rates) run $98 for adults, $78 for seniors 65 and older, $88 for youths 13 to 17, and $54 for children 7 to 12. Early-season lift tickets are about 40 percent less and holidays are a bit pricier; they are free for kids under 7 all season long. The resort is usually open from late November to early April daily from 9am to 4pm.

For serious powder hounds, contact **Irwin** (✆ **970/349-7761;** www.irwincolorado.com), offering snowcat skiing 12 miles west of Crested Butte. This place often gets 600 inches of snow a year, more than any of Colorado's lift-served resorts, but the price is commensurate: $550 per person per day (about 10 runs).

CROSS-COUNTRY SKIING & SNOWSHOEING The **Crested Butte Nordic Center,** based at Big Mine Park, Second Street and Whiterock Avenue in downtown Crested Butte (✆ **970/349-1707;** www.cbnordic.org), maintains about 55 miles of marked and groomed trails and organizes backcountry tours. A day pass costs about $18, $10 for children and seniors; lessons and rentals are available. The center also maintains several backcountry huts available for overnight rentals.

More Outdoor Activities

This is rugged country, surrounded by **Gunnison National Forest,** three wilderness areas, and towering 12,000- to 14,000-foot peaks. For maps and tips on the many activities available, contact the Gunnison Ranger District office at 216 N. Colorado St. in Gunnison (✆ **970/641-0471**).

A good base for exploring this area is **Almont,** located 10 miles north of Gunnison where the East and Taylor rivers meet and form the Gunnison River, and home to several lodgings and outfitters, including **Three Rivers Resort and Outfitting,** 17 miles south of Crested Butte (✆ **888/761-3474** or 970/641-1303; www.3riversoutfitting.com). Three Rivers offers fishing, kayaking, and rafting trips and also has fully equipped and furnished cabins and lodge rooms. There is also a good restaurant here on a riverside patio.

The lifts at **Crested Butte Mountain Resort** (✆ **800/810-7669;** www.skicb.com) don't stop just because the snow's gone, but operate daily from mid-June through early September for hikers, mountain bikers, or those who simply want to enjoy the beautiful mountain scenery without effort. Single trips cost $20 for adults, $17 for children 7 to 17, and $19 seniors 65 and older; all-day passes cost $39, $33, and $37, respectively. Kids under 7 ride free. Also at the resort when the snow's gone are zip lines, a moun-tain-bike course, Frisbee golf, bungee trampolines, a climbing wall, and miniature golf. Adventure Tickets include unlimited lift rides plus these activities for $39 for adults, $31 for children 7 to 17, and $37 for seniors 65 and older.

GOLF The 18-hole course at the **Club at Crested Butte,** 2 miles south of Crested Butte off Colo. 135 (✆ **970/349-8603;** www.theclubatcrestedbutte.com), is one of Colorado's best mountain courses. The fee for 18 holes, including the mandatory cart, is $95 to $149 in summer. In Gunnison, the **Dos Rios Golf Club,** 501 Camino Del Rio (✆ **970/641-1482;** www.dosriosgolf.net), is a scenic course with green fees of $40 to $70 for 18 holes, cart included.

HIKING   There are practically unlimited opportunities for hiking and backpacking in the Crested Butte area. Some of the best are in the **Maroon Bells–Snowmass Wilderness Area,** accessible from the trailhead at Gothic, above Mt. Crested Butte, where you can hike to Aspen if properly motivated. Another good trail is located off Cement Creek Road: The **Farris Creek Trail** (also known as the Caves Trail) takes hikers up to a great vantage point of some cavelike geological formations and a great view of the area's original and long-closed Pioneer ski area. Another option: Ride the chairlift at Crested Butte Mountain Resort and hike to the peak of Mt. Crested Butte. Ask the chamber of commerce for other trail suggestions, or contact the Gunnison National Forest office (© **970/641-0471**).

HORSEBACK RIDING   Guided rides are offered year-round by **Fantasy Ranch Horseback Adventures** in Mt. Crested Butte (© **970/349-5425;** www.fantasy ranchoutfitters.com). Trips go into three different mountain wilderness areas, at elevations from 7,000 feet to 12,700 feet, including the incredibly beautiful Maroon Bells. Rides run $65 to $135. In Almont, 17 miles south of town, you'll find **Harmel's Ranch Resort** (© **800/235-3402** or 970/641-1740; www.harmels.com), which offers hayrides for $15 per person, hour-long horseback rides for $40, and half-day rides for $80. They also offer cabins, lodge rooms, riverside dining, and fishing.

MOUNTAIN BIKING   One of the towns that lays claim to the sport's invention, **Crested Butte** has established a firm reputation as the place to mountain bike in Colorado. From single-track trails to jeep roads, there's something here to please every ability level. Among local shops where you can get trail information, maps, and mountain-bike rentals (from about $35 per day), I recommend **Big Al's Bicycle Heaven,** 207 Elk Ave. (© **970/349-0515;** www.bigalsbicycleheaven.com), in Crested Butte. At **Crested Butte Mountain Resort** (© **800/810-7669;** www.skicb.com), you will find lift-served mountain biking at **Evolution Bike Park,** with more than 25 trails for every skill level and a rental shop; riders need a lift ticket (p. 229). Guided mountain-bike tours are offered by **Crested Butte Mountain Guides,** 416 Sopris Ave. (© **970/349-5430;** www.crestedbutteguides.com), which charges $200 for two riders for a half-day guided ride, not including bike rental.

Popular choices include the **Strand Hill** route, which runs for 18 miles and is considered upper intermediate. Better for lower intermediates is the **Lower Loop** (18 miles), accessible from Crested Butte Mountain Resort. Advanced mountain bikers will love **Trail No. 401,** one of the best trails in the area, a 26-mile round trip that climbs to 11,500 feet through some incredible mountain scenery.

RIVER RAFTING & KAYAKING   For trips on the Taylor and other rivers, check with **Three Rivers Resort and Outfitting** (© **888/761-3474;** www.3riversoutfitting.com). Rates for 3-hour raft trips over relatively calm stretches are about $50 per person.

Festivals & Nightlife

Spring to fall, festivals are a big deal in Crested Butte. In between the spring and fall equinoxes are **Crested Butte Bike Week** (www.cbbikeweek.com) in late June, the **Crested Butte Wildflower Festival** (www.crestedbuttewildflowerfestival.com) in July, the **Crested Butte Wine and Food Festival** (www.crestedbuttewine.com) in late July, and the **Crested Butte Arts Festival** (www.crestedbutteartsfestival.com) in early August. Only the bookends to festival season need explanation. In spring, **Flauschink** toasts the end of ski season with polka, a parade, and other events. **Vinotok** is the annual goodbye to summer, involving a street party and the trial of the Grump, a

curecanti NATIONAL RECREATION AREA

Dams on the Gunnison River, just below Gunnison, have created a series of three very different reservoirs, extending 35 miles to the mouth of the **Black Canyon of the Gunnison** (p. 191). **Blue Mesa Reservoir** (elevation 7,519 ft.), the easternmost (beginning 9 miles west of Gunnison), is the largest body of water in Colorado when filled to capacity, and popular for fishing, boating, and other activities. **Morrow Point Reservoir** (elevation 7,160 ft.) and **Crystal Reservoir** (elevation 6,755 ft.) fill long, serpentine canyons accessible only by trail and limited to use by hand-carried boats.

There are two full-service marinas, offering fuel, supplies, boat rentals, and guided fishing trips. **Elk Creek Marina** is on Blue Mesa Lake, 16 miles west of Gunnison off U.S. 50 (✆ **970/641-0707;** www.bluemesares.com), and **Lake Fork Marina** (✆ **970/641-3048;** www. bluemesares.com) is 25 miles west of Gunnison, at the reservoir's west end.

The **Morrow Point boat tour** leaves the Pine Creek Trail dock at 10am and 12:30pm daily except Tuesday in summer, to explore the Upper Black Canyon of the Gunnison. Keep in mind there is a short hike down to the dock, which has to be repeated in reverse after the boat ride. Rates are $16 adults, $8 children 12 and under. Reservations are required; stop at the Elk Creek Visitor Center or call (✆ **970/641-2337,** ext. 205).

The recreation area has 10 developed **campgrounds,** with about 350 sites for $12 to $18 nightly; a few primitive sites are free. Reservations are available in summer through **www.recreation.gov,** or by phone (✆ **877/444-6777**). Admission to the recreation area is free except for those entering via the East Portal, where a $15 fee is charged. For a brochure and other information before your trip, contact **Curecanti National Recreation Area** (✆ **970/641-2337;** www.nps. gov/cure).

beastly looking effigy who ends up in the middle of a bonfire before it is all said and done—highly recommended. Contact the **Gunnison/Crested Butte Tourism Association** (✆ **877/448-1410**) for more information.

Definitely stop in at **Montanya Distillers,** 212 Elk Ave. (✆ **970/799-3206**), serving handcrafted rum cocktails and small plates. Of the watering holes, I like the rough-and-tumble second-story bar and brewery, the **Eldo,** 215 Elk Ave. (✆ **970/349-6125**), and **Dogwood Cocktail Cabin,** a slick place specializing in creative martinis and mixed drinks, 309 Third St. (✆ **970/349-6338**).

SALIDA ★★

138 miles SW of Denver, 96 miles W of Pueblo, 82 miles N of Alamosa

With a strategic location on the upper Arkansas River, it was natural that Salida (elevation 7,080 ft.) should become an important farming, ranching, and transportation center in its early days, and a major river-rafting and kayaking center today. When Leadville boomed on silver in the late 1870s, the Denver & Rio Grande Railroad built a line up the Arkansas from Pueblo, and the town of Salida was founded at a key point on the line. The vibrant downtown has historic ambience, with a growing arts community, and the city also serves as a base camp for outdoor recreation enthusiasts, namely river rats. About 25 miles north, Buena Vista is another river-rafting hub.

Essentials

GETTING THERE **By Car** U.S. 50 connects Salida with Gunnison, 66 miles west, and Pueblo, 96 miles east on I-25. Colo. 291 heads north from Salida, providing a vital 9-mile link between U.S. 50 and U.S. 285, which runs north-south 5 miles west of Salida (through Poncha Springs), connecting Alamosa with Buena Vista and eventually Denver.

By Plane The nearest commercial airport is in **Gunnison,** 65 miles west.

GETTING AROUND Salida sits on the southwestern bank of the Arkansas River. U.S. 50 (Rainbow Blvd.) marks the southern edge of town. At the eastern city limit, Colo. 291 (Oak St.) turns north off U.S. 50, and turns northwest as First Street through downtown.

VISITOR INFORMATION Consult the **Salida Colorado Chamber of Commerce,** 406 W. Rainbow Blvd. (U.S. 50; 𝒞 **877/772-5432** or 719/539-2068; www. salidachamber.org).

FAST FACTS The **Heart of the Rockies Regional Medical Center,** 1000 Rush Dr. (𝒞 **719/530-2200**), provide 24-hour emergency care. The **post office** is at 310 D St.

Where to Stay

The **Simple Lodge & Hostel,** 224 E. First St. (𝒞 **719/650-7381;** www.simplelodge. com), is the best value in town, offering bunks for $21 to $24 a night and private rooms for $55 to $160 a night in a slickly restored 1883 railroad boardinghouse just 2 blocks from the town center.

Northwest of Salida, **Mount Princeton Hot Springs Resort,** 15870 C.R. 162, Nathrop (𝒞 **888/395-7799** or 719/395-2447; www.mtprinceton.com), features several soaking pools (admission is $12–$22 for nonguests; overnight guests are free). Lodge rooms are $180 to $225 in peak season, and cabins $325 to $450. There is also a restaurant and good access to hiking.

Or you can drive a bit further on C.R. 162 and stay in St. Elmo, a ghost town that sits at the end of Chalk Creek Road northwest of Salida. (Only 4-by-4s need test the mountain passes beyond.) Take your pick of cabins from the **St. Elmo General Store** (𝒞 **719/395-2117;** www.st-elmo.com) for $79 a night or rooms in the stately **Ghost Town Guest House,** 25850 C.R. 162 (𝒞 **719/395-2120;** www.ghosttownguesthouse. com), with rooms for $175 to $195 double.

MODERATE

Woodland Motel ★ This family-run motel is a first-rate operation in winter or summer, and my top pick for lodging in Salida. A short walk or dive from downtown, the location is good (and much quieter than the motels that line U.S. 50 a few miles away). Rooms range from dinky to spacious—the largest sleeps six—but the upkeep (and comfort of the beds) is second to none.

903 W. First St., Salida. 𝒞 **800/488-0456** or 719/539-4980. www.woodlandmotel.com. 18 units, including 3 condos. Summer and winter weekends $67–$128 double; $105–$205 condo. Lower rates spring, fall, and winter weekdays. Pets accepted (free). **Amenities:** Outdoor Jacuzzi; free Wi-Fi.

Where to Eat

MODERATE

The Fritz ★★ GASTROPUB The Fritz occupies a pleasant historic room with a bar, original art, and an even better dog-friendly, heated patio. The ever-changing menu includes unusual sandwiches like chicken and brie and prosciutto and pear; small plates such as scrumptious bacon-wrapped dates and provolone-parmesan mac and cheese with bacon; and pasta and chicken entrees. The Steak Fritz is a specialty, with grilled onions, fries, and hollandaise. The full-service bar serves a number of local beers as well as tall-boy PBRs.

113 E Sackett St. *©* **719/539-0364.** www.thefritzdowntown.com. Main courses $10–$17. Daily 11am–11pm. Bar open later.

Exploring Salida

Salida is a fun town to explore for a day or two, and more if rafting is on the agenda The **Salida Art District** (www.salidaartists.com) encompasses nearly 20 galleries in downtown Salida. A walking-tour brochure is available at the visitor center. To the northwest of Salida the terminus of C.R. 162, **St. Elmo** is a ghost town that was home to 2,000 in 1880. Now there are only a few people and a smattering of structures, with a few operating businesses and hiking opportunities. Contact **Buena Vista Heritage** (*©* **719/395-8458;** www.buenavistaheritage.org) for tour and other information.

Monarch Crest Scenic Tramway ★   Climbing from 11,312-foot Monarch Pass to the Continental Divide at an altitude of 12,012 feet, this tram offers views of five mountain ranges—up to 150 miles away—when skies are clear. The tram includes six four-passenger gondolas. At the top is a gift shop. Pets are welcome. Allow 1 hour.

Monarch Pass, U.S. 50, 22 miles west of Salida. *©* **719/539-4091.** Admission $10 adults, $8 seniors over 55, $5 children 3–12, and free for children under 3. Mid-May to mid-Sept, weather permitting, daily 8:30am–5:30pm.

Mt. Shavano Fish Hatchery ★   This state-run fish hatchery, about a half-mile northwest of town off Colo. 291, produces more than 2 million trout each year, used to stock Colorado's numerous streams and lakes. Visitors can walk among the fish raceways and ponds and feed the fish (food provided from coin-operated machines). Allow 30 minutes to an hour.

7725 C.R. 154. *©* **719/539-6877.** Free admission. Daily 8am–4pm.

Salida Hot Springs ★   Colorado's largest indoor hot springs have been in commercial operation since 1937, when the Works Progress Administration built the pools as a Depression-era project. Ute tribes considered the mineral waters, rich in bicarbonate, sodium, and sulfate, to be sacred and medicinal. Allow 1 hour.

410 W. Rainbow Blvd. (U.S. 50). *©* **719/539-6738.** www.salidarec.com. Admission $11 adults, $9 seniors 60 and older, $5 children 6–17, $3 children 5 and under. Memorial Day to Labor Day Mon–Fri noon–8pm, Sat–Sun noon–9pm; call or check website for winter hours.

River Rafting

Considered the white-water rafting center of the Rockies, Salida is the perfect base for enjoying the **Arkansas Headwaters Recreation Area,** a 148-mile stretch of river from Leadville to Pueblo Lake. With headquarters off Colo. 291 in downtown Salida at 307 W. Sackett Ave. (*©* **719/539-7289;** www.parks.state.co.us), the recreation area includes about 20 developed sites along the river, offering raft and kayak access, fishing, hiking, camping, and picnicking. There are also undeveloped areas that offer access to the river, but be careful not to trespass on private property. User fees are $7 per vehicle per day, $3 walk-in, plus $16 per night for camping.

The busiest stretch of the river is Browns Canyon, a granite wilderness between Buena Vista and Salida, with Class III and IV rapids (moderately difficult to difficult) along a 10-mile stretch of river from Nathrop to Stone Bridge.

Most people explore Colorado's rivers with experienced rafting companies, which provide trips on stretches of river that range from practically calm and suitable for everyone to extremely difficult, with long, violent rapids that are recommended only for skilled whitewater boaters. Leading outfitters in the Salida and Buena Vista area include **Dvorak Expeditions** (✆ **800/824-3795;** www.dvorakexpeditions.com), **Wilderness Aware** (✆ **800/462-7238;** www.inaraft.com), and **River Runners** (✆ **800/723-8987;** www.whitewater.net). Generally, adult rates for half-day raft trips are $60 to $80; full-day trips including lunch are in the $90 to $125 range, and multiday excursions start at about $175 per day. Prices for children are about 20 percent less.

For kayaking classes, duckie (inflatable kayak) rentals and tours, and other rafting-related needs, the **Rocky Mountain Outdoor Center,** 228 N. F St. (✆ **800/255-5784;** www.rmoc.com), is the spot. Two-day group lessons for beginning and intermediate paddlers cost $250, duckies rent for $50 a day, and guided full-day trips are $74 to $119. For practice, the **Arkansas River Whitewater Park** is located on the river downtown.

More Outdoor Activities

FISHING   The Arkansas River is considered by many to be the finest fishing river in Colorado. There's also trout fishing in numerous alpine lakes, including Cottonwood Lake, Twin Lakes, and O'Haver Lake. For tips on the best fishing spots, plus licenses, supplies, and rentals, stop at **ArkAnglers,** 7500 W. U.S. 50, Salida (✆ **719/539-3474;** www.arkanglers.com), which also offers a guide service. Cost for a half-day trip on the Arkansas River for two is $300.

HIKING   There are outstanding trails for all experience levels throughout the region, particularly in the San Isabel National Forest, along the eastern slope of the Continental Divide west of Salida. Of particular interest are hikes into the Collegiate Range (Mts. Harvard, Columbia, Yale, Princeton, and Oxford) off Cottonwood Creek Road west of Buena Vista, and trips from the ghost town of St. Elmo up Chalk Creek Road from Mount Princeton Hot Springs. For maps and other information, stop at the **Salida Ranger District** office, 325 W. Rainbow Blvd. (✆ **719/539-3591**).

MOUNTAIN BIKING   There are numerous trails suitable for mountain biking throughout the area, and they provide stupendous views of the surrounding 14,000-plus-foot peaks. Many locals undertake the short but steep ride up **"S" Mountain** for their daily exercise. **Absolute Bikes,** 330 W. Sackett St. (✆ **719/539-9295;** www.absolutebikes.com), rents, sells, and services mountain bikes and can provide information and maps on nearby trails. Rentals start at $40 per day for mountain bikes.

SKIING & SNOWBOARDING   Among the finest of Colorado's small ski resorts, **Monarch Mountain,** 20 miles west of Salida at Monarch Pass on U.S. 50, serves all levels of ability with 63 trails, with 14 percent rated beginner, 28 percent intermediate, 27 percent advanced, and 31 percent expert. Covering 800 acres, the mountain has a vertical drop of 1,162 feet from its summit of 11,952 feet. It gets about 350 inches of snow annually and has no snow-making equipment. It has one fixed quad and four double chairs. All-day tickets (2013–14 prices) are $65 for adults, $40 for youths 13 to 15 and seniors 62 to 68, $25 for juniors 7 to 12, and free for those under 7 or over 68. The season pass, dubbed **"One Planet—One Pass,"** is worth a look, even for out-of-staters: For about $400, it nets you unlimited skiing at Monarch and free lift tickets and discounts at seven resorts in Colorado, as well as resorts in eleven other states and five other continents. The area is usually open daily from late November to mid-April from 9am to 4pm. For information, contact the resort (✆ **888/996-7669** or 719/530-5000; www.skimonarch.com).

ALAMOSA & THE GREAT SAND DUNES

212 miles SW of Denver, 149 miles E of Durango, 173 miles N of Santa Fe, New Mexico

Founded in 1878 with the extension of the Denver & Rio Grande Railroad into the San Luis Valley, Alamosa was named for the cottonwood (álamo in Spanish) trees that lined the banks of the Rio Grande. Soon rails spread out in all directions from the community, and it became a thriving transportation center for farmers and a supply depot for miners. Farming remains important today, but Alamosa is also an educational center with Adams State College, a 4-year institution founded in 1921. There are numerous legends and mysteries associated with the surrounding valley, from crystal skulls and interdimensional vortexes to UFOs and black helicopters. And if you're looking for Colorado's largest sandbox, here it is: Just 35 miles from Alamosa are the tallest sand dunes in North America, the Great Sand Dunes. Elevation is 7,544 feet, and the population is about 9,000.

Essentials

GETTING THERE   By Car   Alamosa is at the junction of U.S. 160, which runs east 73 miles to I-25 at Walsenburg and west to Durango, and U.S. 285, which extends south to Santa Fe, New Mexico, and north to Denver. Because of a jog in U.S. 285, however, a more direct route from the north is to take Colo. 17 the last 50 miles.

By Plane   The **San Luis Valley Regional Airport (ALS; 𝒞 719/589-4848)**, 2500 State St., 3 miles off U.S. 285 S., has service to and from Denver with **Great Lakes Airlines.**

GETTING AROUND   Alamosa is bisected by U.S. 160, running east-west through downtown as Main Street. On the east side of downtown, Colo. 17 runs north to the Great Sand Dunes.

VISITOR INFORMATION   The **Alamosa Convention & Visitors Bureau,** 610 State Ave. (𝒞 **800/258-7597;** www.alamosa.org), operates a visitor information center that is open daily year-round, except holidays.

FAST FACTS   The **San Luis Valley Regional Medical Center,** with a 24-hour emergency room, is at 106 Blanca Ave. (𝒞 **719/589-2511;** www.slvrmc.org). The **post office** is at 505 Third St.

Where to Stay & Eat

You'll find a number of restaurants along Alamosa's Main Street, many of them chains but also a few good independents. I like the spicy Mexican fare at **Cavillo's,** 400 Main St. (𝒞 **719/587-5500**), and the local Gosar Sausage sandwiches and hoppy microbrews at the **San Luis Valley Brewing Company,** 631 Main St. (𝒞 **719/587-2337;** www.slvbrewco.com), located in a restored historic Art Deco redbrick. Dinner adds steak, seafood, and pasta to the mix, with specialties like jambalaya and green chili pasta Alfredo.

North of town and bordering the Great Sand Dunes National Park and Preserve, **Zapata Ranch,** 5305 Colo. 150, Mosca (𝒞 **719/378-2356;** www.zranch.org), is a historic 110,000-acre ranch that raises cattle and bison in the shadow of the Sangre de Cristos. The ranch limits its occupancy to 25 guests, and emphasizes natural horsemanship, sustainable ranching practices, and overall ecological viability. Three-night to weeklong stays run $1,252 to $2,300 adults for adults and $1,000 to $1,840 for kids 7 and under.

Exploring Alamosa

Alamosa–Monte Vista National Wildlife Refuges ★   These two refuges together have preserved nearly 25,000 acres of vital land for a variety of marsh birds and waterfowl, including many migrating and wintering species. Sandhill and whooping cranes visit in early to mid-October and early March; at other times of the year there may be egrets, herons, avocets, bitterns, and other species. The refuges have self-guided driving tours with a number of viewpoints, and also several hiking trails.

Southeast of Alamosa via U.S. 160 and south of Monte Vista via Colo. 15. © **719/589-4021;** www. fws.gov/alamosa. Free admission. Daily sunrise–sunset.

Colorado Gators ★   Alligators in Colorado? Strangely enough, yes. Geothermal wells keep the temperature a cozy 87°F (31°C) at this alligator farm located 17 miles north of Alamosa off Colo. 17. There are about 350 gators, nearly half of them rescues—topping out at 11 feet long and weighing 600 pounds. Kids love feeding "gator chow" to the resident reptilians; a bucket of the stuff—which looks suspiciously like dog food—costs $2. The farm also raises fish and has a reptile refuge populated with desert tortoises, turtles, and iguanas. Brave souls can pose for a picture with a baby gator in their hands; braver souls can pose for a snapshot with a baby gator or even fork over $100 for a 3-hour alligator-handling class. Early August brings Gatorfest, featuring a gator-wrestling competition. Allow about an hour.

9162 C.R. 9 N., Mosca. © **719/378-2612.** www.gatorfarm.com. Admission $15 adults, $7.50 children 6–12 and seniors 65–79, free for those 5 and under and 80 and over. Memorial Day through Labor Day daily 9am–6pm; spring and fall daily 9am–5pm; winter daily 10am–4pm. Closed Thanksgiving and Christmas.

Rio Grande Scenic Railroad ★★   Over routes more than a century old, the diesel locomotives of the Rio Grande Scenic Railroad haul classic Pullman cars through the mountains and valleys of southern Colorado. The trips include a half-day round trip between Alamosa and Antonito, connecting with the Cumbres & Toltec Scenic Railroad (see sidebar below), but the rails also connect Alamosa and the towns of La Veta to the east and Monte Vista to the northwest. The trains have snack bars and open-air observation cars. Allow at least a half-day.

601 State St. © **877/726-7245** or 719/587-0509. www.coloradotrain.com. Round-trip tickets $19–$99 adults, $9–$89 children 2–12, free for children under 2. More expensive for First and Diamond classes. Train operates from late May to mid-Oct; call for current schedule.

Great Sand Dunes National Park & Preserve ★★★

Just 35 miles northeast of Alamosa, on Colo. 150, is Colorado's fourth national park. It was a national monument until 2004, when final approval came from the federal government for the designation of Great Sand Dunes National Park and Preserve.

Far from any sea or major desert, this 39-square-mile expanse of sand seems incongruous here. The dunes are the tallest on the continent, piled nearly 750 feet high against the western edge of the Sangre de Cristo Mountains—a startling sight. The dunes were created over thousands of years by southwesterly winds blowing across the valley. They formed when streams of water from melting glaciers carried rocks, gravel, and silt down from the mountains. In addition, as the Rio Grande changed its course, it left behind sand, silt, and debris.

Even today the winds are changing the face of the dunes. So-called "reversing winds" from the mountains pile the dunes back upon themselves, building them higher

THE CUMBRES & TOLTEC scenic railroad

Built in 1880 to serve remote mining camps, the **Cumbres & Toltec Scenic Railroad** follows a spectacular 64-mile path through the San Juan Mountains from Antonito, Colorado, to Chama, New Mexico. This narrow-gauge steam railroad weaves through groves of pine and aspen and past odd rock formations before ascending into the striking Toltec Gorge of the Los Piños River. At the rail-junction community of Osier, passengers enjoy lunch while the Colorado Limited exchanges engines with the New Mexico Express. Round-trip passengers return to their starting point in Antonito, while onward passengers continue a climb through tunnels and trestles to the summit of 10,015-foot Cumbres Pass, then drop down to Chama. A joint venture by the states of Colorado and New Mexico, the train is a registered National Historic Site.

A trip from Antonito to Chama (or vice versa), traveling there by train and returning by bus, costs $95 to $179 for adults, $49 to $69 for children 12 and under. A regular round-trip to Osier is a little less, but this omits either the gorge or the pass. Regardless, it's an all-day adventure, leaving in the morning and returning in the late afternoon. Fares include lunch at Osier. The train runs daily from late May to mid-October. For reservations and information, contact the Cumbres & Toltec Scenic Railroad (✆ **888/286-2737;** www.cumbrestoltec. com). The depot is 28 miles south of Alamosa via U.S. 285.

and higher. Though it's physically impossible for sand to be piled steeper than 34 degrees, the dunes often appear sheerer because of deceptive shadows and colors that change with the light: gold, pink, tan, even bluish. Climbing dunes is fun, and the view from the top is one of the best in the state, but it can be tiring at this 8,200-foot altitude. And be careful: The sand's surface can reach 140°F (60°C) in summer.

Among the specialized animals that survive in this harsh environment are the Ord's kangaroo rat, a creature that never drinks water, plus four insects found nowhere else on earth: the Great Sand Dunes tiger beetle and three other beetle varieties. These animals and the flora of the adjacent mountain foothills are discussed in evening programs and guided walks during summer.

For orientation, walk the easy half-mile self-guided nature trail that begins at the visitor center. If you want more of a challenge, hike the dunes—you can get to the top of a 750-foot dune and back in about 90 minutes. Those who make it all the way to the top are rewarded with spectacular views of the dunes and the surrounding mountains. Be sure to bring plenty of water, and perhaps a sled or an old beater snowboard: **Sand-sledding** and **sandboarding** are increasingly popular pursuits here. The best time to attempt it is in the spring, when the sand is fastest. Contact the park for information; sleds specially made sandboards are available for rent for $18 a day at **Kristi Mountain Sports,** 3223 Main St. (✆ **719/589-9759;** www.slvoutdoor.com).

Pinyon Flats Campground, with 88 sites, is open year-round. It has picnic tables, fire grates, flush toilets, and drinking water, but no showers or RV hookups. Campsites are assigned on a first-come, first-served basis, and cost $20 per night; group sites ($65–$80) can be reserved by calling ✆ **877/444-6777** or online at **www.recreation. gov.** Admission to the park for up to a week is $3 per person (free for those 16 and under). The **visitor center** (✆ **719/378-6399**) is open daily year-round (closed on winter holidays). For further information, contact Great Sand Dunes National Park and Preserve (✆ **719/378-6300;** www.nps.gov/grsa).

creede: OUTLAWS, MINERS & ACTORS

Among the best preserved of all 19th-century Colorado mining towns, Creede had a population of 10,000 in 1892 when a balladeer wrote, "It's day all day in the daytime, and there is no night in Creede." Over $1 million in silver was mined every day, but the Silver Panic of 1893 eclipsed Creede's rising star. For most of the next century, area mines produced just enough silver and other minerals to sustain the community until the 1960s, when tourism and outdoor recreation became paramount. Today this mountain town, at an elevation of 8,838 feet, has a population of about 400. It's fairly easy to see most of the town in a day.

To get to Creede from Alamosa, drive west on U.S. 160 about 48 miles to South Fork, and turn north on Colo. 149, which follows the Rio Grande about 23 miles to Creede. You can obtain information on what to see and do, as well as lodging and dining options, from the **Creede & Mineral County Chamber of Commerce,** in the County Annex building at the south end of town at 904 S. Main St. (© **800/327-2102;** www. creede.com). Another good source for information is the **Divide Ranger District office** of the Rio Grande National Forest, 304 S. Main St. (© **719/658-2556**), which can provide maps and information on hiking and all sorts of other outdoor activities in the nearby San Juan and Rio Grande national forests. Ask for directions to the **Wheeler Geologic Area,** region of volcanic rock formations accessible only by 4X4, horseback, or a 5-hour hike, or **North Creede Canyon,** where remnants of the **Commodore Mine,** whose workings

seem to keep a ghostly vigil over the canyon.

The **Creede Historic Museum,** located in the old railroad depot behind City Park (© **719/658-2004;** www. creedehistoricalsociety.com), offers the outlaws, saloon shootouts, and other stories of the one-time boomtown. The museum is typically open daily from 10am to 4pm from Memorial Day to Labor Day with $2 admission for adults, $1 for seniors, and $5 for families.

The **Underground Mining Museum,** on the north edge of town (© **719/658-0811;** www.undergroundminingmuseum. com), is contained in a series of rooms and tunnels blasted into a cliff face. Inside this subterranean world are exhibits that trace the history of mining. Guided tours are offered at 10am year-round, as well as 3pm in summer ($15, reservations recommended). The museum is open daily from 9am to 4pm in summer and 9am to 3pm Monday through Friday the rest of the year. Admission costs $7 for adults, $6 for seniors 60 and over, and $5 for children 6 to 11; kids 5 and under are free. Bring a jacket.

Rugged wilderness, outlaws, and miners aside, the absolutely best way to spend some time here is to take in a production by the **Creede Repertory Theatre,** 124 N. Main St. (© **866/658-2540** or 719/658-2540; www.creederep. org). Established in 1966 by a small troupe of young actors from the University of Kansas, this theater company is now nationally acclaimed, and offers matinee and evening performances from late May through September. Tickets are $11 to $35.

From Alamosa, there are two main routes to Great Sand Dunes: east 14 miles on U.S. 160, then north on Colo. 150, or north 14 miles on Colo. 17 to Mosca, then east on Six Mile Lane to the junction of Colo. 150.

Outdoor Activities

Many of the best outdoor activities in this part of the state take place in the **Rio Grande National Forest,** with the Supervisor's Office at 1803 W. U.S. 160, Monte Vista (*C* **719/852-5941**). For equipment for a variety of outdoor activities (including mountain bike and ski rentals), visit **Kristi Mountain Sports,** 3223 Main St., Alamosa (*C* **719/589-9759**).

FISHING   The Rio Grande is an outstanding stream for trout, walleye, and catfish; there are also numerous high mountain lakes and streams throughout the Rio Grande National Forest where you're apt to catch rainbow, brown, brook, cutthroat, and Rio Grande cutthroat trout. For information, contact the Forest Service office (*C* **719/852-5941**). You can get licenses, tackle, and advice at **Walmart,** 3333 Clark St., off U.S. 160 about 3 miles east of downtown Alamosa (*C* **719/589-9071**).

HIKING   The best opportunities in the region are found in the surrounding **Rio Grande National Forest,** with nearly 2 million acres. One of the most popular hikes, with easy access, is **Zapata Falls,** reached off Colo. 150, about 20 miles northeast of Alamosa and south of Great Sand Dunes. This cavernous waterfall on the northwest flank of 14,345-foot Mount Blanca freezes in winter, turning its cave into a natural icebox that often remains frozen well into summer.

PLANNING YOUR TRIP TO COLORADO

The beauty of a Colorado vacation is that there's truly something for everyone. Depending on where you choose to go, you can have an affordable and fun time, or you can spend a bit more and have a truly world-class experience. The more expensive resorts—Vail, Aspen, Steamboat, and Telluride—tend to fill up quickly, especially during ski season (and even more so in late Dec and early Jan, when ski-in/ski-out room rates hit their zenith); you'll want to book as far in advance as possible. The same is true for the state's most popular attractions, such as the national parks—which are especially busy over school summer vacations. This chapter gives you the information you need to get started.

Getting There

BY PLANE

Those flying to Colorado will probably land at Denver International Airport or Colorado Springs Airport. Each airport is on the fringe of its respective city, so, depending on your itinerary, it can be a tossup as to which is best. Denver certainly has the better average airfares. Both offer car rentals and shuttle services to hotels.

Denver International Airport (DIA) is 23 miles northeast of downtown, usually a 35- to 45-minute drive. The airport, which covers 54 square miles and has six full-service runways, handles around 50 million passengers annually, making it the 15th-busiest airport in the world.

Most major airlines serve Denver, including American, Delta, JetBlue, Southwest, United, and US Airways. **International airlines** include Air Canada, British Airways, Lufthansa, Icelandair, and Aeromexico. **Regional** and **commuter airlines** connecting Denver with other points in the Rockies and Southwest include Alaska, Frontier, and Great Lakes. For other information, call the Denver International Airport **information line** (© **800/247-2336** or 303/342-2000; www.flydenver.com).

Also check fares for **Colorado Springs Airport,** located north of Drennan Road and east of Powers Boulevard in the southeastern part of the city (© **719/550-1900;** www.flycos.com).

BY CAR

An excellent road system, connecting to interstate highways heading in all directions, makes driving a good and economical choice. This is especially true for those planning excursions outside of the Denver, Boulder, or Colorado Springs city limits.

Some 1,000 miles of interstate highways form a star on the map of Colorado, with its center at Denver. **I-25** crosses the state from south to north, extending from New Mexico to Wyoming; over its 300 miles, it goes through nearly every major city of the Front Range, including Pueblo, Colorado Springs, Denver, and Fort Collins. **I-70** crosses from west to east, extending from Utah to Baltimore, Maryland. It enters Colorado near Grand Junction, passes through Glenwood Springs, Vail, and Denver, and exits just east of Burlington, a distance of about 450 miles. **I-76** is an additional 190-mile spur that begins in Denver and extends northeast to Nebraska, joining I-80 just beyond Julesburg.

BY TRAIN

Amtrak (© **800/872-7245;** www.amtrak.com) has two routes through Colorado. The California Zephyr, which links San Francisco and Chicago, passes through Grand Junction, Glenwood Springs, Granby, Winter Park, Denver, and Fort Morgan en route to Omaha, Nebraska. The Southwest Chief, which runs between Los Angeles and Chicago, travels from Albuquerque, New Mexico, via Trinidad, La Junta, and Lamar before crossing the southeastern Colorado border into Kansas.

BY BUS

Greyhound (© **800/231-2222;** www.greyhound.com) is the sole nationwide bus line. The station in Denver is at 1055 19th St. (at Arapahoe St.).

Getting Around

Since most visitors to Colorado will probably be traveling between cities and also into surrounding areas, you will most likely want to rent a car. However, you can save a bit of cash by doing your downtown city exploring, which can be done quite conveniently using public transportation, at either the beginning or the end of your stay, and only renting a car when you plan to leave town.

Each of the individual city chapters in this book contains information on car rentals and public transportation.

BY PLANE

Although you can fly between Denver and Colorado Springs, it's not nearly as economical as driving the 70 miles. Other trips may be worth it, depending on your budget. You can save several hours by flying from Denver to Durango or Telluride, but you will pay for the convenience—and miss the scenic drive.

BY CAR

In Colorado, the most cost-effective way to travel is by car, but Denver, Boulder, and Colorado Springs have pedestrian- and bicycle-friendly routes and at least decent public transportation, as do Summit County, the Vail Valley, Aspen, and other ski areas.

At press time, the cost of gasoline was about $3.50 a gallon in Denver and vicinity, and up to $5 per gallon for the most remote mountain towns. Gas stations are numerous and usually located near highway exits and on major commercial thoroughfares throughout the state. Taxes are already included in the printed price.

BY TRAIN

Although you can catch an Amtrak train from Union Station in Denver, it's not a particularly good method of travel between the Front Range and other areas. You can access Winter Park, Glenwood Springs, and a few other tourism hotspots, however, on the California Zephyr, making it a viable means of travel for a cross-country trip to Colorado. In Denver, existing light rail is useful for navigating certain attractions. And of course, Durango and Silverton can be accessed by the Durango & Silverton Narrow Gauge Railroad, but those are its endpoints. The same can be said for tourist trains in other regions of the state. International visitors can buy a **USA Rail Pass,** good for 15, 30, or 45 days of unlimited travel on **Amtrak** (✆ **800/872-7245;** www.amtrak.com).

BY BUS

Bus travel is often the most economical form of public transit for short hops between U.S. cities, but it's certainly not an option for everyone (particularly when Amtrak, which is far more luxurious, offers similar rates). There are good bus systems in the major cities as well as Summit County, Aspen, Vail, and other resort towns. See individual chapters for details. Greyhound (www.greyhound.com; ✆ 800/231-2222 in the U.S., ✆ **001/214/849-8100** outside the U.S. with toll-free access) is the sole nationwide bus line.

[FastFACTS] COLORADO

ATMs/Banks ATMs and banks are plentiful in cities and towns in Colorado, but hard to find in some of the most remote corners of the states. Banks are usually open weekdays from 9am to 5pm, occasionally a bit later on Friday, and sometimes on Saturday. There's 24-hour access to automated teller machines (ATMs) at most banks, plus in many shopping centers and other outlets.

Business Hours Generally, businesses are open weekdays from 9am to 5pm and government offices are open from 8am until 4:30 or 5pm. Stores are open 6 days a week, with many also open on Sunday; department stores usually stay open until 9pm at least 1 day a week. Discount stores and supermarkets are often open later than other stores, and some supermarkets are open 24 hours a day.

Disabled Travelers Most disabilities shouldn't stop anyone from traveling in the U.S. Thanks to provisions in the Americans with Disabilities Act, most public places are required to comply with disability-friendly regulations. Almost all public establishments (including hotels, restaurants, museums, and so on, but not including certain National Historic Landmarks), and at least some modes of public transportation provide accessible entrances and other facilities for those with disabilities.

The **America the Beautiful—National Park and Federal Recreational Lands Pass—Access Pass** gives visually impaired or permanently disabled persons (regardless of age) free lifetime entrance to federal recreation sites administered by the National Park Service, including the Fish and Wildlife Service, the

Forest Service, the Bureau of Land Management, and the Bureau of Reclamation. This may include national parks, monuments, historic sites, recreation areas, and wildlife refuges.

Drinking Laws The legal age for purchase and consumption of alcoholic beverages is 21; proof of age is required and often requested at bars, nightclubs, and restaurants, so it's always a good idea to bring ID when you go out. Do not carry open containers of alcohol in your car or any public area that isn't zoned for alcohol consumption. The police can fine you on the spot. Don't even think about driving while intoxicated. Bars legally close at 2am in Colorado, liquor stores at midnight. Supermarkets and convenience stores sell beer that is 3.2 percent alcohol, while liquor stores sell stronger beers.

Electricity Like Canada, the United States uses 110–120 volts AC (60 cycles), compared to 220–240 volts AC (50 cycles) in most of Europe, Australia, and New Zealand. Downward converters that change 220–240 volts to 110–120 volts are difficult to find in the United States, so bring one with you.

Emergencies Call ☎ **911.** For the Colorado Poison Center, call ☎ **303/739-1123.** For the Rape Crisis and Domestic Violence Hotline, call ☎ **303/318-9989.**

Family Travel Denver, Boulder, and Colorado Springs are loaded with family attractions, although their downtown dining and nightlife tends to focus more on adult pursuits. Nonetheless, such kids' landmarks as Tiny Town, Casa Bonita, Elitch Gardens, and the North Pole continue to thrive. See "Especially for Kids" write-ups throughout the book.

Health Colorado's Front Range has its fair share of regional health concerns to be aware of before your trip, most of them relating to the altitude and the wildlife, but these can easily be avoided in most cases.

Altitude Sickness: About two-thirds of Colorado is more than a mile above sea level, which means there is less oxygen and lower humidity than many travelers are accustomed to. This creates a unique set of problems for short-term visitors, such as shortness of breath, fatigue, nausea, and other physical concerns. Those not used to higher elevations should get sufficient rest, avoid large meals, and drink plenty of nonalcoholic fluids, especially water. Individuals with heart or respiratory problems should consult their personal physicians before planning a trip to the Colorado mountains. Those in generally good health need not take any special precautions, but it is best to ease the transition to high elevations by changing altitude gradually. Because the sun's rays are more direct in the thinner atmosphere, they cause sunburn more quickly. The potential for skin damage increases when the sun reflects off snow or water. A good sunblock is strongly recommended, as are good-quality ultraviolet-blocking sunglasses. Remember that children need more protection than adults.

Hantavirus: State health officials warn outdoor enthusiasts to take precautions against the Hantavirus, a rare but often fatal respiratory disease first recognized in 1993. About half of the country's confirmed cases have been reported in the Four Corners states of Colorado, New Mexico, Arizona, and Utah. The disease is usually spread by the urine and droppings of deer mice and other rodents, and health officials recommend that campers avoid areas with signs of rodent droppings. Symptoms of Hantavirus are similar to flu and lead to breathing difficulties and shock.

West Nile Virus: Colorado has also had its share of cases of the West Nile virus illness. The best prevention is mosquito repellent. Though it's typically not fatal, the virus has been in some cases. Symptoms include fever, headache, and body aches.

Insurance Although it's not required of travelers, **health insurance** is highly recommended. Most health insurance policies cover you if you get sick away from home—but check your coverage before you leave. International visitors to the U.S. should note that unlike many European countries, the United States does not usually offer free or low-cost medical care to its citizens or visitors. Doctors and hospitals are expensive, and in most cases will require advance payment or proof of coverage before they render their services. Good policies will cover the costs of an accident, repatriation, or death.

Internet Access Wi-Fi is readily available at hotels, cafes, and some public places in Colorado. Most major airports have **Internet kiosks** that provide basic Web access for a per-minute fee that's usually higher than cybercafe prices.

Legal Aid While driving, if you are pulled over for a minor infraction (such as speeding), never attempt to pay the fine directly to a police officer; this could be construed as attempted bribery, a much more serious crime. Pay fines by mail, or directly into the hands of the clerk of the court. If accused of a more serious offense, say and do nothing before consulting a lawyer. In the U.S., the burden is on the state to prove a person's guilt beyond a reasonable doubt, and everyone has the right to remain silent, whether he or she is suspected of a crime or actually arrested. Once arrested, a person can make one telephone call to a party of his or her choice. The international visitor should call his or her embassy or consulate.

LGBT Travelers In general, gay and lesbian travelers will find they are treated just like any other travelers in Colorado. Even cities such as Colorado Springs, home of Focus on the Family and other conservative groups, have become somewhat more open-minded about alternative lifestyles recently. Those with specific concerns can contact **Gay, Lesbian, Bisexual, and Transgender Community Center of Colorado,** aka "The Center" (*C* **303/733-7743;** www. glbtcolorado.org), in Denver; the organization can also provide information on events and venues of interest to gay and lesbian visitors. The **International Gay and Lesbian Travel Association (IGLTA;**

C **954/630-1637;** www. iglta.org) is the trade association for the gay and lesbian travel industry, and offers an online directory of gay-friendly travel businesses.

Mail & Postage At press time, domestic postage rates were 34¢ for a postcard and 49¢ for a letter. For international mail, a first-class letter of up to 1 ounce costs $1.15; a first-class postcard costs the same as a letter. For more information go to **www. usps.com**. If you aren't sure what your address will be in the United States, mail can be sent to you, in your name, c/o General Delivery at the main post office of the city or region where you expect to be. (Call *C* **800/275-8777** for information on the nearest post office.) The addressee must pick up mail in person and must produce proof of identity (driver's license, passport, and so on). Most post offices will hold mail for up to 1 month, and are open Monday to Friday from 8am to 5pm, and Saturday from 9am to 3pm. Always include zip codes when mailing items in the U.S. If you don't know the zip code, visit www.usps.com/zip4.

Mobile Phones All major U.S. cellular networks work fine on the Front Range, but things quickly get spotty outside the

urban cores. If you're not from the U.S., you'll be appalled at the poor reach of the **GSM (Global System for Mobile Communications) wireless network,** which is used by much of the rest of the world. Your phone will probably work in most major U.S. cities; it definitely won't work in many rural areas. To see where GSM phones work in the U.S., check out **www.t-mobile.com/coverage**. And you may or may not be able to send SMS (text messaging) home. Your best bet for a phone in Denver if you need a replacement is not a rental, but a cheap pay-as-you-go model from local mass-market stores.

Money & Costs In general, Colorado is not particularly expensive, especially compared with destinations on the East and West coasts. In most cities, you'll find a wide range of prices for lodging and dining; admission to most attractions is less than $15 and sometimes free. Those traveling away from the major cities will discover prices in small towns are usually quite reasonable, but ski resorts such as Vail and Aspen can be rather pricey, especially during winter holidays. **Traveler's checks** and **credit cards** are accepted at almost all hotels, restaurants, shops, and attractions, plus many grocery stores.

WHAT THINGS COST IN COLORADO

	US$
Taxi from the airport to downtown Denver	51.00
Double room, moderate	150.00
Double room, inexpensive	85.00
Double room in Aspen during ski season	225.00 and up
Double room near small resorts, ski season	125.00–200.00
1-day ski lift ticket at Vail or Aspen	100.00–130.00
1-day ski lift ticket at Loveland or Wolf Creek	50.00–70.00
Half-day white-water rafting trip	About 50.00
Three-course dinner for one without wine, moderate	35.00–50.00
Pint of local microbrew	4.00–6.00
Cup of coffee	1.00–3.00
1 gallon of premium gas	About 3.50
Admission to most museums	5.00–15.00
Admission to Rocky Mountain National Park	20.00 for 7 days

Newspapers & Magazines   After the "Rocky Mountain News" shut down in 2009, the "Denver Post" became Denver's sole daily newspaper. The "Gazette" is Colorado Springs' daily and the "Boulder Daily Camera" serves Boulder. The alternative weeklies are "Westword" (Denver), the "Colorado Springs Independent," and the "Boulder Weekly." The most prominent local magazine in Denver (and along the entire Front Range) is "5280," but you'll find many more publications focusing on local arts, dining, and business in all three cities. Most smaller cities and resort towns have daily newspapers, and the glitzier ski areas have numerous glossy magazines dedicated to style, dining, and architecture.

Packing   Weather in Colorado can change in an instant, so pack several layers of clothing, including a winter jacket and long underwear, and be prepared for anything.

Police   Call ⓒ **911** for emergencies.

Safety   While there are many reasons to visit Colorado, two of the reasons most often cited are its historic sites and its magnificent outdoor activities. However, visiting historic sites and participating in outdoor activities can lead to accidents. When visiting such historic sites as ghost towns, gold mines, and railroads, remember that they were probably built more than 100 years ago, when safety standards were extremely lax, if they existed

at all. Never enter abandoned buildings, mines, or railroad equipment on your own. When you're visiting commercially operated historic tourist attractions, use common sense and don't be afraid to ask questions. When heading to the great outdoors, remember that injuries often occur when people fail to follow instructions. Pay attention when the experts tell you to stay on established ski trails, hike only in designated areas, carry rain gear, and wear a life jacket when rafting. Mountain weather can be fickle, and many of the most beautiful spots are in remote areas. Be prepared for extreme changes in temperature at any time of year, and watch out for sudden summer-afternoon thunderstorms that can leave you drenched and shivering.

Senior Travel   Many Colorado hotels and motels offer special rates to seniors, and an increasing number of restaurants, attractions, and public transportation systems offer discounts as well, some for "oldsters" as young as 55. The U.S. National Park Service offers an **America the Beautiful—National Park and Federal Recreational Lands Pass—Senior Pass** (formerly the **Golden Age Passport**), which gives seniors 62 years or older lifetime entrance to all properties administered by the National Park Service— national parks, monuments, historic sites, recreation areas, and national wildlife refuges—for a one-time fee of $10. The pass must be purchased in person at any NPS facility that charges an entrance fee or via mail for an extra $10.

Smoking   Since 2006, smoking has been banned in all public places in Colorado, including restaurants and bars. Recreational marijuana has been legal since 2014. You must be 18 to buy tobacco products or 21 to buy marijuana, which may not be smoked in public.

Student Travel   A valid student ID will often qualify students for discounts on airfare, accommodations, and admission to museums, events, movies, and more in Colorado.

Taxes   Colorado has a 2.9 percent state sales tax; local jurisdictions often add another 4 or 5 percent. Lodging tax is typically about 10 to 15 percent. The United States has no value-added tax (VAT) or other indirect tax at the national level. Every state, county, and city may levy its own local tax on all purchases, including hotel and restaurant checks and airline tickets. These taxes will not appear on price tags.

Tipping   Across Colorado, tips are a very important part of certain workers' income, and gratuities are the standard way of showing appreciation for services provided. (Tipping is certainly not compulsory if the service is poor!) In hotels, tip **bellhops** about $1 per bag ($2–$3 if you have a lot of luggage) and tip the **chamber staff** $1 to $2 per day (more if you've left a big mess for him or her to clean up). Tip the **doorman** or **concierge** only if he or she has provided you with some specific service (for example, calling a cab for you or obtaining difficult-to-get theater tickets). Tip the **valet-parking attendant** $1 every time you get your car. In restaurants, bars, and nightclubs, tip **service staff** and **bartenders** 15 to 20 percent of the check, tip **checkroom attendants** $1 per garment, and tip **valet-parking attendants** $1 per vehicle. As for other service personnel, tip **cabdrivers** 15 percent of the fare; tip **skycaps** at airports at least $1 per bag ($2–$3 if you have a lot of luggage).

Toilets   You won't find public toilets or "restrooms" on the streets in most U.S. cities but they can be found in hotel lobbies, bars, restaurants, museums, department stores, railway and bus stations, and service stations. Large hotels and fast-food restaurants are often the best bet for clean facilities. Restaurants and bars may reserve their restrooms for patrons.

Index

See also Accommodations and Restaurant indexes, below.

General Index

A

Accommodations. *See also* Accommodations Index
  best, 2
Air travel, 18–19, 240, 241
Alamosa and Great Sand Dunes, 235–239
Alamosa-Monte Vista National Wildlife Refuges, 236
Almont, 229
Alpine slide, Winter Park, 144
American Cowboy Museum (Colorado Springs), 83
American Museum of Western Art (Denver), 40
Anheuser-Busch Brewery (Fort Collins), 113, 115
Animas Museum (Durango), 201
Arapahoe Basin, 3, 150
Arcade Amusements (Manitou Springs), 80–81
Argo Gold Mine, Mill, and Museum (Idaho Springs), 65
Arkansas Headwaters Recreation Area, 233
Armory (Golden), 61
The Art Center (Grand Junction), 180
Art on the Corner (Grand Junction), 180
Aspen, 3, 14, 16, 168–177
Aspen Art Museum, 173
Aspen Highlands, 175
Aspen Historical Society, 173
Aspen Music Festival and School, 177
Aspen Walking Tours, 173
Astor House Museum (Golden), 62
Auto racing, Colorado Springs, 90
Avalanche Ranch (Redstone), 188–189

B

Baby Doe Tabor Museum (Leadville), 166
Bachelor-Syracuse Mine Tour (Ouray), 223
Backpacking. *See* Hiking and backpacking
Ballooning, 48, 84–85, 107, 176
Banjo Billy's Bus Tours (Boulder), 102–103
Barker Reservoir (Boulder), 107
Beaver Creek, 154, 158, 160–161
Betty Ford Alpine Gardens (Vail), 159

Biking and mountain biking, 1
  Aspen, 176
  Boulder, 95, 107
  Breckenridge area, 152, 153
  Colorado Springs, 84–86
  Crested Butte, 230
  Denver, 23, 47, 48
  Durango, 203
  Fort Collins, 116
  Glenwood Springs, 190
  Leadville, 167
  Paonia, 195
  Rocky Mountain National Park, 121
  Salida, 234
  Steamboat Springs, 137
  Telluride, 218
  Vail, 162–163
  Winter Park, 144–145
Bird-watching, Rocky Mountain National Park, 123
Black Canyon of the Gunnison, 191–194
Bluebird Theater (Denver), 59
Boating, 48, 152–153, 231. *See also* Kayaking; Rafting
Boettcher Mansion (Golden), 62
Boulder, 14, 93–117
Boulder Bach Festival, 111
Boulder Beer Company, 105
Boulder Canyon Pioneer Trail, 103
Boulder Creek Path, 103
Boulder Creek Stream Observatory, 103
Boulder History Museum, 103–104
Boulder Museum of Contemporary Art, 104
Boulder Outdoor Cinema, 104
Boulder Philharmonic Orchestra, 111
Boulder Reservoir, 107, 109
Box Canyon Falls & Park (Ouray), 222
Bradford Washburn American Mountaineering Museum (Golden), 62
Bravo! Vail Music Festival, 163
Breckenridge and Summit County, 15, 145–154
Breckenridge Festival of Film, 154
Breckenridge Music Festival, 154
Breckenridge National Historic District, 149
Breckenridge Ski Resort, 150–152
Bridal Veil Falls, 217
The Broadmoor (Colorado Springs), 80
Buffalo Bill Museum & Grave (Golden), 62
Buntport Theater (Denver), 56
Bus travel, 19, 241, 242
Butterfly Pavilion (Westminster), 106
Buttermilk Mountain, 175
Byers-Evans House (Denver), 40

C

Camping, 1234, 127–128, 211, 217, 231, 237
Cañon City, 91, 92
Canyons of the Ancients National Monument, 212
Car travel, 19, 240–241
Castlewood Canyon State Park, 51
Cattle drives (roundups), 137, 162
Cave of the Winds (Manitou Springs), 81
Celestial Seasonings (Boulder), 105
Central City, 61
Central Park (Boulder), 103
Charles A. Heartling Sculpture Garden (Boulder), 103
Chatfield State Park, 51
Cherry Creek Shopping Center (Denver), 53
Cherry Creek State Park, 52
Cheyenne Mountain State Park, 86
Cheyenne Mountain Zoo (Colorado Springs), 4, 80
Children's Museum of Denver, 40
Chimney Rock National Monument, 224
The Church (Denver), 59
Clear Creek History Park (Golden), 62
Cleo Parker Robinson Dance (Denver), 56
Cliff Palace, 210–211
Climate, 9–10
Climbing, bouldering, mountaineering, 107, 121, 193, 203, 222
Clyfford Still Museum (Denver), 40
Colorado Avalanche (Denver), 61
Colorado Ballet (Denver), 56
Colorado Gators (Mosca), 236
Colorado MahlerFest (Boulder), 111
Colorado Mountain School (Estes Park), 121
Colorado Music Festival (Boulder), 111
Colorado National Monument, 184–186
Colorado Railroad Museum (Golden), 62–63
The Colorado Rapids (Denver), 61
Colorado Rockies (Denver), 60
Colorado School of Mines Geology Museum (Golden), 63
Colorado Shakespeare Festival (Boulder), 111
Colorado Ski Museum-Ski & Snowboard Hall of Fame (Vail), 159
Colorado Springs, 16, 68–92
Colorado Springs Dance Theatre, 89
Colorado Springs Fine Arts Center, 79, 88

INDEX